INTERNATIONAL
COOKING
MADE EASY

INTERNATIONAL COOKING MADE EASY

Over 500 unusual recipes

BY MAJ-GRETH WEGENER

Illustrations by

CLAUDIA SMITH FARKAS

NORTH CASTLE BOOKS, GREENWICH, CONN. 06830
Distributed by
Hastings House, Publishers, Inc., New York

ISBN 0-8038-3422-5

Library of Congress Catalog Card Number 78-71120

(CIP data on final page)

Designer: Ernst Reichl
Typography by York Graphic Services
Printing by Halliday Lithograph
Binding by Tapley-Rutter

Manufactured in the United States of America

TO MY MOTHER,

whose good cooking will always be in my memory,

and who taught me, and

inspired me.

Contents

ACKNOWLEDGEMENTS Many people have helped me, not only with recipes, but also in tasting and advice. I just hope I have in mind at least those who have supplied me with recipes and information about eating habits of certain countries, and also hope that any I may have overlooked will please forgive. Both my memory and my files are overcrowded as we go to press, so that I may miss even some of the friendliest and most helpful.

But here are the ones that I remember:

Joan Adams, Svea Andersson, Donna Archino, Bridget Bohannon, Jane Boers, Hsaio-Wen Chen, Daman Chopra, Ritu Chopra, Elena O. de Sanz, Kay Farmer, Ilse Feldstein, Reidun Fuglesang, Michelle Gautier, Elinor Goldberg, Inez Garcia, Mary Green, Aase Jensen, Nancy Joof, Maria Janek, Paula Kowalski, Ingrid Lunden, Betty Minasi, Ms. Miyamoti, Ann Montevano, Rosemarie Moustakas, Beryl Nelson, Bibi Nestor, Herbert Nichols, Tyra Odqvist, Pauline Palamaruk, Vera Perret, Ann Romeo, Angela Santivasi, Sarah Secka, June Waters, Liz Yung.

Measurements

THE recipes in this book are given in American measurements, mostly spoons and 8-ounce cups; and in metric measurements, chiefly spoons, milliliters and grams. The tablespoon, holding $\frac{1}{2}$ fluid ounce, and the teaspoon of $\frac{1}{6}$ ounce are not official measurements, but are used internationally in cooking and have about the same capacity everywhere except in British imperial areas.

Metric amounts have often been approximated to avoid inconvenient numbers and over-fine measurement. All recipes have been tested both ways. There are tables of measurement, weight and temperature in the Appendix for those who are interested in knowing the exact equivalents.

If you are using a British imperial cup, which holds 10 fluid ounces, take $\frac{3}{4}$ of the cup measurements in these recipes. The official British tablespoon holds one ounce, and equals two American tablespoons. There is also an unofficial British tablespoon which holds $\frac{2}{3}$ of an ounce, or $1\frac{1}{3}$ American tablespoons. The British teaspoon holds either $\frac{1}{4}$ or $\frac{1}{6}$ ounce, while an American teaspoon holds $\frac{1}{6}$ ounce. If you have the unofficial size spoons, the error in using American measurements directly will be quite small.

Abbreviations

tbs	tablespoon		**mL**	milliliter
ts	teaspoon		**dl**	deciliter
lb	pound		**L**	liter
″	inch		**g**	gram
F	Fahrenheit		**hg**	hectogram
C	Celsius (Centigrade)		**kg**	kilogram
	cm	centimeter		

Introduction

During the last ten years there has been a great upsurge in interest in foreign foods in the United States. I feel that this awakening is closely connected to increased foreign travel by Americans. Exposure to foreign delicacies abroad results in a desire to enjoy them at home also.

But you may wonder why anyone would make another cookbook, when there are so many of them already on the market. As a beginning, every cookbook author has the idea that her (or his) group of recipes are generally better than others. Then, when I started it, this particular project differed from most other books on foreign cooking in not being limited to only one country.

Why not, I thought, have one book of first class representatives of good and easy dishes from many countries? One cookbook on the shelf, opening doors to many different cuisines, instead of a whole row of books, one from each country? This may well fill your needs, until you get so hooked on the style of some one country that you want its whole story. Now, I hear, others have had the same idea, but I can still hope that these recipes are better than theirs.

This cookbook is, of course, intended for those who may like to experiment with foods and flavors from other countries; not for the type of American I sat next to on a return trip from Spain (and its glorious cuisine). When I asked her what she thought of Spain, she answered with a sigh and, "I did not have a decent hamburger for three weeks . . ." I like to think that this type of food-thinking is becoming more rare.

It has been great fun to get these recipes together, not only that it was an extra excuse to travel—my Viking blood never seems to get enough of that—but I also met so many interesting people, most of them interested and helpful as soon as I mentioned my project.

Living in Greenwich, Connecticut, I am fortunate in having at my elbow many people from different countries. Even my short street seems like a United Nations in miniature. A helpful circumstance is that IBM's world headquarters is nearby. Their employees say that these initials mean, "I've Been Moved." Certainly many of them have come and gone during the years I have been preparing this book. Just as I decided it was hopeless to try to get to Australia, IBM moved an Australian and his delightful family into my immediate neighborhood. They provided a wealth of delicious home-cooking recipes from that continent.

I am afraid I may be criticized for the title of this book in respect to the "EASY", as some people may think that parts of it are not easy at all. I acknowledge that I am assuming that my readers have some knowledge of cooking, and pleasure in doing it, before going into these recipes. And perhaps a few of them do stretch the "easy" at the first try, but thereafter you should find the title justified. Basically, just use common sense and follow directions, handling it item by item.

You may wonder about the metric column. Well, we are going to have to use the metric system sooner or later. There is still some resistance, but many indicators, including most of the cans in the supermarkets, tell us that it is on its way. By including both our present measurements and the ones that will come, I feel that this book will aid in the transition. Metric use is appropriate, as most of the original recipes were metric in their own countries.

Conversions between the two systems have been rounded off for convenience. All recipes have been tested each way, and no significant differences were found.

I have followed the advice of our Metric Council in Washington in expressing the metric measurements. They are not handled just the same way as they are in Europe, where for example one liter is first divided into deciliters (tenths). The American way will be to avoid the deciliter, and divide it right into milliliters (thousandths), which are abbreviated as mLs. To me, this is not the easy way, but since that is how it is going to be, what else can I do?

I am not including a bibliography in this book because none of the recipes have been derived directly from other cookbooks. However, I have read and studied most of the available books on international cooking, to check my direct research.

INTERNATIONAL COOKING MADE EASY

Africa

THIS vast continent with its many different tribes and nations, its many different climates, its history before and during colonization, going back thousands of years, cannot possibly be fairly represented in this book as far as its culinary culture is concerned. There are too many good things to eat that are hidden for the casual visitor.

Furthermore, it is hard to decide how to present the recipes I do have in regard to their geographic origins. I have, for example pulled out from this chapter what I have from the African countries bordering the Mediterranean as the eating habits in these Moslem countries are so close to those of the Middle East that they quite often overlap.

Africa has left its imprint on our American cooking, going back hundreds of years. The slaves that were brought to the Western Hemisphere did not give up their native ideas of eating in their new environment and it is almost eerie to see how closely some of the dishes of the western African countries resemble some of those of our Southern cooking.

But the colonizers and other settlers in Africa have also left their imprint on today's eating habits throughout the continent, so there are definite trends of Portuguese, Dutch, English and East Indian cooking wherever these different people have been.

If I should point to some similarity between the many different African countries of today, I think the most important ones are their almost universal use of peanuts (called groundnuts in Africa), coconuts, and hot peppers for seasoning. Peanut growing is a very important part

1

of the agriculture and the whole economy of some of the smaller countries is based on it, as it is an important export, besides providing protein for eating and oil for cooking. And the coconut palm is not far behind in importance. This is even used in making palm-wine, an intoxicant. The reason why hot peppery seasoning is so popular is probably the same as in other countries where refrigeration is a luxury most people cannot afford—if the meat should not be as fresh as it should be, the spices will adequately hide any off flavor.

All around the African coast there are fish to be caught, but due to transportation problems it is mainly the people along the coast itself who can take advantage of them. But they are so used to their hot seasonings that even freshly caught, tasty fish is often cooked with an abundance of hot spices.

In choosing things to represent Africa there seemed to be a narrower choice because of the fact that many ingredients are almost impossible to get in this country and are difficult to substitute but what follows should not create any difficulties as far as ingredients are concerned.

PEANUT SOUP	*Groundnut Soup*	Gambia
YAM SOUP		Senegal
BEAN STEW		Gambia
WEST AFRICAN FISH STEW	*Nsonlo Sutulu*	Ghana
BEEF STEW WITH PEANUT SAUCE	*Groundnut Chop*	Senegal
BEEF AND RICE STEW	*Jollof Rice*	Gambia
CURRIED CHOPPED MEAT CASSEROLE	*Bobotie*	South Africa
YAM FRITTERS	*Ntomo Krakro*	Ghana
CORN PATTIES	*Akamu*	Nigeria
RICE CAKES		Nigeria
MASHED POTATOES WITH PEAS AND CORN	*Irio*	Kenya
PEANUT SAUCE	*Groundnut Sauce*	Kenya
COCONUT DELIGHT		Sierra Leone
LEMON COCONUT COOKIES		Ghana
ALMOND SPICE COOKIES	*Soetkoekies*	South Africa

PEANUT SOUP

Gambia   *(Groundnut Soup)*

Peanuts are one of the main crops in Gambia—and also in many other African countries. And peanut soup is a popular and good way to cook them.

8 oz	*(250 g)*	roasted and shelled peanuts (unsalted)
3 cups	*(750 mL)*	beef or chicken stock
1	*(1)*	small onion, finely minced (½ cup or 125 mL)
1 tbs	*(1 tbs)*	salad oil
1 cup	*(250 mL)*	light cream (or half and half)
2 ts	*(2 ts)*	corn starch
½ ts	*(½ ts)*	salt
¼ ts	*(¼ ts)*	ground red pepper
For sprinkling:		chopped parsley or chives

Grind peanuts to a fine meal, either in a nut grinder or an electric blender. In a large sauce pan sauté onion in butter or margarine until transparent, then add stock and ground peanuts. Bring to a boil, turn down heat to very low and simmer for about 1 hour, stirring off and on to avoid mixture sticking to the bottom of the pan. Purée mixture in an electric blender, or pass through a sieve, and discard any coarse pieces of nuts.

Return mixture to pan. Mix corn-starch with ¼ cup (60 mL) of the cream, add to the soup and bring to a boil. Boil, while stirring continuously, for 1 minute, then add remaining cream, a little at a time, and seasonings. Simmer for 20 minutes, but make sure soup does not boil. Serve soup sprinkled with chopped chives or parsley.   Serves 4–5.

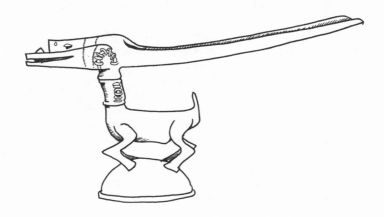

Senegal   YAM SOUP

*A rich and spicy soup which is popular in some version among practically all
the countries on Africa's west coast.*

1	(1)	large onion, finely chopped (about ¾ cup or 180 mL)
2 tbs	(2 *tbs*)	salad oil
2	(2)	small hot chilies, finely chopped (seeds removed if a too-spicy mixture is not wanted) or ⅛–¼ ts cayenne, according to taste
2	(2)	medium tomatoes, peeled and chopped (or 1 cup or 250 mL canned tomatoes)
1 lb	(½ *kg*)	yams or sweet potatoes, cut in small cubes (about 2 cups or 500 mL)
3 cups	(750 *mL*)	beef stock
1 ts	(1 *ts*)	salt
For sprinkling:		Finely chopped parsley

Sauté onion in oil until transparent, add peppers and tomatoes and cook for about 5 minutes. Add yams, beef stock and salt, bring to a boil, lower heat and simmer for 20–30 minutes, or until yams are soft. Purée soup in an electric blender, or pass through a sieve. Return to pot and heat thoroughly. Serve in soup bowls, sprinkled with parsley.   For 4–5.

Gambia   BEAN STEW

*Dried beans are one of the cooking staples in Africa—as well as in other
countries. Many good things are made with them. Like this stew.*

1 lb	(½ *kg*)	dried navy beans (or lima beans)
¾ lb	(350 *g*)	stewing beef, cut into ½" (12 mm) cubes
1	(1)	large onion, finely chopped (1 cup—250 mL)
2	(2)	medium tomatoes, peeled and finely chopped (or 1 cup or 250 mL chopped canned tomatoes)
3 tbs	(3 *tbs*)	salad oil
1 tbs	(1 *tbs*)	tomato paste
¼–½ ts	(¼–½ *ts*)	cayenne pepper, according to taste salt to taste

Soak beans overnight or for several hours, then boil in slightly salted water until tender, adding more water if they should cook dry and draining excess water, if any, when they are ready.

Brown beef slightly in oil, then add onion and sauté until transparent. Add tomatoes and cook together about 15 minutes, then combine with beans. Add tomato paste, pepper and salt and simmer about 30 minutes, adding hot water if the stew tends to get too thick or starts to stick to the bottom of the pot. Serve with boiled rice. Serves 4–6.

VARIATION:

The above dish can also be made with dried fish instead of meat. For this, soak ½ lb (¼ kg) dried, salted fish overnight, drain water, bring to a boil with fresh cold water, then simmer until fish is tender. Otherwise follow the instructions as above.

WEST AFRICAN FISH STEW

Ghana   (*Nsonlo Sutulu*)

A nice, spicy fish dish.

1½–2 lbs	(¾–1 kg)	ocean perch fillets (other salt water fish may be substituted)
		salt to taste
2 tbs	(2 tbs)	flour
2 tbs	(2 tbs)	cooking oil
1	(1)	small onion, finely chopped (½ cup or 125 mL)
2	(2)	medium size tomatoes, peeled and chopped (or 1 cup or 250 mL chopped, canned tomatoes)
1 tbs	(1 tbs)	tomato paste
¼ ts	(¼ ts)	crushed red pepper (or more if a really hot sauce is desired)
½ cup	(125 mL)	water
For sprinkling:		chopped parsley

Cut fish into serving pieces. Mix together flour and salt and dredge fish pieces in this. Heat oil in a deep skillet and lightly brown fish on both sides, then remove. Sauté onion in skillet until transparent, add tomatoes and water and cook together about 10 minutes.

Add tomato paste and red pepper, stir well to mix, add fish, bring to a boil, then turn down heat and simmer for 10 minutes. If sauce does not cover fish pieces completely, they should be turned a couple of times during the simmering period. Serve, sprinkled with parsley, over boiled rice.

For 5–6.

BEEF STEW WITH PEANUT SAUCE

Senegal (*Groundnut Chop*)

This is a traditional stew in many African countries. It has several variations, all of which are served with simple side dishes of different kinds as mentioned below.

2 lbs	(*1 kg*)	stewing beef
3 tbs	(*3 tbs*)	salad oil
2	(*2*)	medium size onions (1 chopped ¾ cup (180 mL) and 1 sliced)
		salt to taste
¼ lb	(*125 g*)	peanut butter
3–4	(*3–4*)	hot chilies, seeded and finely chopped or ¼ ts (or more, according to taste) ground red pepper
4 cups	(*1 L*)	canned tomatoes
2	(*2*)	hard-boiled eggs, chopped

Cut meat into ¾" (18 mm) cubes and brown in the oil in a skillet. Remove meat and sauté chopped onion for 5 minutes, return meat to skillet and add salt, chilies and tomatoes, bring to a boil and simmer for 30 minutes. Remove some of the broth and mix with the peanut butter to a smooth paste, add this, a little at a time to the skillet and stir well.

Add eggs and simmer for 1 hour or until meat is very tender. If sauce should become too thick, add a little hot water. Serve to 5–6 with plain boiled rice and side dishes, such as:

Sliced oranges, bananas, or both
Chopped fresh tomatoes
Chopped green peppers
Sliced cucumbers
Grated fresh coconut
Diced fresh pineapple
Sour-sweet chutney
Roasted peanuts
Chopped fried okra
Chopped fried eggplant

BEEF AND RICE STEW

Gambia   *(Jollof Rice)*

A satisfying meal which can be made hot or more or less spicy with hot peppers, you have to be your own judge about how much your family can take.

1½ lbs	(¾ kg)	stewing beef
¼ cup	(60 mL)	salad oil
2	(2)	medium size onions, chopped (1½ cups or 375 mL)
3	(3)	large tomatoes, peeled and chopped
1	(1)	hot green or red chili, seeds removed (or ¼ ts ground red pepper, or more according to taste)
1	(1)	6 oz (180 mL) can tomato paste
2 cups	(500 mL)	water
1	(1)	bay leaf
2 cups	(500 mL)	rice
1 cup	(250 mL)	frozen peas (½ package)

Cut meat into ¾″ (18 mm) cubes then brown slightly in a skillet in half the salad oil. Transfer meat into a heavy pot. Add remaining oil to skillet, sauté onion for 5 minutes, then add tomatoes and chili and cook for a few minutes, then add to the meat. Add remaining ingredients, except rice and peas, bring to a boil, then turn down heat to very low and simmer about 45–50 minutes, or until meat is tender.

Remove meat, keep it hot, add rice to the pot and cook under cover for 10–15 minutes, or until rice is tender. If mixture should be too dry, add more water. Stir off and on to prevent sticking. Add peas and cook for about 10 minutes more. Put the meat in the middle of a serving dish, then pile the rice around it.   Serves 5–6.

VARIATIONS:

Instead of beef, use 1½ lbs (¾ kg) fish cut into bite size pieces or 1 2½–3 lbs (1–1½ kg) chicken, cut into serving pieces.

CURRIED CHOPPED MEAT CASSEROLE

South Africa   *(Bobotie)*

This very tasty casserole definitely shows an Indian influence.

2 lbs	(*1 kg*)	chopped chuck beef
2 tbs	(*2 tbs*)	butter or margarine
2	(*2*)	medium size onions, finely chopped
1	(*1*)	apple, peeled and diced
2	(*2*)	slices white bread
½ cup	(*125 mL*)	water
2	(*2*)	eggs
¼ cup	(*60 mL*)	raisins
2 tbs	(*2 tbs*)	curry powder
2 tbs	(*2 tbs*)	vinegar
2 tbs	(*2 tbs*)	sugar
		salt and pepper to taste
6	(*6*)	bay leaves
1 cup	(*250 mL*)	milk

Brown meat in butter or margarine in a large skillet, then push towards the sides and sauté onion for five minutes, add apple and sauté an additional 5 minutes. Soak bread in water, squeeze out excess. In a bowl put together meat, onion, apple, bread, one of the eggs, raisins, curry, vinegar, sugar, salt and pepper and mix well.

Put in a greased baking dish and insert the bay leaves in an upright position. Bake in a 350°F (175° C) oven for 45 minutes. Beat the second egg slightly and mix well with milk, then pour over casserole and bake an additional 10 minutes or until egg mixture has coagulated. Remove bay leaves and serve with rice and chutney, to 6–8.

YAM FRITTERS

Ghana   *(Ntomo Krakro)*

A nice way of serving a vegetable with fried fish or meat.

1 cup	(*250 mL*)	cooked, mashed yams (sweet potatoes may be substituted)
1	(*1*)	egg, slightly beaten
1 tbs	(*1 tbs*)	light cream (or evaporated milk)

(Continued on next page)

(Yam Fritters, cont.)

2 tbs	(2 tbs)	finely minced onion
½ ts	(½ ts)	salt
		pinch of cayenne, or, if preferred, ¼ ts black pepper
¼ cup	(60 mL)	flour
¼ ts	(¼ ts)	baking powder
		oil for deep frying

Mix together yams, egg, cream, onion and seasonings. Sift together flour and baking powder and add to yam mixture. Heat oil to 375° F (190° C), then drop yam mixture, about ½ tbs at a time, into oil and cook until golden brown on all sides, 3–5 minutes in all. Serve with meat or fish. Serves 4–5.

CORN PATTIES

Nigeria   *(Akamu)*

Some of the food in western Africa seems to have much in common with our southern cooking. Probably the people brought their way of cooking with them when they were brought here. It is interesting to find things that look familiar. For example, this recipe somewhat resembles hush puppies.

2 cups	(500 mL)	corn meal (white or yellow)
⅔ cup	(160 mL)	flour
2 ts	(2 ts)	baking powder
1 ts	(1 ts)	salt
¼ ts	(¼ ts)	cayenne pepper
1½ tbs	(1½ tbs)	sugar
2	(2)	eggs, well beaten
2 tbs	(2 tbs)	grated onion (about 1 small onion)
½–¾ cup	(125–180 mL)	water
		oil for deep frying

Sift together all dry ingredients into a mixing bowl. Add eggs, onion and ½ cup (125 mL) water and mix well. The dough should be fairly stiff, but if it is *too* stiff, add a little more water. Dust hands with flour and roll dough into balls, the size of walnuts, then flatten them into patties and cook in a deep fryer, or in about 1″ (25 mm) oil in a skillet at 375° F (190° C) until golden in color. Remove, and drain on paper toweling. Makes 20–25 patties, for 4–6 people. Serve with fried fish.

RICE CAKES

Nigeria

So many things in Africa are flavored with grated coconut, but of course there is an abundance of coconut palms where the recipes originate.

1½ cups	(375 mL)	well cooked rice (it should even be a bit sticky from over-cooking)
1	(1)	egg well beaten
2 tbs	(2 tbs)	sugar
2 tbs	(2 tbs)	flour (or rice flour, if available)
2 tbs	(2 tbs)	grated coconut
½ ts	(½ ts)	grated nutmeg

For dredging:

¼ cup	(60 mL)	flour or rice flour, or slightly more oil for frying

Mix together rice, egg, sugar, flour and grated coconut, then shape into patties and dredge in flour mixed with nutmeg. Fry in shallow hot oil in a frying pan (375° F (190° C)), turning them once to get both sides done, until they are golden brown. Remove and drain on paper toweling.

Serves 4–5.

MASHED POTATOES WITH PEAS AND CORN

Kenya   *(Irio)*

In Kenya what is called irio exists in many versions—it is a mixture of different vegetables, sometimes changing with the location and sometimes with what is available. This is a nice version and a colorful way to serve mashed potatoes.

3 cups	(750 mL)	mashed potatoes
1 cup	(250 mL)	cooked green peas with ½ cup (125 mL) cooking liquid
2 tbs	(2 tbs)	butter or margarine
		salt and pepper to taste
1 cup	(250 mL)	cooked kernel corn, drained

Cook raw potatoes, or use instant mix, to make mashed potatoes. Make a purée of peas and liquid in a blender and add to potatoes together with butter and seasonings and mix well. Fold in corn. This dish is traditionally served in individual mounds, slightly flattened and scooped out on top to resemble a volcano. This hollow is filled with strips of steak or other meat.

Serves 4–5.

PEANUT SAUCE

Kenya   *(Groundnut Sauce)*

When a dish itself does not contain peanuts, a sauce containing them may be served with it. This sauce is used on meat, chicken or even plain rice.

⅓ cup	*(80 mL)*	roasted peanuts
1 tbs	*(1 tbs)*	butter or margarine
1 tbs	*(1 tbs)*	flour
1 cup	*(250 mL)*	chicken or beef stock
		salt and pepper to taste
		pinch of sugar (optional)

Grind peanuts to a fine meal in a nut grinder or a blender. Brown butter in a small saucepan, add flour, stirring constantly until mixture browns slightly. Add ground peanuts and mix well. Heat stock and add, a little bit at a time, stirring constantly to make a smooth sauce. Add seasonings and cook an additional five minutes. If a thinner sauce should be desired, add a bit more stock or plain water. Serve over rice with meat or chicken.

COCONUT DELIGHT

Sierra Leone

Farina is a popular ingredient in dessert puddings in many parts of the world. This African version has coconut added.

2 cups	*(500 mL)*	milk
¼ ts	*(¼ ts)*	salt
⅓ cup	*(80 mL)*	sugar
3 tbs	*(3 tbs)*	farina
1 ts	*(1 ts)*	vanilla flavoring (optional)
1 cup	*(250 mL)*	flaked or grated coconut
		(fresh or dried)
For serving:		Strawberry preserves or
		frozen strawberries
		(optional)

Bring milk, sugar and salt to a boil in a saucepan, add farina and cook until thickened (amount of time depends on what kind of farina is used, so let yourself be guided by package instructions), stirring off and on to make sure the mixture does not get scorched. Add coconut and continue cooking an additional 10 minutes, then add vanilla and pour into a serving dish and chill. Serve either plain or with strawberry preserves or frozen strawberries.

Serves 4–6.

LEMON COCONUT COOKIES

Ghana

A nice coconut cookie with a subtle lemon flavor.

½ cup	*(125 mL)*	butter or margarine
½ cup	*(125 mL)*	sugar
½ cup	*(125 mL)*	finely grated coconut (if only shredded coconut is on hand, it can be grated in a blender or chopped finely on a chopping board)
2 ts	*(2 ts)*	lemon juice
		grated rind from one lemon
1	*(1)*	egg, slightly beaten
1½ cup	*(375 mL)*	flour
½ ts	*(½ ts)*	baking powder

Cream butter and sugar until light and fluffy, add coconut, lemon juice and rind, then beaten egg and mix well. Sift together flour and baking powder and add to butter mixture and mix well.

Wrap dough in plastic wrap and let rest in refrigerator for ½ hour.

Make cookies by rolling about 1 ts of dough into a ball, then flatten it out in a criss-cross fashion with a fork, dipped in flour. It can also be rolled out onto a well floured board into a thin sheet and cut with a cooky cutter into any shape desired, but because of the coconut it is difficult to get even edges.

Bake on a greased baking sheet in a 350° F (175° C) oven 6–8 minutes, or until golden brown. Makes 4 dozen.

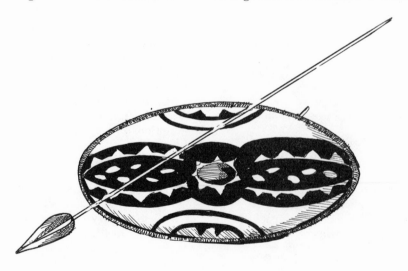

ALMOND SPICE COOKIES

South Africa   (*Soetkoekies*)

½ cup	(*125 mL*)	butter or margarine
1 cup	(*250 mL*)	brown sugar
1	(*1*)	egg, well beaten
2 tbs	(*2 tbs*)	red wine
2 cups	(*500 mL*)	flour
½ ts	(*½ ts*)	baking soda
1 ts	(*1 ts*)	cinnamon
½ ts	(*½ ts*)	ginger
½ cup	(*125 mL*)	finely chopped almonds

Cream butter with brown sugar until light and fluffy, then add about half of the egg and all the wine and mix well. Sift together flour, baking soda and spices and add to mixture, then work it in until well blended. Add almonds and stir to mix well. Form dough into a ball, wrap it in plastic and let rest in refrigerator for several hours.

Roll out dough on a floured baking board to about ¼" (6 mm) thickness and cut out with a cookie cutter or simply a small glass, dipped in flour between cookies. Brush with remaining beaten egg, place on a cookie sheet and bake in a 375° F (190° C) oven about 8 minutes, then remove and cool on a rack. Store in air-tight container.

Makes about 3 dozen.

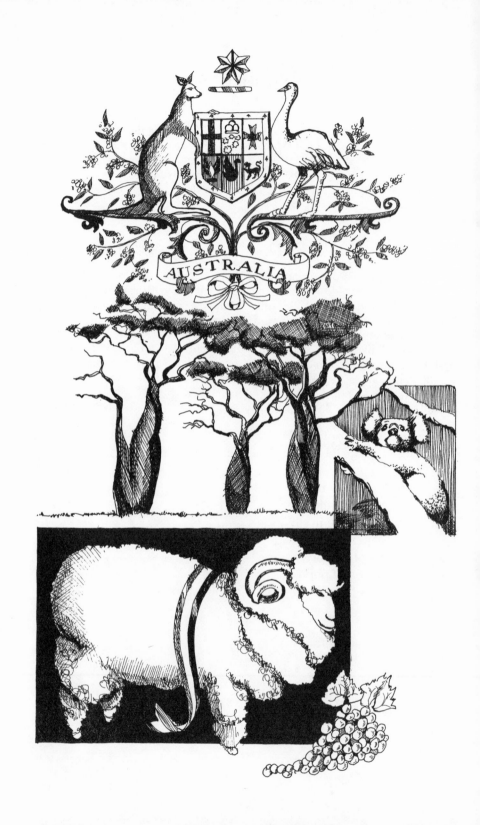

Australia

THE cuisine of Australia is not what you would think—that of a far-away, exotic place. Instead, the eating habits of the Australians closely resemble those of the Americans.

Their mostly British heritage, however, shows up in their breakfast, which generally is a substantial one, often consisting of bacon and eggs.

Their luncheon meal is usually a light one, a sandwich, some soup etc. However, the typical Saturday lunch is different, often a hot meat pie, especially looked forward to by the men to be eaten with their favorite drink, beer, before going to the "football game"—which is not our American variety but something completely their own, somewhat like soccer but with eighteen players on each team.

The big difference in their main meals is that salads are never part of the dinner menu. They are mainly served as part of a party buffet with meat and salads only. Salads are also served at barbecues together with grilled beef and pork sausages, which by the way are very different from our hot dogs. Barbecues are a very popular way of entertaining in Australia as this fits in with their casual way of life, in dress and otherwise.

A formal dinner consists of an appetizer, such as a seafood cocktail, or very often fresh fruit such as fruit cocktails, melons and avocados, or soup, then the main course and a dessert. One of the popular soups is kangaroo tail soup. However, I have not included a recipe for this as for obvious reasons—the ingredients are not as abundant here as in Australia! But oxtail soup is also popular, and so is barley soup which, of course, has travelled there from Scotland where it had originated.

Desserts are most often some baked delicacy, of which I have given several examples, the most popular being Pavlova, the national favorite, which is a delicious meringue concoction, always filled with fruits, exotic or native, and lots of whipped cream. One of their special touches is to spread the fresh, sliced fruit with either fresh or canned pulp of the passion fruit—and this makes it extra delectable.

As in England, tea is a very popular drink but they do not as a rule make a main meal around it. Except for Sunday afternoons when tea and pastries are served—sometimes called Devonshire tea. At this time scones, topped with jam and whipped cream are served together with other pastries. And, as in England, beer is the one favorite among the men but unlike England, it is served ice-cold as it is here in the U.S.

SWEET AND SOUR LAMB CHOPS	*Jarred Chops*
STEAK AND PINEAPPLE CASSEROLE	
CHICKEN WITH LEMON SAUCE	
VEAL AND HAM PIE	
CHEESE AND ONION PIE	
PAVLOVA MERINGUE DESSERT	*Pavlova*
COCONUT PUDDING	
CHOCOLATE SAUCE PUDDING	
RUM CAKE	
MELTING MOMENTS (YOYOS)	
CINNAMON SQUARES	
RASPBERRY SQUARES	
CONTINENTAL SQUARES	
CHOCOLATE PEPPERMINT SQUARES	
HEDGEHOG SQUARES	

SWEET AND SOUR LAMB CHOPS

Australia   *(Jarred Chops)*

Lamb is one of the most popular meats in Australia and their "Jarred Chops" is an easy and delicious way to prepare it.

5	(5)	shoulder lamb chops (2-2½ lbs or 1-1¼ kg)
1½ tbs	(1½ tbs)	flour
2 ts	(2 ts)	sugar
		salt and pepper to taste
2 tbs	(2 tbs)	Worcestershire sauce
3 tbs	(3 tbs)	tomato sauce
1 tbs	(1 tbs)	vinegar

Dredge chops in mixture of flour, sugar, salt and pepper then place them in a baking dish. Mix together Worcestershire sauce, tomato sauce and vinegar and pour over chops, cover dish and bake in a 350° F (175 °C) oven 1½-2 hours, or until meat is thoroughly tender.

Serves 4-5.

STEAK AND PINEAPPLE CASSEROLE

Australia

A very tasty casserole and nice for company as it can be made well ahead of time.

2 lbs.	(1 kg)	round steak or other boneless cut of beef
3 tbs	(3 tbs)	flour
		salt and pepper to taste
1	(1)	medium onion, chopped (¾ cup or 180 mL)
3 tbs	(3 tbs)	butter or margarine
1	(1)	can pineapple chunks (about 16 oz or 500 g)
3 tbs	(3 tbs)	tomato paste
⅓ cup	(80 mL)	water

Cut steak into 1" (25 mm) cubes and dredge in the flour, seasoned with salt and pepper. Brown meat well on all sides in a skillet, then remove meat and put it into a buttered baking dish. Sauté onion in the same skillet for about 5 minutes, then add to meat. Add pineapple with juice, tomato paste and water to the baking dish, cover and bake in a 350° F (175° C) oven for 1½ hours, or until meat is thoroughly tender.

Serves 5-6.

CHICKEN WITH LEMON SAUCE

Australia

1	(*1*)	frying chicken (3–3½ lbs or 1½–1¾ kg), cut into serving pieces
2 tbs	(*2 tbs*)	flour
2 ts	(*2 ts*)	paprika
		salt and pepper to taste
3 tbs	(*3 tbs*)	butter or margarine

Mix together flour, paprika, salt and pepper and dredge chicken pieces in this. Arrange chicken, skin side down, single layer, in a large baking dish. Melt butter and brush on chicken pieces. Bake uncovered for 30 minutes in a 350° F (175° C) oven, then turn over pieces, pour sauce over them, making sure every piece gets a share, and continue baking an additional 30 minutes or until chicken is golden brown and tender.

Serves 4–5.

Sauce:

3 tbs	(*3 tbs*)	salad oil
1 tbs	(*1 tbs*)	soy sauce
¼ cup	(*60 mL*)	lemon juice
		grated rind of 1 lemon
½ ts	(*½ ts*)	salt
¼ ts	(*¼ ts*)	pepper
1	(*1*)	clove garlic, finely minced

Combine all the ingredients and mix well. Refrigerate for at least 1 hour before using, to blend flavors.

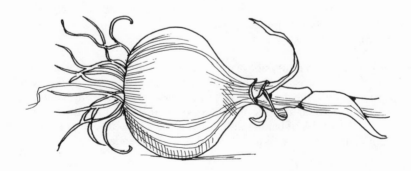

VEAL AND HAM PIE

Australia

An excellent way to use left-over veal roast.

1 lb	(½ kg)	thinly sliced veal (meat may be raw or cooked)
¼ lb	(125 g)	thinly sliced ham
		salt and pepper to taste
2 tbs	(2 tbs)	parsley
3	(3)	medium size potatoes, peeled and thinly sliced
¾ cup	(180 mL)	meat stock (may be made from bouillon cubes)
2 tbs	(2 tbs)	butter or margarine
		single pie crust (see page 54)

Put ⅓ of the meat on the bottom of a 2 quart (2 L) casserole, sprinkle with some of the parsley and salt and pepper. Add ⅓ of the potatoes and continue the layers until all is used up, ending with potatoes. Add stock, dot with butter. Roll out pastry dough to fit top of casserole, make a couple of slits to let steam escape, then bake in a 350° F (175° C) oven for 1½ hours. Serve immediately to 4–5.

CHEESE AND ONION PIE

Australia

		double pie crust (see page 54)
2 lbs	(1 kg)	white onions, peeled and coarsely chopped
½ lb	(¼ kg)	mild flavored cheese (Muenster or mild cheddar)
2 tbs	(2 tbs)	milk
		salt and pepper to taste

Bring chopped onions to a boil in a saucepan, then turn down heat and simmer for 10 minutes. Drain. Grate the cheese. Line a 9″ (220 mm) pie dish with half the pastry, place half the drained onions in this, then cover with a layer of half the cheese. Sprinkle with salt and pepper, then repeat the layers once more. Sprinkle with the milk and place remaining crust on top. Cut a few slits in top crust to enable steam to escape. Bake in a 375° F (190° C) oven for about 25 minutes or until pastry is golden in color. Serves 6 as a side dish, 4 if served as a main luncheon course.

PAVLOVA MERINGUE DESSERT

Australia   *(Pavlova)*

I do not know how this dessert got its name—maybe because it is light, fluffy and airy like the famous ballerina. Anyhow, it is the dessert of Australia and there are many versions of it. If a small can of passion fruit can be obtained and spread over sliced bananas for the filling, it is a heavenly concoction indeed.

2	*(2)*	egg whites
1 ts	*(1 ts)*	vinegar
1 ts	*(1 ts)*	corn starch
1 ts	*(1 ts)*	vanilla extract
4 tbs	*(4 tbs)*	boiling water
1 cup	*(250 mL)*	sugar

In an electric mixer beat under low speed all the ingredients except sugar for a few minutes, increase speed to medium, then add sugar, a little at a time and keep on beating until mixture forms a stiff meringue. Carefully grease a piece of aluminum foil and place it on a baking sheet. Use a 9" (220 mm) cake pan and draw a line around it on the foil to get the outline, then pile meringue inside the circle, making it a little higher towards the edge. Bake in a 250° F (120° C) oven about 30 minutes. Turn off heat and let meringue cool in the oven.

Filling:

1–3 cups	*(250–750 mL)*	fresh or canned fruit, of any kind, as desired, such as bananas, pineapples, peaches, strawberries etc. either mixed or of only one variety.

Topping:

1 cup	*(250 mL)*	heavy cream, whipped

Australia   **COCONUT PUDDING**

A light-as-a-feather pudding and you wonder what happened to the bread as it seems not to be in it at all.

1	*(1)*	slice white bread, crust removed, and cubed
½ cup	*(125 mL)*	shredded coconut
2 cups	*(500 mL)*	milk, scalded

(Continued on next page)

(Coconut Pudding, cont.)

1	(1)	egg, separated
3 tbs	(3 tbs)	sugar
		pinch of salt
1 tbs	(1 tbs)	melted butter

Soak bread cubes and coconut in scalded milk for a few minutes. Beat egg yolk slightly, add sugar, salt and melted butter. Stir well and combine with milk mixture. Beat egg white until stiff and fold in. Pour into greased one quart (1 L) baking dish, place same in a basin with boiling water up to within 1″ (25 mm) of its top, put in the oven and bake at 350° F (175° C) 35–40 minutes. Serve slightly warm or cold, to 4.

CHOCOLATE SAUCE PUDDING
Australia

I must say I was kind of dubious when I got this recipe. It just did not make sense to me as I had never come across anything like it before. But after I had made it-surprise!-there was the pudding, or rather cake with its own ready-made sauce, and very delicious too.

2 tbs	(2 tbs)	butter or margarine
½ cup	(125 mL)	sugar
1	(1)	egg
½ cup	(125 mL)	milk
1 cup	(250 mL)	flour
½ ts	(½ ts)	baking powder

Cream butter and sugar, add egg and mix well then add flour mixed with baking powder and milk alternately while stirring. Place batter in a greased 8″ (200 mm) pie dish.

Sauce:

2 tbs	(2 tbs)	cocoa
½ cup	(125 mL)	sugar
1½ cup	(375 mL)	boiling water

Mix together sugar and cocoa and sprinkle over batter in pie dish. Gently pour boiling water over it and bake in a 350° F (175° C) oven for 30 minutes. Serve warm with cream or ice cream. Serves 4–5.

Australia   RUM CAKE

A delectable "rummy" cake, or if you use the variation you may call it pudding.

Sponge cake:

3	(3)	eggs
1½ cups	(375 mL)	sugar
¾ cup	(180 mL)	milk
3 tbs	(3 tbs)	butter or margarine
1 ts	(1 ts)	vanilla extract
1½ cups	(375 mL)	flour
2 ts	(2 ts)	baking powder
¼ ts	¼ ts	salt

Beat eggs until thick and foamy, gradually add sugar. Continue beating until mixture is very light and fluffy. Melt butter in a saucepan, add milk and heat but do not let it come to a boil. Sift together flour, baking powder and salt and add to egg mixture and mix well. Add the hot milk mixture and stir batter only until it is smooth. Pour batter into two greased and floured 8″ (200 mm) baking pans and bake in a 350° F (175° C) oven for about 25 minutes or until done. Turn out on racks to get completely cool.

Filling:

1 tbs	(1 tbs)	cocoa
¾ cup	(180 mL)	sugar
2 tbs	(2 tbs)	milk
2	(2)	eggs, separated
½ cup	(125 mL)	butter or margarine
¼ cup	(60 mL)	rum

Put cocoa, ¼ cup (60 mL) sugar, milk and egg yolks in a small saucepan and cook until thickened but without boiling, then let it cool.

Cream butter with remaining sugar until light and fluffy, add cocoa mixture and beat well, then add rum and mix well. Beat egg whites until stiff, and fold in.

Assembly:

¼ cup	(60 mL)	rum
1 cup	(250 mL)	heavy cream
1 tbs	(1 tbs)	confectioners' sugar
		shaved chocolate

(Continued on next page)

(Rum Cake, cont.)

Sprinkle each layer with rum, then add half of filling on top of each layer, refrigerate for a couple of hours, then put one layer on top of the other, beat cream with confectioners' sugar and spread all over cake.

Decorate the cake with chocolate shavings.

VARIATION:

Instead of using two cake layers, use either pound cake or other loaf cake, cut into slices. Line a bowl with some of these slices, sprinkle with rum then pour rum filling on top. Cover with remaining cake. Put in refrigerator over-night, turn out of bowl, cover with whipped cream, decorate.

MELTING MOMENTS (YOYOS)

Australia

1 cup	(*250 mL*)	butter
1 cup	(*250 mL*)	confectioners' sugar
¼ cup	(*60 mL*)	corn starch
2 cups	(*500 mL*)	flour
		pinch of salt
1 ts	(*1 ts*)	vanilla extract

Cream butter and sugar until light and fluffy, add vanilla extract. Sift together flour, cornstarch and salt and add to butter mixture and mix well. Roll into small balls about ¾″ (18 mm) in diameter and place on a well greased baking sheet. Dip a fork in flour and press each ball to flatten, making a criss-cross pattern. Bake in a 350° F (175° C) oven until golden colored, about 10–12 minutes. When cold, sandwich the cookies together with the following lemon filling.

Filling:

4 tbs	(*4 tbs*)	butter
1 cup	(*250 mL*)	confectioners' sugar
		juice of ½ lemon

Cream butter and sugar then add lemon juice and blend into a smooth paste.   Makes about 3 dozen.

CINNAMON SQUARES

Australia

Australia has a number of nice recipes for brownie-type cakes, cut into squares or bars. Here are several versions.

½ cup	*(250 mL)*	butter or margarine
¾ cup	*(180 mL)*	sugar
1	*(1)*	egg, separated
1 cup	*(250 mL)*	flour
½ ts	*(½ ts)*	baking powder
2 ts	*(2 ts)*	cinnamon
1 ts	*(1 ts)*	vanilla extract
1 cup	*(250 mL)*	raisins

Beat sugar and butter until light and fluffy, then beat in egg. Add flour sifted together with baking powder and cinnamon and mix well. Add vanilla and raisins and mix, then spread evenly in a square 9″ (220 mm) baking pan. Bake for 20–25 minutes in a 350° F (175° C) oven. Cut into squares while warm and leave in pan to cool.

RASPBERRY SQUARES

Australia

½ cup	*(125 mL)*	butter or margarine
1 cup	*(250 mL)*	sugar
2	*(2)*	eggs, separated
1 tbs	*(1 tbs)*	milk
2 cups	*(500 mL)*	flour
1 ts	*(1 ts)*	baking powder
5 tbs	*(5 tbs)*	raspberry jam
1 cup	*(250 mL)*	grated coconut

Cream butter and one-half the sugar until light and fluffy, then add egg yolks and milk and mix well. Sift flour, and baking powder together, add and mix. Press dough into a 8 x 13″ (200 x 300 mm) baking pan. Spread top with raspberry jam. Beat egg whites until stiff, add remaining sugar, a little at a time, then fold in coconut. Spread this on top of raspberry jam. Bake in a 350° F (175° C) oven for 25 minutes. Cut into squares when cool.

CONTINENTAL SQUARES

Australia

½ cup	*(125 mL)*	butter or margarine
⅓ cup	*(80 mL)*	sugar
3 tbs	*(3 tbs)*	apricot jam
1 cup	*(250 ml)*	grated coconut
2 tbs	*(2 tbs)*	cocoa
1 cup	*(250 mL)*	flour
1 ts	*(1 ts)*	baking powder

Cream butter and sugar until light and fluffy, add coconut, cocoa, and 1 tbs of the jam. Sift together flour and baking powder and add to butter mixture and blend well. Press into a 9 x 9" (220 x 220 mm) square baking pan and bake in a 350° F (175° C) oven for 25 minutes. While still hot, spread top with apricot jam, then spread with chocolate icing. Cut into squares when cold.

Chocolate Icing:

1 oz	*(30 g)*	unsweetened chocolate (1 square)
2 tbs	*(2 tbs)*	butter or margarine
1 tbs	*(1 tbs)*	milk
1 cup	*(250 mL)*	confectioners' sugar

Melt butter and chocolate in a small dish, set in hot water, add milk and sugar and beat well until mixture is smooth.

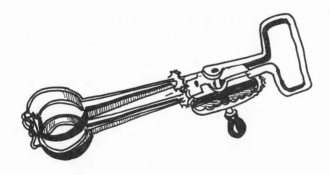

CHOCOLATE PEPPERMINT SQUARES

Australia

Australia also has several kinds of cakes or cookies, that can be made without the use of an oven, which can be handy at times. They are all good and if you like a faint flavor of peppermint, this first one is a must to try.

Bottom layer:

½ cup	(*125 mL*)	butter or margarine
8 oz	(*250 g*)	crushed tea biscuits (about 2½ cups or 625 mL) (or use graham cracker crumbs)
7 oz (scant cup)	(*225 mL*)	sweetened condensed milk (½ can)
¾ cup	(*180 mL*)	grated coconut
1 tbs	(*1 tbs*)	cocoa

In a medium size saucepan melt butter or margarine then add remaining ingredients and mix well. Press into a greased 7 x 12″ (180 x 300 mm) baking dish.

Filling:

1 cup	(*250 mL*)	confectioners' sugar
2 tbs	(*2 tbs*)	melted butter
1 ts	(*1 ts*)	peppermint flavoring
1 ts	(*1*)	cream

Sift sugar and mix with remaining ingredients then spread in a thin layer over the crumb mixture of the bottom layer.

Topping:

2 tbs	(*2 tbs*)	butter
2 oz	(*60 g*)	semi-sweet chocolate (2 squares)
¼ cup	(*60 mL*)	confectioners' sugar
1 ts	(*1 ts*)	vanilla extract

Melt butter and chocolate over hot water, then add sugar and vanilla and mix well. Spread on top of the filling and place the dish in refrigerator for at least a couple of hours before cutting into squares and serving. If serving is delayed, keep in refrigerator in order to keep the topping firm.

HEDGEHOG SQUARES

Australia

½ cup	(*125 mL*)	butter or margarine
½ cup	(*125 mL*)	sugar
1 tbs	(*1 tbs*)	cocoa
½ lb	(*250 lb*)	crushed tea biscuits (about 2½ cups or 625 mL) (or use graham cracker crumbs)
¾ cup	(*180 mL*)	chopped nuts (any kind)
1	(*1*)	egg, well beaten
1 ts	(*1 ts*)	vanilla extract

Place butter and sugar in a small saucepan and melt over low heat, stirring off and on to make sure that the mixture does not brown. Sift cocoa and add together with crumbs, nuts, beaten egg and vanilla, and mix well. Spread mixture into a greased 7 x 12″ (180 x 300 mm) baking dish. Press well with a spoon, and spread with the topping in the preceding recipe. Let set in the refrigerator for at least two hours before cutting into squares and serving. It is also best to keep the squares in the refrigerator for re-serving, in order to keep the topping firm.

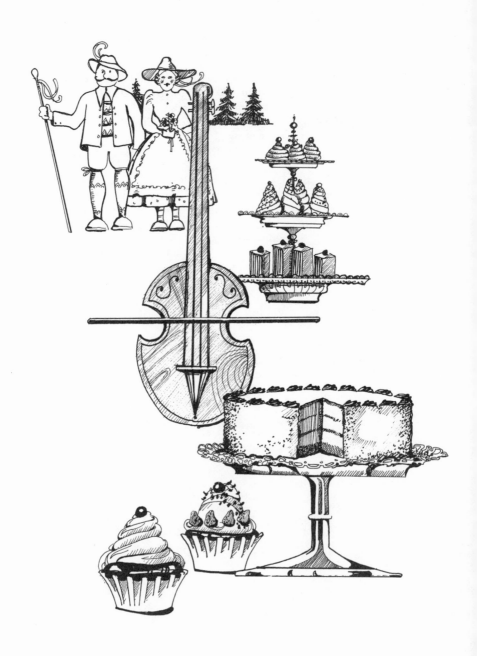

Austria

SITUATED as Austria is in the middle of Europe, its eating and cooking habits are, of course, influenced by the surrounding countries. It was united with Hungary for several hundred years and many dishes are practically the same in these two countries.

Still it managed to develop specialties of its own, and some have become so popular and widely spread that they have kept their original names wherever they are served—I am thinking of *Wienerschnitzel* and *Wieners*, but I am afraid that the wieners we get in our country only have the name in common with their ancestor sausages in Austria.

Soups play an important part of the eating habits and are often of such substantial kind that they are meals in themselves, especially as the Austrian specialties of *knoedels* (dumplings), pastas or small meatballs are added to the soup stock.

But most of all when we think of Austria, it is their baked products that come to mind, because they are so outstanding. Visitors to that country will remember the little *konditoreis*, where coffee or tea is served together with fabulous pastries or slices of wonderful *tortes* such as *Sachertorte* or *Linzertorte*, and almost always served with *schlag*, that is rich, whipped cream.

BAKED FISH PAPRIKA	*Paprika Fisch*
VEAL CUTLET FROM VIENNA	*Wienerschnitzel*
DESSERT OMELET FROM	
SALZBURG	*Salzburger Nockerl*
LINZER TORTE	*Linzer Torte*

(*Continued on next page*)

SACHER TORTE	*Sacher Torte*
SIMPLIFIED SACHER TORTE	
OLD VIENNA TORTE	*Alt Wiener Torte*
APPLE TART	*Apfel Torte*
STRAWBERRY TART	*Erdbeer Torte*
FILBERT BARS	*Haselnuss Stangerl*

BAKED FISH PAPRIKA

Austria   *(Paprika Fisch)*

2 lbs.	*(1 kg)*	fish fillets (preferably fresh water fish, but salt water fish will do)
		salt and pepper to taste
2 tbs	*(2 tbs)*	butter or margarine
1	*(1)*	large onion, finely chopped (about 1 cup or 250 mL)
1½ tbs	*(1½ tbs)*	paprika
⅔ cup	*(160 mL)*	light cream

Cut fish into serving pieces and sprinkle with salt and pepper. Sauté onion in butter or margarine until translucent, then put in a buttered baking dish (a 9 x 9″ (220 x 220 mm) square baking dish fits well with this). Place fish on top, sprinkle with paprika and carefully pour the cream over. Bake in a 350° F (175° C) oven about 20–25 minutes, or until fish is flaky, basting at least three times. Serve with potatoes or noodles.

Serves 5–6.

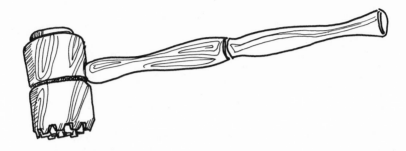

VEAL CUTLET FROM VIENNA

Austria   *(Wienerschnitzel)*

Wienerschnitzel (actual translation, Cutlet from Vienna) is probably the most well-known of Austria's contribution to America's cuisine, and it definitely deserves to be so.

1½ lbs	(¾ kg)	veal cutlets, ⅓" (8 mm) thick, cut from top of leg
		salt and pepper to taste
2 tbs	(2 tbs)	flour
1	(1)	egg, slightly beaten
½-⅔ cup	(125-160 mL)	dry breadcrumbs
2 tbs	(2 tbs)	butter or margarine

For garnish:

4	(4)	lemon slices
4	(4)	rolled up anchovy fillets
2 ts	(2 ts)	capers

Flatten out meat slightly by pounding it with a mallet or the bottom of a heavy carving knife, season with salt and pepper, turn it in the flour, then in the egg and finally in the breadcrumbs. Brown meat in the butter or margarine on both sides until golden brown, then continue cooking for a few more minutes, or until desired done-ness. Garnish each slice by putting one slice of lemon, one rolled-up anchovy fillet and ⅓ ts capers on top.

Serves 4.

DESSERT OMELET FROM SALZBURG

Austria   *(Salzburger Nockerl)*

An unusual but delicious dessert—perfect to follow a meal whose main dish is soup.

3 tbs	(3 tbs)	butter, at room temperature
½ cup	(125 mL)	sugar
5	(5)	eggs, separated
3 tbs	(3 tbs)	flour
½ cup	(125 mL)	milk
For dusting:		confectioners' sugar

Cream butter and sugar until light and fluffy, add egg yolks one at a time, beating well after each addition. Beat egg whites until very stiff. Add flour to egg mixture and beat well, then fold egg whites into batter. Bring milk to a boil and pour into a 10″ (250 mm) all-iron skillet, if available, otherwise use a 9″ or 10″ (220 or 250 mm) pie dish. Pour batter into hot milk and put in a preheated 425° F (220° C) oven but turn down heat immediately to 400° F (205° C) and bake for 5–8 minutes until golden on top. Mixture should be firm on the outside but light and slightly moist on the inside. Dish out immediately with a large spoon and dust each serving with confectioners' sugar. It is important that this dish is served without delay, because, like a soufflé, it will collapse in minutes.   Serves 4–5.

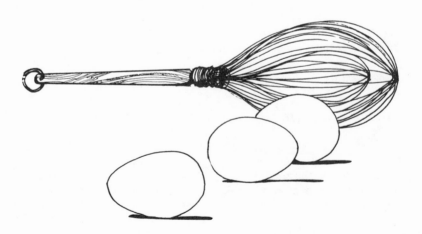

LINZER TORTE

Austria   *(Linzer Torte)*

*Linzer Torte is one of the classical cakes of Austria, and I suggest that it should
not be baked and served the same day, as it is rather hard at first. Therefore let
it "mellow" for at least two days, and preferably 3–4 days before it is used.
Thus (and then) it makes a nice dessert for dinner for a busy person who avoids
last minute rush with the dessert.*

1¼ cup	(310 mL)	flour
2½ cups	(625 mL)	ground, blanched almonds
		(about 1½ cups (375 mL) unground)
⅓ cup	(80 mL)	sugar
½ cup	(125 mL)	butter
1	(1)	egg, slightly beaten
		grated rind of 1 lemon
1	(1)	egg white
¼ cup	(60 mL)	currant jelly or raspberry jam

Mix together flour, ground almonds and sugar. Cut in butter with a pastry blender, until mixture has the texture of coarse crumbs. Add beaten egg and stir until well mixed, then knead with your hands on a baking board for about one minute till you get a smooth dough. Form into a ball and chill at least 1 hour in refrigerator.

When ready to use, set aside ⅓ of dough and roll out remainder on a floured baking board to fit into the bottom of an 8″ (200 mm) baking pan, preferably a spring pan. Take some of the dough that was set aside and role it between your hands to make a long thin roll, about ¼″ (6 mm) thick and place it around the torte to make an edge. Cover the bottom of the shell with jam or jelly. Use remaining dough to make more thin rolls and make a lattice and put on top, criss-cross fashion. Carefully brush lattice rolls with slightly beaten egg white.

Bake in a 375° F (190° C) oven for 15 minutes, then reduce heat to 350° F (175° C) and bake 20–25 minutes longer or until torte is golden in color and shrinks away from sides of pan. Before serving, refill spaces in the lattice with some more jam or jelly, then dust with confectioners' sugar.   Serves 8–10.

SACHER TORTE

Austria   *(Sacher Torte)*

*Sacher Torte is one cake that almost every family in Austria makes differently.
All versions seem to be good, and share a wonderful keeping quality.*

3	(3)	squares semi-sweet chocolate (3 oz or 85 g)
1 tbs	(1 tbs)	hot water
½ cup	(125 mL)	butter
⅓ cup	(80 mL)	sugar
4	(4)	eggs, separated
1 cup	(250 mL)	flour

Melt chocolate together with hot water in a double boiler. Cream butter and sugar until light and fluffy, then add egg yolks one at a time while beating, to get them thoroughly incorporated into mixture, which should be very light and fluffy before the melted chocolate is added. Continue beating until well blended. Beat egg whites until stiff, then carefully fold into batter. Bake in a greased and floured 9″ (220 mm) baking pan in a 350° F (175° C) oven 35–40 minutes or until tested as done.

Glaze:

| ¼ cup | (60 mL) | apricot jam |

Heat jam over low heat while stirring until it becomes somewhat thinner. Spread smoothly on the cake while it is still hot.

Icing:

| 6 tbs | (6 tbs) | butter |
| 3 | (3) | squares semi-sweet chocolate (3 oz or 85 g) |

Melt chocolate in a double boiler, then add butter. Keep stirring to obtain a smooth mixture. Spread icing right over apricot glaze and on sides. Cool cake thoroughly, for several hours or overnight.

SIMPLIFIED SACHER TORTE

Austria

The simplified version of the Sacher Torte is good, but it does not keep as well as the real McCoy and should be eaten within a day or so after it is made.

½ cup	(*125 mL*)	butter or margarine
2 tbs	(*2 tbs*)	cocoa
½ cup	(*125 mL*)	milk
¼ cup	(*60 mL*)	strong coffee
2	(*2*)	eggs
¾ cup	(*180 mL*)	sugar
1¼ cup	(*310 mL*)	flour
1 ts	(*1 ts*)	baking powder

Melt butter or margarine, add cocoa, then milk and coffee and mix well. Bring to a boil then cool mixture to luke-warm. Beat eggs and sugar until light and fluffy, add flour sifted together with baking powder alternately with butter mixture. Bake in a 9″ (220 mm) baking pan that has been greased and floured, in a 350° F (175° C) oven about 30–35 minutes, or until tested as done. Let cake cool thoroughly, then proceed as for the previous recipe in regard to glaze and icing.

OLD VIENNA TORTE

Austria   (*Alt Wiener Torte*)

The cakes of Austria are all so good! Here is one that has an unusual filling and frosting made from chestnuts. Here in United States chestnuts seldom are used in pastries. Although this cake entails a lot of details, it is not too hard to do, if you take one step at a time.

Sponge layer:

2	(2)	eggs
½ cup	(125 mL)	sugar
1 tbs	(1 tbs)	butter or margarine
¼ cup	(60 mL)	milk
½ cup	(125 mL)	flour
1 ts (scant)	(1 ts)	baking powder

Beat eggs until thick and fluffy, gradually add sugar. Do not underbeat, because the longer the beating, the better the cake will be. Melt butter in a saucepan, add milk and heat until hot, but do not let it boil. Sift together flour and baking powder and add to egg mixture, then add hot milk mixture and stir only until batter is smooth. Pour into a greased and floured 9″ (220 mm) round cake pan and bake in a 350° F (175° C) oven about 25 minutes, or until tested dry.

Chocolate hazelnut layer:

2	(2)	squares (2 oz or 60 g) semi-sweet chocolate, melted
4 tbs	(4 tbs)	butter, softened
¼ cup	(60 mL)	sugar
3	(3)	eggs, separated
1¼ cups	(310 mL)	toasted, blanched and finely ground hazelnuts
¼ cup	(60 mL)	flour

Melt chocolate in a glass dish in hot water in saucepan. Cream butter and sugar until light and fluffy. Add egg yolks, one at a time, beating well after each addition until mixture is creamy. Stir in melted and slightly cooled chocolate. Fold in nuts and flour. Beat egg whites until very stiff, then fold into batter and blend well, but lightly. Pour into a greased and floured 9″ (220 mm) round baking pan and bake in a 350° F (175° C) oven about 25 minutes. Let cool for 10 minutes, then carefully remove from pan and cool some more.

(*Continued on next page*)

(Old Vienna Torte, cont.)

Chestnut Cream Filling and Frosting:

½ cup	(125 mL)	butter, softened
¾ cup	(180 mL)	verifine sugar
1	(1)	egg yolk
1½ lb	(¾ kg)	raw chestnuts
3 cups	(750 mL)	water
3 tbs	(3 tbs)	cognac

Boil chestnuts for about 20 minutes, then remove them while water is still hot, one by one, and peel them. You may want to have a bowl with cold water to dip your fingers in while doing this, but the main thing is to peel them while very hot, as soon as they get luke-warm it becomes diffi-cult. Put the chestnuts through a potato ricer or a food grinder, using the finest blade.

Beat butter with sugar until light and fluffy, add egg yolk and continue beating. Stir in riced or ground chestnuts and add cognac, a spoonful at a time. Mix until very creamy.

Chocolate Icing:

1	(1)	square semi-sweet chocolate (1 oz or 30 g)
1 ts	(1 ts)	hot water
2 tbs	(2 tbs)	butter, softened

Melt chocolate over hot water in a glass dish. When soft, add hot water and butter and stir until smooth.

Assembly:

When layers are completely cool, put chocolate layer on a cake plate, then spread with about ⅓ of the frosting mixture. Place sponge layer on top and refrigerate for a couple of hours, then spread with remaining frosting on top and sides. Decorate with the chocolate icing, using a cake decorator with the smallest tube-like opening, squeezing first a circle around the cake, then vertical and horizontal lines across the top. Keep in refrigerator until ready to serve.

Serves 10–12.

APPLE TART

Austria   *(Apfel Torte)*

When you wish to serve an apple dessert with a certain elegance, try this recipe.

Tart shell:

1 cup	(*250 mL*)	flour
3 tbs	(*3 tbs*)	sugar
		pinch of salt
		grated rind of ½ lemon
6 tbs	(*6 tbs*)	butter or margarine
1	(*1*)	egg, slightly beaten
½ tbs	(*½ tbs*)	vinegar
1 tbs	(*1 tbs*)	cold water

Sift together flour, sugar and salt and add grated rind. Cut in butter or margarine with a pastry cutter until mixture resembles coarse crumbs. Add egg, vinegar and water and mix thoroughly, scraping up loose pieces around the bowl with the ball of dough. Turn out on a lightly floured baking board and knead for a few minutes until a medium-firm dough has been obtained. If necessary, add a bit more flour. Shape into a ball, wrap in plastic wrap and refrigerate for 20–30 minutes.

Filling:

2	(*2*)	large apples
¼ cup	(*60 mL*)	light raisins
¼ cup	(*60 mL*)	finely chopped nuts (almonds, walnuts or pecans)
½ cup	(*125 mL*)	sugar
1 ts	(*1 ts*)	cinnamon
2 tbs	(*2 tbs*)	melted butter

Peel and core apples, then cut into thin slices. Put in a bowl with water mixed with a little lemon juice or ascorbic acid to prevent discoloring.

For sprinkling:

½ tbs	(*½ tbs*)	confectioners' sugar

(Continued on next page)

(Apple Tart, cont.)

Assembly:

Roll out dough on a floured baking board to fit a 9″ (220 mm) pan, preferably with removable sides, or a pie dish, with about ½″ (12 mm) of the dough hanging over the edge. Cover dough with one layer of apples, slightly overlapping each other, leaving a 1″ (25 mm) margin all around. Sprinkle half of the nuts, raisins and sugar mixed with cinnamon over the apples, then cover with a second layer of apples and sprinkle with remaining nuts, raisins and sugar-cinnamon mixture. Fold the overlapping edge over towards the apples, and spoon melted butter over filling. Bake in a 350° F (175° C) oven 30–35 minutes or until golden brown and the apples are tender. Serve slightly warm or cold, sprinkled with confectioners' sugar.   Serves 6–8.

STRAWBERRY TART

Austria   *(Erdbeer Torte)*

Tart:

1 cup	(250 mL)	flour
3 tbs	(3 tbs)	sugar
		grated rind of 1 lemon
6 tbs	(6 tbs)	butter or margarine
		pinch of salt
1	(1)	egg, slightly beaten
1-2 tbs	(1-2 tbs)	water

Cut butter into flour with a pastry blender until mixture resembles coarse crumbs, add lemon rind, salt and whole egg. Add enough water to hold dough together and work together into a ball, using this to scrape sticky dough off the sides of the bowl. Cover with a plastic wrap and chill in refrigerator for at least ½ hour.

Roll out dough between two sheets of waxed paper and fit it into a 9″ (220 mm) spring pan or pie pan. Crimp edges for decoration as for a pie crust. Prick bottom and sides of dough with a fork to prevent air bubbles from forming while baking. Bake in a 350° F (175° C) oven about 15–20 minutes, or until crust shrinks from the sides of the pan. Let cool completely before filling.

Vanilla Cream:

1 cup	(250 mL)	milk
3	(3)	egg yolks
¼ cup	(60 mL)	sugar
2 tbs	(2 tbs)	corn starch
1 ts	(1 ts)	vanilla extract

Topping:

| 4 cups | (1 L) | strawberries |
| ¼ cup | (60 mL) | currant jelly |

Mix corn starch with milk and sugar, then stir in egg yolks. Heat in a double boiler or a thick bottom saucepan while stirring until cream becomes thick, but do not bring to a full boil. If a saucepan is used, set it in cold water immediately to stop cooking action, then add vanilla. Cool mixture, stirring it from time to time.

When entirely cool, pour vanilla cream into tart. Put a layer of hulled and cleaned strawberries to cover entire surface. Heat currant jelly carefully and spoon this over strawberries. Cool to let set, then serve.

Serves 6–8.

FILBERT BARS

Austria   (*Haselnuss Stangerl*)

What makes people remember most from a visit in Austria is that country's wonderful skill in baking pastries and cakes. They make a lot of use of nuts, and filberts are favorites. Here is a recipe for bars where both filberts and cocoa are used in a delicious blend of flavors.

1¾ cup	(*430 mL*)	ground filberts (about 1 cup or 250 mL unground nuts) (Reserve ½ cup or 125 mL for the filling)
5 tbs	(*5 tbs*)	sugar
4 tbs	(*4 tbs*)	flour
3	(*3*)	egg whites
2 tbs	(*2 tbs*)	butter, melted

Filbert Cocoa filling:

2 tbs	(*2 tbs*)	butter, softened
2 tbs	(*2 tbs*)	sugar (verifine)
2 ts	(*2 ts*)	cocoa
		ground filberts (½ cup or 125 mL, above)

Mix sugar, 1¼ cup (310 mL) ground filberts and flour together. Beat egg whites until stiff and carefully combine with nut mixture and melted butter. Press dough through a cookie press, using the tube-like attachment, onto a buttered baking sheet and make bars about 1½″ (38 mm) long. Bake in a 350° F (175° C) about 15 minutes. The bars will still be soft but will harden as they cool. Let rest on the baking sheet until slightly cool, then loosen with a knife or spatula and remove and cool them completely. Spread filling between the bottoms of two bars and sandwich them together.

Makes 20–25 bars.

Filling:

Cream butter and sugar until light and fluffy, add cocoa and mix well, then add remaining ground filberts and mix until well blended.

Belgium

BELGIAN cooking is to a considerable extent influenced by its neighbor to the South and a number of dishes commonly made in Belgium are practically the same as those in France. And some dishes made in the North are very similar to those made in Holland. But I guess this is a natural consequence for a small country friendly with its neighbors and having a language in common.

There are, of course, many things in the Belgian cuisine that are completely their own. Among them the most famous is Waterzooie which is a thick soup—or a thin stew—whichever you would like to call it, made with either chicken or fish.

One popular item in Belgium is mussels and French fries—Moules et Frites—which are commonly sold from push-carts in the streets.

There are several vegetables which are a specialty of the Belgian farms and the most important one of these is endive, which is used both in salads and cooked. An excellent variety of asparagus is grown in large quantities. It is often eaten with a sauce made of the yolk of hard-boiled eggs mixed with butter, or simply with a soft-boiled egg.

SHRIMP STUFFED TOMATOES	*Tomatoes aux Crevettes*
FLEMISH BRUSSEL SPROUT PURÉE	*Purée Flamande de Choux de Bruxelle*
MUSSEL STEW	*Matelote de Moules*
SHRIMP CROQUETTES	*Croquettes de Crevettes*
BELGIAN CHICKEN STEW	*Waterzooi van Kip*
FLEMISH BEEF STEW	*Carbonnade des Flamands*
FLEMISH WAFFLES	*Gaufres à la Flamande*
MOCHA CHEESE MOLD	*Crème Fromage au Café*

SHRIMP STUFFED TOMATOES

Belgium   *(Tomates aux Crevettes)*

This is quite a simple appetizer, but is so popular in Belgium that I felt I had to include it. But make it with the home-made "lemony" mayonnaise below, to make it extra special.

6	(6)	large tomatoes, fully ripe but firm
3 cups	(750 mL)	tiny size shrimp (if larger shrimp are used, cut into pieces) or use 3 cans of the 8 oz (500 g) size
1 cup	(250 mL)	mayonnaise
		salt and pepper to taste
½ cup	(125 mL)	minced parsley

Cut a slice off the stem end of the tomatoes, then with a teaspoon carefully scoop out seeds. Let them drain for ten minutes. If fresh shrimp are used, bring them to a boil in a small amount of water, then immediately remove from heat and let them stand for a few minutes, at which time they will have turned pink. If canned shrimp are used, let them drain well. Mix shrimp and mayonnaise with salt and pepper, then stuff each tomato with the mixture. Sprinkle with parsley and serve on a bed of lettuce leaves, as an appetizer. Six servings.

Mayonnaise:

1	(1)	egg, at room temperature
1 ts	(1 ts)	dry mustard
½ ts	(½ ts)	salt
1 cup	(250 mL)	salad oil
2 tbs	(2 tbs)	lemon juice
½ ts	(½ ts)	sugar, optional

Heat bowl of electric mixer with hot water for a few minutes, then beat egg with mustard and salt until thick and lemon colored. Add salad oil, first a few drops at a time, then in an even thin stream until it is well incorporated into mixture. Add lemon juice, and sugar if used, and mix until well blended. Makes a little more than one cup mayonnaise.

FLEMISH BRUSSELS SPROUT PUREE

Belgium   (*Purée Flamande de Chous de Bruxelle*)

1 lb	(½ kg)	Brussels sprouts
4 tbs	(4 tbs)	butter or margarine
2	(2)	medium size potatoes, peeled and cubed
4 cups	(1 L)	chicken stock
½ cup	(125 mL)	light cream
		salt and pepper to taste

Boil Brussels sprouts in salted water about 5 minutes, then drain. Then sauté them in 2 tbs butter in a heavy saucepan for a couple of minutes, add potatoes and chicken stock and bring to a boil, turn down heat and simmer 10–15 minutes, or until vegetables are tender. Mash mixture thoroughly, then puré in a blender, or pass through a sieve, and return mixture to pot. Add cream and remaining 2 tbs. butter and heat, but do not let it come to a boil.   Serves 5–6.

Belgium   MUSSEL STEW   (*Matelote de Moules*)

4–5 doz	(4–5 doz)	mussels
1	(1)	large onion, sliced
1½ cups	(375 mL)	dry white wine
1	(1)	bay leaf
2 tbs	(2 tbs)	chopped fresh parsley
¼ lb	(125 g)	fresh mushrooms, sliced
3 tbs	(3 tbs)	butter or margarine
2 tbs	(2 tbs)	flour
		juice of ½ lemon
		salt and pepper to taste

Scrub mussels with a stiff brush and scrape off beards. Put them in a large pot together with onion, wine, bay leaf and parsley and cook under cover until their shells open, about 4–5 minutes. Remove mussels from shells. Strain the liquid through double cheesecloth and set aside. Sauté mushrooms in butter for 5 minutes, add flour and mussel liquid and cook until thickened. Add mussels, lemon juice, salt and pepper and heat only until thoroughly hot. Serve on toast triangles to 4–6.

SHRIMP CROQUETTES

Belgium   (*Croquettes de Crevettes*)

½ lb	(¼ *kg*)	cooked shrimp
2 tbs	(*2 tbs*)	butter or margarine
⅓ cup	(*80 mL*)	flour
1 cup	(*250 mL*)	milk
2	(*2*)	egg yolks
		salt and pepper to taste
1 ts	(*1 ts*)	Worcestershire sauce
		pinch of nutmeg

For dredging:

¼ cup	(*60 mL*)	flour
2	(*2*)	egg whites, slightly beaten
1 cup	(*250 mL*)	dry bread crumbs
		oil for deep frying

Chop cooked shrimp finely and set aside. In a saucepan, melt butter, add flour while stirring continuously, then add milk, a little at a time. Stir until a smooth mixture has been obtained. Cook for about 5 minutes, remove from heat. Slightly beat egg yolks, add a little bit of the mixture from saucepan and stir, then stir the egg mixture into the saucepan. Add shrimp. Cool, then chill in refrigerator for 2–3 hours, until fairly firm.

Heat oil to 375° F (190° C). Shape into balls or cone shape croquettes, roll first in flour, then in beaten egg whites, then coat with bread crumbs. Fry in deep fat, a few at a time, until golden brown. Drain on paper towels, and serve as quickly as possible, or keep warm in a 200° F (100° C) oven for a few minutes while the rest are being cooked.   Serves 4–5.

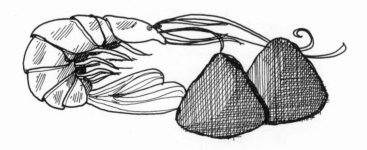

BELGIAN CHICKEN STEW

Belgium   *(Waterzooi van Kip)*

A richly flavored chicken dish that is well worth the extra effort of finely chopping some of the ingredients.

1	(*1*)	frying chicken, 3–3½ lb or 1½ kg cut into serving pieces
		salt and pepper to taste
3 tbs	(*3 tbs*)	butter
3	(*3*)	stalks celery, finely chopped (1½ cups or 375 mL)
1	(*1*)	medium onion, finely chopped (¾ cup or 180 mL)
2	(*2*)	medium size carrots, peeled and finely chopped (about 1 cup or 250 mL)
2 tbs	(*2 tbs*)	finely chopped parsley
8	(*8*)	whole peppercorns
2 cups	(*500 mL*)	chicken broth
2	(*2*)	egg yolks
		juice of ½ lemon
½ cup	(*125 mL*)	heavy cream
For sprinkling:		2 tbs finely chopped parsley

Sprinkle chicken with salt and pepper and sauté in butter for about 10 minutes, but do not let chicken brown. In a heavy bottom pot or flameproof casserole, place chopped vegetables on the bottom, then chicken pieces on top. Add peppercorns, bring chicken broth to a boil and pour over, then bring it all to a boil, turn down heat to very low and simmer for about 40–45 minutes, or until chicken is tender. Remove chicken and keep hot. Beat the egg yolks slightly, add a little bit of broth to them, then put it all in the broth. Cook, stirring constantly until mixture thickens. Add lemon juice and cream, but do not let this mixture boil as it would curdle. Serve in soup bowls with the chicken sprinkled with chopped parsley and boiled rice.

Serves 4–5.

FLEMISH BEEF STEW

Belgium   *(Carbonnade des Flamands)*

Many countries have a version of beef stew made with beer. I think this recipe from Belgium is one of the best.

2 lbs	*(1 kg)*	stewing beef, cut into 1–1½″ or (25–35 mm) cubes
3 tbs	*(3 tbs)*	butter or margarine
		salt and pepper to taste
4	*(4)*	medium size onions, thinly sliced (about 3 cups or 750 mL)
1	*(1)*	clove garlic, finely minced
1	*(1)*	bay leaf
¼ ts	*(¼ ts)*	thyme
2 tbs	*(2 tbs)*	parsley, finely minced
1 ts	*(1 ts)*	brown sugar
1 tbs	*(1 tbs)*	wine vinegar
one 12 oz.	*(375 mL)*	bottle or can of beer
1 tbs	*(1 tbs)*	flour, mixed with ¼ cup (60 mL) water

In a large skillet brown meat on all sides, a few pieces at a time, and sprinkle with salt and pepper. Remove meat and place in a heavy-bottom saucepan or stew pot. Sauté onion and garlic in skillet until onion is transparent, then transfer to meat pan and mix well. Add bay leaf, thyme, parsley, brown sugar, vinegar and beer and bring to a boil. Turn down heat very low and simmer under cover about 1½ hours or until meat is fork-tender. Add flour mixture and stir to blend, then cook for an additional five minutes. Serve with noodles or boiled potatoes.

Serves 4–6.

FLEMISH WAFFLES

Belgium   *(Gaufres à la Flamande)*

For many people who visited the Worlds Fair in New York in 1963–64 the memory of the waffles served by the Belgian Pavilion remains a sweet memory. They were not only tender but loaded with fresh sliced strawberries and lots of whipped cream. They are not hard to make at all and may bring on a bit of nostalgia for that "good old time."

2 cups	*(500 mL)*	flour
4	*(4)*	eggs, separated
3 tbs	*(3 tbs)*	confectioners' sugar
		pinch of salt
1 cup	*(250 mL)*	milk
4 tbs	*(4 tbs)*	butter, melted
1 ts	*(1 ts)*	vanilla extract

Mix together flour, sugar and salt, add egg yolks and milk and blend into a smooth batter. Add melted butter and vanilla and mix well. Beat egg whites until stiff and carefully fold into batter, which will be quite thick.

Bake waffles in a buttered waffle iron in accordance with directions for the appliance. Serve warm, either sprinkled with confectioners' sugar, or with sliced strawberries or peaches and whipped cream.

Makes 10–12 waffles.

MOCHA CHEESE MOLD

Belgium   *(Creme Fromage au Café)*

¼ cup	*(60 mL)*	cold, strong coffee
1	*(1)*	envelope unflavored gelatin
1 cup	*(250 mL)*	hot, strong coffee
¼ cup	*(60 mL)*	sugar
¼ cup	*(60 mL)*	rum
1½ cups	*(375 mL)*	cottage cheese
2	*(2)*	eggs, separated
1	*(1)*	egg white

Soften gelatin in cold coffee, then mix with hot coffee, sugar and rum, then cool until syrupy in consistency. Press cottage cheese through a sieve, then cream with egg yolks until thoroughly blended and light in texture. Mix with coffee syrup. Beat egg whites until stiff, then fold into mixture and blend well. Put into a buttered mold and chill for at least 3 hours. Before serving, unmold on platter and serve either with sliced fresh fruits, canned fruits or whipped cream. Serves 5–6.

Canada

CANADA is very much like the U.S. in having a population consisting of people from many countries with different cultural backgrounds, so the Canadian cuisine is quite varied also. The eating habits of different ethnic groups are similar to those of similar background in the U.S. There are, of course, more people in Canada with a French or British heritage, with the French Canadians in Quebec, and lots of people with Scotch descent in the provinces along the Atlantic Ocean.

There are several dishes that are purely French-Canadian in origin, the most well-known being the *tourtière* (a pork-pie), which is the pride of the Quebec province.

With large numbers of sugar maples to tap, maple syrup has become a popular ingredient in many Canadian desserts, in sauces and pies, and it is often used plain as a topping for ice cream.

HABITANT PEA SOUP

NOVA SCOTIA FISH CHOWDER

FRENCH CANADIAN PORK PIE   *Tourtiere*

DOUBLE CRUST PIE SHELL

SINGLE CRUST PIE SHELL

BLUEBERRY CRISP

MAPLE SYRUP PIE

Canada   HABITANT PEA SOUP

2 cups	(500 mL)	dried, whole yellow peas (about 1 lb or ½ kg)
8 cups	(2 L)	water, approximately
½ lb	(¼ kg)	salt pork
1	(1)	large onion, finely chopped (1 cup or 250 mL)
1 or 2	(1 or 2)	carrots, scraped and diced (about 1 cup or 250 mL)
1 tbs	(1 tbs)	salt, approximately (more or less according to taste)
1 ts	(1 ts)	dried savory

Rinse and pick over peas to remove damaged or discolored ones. Add water, bring to a boil, turn off heat and let peas soak for at least two hours. Cut pork into thick slices and add to peas together with onion, carrots and seasonings.

Bring to a boil again, turn down heat and skim off foam, if necessary, then cook over low heat 2–3 hours, or until peas are tender, stirring occasionally to scrape the bottom of pan to avoid scorching. If soup should get too thick, add additional water.

Serve hot, with or without the pork slices, depending on preference, as some people like the cooked fat pork and others cannot stand it.

Serves 6–8.

Canada   NOVA SCOTIA FISH CHOWDER

From the rich fishing banks off the east coast of Canada the boats bring back haddock and cod. What better use of it for a cold winter's day than a nice, rich chowder?

1½ lb	(¾ kg)	haddock (or cod) fillets
¼ lb	(125 g)	salt pork, finely diced
1	(1)	medium size onion, cut in half and thinly sliced
2 cups	(500 mL)	water
3 cups	(750 mL)	potatoes, cut in ¼″ (6 mm) cubes
3 cups	(750 mL)	milk
6	(6)	soda crackers, crumbled
		salt and pepper to taste
2 tbs	(2 tbs)	butter
1 cup	(250 mL)	cream
2 tbs	(2 tbs)	finely chopped parsley

(Continued on next page)

(Nova Scotia Fish Chowder, cont.)

Cut fish into bite size pieces. Sauté salt pork until brown and very crisp, then remove whole pieces. Add onion to pork fat and sauté until tender, but do not let it get brown. Add water and potatoes and cook for 10 minutes, or until potatoes are almost tender, then add fish, salt and pepper, bring to a boil, turn down heat and simmer for 10 minutes.

In another pot mix together milk and crumbled crackers, heat to scalding point, then blend into fish mixture together with cream. Do not allow it to boil again as it may then curdle. Pour into a soup tureen, add butter and sprinkle parsley on top. (It is also nice to crumble one or more soda crackers on top of each serving.)
Serves 5–6.

Canada   **FRENCH CANADIAN PORK PIE**   (*Tourtière Quebec*)

The pork pie is the most French-Canadian of all dishes served in Canada, I believe. This is a nice version of same with a hint of spices that we do not ordinarily connect with pork.

1½ lbs	(¾ kg)	ground pork
1	(1)	medium onion, finely chopped (about ¾ cup or 180 mL)
1	(1)	clove garlic, finely minced
2 tbs	(2 tbs)	butter or margarine
2	(2)	medium size potatoes, peeled and cut in small cubes (optional)
½ ts	(½ ts)	ground cloves
¼ ts	(¼ ts)	cinnamon
1 ts	(1 ts)	allspice, ground
1	(1)	bay leaf
		salt and pepper to taste
½ cup	(125 mL)	boiling water

Double crust pie shell (see following recipe)

Sauté onion and garlic in butter until onion is transparent. Add pork and cook, breaking up meat with a fork until it loses its pink color. Add potatoes, if these are used, spices and water, bring to a boil, turn down heat and simmer for about 30 minutes. Chill mixture thoroughly.

Line a 9″ or a 10″ (220–250 mm) pie pan with half the pastry and add the meat mixture. Cover with remaining pastry and seal the edges. With a small sharp knife make some vents on top of pie to let steam escape during baking. Bake in a 425° F (220° C) oven for 10 minutes, then turn down heat to 350° F (175° C) and bake 35 minutes longer. Serve piping hot.   For 5 or 6.

Canada

DOUBLE CRUST PIE SHELL

2 cups	(*500 mL*)	flour
1 ts	(*1 ts*)	salt
⅔ cup	(*160 mL*)	shortening (preferably vegetable shortening such as Spry or Crisco. Lard may also be used. With butter or margarine, crust will not be quite as flaky)
¼ cup	(*60 mL*)	ice-cold water

Sift flour and salt into a bowl and cut in shortening with a pastry blender or two knives until mixture consists of crumbs the size of small peas. Sprinkle with ice water and stir lightly with a fork until mixture is evenly moist, then squeeze together with your hand into a ball; scraping around the walls of the bowl to get all the crumbs.

The dough may be rolled out immediately or put in the refrigerator for about 15 minutes. Divide into halves and roll out to fit a 9″ or 10″ (220–250 mm) pie pan.

Canada

SINGLE CRUST PIE SHELL

1 cup	(*250 mL*)	flour
½ ts	(*½ ts*)	salt
⅓ cup	(*80 mL*)	shortening (see note in Double Crust recipe, above)
2 tbs	(*2 tbs*)	ice-cold water

Proceed as above, but roll out all the dough to fit a 9″ or 10″ (220–250 mL) pie pan.

Canada   BLUEBERRY CRISP

As American as blueberry pie, we say. However, many countries feel that blueberries are something very much their own. Canadians do have a special way with them, and their Blueberry Crisp is an example.

3 cups	*(750 mL)*	fresh or frozen blueberries
½ cup	*(125 mL)*	sugar
1 tbs	*(1 tbs)*	lemon juice
⅓ cup	*(80 mL)*	flour
⅓ cup	*(80 mL)*	brown sugar
4 tbs	*(4 tbs)*	butter or margarine
⅔ cup	*(160 mL)*	oatmeal
For serving:		whipped cream

Put blueberries in a one quart (1 L) baking dish, sprinkle with sugar and lemon juice. Mix together brown sugar and flour, then cut in butter with a pastry blender until mixture has the texture of coarse crumbs, mix in oatmeal and spread on top of blueberries. Bake in a 375° F (190° C) oven for 30 minutes. Serve with whipped cream while still slightly warm.   Serves 6.

Canada   MAPLE SYRUP PIE

Sugar maples must be as prevalent in eastern Canada as in our northeastern states. They use their boiled-down sap for more than pancakes. Their Maple Syrup pie is similar to our southern pecan pie in texture. If walnuts or pecans are used for sprinkling on top, it would be very much like it. It is rich as anything, so forget about calories if you want to indulge in it.

		Pastry for single crust pie shell (see above)
1 cup	*(250 mL)*	pure maple syrup
1 tbs	*(1 tbs)*	corn starch
2 tbs	*(2 tbs)*	cold water
2	*(2)*	eggs, well beaten
½ cup	*(125 mL)*	heavy cream
For serving:		whipped cream

Roll out dough and fit into an 8″ (200 mm) pie pan. Dissolve corn starch in water, then add to maple syrup and stir until well blended. Mix together eggs and heavy cream and add to syrup mixture. Pour into the pie shell and bake in a 350° F (175° C) oven for about 40 minutes or until the top of the pie gets dark and becomes a bit crinkly in appearance. Serve cold with whipped cream.   Serves 6–8.

Caribbean

So many different countries colonized this area that each separate island group developed a cuisine of its own. However, there are many similarities between the cooking on the various islands. They all have abundant and wonderful raw materials to work with, from the fish in the sea to their rich variety of vegetables, spices and exotic fruits.

I will treat the area as one unit but will identify each island in the recipes. I am afraid it will be easy to see which islands I have visited.

PICKLED FISH	*Escovitched Fish*	Jamaica
PUMPKIN SOUP		Jamaica
COCONUT SOUP		Jamaica
SHRIMP SOUP	*Asopao*	Puerto Rico
BLACK BEAN SOUP	*Sopa Frijoles*	Cuba
RICE WITH SHRIMP	*Pilau de Camarones*	Dominican Republic
CHICKEN WITH PINEAPPLE	*Pollo con Piña*	Cuba
CHICKEN IN ORANGE SAUCE		Trinidad
BAKED CHICKEN WITH RUM		Jamaica
CHICKEN FRICASSEE		Jamaica
PORK ROAST CALYPSO		Jamaica
RICE WITH PORK	*Arroz con Carne de Cerdo*	Dominican Republic
BARBADOS PORK STEW		Barbados
SAUSAGE ROLL	*Pulpeta*	Cuba

(*Continued on next page*)

GROUND BEEF AND POTATO CASSEROLE	*Gâteau de Pommes de Terre)*	Haiti
RICE AND KIDNEY BEANS		Jamaica
COCONUT MILK		Jamaica
PITCH LAKE MOUSSE	*Black Devil's Mousse*	Trinidad
COCONUT MOLD		Aruba
BAKED BANANAS WITH RUM		Haiti
SWEET POTATO CAKE	*Gâteau de Patate*	Haiti
ORANGE BREAD		Jamaica
BANANA FRITTERS		Monserrat

PICKLED FISH

Jamaica   **(Escovitched Fish)**

A spicy appetizer from Jamaica. As the Caribbean islands grow abundant allspice, it is used very much all through them and is a nice flavor to get "hooked" on.

1 lb	(½ kg)	fish fillets (haddock, cod or ocean perch)
2 tbs	(2 tbs)	butter or margarine
1 cup	(250 mL)	cider vinegar
1	(1)	small onion, finely chopped (½ cup or 125 mL)
1	(1)	clove garlic, finely minced
¼ cup	(60 mL)	green pepper, finely chopped
1 ts	(1 ts)	salt
½ ts	(½ ts)	whole allspice
½ ts	(½ ts)	whole black pepper
1	(1)	small red chili (or ½ ts dried red pepper flakes)

Cut fish fillets into bite size pieces and sauté in butter on both sides. Put into a bowl. Bring vinegar, onion, garlic, green pepper and seasonings to a boil in a sauce pan, then immediately pour over fish and cover. Marinate in refrigerator for 24 hours. Serve as an appetizer on toasted small squares of bread or crackers.

Serves 6–8.

PUMPKIN SOUP

Jamaica

A rich and filling soup using pumpkin, which unfortunately is mostly limited to pies or Jack'o'Lanterns in the U.S.

1 cup	(*250 mL*)	cooked mashed pumpkin (half of 1 lb or ½ kg can)
2 cups	(*500 mL*)	chicken broth
1 ts	(*1 ts*)	salt
1 tbs	(*1 tbs*)	flour
⅛ ts	(*⅛ ts*)	ground ginger
⅛ ts	(*⅛ ts*)	ground allspice
⅛ ts	(*⅛ ts*)	ground nutmeg
1	(*1*)	egg, well beaten
1 cup	(*250 mL*)	light cream, half and half or evaporated milk

For sprinkling: 1 tbs chopped parsley

Mix pumpkin with chicken broth in a saucepan and cook for about 10 minutes. Put together flour and spices with ¼ cup (60 mL) of cream or milk and mix well, stir into saucepan and bring to a boil, then simmer over low heat about five minutes.

Mix well-beaten egg with remaining cream and a little of the pumpkin mixture, then pour it all back into the saucepan and heat to almost boiling, but do not let it really boil, as the mixture then might curdle. Put in soup bowls and sprinkle with chopped parsley.

Serves 4–5.

COCONUT SOUP

Jamaica

A light soup with the delicate flavor of the coconut.

2 cups	(*500 mL*)	grated fresh coconut
4 cups	(*1 L*)	chicken stock
2 tbs	(*2 tbs*)	butter or margarine
2 tbs	(*2 tbs*)	flour
½ cup	(*125 mL*)	heavy cream salt and pepper to taste

(*Continued on next page*)

(Coconut Soup, cont.)

Combine the coconut and chicken stock in a heavy saucepan, bring to a boil, turn down heat, cover and simmer gently for 30 minutes. Strain through a sieve, pressing with the back of a spoon to extract all the liquid, then discard the coconut.

Cream together butter and flour, add stock a little at a time, stirring constantly to make a smooth mixture, then cook until soup is thickened, about 5 minutes. Remove from heat, then add heavy cream and seasoning. Serves 4–5.

SHRIMP SOUP

Puerto Rico   *(Asopao)*

In Puerto Rico soup with rice, so thick that it can almost be considered as a stew, is very common. It is usually made with shrimp, but almost as often with chicken, fish or turtle.

2	*(2)*	slices bacon, cut into small pieces
½ cup	*(125 mL)*	diced ham
1	*(1)*	medium size onion, finely chopped (¾ cup or 180 mL)
1 cup	*(250 mL)*	chopped green peppers
2	*(2)*	medium size tomatoes, peeled and chopped (or 1 cup—250 mL—canned tomatoes)
⅓ cup	*(80 mL)*	chopped green olives
1 tbs	*(1 tbs)*	capers
1 cup	*(250 mL)*	tomato sauce (one 8 oz or 250 mL can)
1 ts	*(1 ts)*	oregano
2 tbs	*(2 tbs)*	ground coriander
		salt and pepper to taste
4 cups	*(1 L)*	boiling water
1 cup	*(250 mL)*	rice
1 lb	*(½ kg)*	shrimp, peeled and de-veined

In a large, heavy saucepan cook the bacon and ham for about five minutes, then add onion and sauté until onion is transparent. Add peppers, tomatoes, olives, capers, tomato sauce and seasonings, and stir to mix well. Add water and rice and cook about 15 minutes or until rice is tender. Add shrimp and cook five more minutes. Serve in soup bowls.   Serves 5–6.

BLACK BEAN SOUP

Cuba   *(Sopa Frijoles)*

A rich, flavorful and filling soup and an important addition for those who love beans in any form.

1 lb	(½ kg)	black, dried beans (about 2 cups or 500 mL)
3 qts	(3 L)	water
1	(1)	ham hock or ham bone with some meat left on
1	(1)	medium onion, finely chopped (¾ cup or 180 mL)
1	(1)	clove garlic, finely chopped
1	(1)	rib celery, finely chopped salt and pepper to taste
½ ts	(½ ts)	dry mustard
1 ts	(1 ts)	cumin, crushed
1½ tbs	(1½ tbs)	lemon juice
¼ cup	(60 mL)	sherry
1	(1)	hard boiled egg, chopped

Wash beans and remove defective ones. Soak in cold water 3–4 hours or overnight. Drain and add 3 qts (3 L) water, ham hock or bone, onion, garlic, and celery and bring to a boil. Turn down heat and simmer until beans are soft but not mushy, 2½–3 hours.

Add salt and pepper, dry mustard, cumin and lemon juice and simmer another 20 minutes. Remove ham hock or bone and put remaining contents in an electric blender, a little at a time or pass through a sieve, blend well, then return to saucepan, add sherry, and heat carefully. (If desired, only half of the bean mixture may be put through the blender, and the remaining beans left whole). Put in soup bowls and sprinkle chopped egg on top.

Serves 5–6.

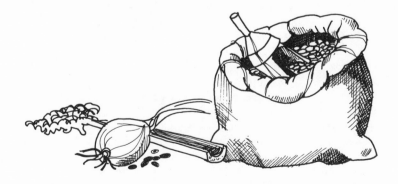

RICE WITH SHRIMP

Dominican Republic   (*Pilau de Camarones*)

6	(*6*)	slices bacon, cut up into small pieces
1	(*1*)	large onion, finely chopped (1 cup or 250 mL)
1	(*1*)	clove garlic, finely minced
1 tbs	(*1 tbs*)	fresh red or green chili, seeded and finely chopped (or ¼ ts crushed, dried hot pepper)
1½ cups	(*375 mL*)	rice
5-6	(*5-6*)	medium size tomatoes (about 2 lbs. (1 kg), peeled, seeded and chopped
3 cups	(*750 mL*)	chicken stock
1½ lbs	(*¾ kg*)	shrimp, peeled, de-veined and cut into small pieces
2 tbs	(*2 tbs*)	butter or margarine
3 tbs	(*3 tbs*)	finely chopped parsley salt and pepper to taste
For serving:		grated parmesan cheese

In a large skillet or electric frying pan fry bacon pieces until crisp, then remove with a slotted spoon. Sauté onion, garlic and chili in bacon fat over low heat until onion is transparent. Add rice and cook while stirring for about 5 minutes or until rice grains are coated with fat. Do not let it brown. Add tomatoes, stock, salt and pepper and bring to a boil, then turn down heat and simmer for 20 minutes, or until rice is tender.

In another small frying pan or saucepan sauté shrimp in butter or margarine until they turn pink, about 5 minutes. Mix together shrimp, bacon and parsley, add to rice mixture and heat only until it is thoroughly warm, as prolonged cooking would make the shrimp tough. Serve sprinkled with parmesan cheese.

Enough for 6.

CHICKEN WITH PINEAPPLE

Cuba   (*Pollo con Piña*)

1	(*1*)	frying chicken, 3-3½ lbs (1½-1¾ kg)
		juice and grated rind of one lemon or lime
		salt and pepper to taste
3 tbs	(*3 tbs*)	salad oil
1	(*1*)	medium size onion, chopped (¾ cup or 180 mL)
1	(*1*)	clove garlic, finely minced
2	(*2*)	medium size tomatoes, peeled and chopped
2 tbs	(*2 tbs*)	raisins
1	(*1*)	small fresh chili, seeded and chopped, or ¼ ts cayenne pepper
½ ts	(*½ ts*)	oregano
1	(*1*)	bay leaf
2 cups	(*500 mL*)	chopped fresh pineapple with juice or chopped canned unsweetened pineapple
¼ cup	(*60 mL*)	rum

Cut chicken into serving pieces then rub with lemon or lime juice and rind. Let stand for 30 minutes. Brown chicken in 2 tbs oil, season with salt and pepper, then transfer into heavy pan. Sauté onion and garlic in remaining oil until onion is transparent, add tomatoes, raisins, pepper, oregano and bay leaf and cook for 5 minutes, stirring off and on.

Pour this mixture over chicken in pan, cover and cook over slow heat until chicken is tender, about 45 minutes. If fresh pineapple is used, cook with the juice in small sauce pan for 10 minutes, add rum and mix well. Pour over chicken and cook for 5 more minutes. Serve with rice.

Serves 5–6.

CHICKEN IN ORANGE SAUCE
Trinidad

1	(*1*)	frying chicken (3-3½ lbs or 1½-1¾ kg) cut into serving pieces
⅓ cup	(*80 mL*)	flour
		salt and pepper to taste
¼ cup	(*60 mL*)	salad oil
2	(*2*)	cloves garlic, finely minced
2 cups	(*500 mL*)	orange juice
2 tbs	(*2 tbs*)	brown sugar
2 tbs	(*2 tbs*)	vinegar
1 ts	(*1 ts*)	ground nutmeg
1 ts	(*1 ts*)	finely minced fresh basil (or ½ ts dried)
3	(*3*)	oranges, peeled, sectioned and membranes removed

Mix salt and pepper with the flour, then use to dredge chicken pieces heavily. Heat oil in large skillet and sauté chicken pieces until golden brown on both sides. As they are done, transfer them to a baking dish. Sauté garlic for a few minutes in remaining oil, then remove same and add to baking dish.

Pour off excess oil in skillet, then scrape loose any brown bits sticking to pan, softening with a little of the orange juice, if necessary, and add together with remaining ingredients, except the orange sections, to baking dish. Bake in a 350° F (175° C) oven 45 minutes. (Or instead of a baking dish, use a heavy-bottom casserole and cook on top of stove over very low heat). Add orange sections and cook 5 minutes longer. Serve with plain boiled rice.   For 5-6 people.

BAKED CHICKEN WITH RUM
Jamaica

A simple but good way to bake chicken.

1	(*1*)	frying chicken, 3-3½ lbs (1½-1¾ kg)
Marinade:		
⅓ cup	(*80 mL*)	soy sauce
		juice of one lemon
3 tbs	(*3 tbs*)	rum
½ ts	(*½ ts*)	ginger

(*Continued on next page*)

(Baked Chicken with Rum, cont.)

For dredging: ½ cup (*125 mL*) flour
                                     salt and pepper to taste

Cut the chicken into serving pieces, then place them in a shallow dish. Mix marinade ingredients together and pour over chicken, then place in refrigerator for about 3 hours. Turn over pieces several times to make marinade do its work on all sides. When ready to cook, remove from marinade and let drip off for a few minutes. Mix together flour with salt and pepper and dredge chicken pieces in this.

Place in a large baking dish, so that chicken pieces do not touch each other and bake in a 350° F (175° C) oven for 35–45 minutes or until chicken is tender.

Serves 4–5.

CHICKEN FRICASSEE

Jamaica

A stewing chicken will do equally well for this recipe, just cook it a little longer so that the meat is tender.

1	(*1*)	frying chicken (3–3½ lbs or 1-½-1¾ kg)
3	(*3*)	cloves garlic, finely minced
1 ts	(*1 ts*)	ginger
1 ts	(*1 ts*)	paprika
		salt and pepper to taste
3 tbs	(*3 tbs*)	salad oil
2	(*2*)	large onions, chopped (2 cups or 500 mL)
3	(*3*)	medium size tomatoes, peeled and coarsely chopped (2 cups or 500 mL)
1	(*1*)	fresh chili, preferably red, or ¼ ts cayenne pepper

Cut the chicken into serving pieces, rub them with garlic and seasonings, then let stand in refrigerator for at least 6 hours. Scrape off seasonings and set them aside. Brown chicken in 2 tbs oil until golden in color, then place in a heavy casserole. Sauté onion in remaining oil until transparent, then add to casserole together with tomatoes, the reserved seasonings and the fresh chili, which should be left whole, with stem and all.

Cover casserole and bake in a 350° F (175° C) oven, or simmer on top of stove over very low heat (but be sure casserole is flame-proof) until chicken is tender, about 1 hour, adding a little water if the mixture should look too dry. Remove and discard chili before serving with rice or Rice and Kidney Beans, page 70.

For 4–6 portions.

Jamaica   PORK ROAST CALYPSO

Pork does very well with some extra spices added. In Jamaica they do it this way.

4-5 lbs	(2-2½ kg)	loin of pork
		salt and pepper to taste
½ ts	(½ ts)	ground ginger
½ ts	(½ ts)	ground cloves
1	(1)	clove garlic, finely minced
1	(1)	bay leaf, crumbled
⅔ cups	(180 mL)	rum
1 cup	(250 mL)	chicken stock (may be made with bouillon cubes)
⅓ cup	(80 mL)	brown sugar
¼ cup	(60 mL)	lime juice (or lemon juice)
For gravy:		2 tbs flour mixed with ¼ cup or 60 mL cold water

Score surface of meat in a diamond pattern. Mix together salt, pepper, ginger, cloves and garlic and rub into surface. Place crumbled bay leaf on top and put in a roasting pan in a 325° F (165° C) oven for 30 minutes without cover.

Heat rum and chicken stock, add brown sugar and lime juice, add to roasting pan and cover same. Continue cooking, about 30 minutes per lb (one hour per kg), until done (registers 185° F or 75° C on meat thermometer). Baste with pan juices at least 4 times during baking.

When roast is done, remove bay leaves from top, then keep it warm. Remove excess fat from pan drippings and add flour mixture, stirring continuously to make a smooth gravy. Add a bit of water, if it should be too thick. Serve gravy from gravy bowl. For 5-6 people.

RICE WITH PORK

Dominican Republic   (*Arroz con carne de Cerdo*)

1½ lb	(¾ kg)	boneless pork, cut into ¾″ (18 mm) cubes
3	(3)	slices bacon, coarsely chopped
1	(1)	medium size onion, finely chopped (¾ cup or 180 mL)
2	(2)	cloves garlic, finely minced
1	(1)	fresh red or green chili, seeded and chopped, or ¼ ts dried hot crushed pepper

(*Continued on next page*)

(Rice with Pork, cont.)

1	(1)	bay leaf, finely crumbled
1 tbs	(1 tbs)	finely minced parsley
2 tbs	(2 tbs)	vinegar
		salt to taste
3 tbs	(3 tbs)	butter or margarine
1/4 cup	(60 mL)	tomato paste
1½ cups	(375 mL)	rice
10-15	(10-15)	small pimiento-stuffed green olives, cut into halves
3-3½ cups	(750-900 mL)	water

Stir together bacon, onion, garlic, chili, bay leaf, parsley, vinegar and salt, then add meat and mix well. Put in refrigerator about 2 hours. Heat butter in a heavy saucepan and sauté meat mixture for 5 minutes over medium heat, then turn down heat and cook an additional 15 minutes.

Add tomato paste, rice, olives and 3 cups (750 mL) water, bring to a boil, cover, turn down heat to a very low and simmer until rice is tender, about 15 minutes. If mixture should get too thick, add some or all the remaining water.

Serves 5-6.

Barbados **BARBADOS PORK STEW**

A delicious way to incorporate bananas into a stew, coming from one of the lovely Caribbean isles.

1½ lbs	(¾ kg)	boneless pork, cut into 1" (250 mm) cubes
1/3 cup	(80 mL)	flour
		salt and pepper to taste
2 tbs	(2 tbs)	salad oil
1	(1)	large onion, sliced
½ cup	(125 mL)	chopped celery
2/3 cup	(160 mL)	chopped green pepper
1	(1)	clove garlic, finely minced
1	(1)	small fresh green chili, seeded and finely chopped; or ¼-½ ts cayenne
1½ cups	(375 mL)	water
1	(1)	medium size cucumber, peeled, seeded and diced
3	(3)	medium size tomatoes, peeled and diced
3	(3)	firm but ripe bananas

(Continued on next page)

(Barbados Pork Stew, cont.)

Dredge pork cubes in flour, mixed with salt and pepper, then brown well in salad oil. Remove meat, then sauté onion, green pepper, garlic and chili for 10 minutes, return meat to pan and add water. Bring mixture to a boil, then turn down heat to low and simmer until meat is tender, about 45–60 minutes. Add cucumber and tomatoes and cook an additional 10 minutes, then add sliced bananas and leave on heat only until thoroughly hot. Serve with rice.

Serves 5–6.

SAUSAGE ROLL

Cuba   *(Pulpeta)*

1½ lbs	(¾ kg)	ground beef (chuck)
¼ lb	(125 g)	ground lean pork
¼ lb	(125 g)	ground ham
1	(1)	medium onion, finely chopped (¾ cup or 180 mL)
2	(2)	cloves garlic, finely minced
¼ cup	(60 mL)	finely minced parsley
2	(2)	slices white bread, cubed
⅓ cup	(80 mL)	milk
2	(2)	eggs
		salt and pepper to taste
¼ ts	(¼ ts)	crushed hot pepper (optional)
4	(4)	hardboiled eggs, peeled

For cooking:

		water
1	(1)	medium size onion, sliced
1	(1)	bay leaf
¼ cup	(60 mL)	dry sherry

In a large bowl, soak bread cubes in milk for a few minutes, then add meat, onion, garlic, parsley, raw eggs and seasonings and mix thoroughly until a smooth and light mixture is obtained. Shape into two rectangles, about 4 x 12" (100 x 300 mm) and on one of them place the four hard boiled eggs lengthwise end-to-end in the center. Cover with the second rectangle and shape the meat into a cylinder. Wrap it in cheese cloth, make it into a sausage shape and tie a string at both ends. Put in a large pot, add water half-way up the sausage, then add onion slices, bay leaf and sherry and bring to a boil. Turn down heat to very low and simmer 1½–2 hours, or until sausage feels firm. Unwrap and place on hot serving platter and cut into 1" (25 mm) slices. If desired, serve with tomato sauce (see page 304) or your own favorite kind, either poured over the sausage slices or served separately from a sauce bowl. The sausage may also be served cold.

For 6–8 portions.

GROUND BEEF AND POTATO CASSEROLE

Haiti (*Gâteau de Pommes de Terre*)

A simple but satisfying chopped meat casserole.

5	(5)	medium size potatoes (about 1½ lb or ¾ kg)
½ cup	(125 mL)	milk
2 tbs	(2 tbs)	butter or margarine
1	(1)	clove garlic, finely minced
1 tbs	(1 tbs)	cooking oil
1½ lb	(¾ kg)	ground chuck beef
		salt and pepper to taste
2 tbs	(2 tbs)	lemon juice
1 tbs	(1 tbs)	finely minced parsley
2 tbs	(2 tbs)	tomato paste
1½ cup	(375 mL)	grated cheddar cheese

Peel and cook potatoes until tender, then drain and mash them, adding milk and butter. In the meantime, sauté garlic in the oil for a few minutes, then add ground meat and cook until meat loses its red color, breaking it up with a fork. Add salt and pepper, lemon juice, parsley and tomato paste and bring to a boil, then turn down heat very low and simmer meat for about 15 minutes.

In a buttered 2 qt (2 L) baking dish put half of the mashed potatoes, then half the meat mixture and half the cheese, then repeat layers once more in the same order. Bake in a 350° F (175° C) oven about 30 minutes.

Serves 5–6.

Jamaica   RICE AND KIDNEY BEANS

This rice looks a little "strange" as it picks up the color from the kidney beans and turns pinkish.

½ cup	(*125 mL*)	dried red kidney beans
2-3 cups	(*500-750 mL*)	water
2 tbs	(*2 tbs*)	finely chopped celery
1 tbs	(*1 tbs*)	coconut milk (see below)
		pinch of thyme
		salt to taste
1 cup	(*250 mL*)	rice

Soak the beans in cold water, at least 6 hours or overnight. Drain off water then add 2 cups (500 mL) cold water, celery, and onion; and cook for 45 minutes. Add coconut milk and continue cooking until beans are tender, 1-1½ hours, depending upon the beans. Add rice and seasonings and cook over low heat until rice is tender and all the liquid has been absorbed. Check while cooking the rice to make sure the mixture is not too dry, in that case add more hot water. Serve with chicken or meat.   Serves 5-6.

COCONUT MILK

Coconuts contain a refreshing liquid, often called coconut milk. This is a popular beverage, drunk direct from the nut, throughout tropical countries. However, it is not a suitable cooking ingredient for most recipes, such as those given here. In them, it is replaced by an extract of the coconut meat, without change of name.

1	(*1*)	whole coconut, husk removed
2 cups	(*500 mL*)	boiling hot water

Crack the coconut and pour off the liquid in center, which you may either drink or discard. Then using a sharp knife, pare off the white coconut meat from the shell, cutting away the dark outside coating. Cut the white coconut meat into cubes. Pour one cup (250 mL) of the boiling water into the blender, then add coconut cubes and blend at high speed until thoroughly blended. Line a mixing bowl with cheese cloth and pour the coconut mixture into it, then squeeze and twist the cheese cloth to extract as much juice as is possible. Return the coconut to the blender again, pour on remaining hot water and blend once more, then pour into cheese cloth and squeeze. Discard coconut. The liquid which has been obtained is coconut milk, which should be shaken well before using. Makes about 2 cups. (500 mL).

(*Continued on next page*)

(Coconut Milk, cont.)

VARIATION: COCONUT CREAM

Proceed as above but let the coconut milk stand until the thicker part floats to the top. Skim this off. This is referred to as coconut cream.

PITCH LAKE MOUSSE

Trinidad   (*Black Devils Mousse*)

In Trinidad there is a natural asphalt (pitch) lake. It probably inspired the name for this very dark and chocolaty dessert.

1 tbs	(*1 tbs*)	instant coffee
½ cup	(*125 mL*)	boiling water
⅔ cup	(*160 mL*)	verifine sugar
⅔ cup	(*160 mL*)	cocoa
3	(*3*)	eggs, separated
3 tbs	(*3 tbs*)	dark rum
		pinch of salt
⅔ cup	(*160 mL*)	heavy cream

In the top of a double boiler dissolve coffee in the boiling water, add sugar and stir until dissolved. Add cocoa and put the pot over hot water and cook for 5 minutes, stirring continuously. Add egg yolks, one at a time, and beat vigorously after each addition.

Remove from heat, stir in rum and cool. Add salt to the egg whites and beat until stiff. Carefully fold beaten whites into cooled mixture and pour into a 1 qt (1 L) soufflé dish and refrigerate for several hours, or overnight. Beat heavy cream until stiff and serve over mousse. (If desired, cream may be flavored, after it is beaten, with 1 tbs sugar and 1 tbs rum.)

Serves 6.

COCONUT MOLD

Aruba

Loving coconut flavor, this is one of my favorite desserts.

2 tbs	(*2 tbs*)	gelatin
¼ cup	(*60 mL*)	rum
3	(*3*)	eggs, separated
½ cup	(*125 mL*)	sugar
1 cup	(*250 mL*)	milk
1 cup	(*250 mL*)	coconut milk (see page 70)
1 cup	(*250 mL*)	heavy cream

Soften gelatin in rum. Beat egg yolks with half the sugar in a saucepan until light and fluffy, then stir in milk and coconut milk and mix well. Cook over low heat, stirring constantly, until mixture thickens, but do not let it reach boiling. Add gelatin and mix well. Chill until mixture begins to thicken. Beat egg whites until stiff, adding remaining sugar a little at a time, then carefully add to gelatin mixture. Beat heavy cream until thick, then fold in. Put into a rinsed or slightly oiled mold and chill until firm. Carefully unmold on a serving platter. Serve with Lime Sauce (below).

For 6–8 portions.

Lime Sauce:

1 cup	(*250 mL*)	water
½ cup	(*125 mL*)	sugar
2 ts	(*2 ts*)	cornstarch
		juice and grated rind of 1 lime

Mix together water, sugar and cornstarch and bring to a boil. Remove from heat and stir in lime juice and rind and mix well. Chill before serving.

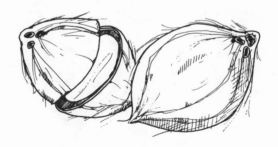

Monserrat BAKED BANANAS WITH RUM

There is always a certain excitement and festivity connected with desserts "flambees." So why not arouse it with this, which is very easily prepared.

6	(6)	ripe, but firm bananas
4 tbs	(4 tbs)	butter
⅓ cup	(80 mL)	brown sugar
2 tbs	(2 tbs)	lemon juice
½ cup	(125 mL)	rum
For serving:		whipped cream, if desired

Melt butter in a baking dish and add the bananas, peeled and cut in halves lengthwise. Sprinkle with lemon juice and brown sugar and bake in a 350° F (175° C) oven about 20 minutes. Just before serving, heat the rum in a small saucepan, pour over the bananas and ignite. Serve as soon as flames have died down, with whipped cream, if desired. Six portions.

SWEET POTATO CAKE

Haiti (*Gâteau de Patate*)

In Haiti they call this a cake, but the texture is more like a pudding. It is a good dessert by whatever name.

2 lbs	(1 kg)	sweet potatoes or yams
1	(1)	large banana
4 tbs	(4 tbs)	butter, melted and slightly cooled
1 cup	(250 mL)	sugar
1 cup	(250 mL)	evaporated milk
½ cup	(125 mL)	molasses
¼ ts	(¼ ts)	nutmeg
¼ ts	(¼ ts)	cinnamon
1 ts	(1 ts)	vanilla
3	(3)	eggs
¼ cup	(60 mL)	seedless raisins

Peel sweet potatoes and cut into pieces, then cook until tender, about 15–20 minutes. Drain well and mash thoroughly. Peel and mash banana and add to sweet potatoes, then add butter, sugar, milk, molasses, nutmeg, cinnamon and vanilla and mix well.

Beat eggs until thick and fluffy and combine with sweet potato mixture, then add raisins and pour into a greased 9 x 5″ (125 x 220 mm) loaf pan and bake in a 350° F (175° C) oven about 1½ hours. Let cool for a few minutes in pan before turning onto a rack.

Makes one loaf.

ORANGE BREAD

Jamaica

2 cups	(*500 mL*)	flour
4 ts	(*4 ts*)	baking powder
½ cup	(*125 mL*)	sugar
½ ts	(*½ ts*)	salt
1	(*1*)	egg, well beaten
1 cup	(*250 mL*)	orange juice
4 tbs	(*4 tbs*)	butter, melted

Sift together dry ingredients and mix well. Mix beaten egg with orange juice and melted butter and pour into flour mixture. Blend only until all the ingredients are moist. Pour batter into a greased and floured 9 x 5" (125 x 220 mm) loaf pan and bake in a 350° F (175° C) oven for 30 minutes or until done. Makes 1 loaf.

If desired, top with an orange glaze (½ cup (125 mL) confectioners' sugar mixed with 1 tbs orange juice). Spread on top after cake has cooled somewhat.

BANANA FRITTERS

Monserrat

From one of the less known of the Caribbean Islands, but probably one of the most beautiful ones, come these fritters, suitable for dessert or a snack.

2 cups	(*500 mL*)	flour
½ ts	(*½ ts*)	salt
1 tbs	(*1 tbs*)	sugar
½ cup	(*125 mL*)	shortening
¼ cup	(*60 mL*)	sour cream
		oil for deep-frying

Mix together flour, salt and sugar then cut in shortening with a pastry cutter until mixture resembles coarse crumbs. Add sour cream and mix well, scraping dough together in a ball. Roll out ⅛" (3 mm) thick and cut out circles, 2½–3" (63–75 mm) in diameter. Put about ½–¾ ts filling off center on each one, then fold over, wet edges then press together with a fork. Fry in 375° F (190° C) for a few minutes until golden brown, then remove and drain on paper towels. Serve slightly warm or cold, sprinkled with confectioners' sugar, if desired.

Filling:

3	(*3*)	medium size ripe bananas
¼ cup	(*60 mL*)	grated coconut, preferably fresh

Mash bananas and mix well with coconut.

Central
and
South America

THIS vast region has much in common with Mexico as far as its cuisine is concerned, as the cooking is based on pretty much the same type of grains and vegetables. Therefore, if you cannot find a recipe for something you may have eaten in any of these countries you may find it in the section for Mexico.

However, as there were more countries than Spain that colonized this area, other influences were brought along. Brazil's cooking style owes much to the Portuguese, and so on.

Fish is a favorite food in most of these countries, and it is quite natural when you think of their long seacoasts. As Argentina is one of the biggest beef producing countries in the world, beef is most popular among the meats in that country, and also in some of the others, but as far as the food for the many poor people all over South America, it is the so-called *corn kitchen* with its variety of preparation that is the staple of life, just as in Mexico.

As the larger part of this region has a tropical climate there are abundance of bananas and other tropical fruits, and of course coconuts, which are used in many ways.

BACON AND EGG STUFFED PEPPERS	*Pimentao Recheio*	Brazil
AVOCADO MOUSSE	*Mousse de Aguacate*	Guatemala
LETTUCE SOUP	*Crema de Alface*	Brazil

(Continued on next page)

77

FISH SOUP	Chupe de Pesces	Peru
SHRIMP AND CORN CASSEROLE		Brazil
CHICKEN WITH RICE	Arroz con Pollo	Costa Rica
BARBECUED BEEF	Anticuchos	Peru
SPICY GROUND BEEF	Pepitoria de Carne Picada	Venezuela
CORN PUDDING	Shipa Guazu	Paraguay
VEGETABLE MIX	Locro	Equador
NUT PUDDING	Postre de Nues	Venezuela
COCONUT CUPCAKES	Mae Bentas	Brazil
COCONUT TURNOVERS	Pastelitos de Coco	Bolivia
CORNMEAL CAKE	Bolo de Fuba	Brazil

BACON AND EGG STUFFED PEPPERS

Brazil (*Pimentao Recheio*)

Peppers may be stuffed with many different things. In Brazil they use bacon and eggs, and the result is as good as it is different for us. They can be served either as an appetizer, or as a luncheon or light supper dish.

4	(4)	sweet green peppers
2 tbs	(2 tbs)	butter or margarine
2 tbs	(2 tbs)	flour
1 cup	(250 mL)	milk
		pinch of salt
2 ts	(2 ts)	prepared mustard
6	(6)	hard boiled eggs
5	(5)	slices bacon
¼ cup	(60 mL)	dry bread crumbs
2 tbs	(2 tbs)	melted butter

Cut peppers in half length-wise, remove seeds and white membranes, then parboil in boiling water for 3 minutes and reserve until the stuffing is prepared.

Then melt butter or margarine in a saucepan, add flour and mix well, then add milk, a little at a time while stirring to make a smooth white sauce. Add salt and mustard and mix well, then cook until sauce has thick-ened, about 5 minutes. Remove from heat and set aside.

Fry bacon until crisp, then crumble it into bits. Chop eggs finely, then mix together with bacon bits and the sauce, and blend well. Fill peppers with this mixture, then sprinkle bread crumbs on top and add melted butter. Bake in a 350° F (175° C) oven for 15–20 minutes or until thoroughly hot. Serve hot to 4–6.

AVOCADO MOUSSE

Guatemala   *(Mousse de Aguacate)*

A wonderfully light and flavorful mousse, which can be used either as a salad course or as a part of a buffet.

1	*(1)*	large, well-ripened avocado
1	*(1)*	small onion, grated (about 1½ tbs)
½ ts	*(½ ts)*	salt
¼ ts	*(¼ ts)*	Worcestershire sauce
1 tbs	*(1 tbs)*	plain gelatin
½ cup	*(125 mL)*	cold water
½ cup	*(125 mL)*	boiling water
¼ cup	*(60 mL)*	heavy cream, whipped
¼ cup	*(60 mL)*	mayonnaise

Peel avocado, remove pit and cut meat into small pieces. In an electric mixer blend avocado, grated onion, salt and Worcestershire sauce until mixture is very smooth. Soften gelatin in ¼ cup (60 mL) cold water, then add ½ cup (125 mL) boiling water and stir until gelatin is dissolved, add remaining ¼ cup (60 mL) cold water and cool mixture until slightly thickened, about the consistency of an egg white. Carefully fold in avocado mixture, whipped cream and mayonnaise and mix well. Pour into a 1 qt (1 L) mold, rinsed with cold water, and refrigerate until set, about 4–5 hours.

Serves six.

LETTUCE SOUP

Brazil   *(Crema de Alface)*

1	*(1)*	head of lettuce, preferably Boston or Bib lettuce
1	*(1)*	small onion, finely chopped (½ cup or 125 mL)
2 tbs	*(2 tbs)*	butter or margarine
4 cups	*(1 L)*	chicken broth
		salt and pepper to taste
⅓ cup	*(80 mL)*	light cream
1	*(1)*	egg yolk

(Continued on next page)

(Lettuce Soup, cont.)

Shred lettuce finely. Sauté onion in butter or margarine until it is transparent, then add chicken broth, salt, pepper and lettuce and bring to a boil, lower heat and simmer for 20 minutes. Mix together cream and egg yolk, then add some hot soup to this and stir well, then add this mixture to the soup but do not let it boil afterward as it might then curdle.

Serves 4–5.

FISH SOUP

Peru   (*Chupe de Pesces*)

1	(*1*)	large onion, chopped (1 cup or 250 mL)
2	(*2*)	cloves garlic, finely minced
2 tbs	(*2 tbs*)	salad oil
1 lb	(½ *kg*)	fish fillets (sole, flounder or haddock)
2 cups	(*500 mL*)	water
		salt to taste
2 tbs	(*2 tbs*)	tomato paste
¼ ts	(¼ *ts*)	cayenne (or more, if a hotter soup is desired)
2	(*2*)	medium size potatoes, peeled and cubed (about 2 cups or 500 mL)
1	(*1*)	16 oz (500 g) can whole-kernel corn
½ lb	(¼ *kg*)	raw shrimp, shelled and de-veined
1 cup	(*250 mL*)	milk
½ cup	(*125 mL*)	heavy cream
For garnish:		chopped fresh mint (optional)

In a large saucepan sauté onion and garlic in oil for five minutes. Poach fish fillets in salted water for five minutes, then tear or cut into bite size pieces. Pour water in which fish was simmered into saucepan with onion, then add tomato paste, cayenne and potatoes and bring to a boil, turn down heat and simmer for 10 minutes, add corn and cook 5 minutes, then shrimp and cook only until they turn pink, about 5 minutes. Mix milk and cream, add, and heat carefully, but do not let the soup boil again. Serve, sprinkled with chopped mint, to 4–6.

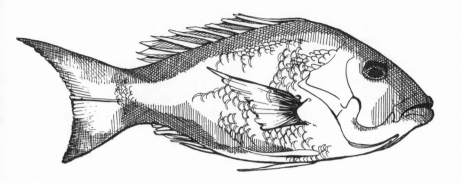

SHRIMP AND CORN CASSEROLE

Brazil

A both tasty and easy casserole.

1 lb	(½ kg)	shrimp, peeled and de-veined
1	(1)	small onion, finely chopped
		(½ cup or 125 mL)
1	(1)	clove garlic, finely minced
2 tbs	(2 tbs)	chopped green pepper
2 tbs	(2 tbs)	olive oil or other salad oil
2 tbs	(2 tbs)	chopped parsley
¼ cup	(60 mL)	tomato sauce
		salt and pepper to taste
2 tbs	(2 tbs)	flour
¼ cup	(60 mL)	milk
2 cups	(500 mL)	cream-style corn
		(about 1 lb or 500 g can)
3 tbs	(3 tbs)	grated parmesan cheese

Sauté onion, garlic and pepper in oil until onion is transparent. Add parsley, tomato sauce, salt and pepper and mix well. Cook for 5 minutes. Add shrimp, then sprinkle with flour, add milk and mix well, bring to a boil turn down heat and simmer for 5 minutes.

Let mixture cool slightly, then pour it into a buttered baking dish, about 1½ qt (1½ L). Put the creamed corn on top, taking care that it stays there in a layer by itself, sprinkle with parmesan cheese and bake in a 350° F (175° C) oven for 20 minutes. Serve immediately, to 4–5.

CHICKEN WITH RICE

Costa Rica   (*Arroz con Pollo*)

Chicken with rice may be considered a classic in most Spanish speaking countries. Here is a good version of it from Costa Rica and if you like it more spicy, just add more chili powder.

1	(*1*)	frying chicken, about 3-3½ lbs. (1½-1¾ kg)
4 cups	(*1 L*)	water
1 tbs	(*1 tbs*)	salt
1	(*1*)	medium size onion, chopped (¾ cup—180 mL)
½ cup	(*125 mL*)	celery, thinly sliced
¼ cup	(*60 mL*)	green pepper, chopped
1 cup	(*250 mL*)	rice
1	(*1*)	can tomato paste (6 oz.—180 mL)
⅓ cup	(*80 mL*)	seedless raisins
½ cup	(*125 mL*)	sliced green olives
1 ts	(*1 ts*)	paprika
1 ts	(*1 ts*)	chili powder (or more, if desired)

Cut chicken into serving pieces and place in a large saucepan together with water, salt, onion and celery and bring to a boil. Turn down heat very low and simmer chicken until tender, about 45 minutes to 1 hour.

Remove chicken, add green pepper and rice and cook for about 15–20 minutes, or until rice is tender. Add remaining ingredients and stir well to blend, then add chicken and cook until thoroughly hot.   Serves 5–6.

BARBECUED BEEF

Peru   (*Anticuchos*)

2 lbs	(*1 kg*)	boneless sirloin, cut into 1″ (25 mm) cubes
2 tbs	(*2 tbs*)	salad oil
Marinade:		
¾ cup	(*180 mL*)	vinegar
½ cup	(*125 mL*)	water
1 ts	(*1 ts*)	chili powder
2	(*2*)	cloves garlic, finely minced salt and pepper to taste

(*Continued on next page*)

(Barbecued Beef, cont.)

In a bowl mix together marinade and add meat cubes. Cover bowl and refrigerate for at least 8 hours or overnight, turning beef cubes a couple of times. Before grilling the meat, let it drain and wipe off excess marinade, then thread meat on skewers and brush with salad oil. Broil meat on a charcoal grill or in the oven until desired doneness, turning the skewers frequently to avoid scorching, and basting with the marinade a couple of times.

Serves 4–5.

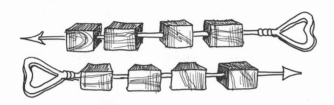

SPICY GROUND BEEF

Venezuela   (*Pepitoria de Carne Picada*)

A good way to make the good old ground beef a bit fancier.

2 tbs	(2 *tbs*)	butter or margarine
2 tbs	(2 *tbs*)	olive oil
2	(2)	medium size onions, chopped (1½ cup or 375 mL)
1 lb	(½ kg)	ground beef
		salt and pepper to taste
¼ ts	(¼ *ts*)	crushed red pepper
½ ts	(½ *ts*)	oregano
		grated rind of one orange
		juice of one orange
½ cup	(125 mL)	raisins
½ cup	(125 mL)	ketchup
½ cup	(125 mL)	water

Sauté onion in butter and olive oil in a large skillet until transparent, add chopped beef and brown lightly, breaking up lumps with a fork. Add salt and pepper, crushed pepper, oregano, orange juice and rind, and simmer for 10 minutes. Add remaining ingredients and bring to a boil, turn down heat very low and simmer an additional 15 minutes, stirring off and on. If meat mixture should get dry, add a little bit more water. Serve with boiled rice.

For 4–5 people.

CORN PUDDING

Paraguay *(Shipa Guazu)*

A non-dessert pudding that goes well with most meats, and which may also be served as a luncheon or light supper dish by itself.

2	(2)	medium onions, finely chopped (1½ cups or 375 mL)
2 tbs	(2 tbs)	salad oil
1	(1)	medium tomato, peeled and cubed
⅔ cup	(160 mL)	flour
½ cup	(125 mL)	yellow corn meal
1½ ts	(1½ ts)	baking powder
1 ts	(1 ts)	salt
1 tbs	(1 tbs)	sugar
1	(1)	whole egg
½ cup	(125 mL)	milk
2 tbs	(2 tbs)	butter or margarine
1	(1)	can creamed corn (1 lb or 500 g size)
2	(2)	eggs, separated
⅓ lb	(150 g)	soft cheese, coarsely grated (Monterey Jack or similar)

Sauté onion in oil until transparent, add tomatoes and cook for 5 minutes. Sift together flour, cornmeal, baking powder, salt and sugar. Add egg, milk and melted butter, then stir only until blended. Add corn, egg yolks, cheese and onion mixture and blend. Beat egg whites until stiff, then carefully fold them into corn mixture.

Bake in a buttered 1½ qt (1½ L) baking dish in a 325° F (160° C) oven for 1 hour. Serve immediately.

For 6.

VEGETABLE MIX

Equador *(Locro)*

A very flavorful vegetable stew in which mashed pumpkin is an ingredient, giving it a very special flavor.

1	(1)	large onion, finely chopped (1 cup or 250 mL)
1	(1)	clove garlic, finely minced
2 tbs	(2 tbs)	butter or margarine

(Continued on next page)

(Vegetable Mix, cont.)

⅓ cup	(80 mL)	tomato sauce
⅓ cup	(80 mL)	water
3	(3)	medium size potatoes
		(about 1 lb or ½ kg)
1 cup	(250 mL)	canned pumpkin
1 cup	(250 mL)	canned or frozen kernel corn, drained
1 cup	(250 mL)	fresh or frozen peas
¾ cup	(180 mL)	milk
		salt and pepper to taste
½ cup	(125 mL)	grated cheese

In a saucepan, sauté onion and garlic in butter or margarine for 10 minutes over low heat. Add tomato sauce and water. Peel and cut each potato in eight pieces and add to saucepan. Bring to a boil, turn down heat and simmer under cover for 20 minutes.

Add pumpkin, corn, peas and milk and stir to mix well, cover and bring to a boil, then turn down heat to very low and cook an additional 20 minutes, stirring off and on to prevent sticking to the bottom. Just before serving, stir in cheese and mix well. Serves 5–6.

NUT PUDDING

Venezuela   (*Postre de Nues*)

¾ cup	(180 mL)	pecans or other nuts, ground
1½ cups	(375 mL)	milk
½ cup	(125 mL)	sugar
3	(3)	egg yolks

For garnish: whipped cream and some
                                              whole pecans

Heat milk and sugar in a saucepan, stirring until sugar has dissolved. Beat egg yolks until light and fluffy, add a little of the hot milk, stirring vigorously, then put it all in the top of a double boiler, adding the ground

nuts, and cook over hot water, stirring off and on, until nut mixture is very thick, about 30–40 minutes. Put pudding in a serving dish and chill. Garnish with whipped cream and whole pecans. Serve to 4–5.

COCONUT CUPCAKES

Brazil (*Mae Bentas*)

Wasn't there a popular song some years ago "they've got an awful lot of coconuts in Brazil"? And they do use their coconuts in a lot of recipes and here follow two good ones.

4 tbs	(*4 tbs*)	butter or margarine
¾ cup	(*180 mL*)	sugar
2	(*2*)	eggs, separated
1 cup	(*250 mL*)	fresh, grated coconut
½ cup	(*125 mL*)	milk
1 cup	(*250 mL*)	flour
1½ ts	(*1½ ts*)	baking powder
¼ ts	(*¼ ts*)	salt
1 ts	(*1 ts*)	vanilla flavoring

Cream butter and sugar until light and fluffy, add egg yolks and keep on beating until mixture is smooth. Add coconut and milk and stir until well mixed. Sift together flour, baking-powder and salt and add to batter and mix. Beat egg whites until stiff and carefully fold them into mixture. Put in greased and floured cupcake pan and bake in a 390° F (200° C) for 12–15 minutes or until done. Makes about 1 dozen.

COCONUT TURNOVERS

Bolivia (*Pastelitos de Coco*)

Pastry:

2 cups	(*500 mL*)	flour
½ ts	(*½ ts*)	baking powder
½ ts	(*½ ts*)	salt
⅔ cup	(*160 mL*)	lard or other soft shortening (Crisco or Spry type)
¼ cup	(*60 mL*)	ice-cold water

For brushing: 1 egg yolk mixed with 1 tbs milk

Sift together flour, baking powder and salt, mix well, then cut in shortening with a pastry-cutter or two knives until mixture is crumbly. Add ice-cold water and mix into a ball, cover with plastic wrap and let rest in refrigerator for at least one hour. Roll out dough on a floured baking board

(*Continued on next page*)

(Coconut Turnovers, cont.)

to a thickness of about ⅛″ (2 mm), then cut in 3″ (70 mm) rounds with either a cookie cutter or a glass, dipped in flour each time before it is pressed into dough. Add about 1 ts filling, slightly off center, wet the edges somewhat shape into half-circles and seal together, pressing down with a fork. Place turn-overs on a greased baking sheet, brush with egg yolk and milk mixture, prick each one with a fork to allow steam to escape, and bake in a 400° F (200° C) oven for 10–12 minutes until golden in color.

Makes about 2 dozen.

Filling:

1 cup	(250 mL)	sweetened flaked coconut
1 tbs	(1 tbs)	flour
3 tbs	(3 tbs)	sugar
⅓ cup	(80 mL)	light cream
2 tbs	(2 tbs)	butter
2	(2)	egg yolks, lightly beaten

Mix together coconut, flour and sugar in a saucepan, add cream, mix well and cook over low heat until mixture thickens. Add butter and cook for a couple of minutes, then remove from heat, add egg yolks and stir well to mix. Let mixture cool before adding to pastry circles.

CORNMEAL CAKE

Brazil   *(Bolo de Fuba)*

½ cup	(125 mL)	butter or margarine
½ cup	(125 mL)	soft shortening (Crisco, Spry or similar)
⅓ cup	(80 mL)	sugar
1	(1)	egg
1 cup	(250 mL)	yellow cornmeal
1 cup	(250 mL)	flour
½ ts	(½ ts)	salt
4 ts	(4 ts)	baking powder
1¼ cups	(310 mL)	milk
½ ts	(½ ts)	anise seeds, crushed
For sprinkling:		cinnamon

Cream shortening with sugar, add egg and continue creaming until mixture is light and fluffy. Sift together cornmeal, flour, salt and baking powder and add to egg-mixture alternately with milk. Add anise and mix well. Pour into a 9″ (220 mm) square baking pan and sprinkle with cinnamon. Bake in a 375° F oven (190° C) for 35–40 minutes.

China

CHINESE restaurants have for many years been very popular with the American public, who have learned to love Chinese foods through them. However, in the homes Chinese cooking has been far behind except for a few dishes, some of them not even of authentically Chinese origin, chop suey among others.

Homemakers have been hesitant to try Chinese cooking partly because they have felt that it is necessary to use a *wok*, as that is what they use in China. It is indeed a very handy vessel for stir-frying Chinese food, but it is not at all a necessity, any large skillet can be used and an electric frying pan will do very well. All other utensils the Chinese cooks use for stirring, chopping etc. can be replaced with what the American cook finds most comfortable. Once when I was taking Chinese cooking lessons, our Chinese instructor had forgotten her chopsticks which she used for stirring and other things in the cooking process and she felt quite lost. She then proceeded, to our amusement, to turn two wooden spoons upside down and hold them like chopsticks while she did her work. This is just an example of how habits get the best of us, and for sure, most of us do much better stirring with our own utensils than with chopsticks.

As China is one of the oldest cultures in the world, it goes without saying that their advanced state of cooking is connected with this, as it has had time to develop not only during centuries but over thousands of years. And in China, as in other countries where the cuisine is held in high esteem, the cooking itself is looked upon as an art, and food is prepared not just to satisfy hunger but for esthetic pleasures as well.

Since fuel shortage has been common in many parts of China, ways of cooking were developed where actual cooking over heat was kept to a minimum. This led to their skill in having every morsel prepared and ready to cook in the last minute. This lends itself quite readily to the American way of entertaining today, with our shortage of help, because the hostess can easily do most of the preparation ahead of time and then be able to stay with her guests until shortly before it is time to sit down and eat.

As China is a large country, each section has quite a different cuisine. We are mainly used to the south-eastern—or Cantonese—style of cooking, as most Chinese restaurants in our country use it. A completely different kind of cuisine is found in northern China where more cereals and grains are used instead of rice. And like in so many other countries in the world, there is a tendency for southern recipes to be more highly spiced (Szechuan cooking).

In our country Chinese restaurants follow our way of eating by serving courses of appetizers, soup, main meal and dessert in that order. However, this is not truly the Chinese way. All food should be put on the table at once, the soup as often as not eaten in the middle of the meal, but for convenience it may be easier to do it the Americanized way, and handle one or two dishes at a time.

You may have noticed in most Chinese cookbooks the almost universal use of monosodium glutamate (msg, also known by the trade name Accent). However, as there are quite a few people with an allergy to this, who develop what is sometimes referred to as the Chinese restaurant syndrome, I have not used monosodium glutamate in any recipes. If the ingredients are of good quality, and Chinese recipes almost take this for granted, I do not think it is necessary.

It has been difficult to choose among the very many delicious Chinese foods for this book, but I have tried to include a little bit of everything for both diversity in the foods themselves and in the methods of preparation. Once you get started on Chinese cooking, however, you will wish to try many more things. Fortunately, there are many excellent cookbooks on the market, containing numerous recipes from the different regions. But this quick coverage should provide at least a good beginning.

SHRIMP TOAST
SHERRY SOY SAUCE
SWEET AND SOUR SAUCE
WONTONS
EGG ROLLS
(SPRING ROLLS)
BARBECUED SPARE RIBS
EGG DROP SOUP
CORN SOUP
WONTON SOUP
LOBSTER CANTONESE
FRIED FISH WITH PEPPERS
SWEET AND SOUR PORK

STIR FRYING
SHREDDED BEEF WITH ONION
PORK WITH MUSHROOMS
PORK WITH NOODLES
RED COOKED CHICKEN
RED COOKED BEEF
SHRIMP FOO YUNG
CANTONESE DUCK
MIXED VEGETABLES
FRIED RICE
HONEY DIPPED APPLE
FRITTERS
ALMOND COOKIES

SHRIMP TOAST
China

A delicious appetizer that can be made well in advance of a party by doing everything except the deep frying ahead of time.

1 lb	(½ kg)	raw shrimp
10	(10)	water chestnuts, finely chopped
1	(1)	scallion, finely chopped
2 ts	(2 ts)	salt, or to taste
1 tbs	(1 tbs)	cornstarch
1 tbs	(1 tbs)	sherry
1	(1)	egg, slightly beaten
10	(10)	slices day-old white bread
		oil for deep-frying

Shell and de-vein shrimp, then wash and drain. Finely chop shrimp then mix well with water chestnuts, scallion, salt, cornstarch, sherry and egg. Trim crusts off bread slices, then cut either into four squares or four triangles, then spread with shrimp mix- ture. Fry in 350° F (175° C) oil, shrimp side down, for 1 minute, or until golden brown in color, then turn over and cook for a few seconds on the other side. Remove and drain on paper toweling. Serve hot as an ap- petizer. Makes 40 pieces.

SHERRY SOY SAUCE

China

¼ cup	(60 mL)	soy sauce
¼ cup	(60 mL)	sherry
½ ts	(½ ts)	sugar

Mix together all the ingredients without heating and blend until sugar is completely melted. Serve in individual bowls.

SWEET AND SOUR SAUCE

China

½ cup	(125 mL)	vinegar
½ cup	(125 mL)	sugar
¼ cup	(60 mL)	soy sauce
2 tbs	(2 tbs)	sherry
¼ cup	(60 mL)	ketchup
1½ tbs	(1½ tbs)	cornstarch
½ cup	(125 mL)	water

Mix together vinegar, sugar, soy sauce, sherry and ketchup in a small saucepan and bring to a boil. Mix corn starch with water and add to saucepan while stirring. Bring to a boil and cook for 1 minute then remove from heat and serve hot or cold according to the recipe you are using.

WONTONS

China

Wontons are mainly known as a soup ingredient, but they also make a nice appetizer when they are deep fried instead of boiled in soup stock.

1 lb	(½ kg)	ground pork
1 lb	(½ kg)	fresh spinach (or one 10 oz (300 g) package frozen spinach), finely chopped
3	(3)	scallions, finely chopped
2 tbs	(2 tbs)	soy sauce
2 tbs	(2 tbs)	sesame oil
2 ts	(2 ts)	salt
1	(1)	egg
5-6	(5-6)	Chinese mushrooms, finely chopped (optional)
10-12	(10-12)	dried shrimp, finely minced (optional)
1 pkg	(1 pkg)	ready-made Wonton wrappers (100 pcs) (a thin dough, cut into squares)

Mix together all the ingredients except the wrappers and blend well. Put about 1 ts of the filling in the middle of each wrapper. With your finger dipped in cold water, run it along the edges of the wrapper, then fold it square in half and pinch together. Fold over about ¼″ (6 mm) along the sealed edge, then fold rectangle in half and pinch together left and right hand corners, again wetting with a bit of water to help seal.

For appetizers:

Preheat cooking oil to 350° F (175° C) and drop in filled wontons, a few at a time, and deep-fry until golden brown in color, turning them over now and then to make sure they get evenly cooked. Drain on paper towels and serve hot. Serve with either Sweet and Sour Sauce or Sherry-Soy Sauce in preceding recipes.

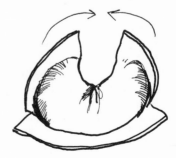

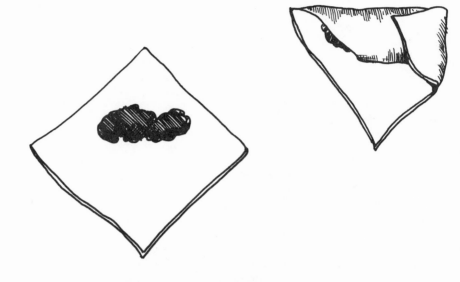

EGG ROLLS (SPRING ROLLS)

China

It is now not too hard to find frozen egg roll wrappers in well-supplied supermarkets, but you can also make your own by using this recipe. If you are somewhat familiar with rolling cookie dough out very thinly, you should not have any difficulties with them. Otherwise you'd better get the ready-made ones.

Wrappers:

1½ cup	(375 mL scant)	plain flour
½ cup	(125 mL)	instant flour (Wondra)
½ ts	(½ ts)	salt
1	(1)	egg, lightly beaten
3–4 tbs	(3–4 tbs)	water
		corn starch for dusting baking board

Sift together flours and salt, add egg and about 2 tbs water and mix well. Add more water a little at a time, to make a smooth dough. Knead dough on board for about 10 minutes, then refrigerate it about one hour. Dust board lightly with the cornstarch, then divide dough in half and roll each half out paper thin, frequently turning the rolled-out dough and dusting with more corn starch to prevent sticking. Cut dough sheets into 7″ (180 mm) squares. Cover with damp cloth until you are ready to fill them, in order to prevent drying out.

(*Continued on next page*)

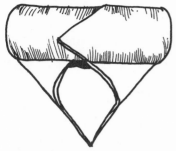

Filling:

½ lb	(¼ kg)	lean pork
¼ lb	(125 g)	raw shrimp
½ cup	(125 mL)	finely minced scallions
¾ cup	(180 mL)	celery, finely chopped
1½ cup	(375 mL)	bean sprouts
10	(10)	water chestnuts, finely chopped
½ cup	(125 mL)	bamboo shoots, shredded
1	(1)	slice fresh ginger, about ⅛″ (3 mm) thick finely minced
3 tbs	(3 tbs)	cooking oil
½ ts	(½ ts)	salt
2 ts	(2 ts)	soy sauce
2 ts	(2 ts)	sherry
1	(1)	egg, slightly beaten
		oil for deep-frying

Cut pork against the grain into very thin slices, then into strips and then mince the strips finely. Clean and shell the shrimp and de-vein, then chop into small pieces. Rinse bean sprouts.

In a wok or large skillet heat 2 tbs cooking oil and stir-fry pork (see page 101) until it loses its pink color, about 2 minutes, then add shrimp and stir-fry for one more minute. Remove, add one more tbs of oil and heat, add scallions, ginger, bamboo, water chestnuts and stir-fry 2 minutes, add bean sprouts and cook one more minute. Return pork and shrimp and mix well. Add salt, soy sauce and sherry, then remove from heat. Put mixture in a colander to drain out excess moisture.

Place about 1½ tbs of this mixture on each wrapper, slightly off center towards you, then make a neat, tight "package" by folding the sides over, then rolling it up and sealing the edges with egg (see illustration). Set them slightly apart on a platter, while you are rolling them up, so that they will not stick to each other. Heat oil in a deep fryer to 375° F (190° C) and fry the egg rolls, a couple at a time, 3–4 minutes or until golden brown, turning them once to make them color evenly. Drain on paper toweling and serve hot.

Makes 14–16 rolls.

BARBECUED SPARERIBS

China

Another Chinese classic. And so easy!

3 lbs	(1½ kg)	spareribs

Marinade:

3	(3)	cloves garlic, finely minced
½ cup	(125 mL)	chicken stock or water
2 tbs	(2 tbs)	soy sauce
2 tbs	(2 tbs)	sherry
3 tbs	(3 tbs)	sugar

Trim fat off spareribs, cut to separate them and with a cleaver cut them into 2″ (50 mm) lengths. Mix ingredients for marinade and place spareribs in it for at least 4 hours. Bake spareribs together with marinade in a 325° F (165° C) oven about 30 minutes, then turn them over and bake 15–20 minutes longer, or until meat is tender. Remove, strain the pan juice into a saucepan, add one ts cornstarch mixed with one tbs water and bring to a boil. Cook one minute then serve spareribs with sauce immediately.

Serves 5–6.

EGG DROP SOUP

China

This simple soup is fun to make—and nice to eat too.

4 cups	(1 L)	chicken broth
1	(1)	egg
1 ts	(1 ts)	water
2	(2)	scallions, finely chopped
1 tbs	(1 tbs)	soy sauce
1 tbs	(1 tbs)	sesame oil

Bring chicken broth to a boil. Beat egg with water vigorously, then drop slowly into the boiling broth while stirring it slowly. The egg will coagulate immediately and form thin threads. Add scallions, and just before serving, soy sauce and sesame oil.

Serves 4–5.

CORN SOUP

China

An easy-to-make soup which should appeal to our corn-loving nation.

1	(*1*)	can cream style corn (about one lb—500 g)
4 cups	(*1 L*)	chicken stock
1 cup	(*250 mL*)	cooked chicken, finely chopped
2 tbs	(*2 tbs*)	corn starch, mixed with one tbs water
		salt to taste
For garnish:		⅓ cup (*80 mL*) boiled ham, cut into fine strips

Bring corn and chicken stock to a boil, add corn starch and salt, stir in chicken and heat thoroughly, then remove from heat. Serve in soup bowls, with about one tbs of ham strips in the middle of each.

Serves 5–6.

WONTON SOUP

China

Preferably you should have a rich, home-made chicken broth for this, but there are also some canned brands that are good.

4 cups	(*1 L*)	chicken broth
2	(*2*)	scallions, thinly sliced, diagonally, or a handful of fresh spinach leaves
12-20	(*12-20*)	wontons (depending upon how many are desired for each serving) see page 93

Cook wontons in 6 cups (1½ L) boiling, salted water for about 10 minutes, but do not cook all of them at once if the larger quantity is used. Heat chicken broth, add cooked wontons and garnish each plateful with either scallions or spinach leaves. Serves 4–5.

LOBSTER CANTONESE

China

An elegant Chinese dish, for special occasions only, as the price of lobster does not allow you to have it often.

2	(2)	lobsters about 1½-2 lbs. ea (¾-1 kg)
		OR
4-5	(4-5)	rock lobster tails (about 6 oz. (170 g) ea
3 tbs	(3 tbs)	scallions, chopped
1	(1)	clove garlic, finely minced
1	(1)	thin slice fresh ginger, finely minced
½ lb	(¼ kg)	ground lean pork
2 tbs	(2 tbs)	cooking oil
1 cup	(250 mL)	chicken stock, or water
1	(1)	egg, slightly beaten
2 tbs	(2 tbs)	soy sauce
¼ cup	(60 mL)	cold water
2 tbs	(2 tbs)	corn starch

In a large pot bring a small amount of water (about 1″ or 25 mm) to a deep boil, add lobsters, cover and bring to a boil again, cook for 10 minutes, then remove lobsters. As soon as they are cool enough to handle, shell them and cut meat into bite size pieces, also remove meat from claws and head, and set aside.

In a wok or a large skillet heat cooking oil and fry scallions, garlic, ginger and pork while continuously stirring for about 8-10 minutes, or until pork loses its pink color. Add lobster meat and chicken stock and bring to boil, then simmer for 10 minutes.

Add egg, while stirring, then blend together soy sauce, water and corn starch and bring to a boil, cook for one minute, then serve immediately with rice.   For 4-6 people.

FRIED FISH WITH PEPPERS

China

*So many people in our country do not like fish, but there are many different
ways to prepare it that are very appealing. Like this one.*

1½ lb	(¾ kg)	fish fillets (flounder, haddock, cod or sole)
1	(1)	thin slice of fresh ginger, finely minced
1 tbs	(1 tbs)	salt
¼ ts	(¼ ts)	sugar
1 ts	(1 ts)	sesame oil
2 tbs	(2 tbs)	sherry
2	(2)	sweet green peppers (or one green and one red)
1	(1)	medium onion, cut in thick slices
1	(1)	egg, lightly beaten
2 tbs	(2 tbs)	corn starch
¼ cup	(60 mL)	cooking oil
1	(1)	clove garlic, finely minced
1 ts	(1 ts)	soy sauce, mixed with one ts sherry

Cut the fish fillets into ½" x 1½"
(12 x 38 mm) pieces. Mix together
ginger, salt, sugar, sesame oil and
sherry in a bowl and marinate the fish
in this for at least 2–3 hours. Cut
peppers in half lengthwise, remove
membranes and seeds, then cut into
1" (25 mm) square pieces. Separate
onions into ¼" (6 mm) rings. Drain
fish and pat dry on paper towels, then
dip in beaten egg and after that in
corn starch. Heat one tbs oil in skillet,
add ginger and garlic and stir-fry for
a few minutes, then remove ginger
and garlic and discard. Add pepper
and onion and stir-fry about 2–3 minutes over medium heat, add sherry
and soy sauce and keep stirring. Remove all from pot and keep hot.

Heat remaining oil, then fry fish on
both sides until crisp. Remove fish
from pan and drain on paper towels,
then place on serving dish, add pepper and onion mixture and serve immediately to 4–5.

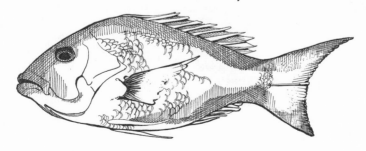

SWEET AND SOUR PORK

China

One of the most popular of all Chinese dishes in our country.

1½ lb	(¾ kg)	pork tenderloin, cut into ¾" (18 mm) cubes
3 tbs	(3 tbs)	corn starch
2 tbs	(2 tbs)	sherry
2	(2)	green peppers
½ cup	(125 mL)	sliced carrots (diagonal slices)
4	(4)	slices canned pinapple
1	(1)	clove garlic, finely minced
¾ cup	(180 mL)	water
⅓ cup	(80 mL)	vinegar
1 tbs	(1 tbs)	soy sauce
⅔ cup	(180 mL)	sugar
		pepper and salt to taste
		oil for deep frying

Dredge pork cubes in 2 tbs corn starch thoroughly, then sprinkle with sherry, creating a paste-like coating and let stand for 20 minutes. Clean and seed peppers and cut into ¾" (18 mm) squares. (If desired, par-boil peppers and carrots in a little water for one minute). Cut pineapple slices into pieces and mince garlic very finely.

Mix vinegar, water, soy sauce, sugar, garlic, salt and pepper in a saucepan and bring to a boil, add peppers, carrots and pineapple and cook for one minute. Add 1 tbs corn starch mixed with 2 tbs water and stir until gravy thickens. Remove from heat and keep warm.

Heat oil in a deep fryer to 375° F (190° C) and drop in pork cubes and cook until they are golden brown and float to the surface, which means they are done. Drain them on a paper towel and add to saucepan with vegetables.

Reheat until boiling, stirring carefully to make sure sauce is covering all ingredients. Serve immediately. If this dish is done right, the pork will be crisp although completely coated with the sauce. Serve with rice. For 5–6.

STIR FRYING

Stir frying means quick frying, with little oil and constant stirring. It is in several recipes, so I would like to give a few pointers about it.

Make sure all the ingredients are cut in small enough pieces so that they do not remain raw after cooking. However, vegetables are supposed to be still crisp and chewy.

Make sure the oil is very hot before anything is added to it, this will make the food crisp instead of soggy.

Make sure you have all ingredients prepared and ready, as the hot oil should not wait while things get cut up and fixed.

When it comes to cooking times, I have tried to give them in minutes, but it will not always work out exactly. Always keep in mind, though, that the vegetables should be cooked only so long as they keep their nice fresh color.

SHREDDED BEEF WITH ONION

China

One of the easiest to prepare—the first one we got to do in Chinese cooking class.

1 lb	(½ kg)	flank beef or London broil
4	(4)	medium size onions, cut in halves and sliced
3 tbs	(3 tbs)	cooking oil
1	(1)	thin slice ginger
1 ts	(1 ts)	sesame oil
		salt to taste

Marinade:

3 tbs	(3 tbs)	soy sauce
1 tbs	(1 tbs)	sherry
2 ts	(2 ts)	sugar
2 ts	(2 ts)	corn starch

Cut the beef against the grain into thin shreds. Mix together ingredients for marinade, add meat and stir to coat all the meat. Keep in marinade for 20 minutes. Heat cooking oil until very hot, place slice of ginger in it, then add beef and stir-fry until light brown. Discard ginger, and remove meat and sauté onions, adding a bit more oil if necessary, add salt to taste and cook until onions are almost tender. Add beef, stir to mix, and reheat. Add sesame oil, mix well and heat only until thoroughly hot. Serve with rice, to 4–5.

PORK WITH MUSHROOMS
China

What makes Chinese dishes economical to prepare is the fact that they do not use great quantities of meat. However, the meat should be of high quality and usually cut against (across) the grain into first thin slices, then into shreds, and it is always marinated, which both tenderizes and gives flavor. Pork is very popular in China, and here are two easy dishes using it.

1 lb	(½ kg)	pork tenderloin, sliced very thin against the grain
3 tbs	(3 tbs)	cooking oil
½ lb	(¼ kg)	fresh mushrooms, thinly sliced
1	(1)	slice fresh ginger, ⅛″ (3 mm) thick
1 tbs	(1 tbs)	corn starch mixed with 2 tbs water
½ ts	(½ ts)	sugar
2 ts	(2 ts)	soy sauce
1 ts	(1 ts)	salt
1½ cup	(375 mL)	chicken stock or water

Marinade:

2 ts	(2 ts)	corn starch
2 ts	(2 ts)	soy sauce
1 tbs	(1 tbs)	sherry
½ ts	(½ ts)	sugar
1 tbs	(1 tbs)	vegetable oil

Mix ingredients for marinade and add pork, making sure all pork surfaces are covered. Set aside for at least 20 minutes. Heat oil in a wok or skillet, add ginger, then pork, and stir-fry for about 5 minutes, or until pork has turned white. Add mushrooms and stock, cover pan and cook about 3 minutes. Thicken with corn starch mixed with sugar, salt and soy sauce and cook for only one minute.

VARIATION:

Other vegetables may be used instead of mushrooms, such as onions, scallions, broccoli, asparagus or Chinese cabbage. The cooking times will vary somewhat and you will have to use the color of the vegetables as your guide as they should not cook so long that they lose their fresh colors.

Serves 4–5.

PORK WITH NOODLES
China

Noodles were eaten in China long before they were known in Europe and are supposed to have been brought to Italy by Marco Polo.

½ lb	(¼ kg)	Chinese noodles or thin spaghetti
5	(5)	Chinese dried mushrooms
¾ lb	(400 g)	pork cutlet
1 cup	(250 mL)	Chinese cabbage, finely shredded
½ cup	(125 mL)	bamboo shoots, finely shredded
3 tbs	(3 tbs)	soy sauce
1 tbs	(1 tbs)	sesame oil
2-3 tbs	(2-3 tbs)	salad oil for frying

Marinade:

1 tbs	(1 tbs)	soy sauce
1 tbs	(1 tbs)	sherry
½ ts	(½ ts)	sugar
1 ts	(1 ts)	corn starch

Soak mushrooms in warm water for 20 minutes, then cut into shreds. Cut meat against the grain into thin shreds. Mix together soy sauce, sherry, sugar and corn starch and add meat to this marinade, stirring to get the meat evenly covered, then leave it for about 20 minutes.

Cook noodles in salted, boiling water for 5-6 minutes. Drain and rinse quickly with cold water, then keep them hot. Heat oil in a wok or large frying pan until very hot, fry meat while stirring until it loses its pink color, then remove it. Add more oil, if necessary, and stir-fry the cabbage, bamboo shoots and shredded mushrooms until vegetables are almost soft, then add one tbs soy sauce.

Add meat to vegetable mixture and let them cook together for a few minutes. Mix sesame oil and 2 tbs soy sauce with the noodles, put them in a serving bowl and pour the pork mixture over them and serve immediately. For 4-5.

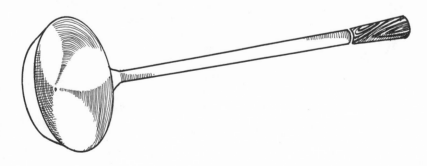

RED COOKED CHICKEN

China

What is called the red-cooking method is a way of slow-cooking chicken or meat in a pot, that somehow gives it a nice reddish-brown color and a lot of flavor. And it is said that some families keep their red-cooking liquid going for years.

1	(1)	frying chicken 3-3½ lb (1½-1¾ kg)
2	(2)	thin slices fresh ginger
1	(1)	clove garlic, finely minced
2 tbs	(2 tbs)	sugar
1	(1)	star anise (or one ts anise seeds) optional
2 tbs	(2 tbs)	sherry
1 cup	(250 mL)	soy sauce
½ cup	(125 mL)	chicken stock, or water

In a Dutch oven mix together all the ingredients except the chicken and bring to a boil. Add the chicken, whole, lying on its side, bring to a boil again, turn down heat then simmer under cover about 1-1½ hours. Turn chicken ¼ turn every 15 minutes. When ready, remove chicken and cut into serving pieces, or remove meat from bones, cut into bite-size pieces and moisten with some of the liquid from the pot.

(Left-over liquid may be strained, then kept in freezer and re-used for other red-cooked dishes).

Serves 4-6.

RED COOKED BEEF

China

The Chinese version of pot roast, just loaded with flavor.

3-4 lbs	(1½-2 kg)	pot roast (eye round, top round, or chuck roast)
2	(2)	thin slices fresh ginger
1	(1)	clove garlic, finely minced
3 tbs	(3 tbs)	salad oil
½ cup	(125 mL)	soy sauce
⅓ cup	(80 mL)	sherry
1	(1)	star anise
1 tbs	(1 tbs)	sugar
		salt and pepper to taste
		water

(Continued on next page)

(Red Cooked Beef, cont.)

Brown meat on all sides in oil in a Dutch oven, then add remaining ingredients with enough water to make the liquid reach $\frac{3}{4}$ to the top of the meat. Bring to a boil, then turn down heat to very low, cover, and simmer until tender.

Cooking time depends on what kind of cut is used, but start testing for done-ness after about 2 hours.

Turn the meat several times during cooking. When ready, slice meat and serve with some of the sauce, after it has been strained.

Remaining sauce may be used over again for similar dishes if kept either in the freezer or in the refrigerator. (If kept in the refrigerator it should be heated to boiling point about every ten days.)   Serves 6–8.

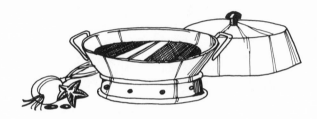

SHRIMP FOO YUNG

China

The variations provide a good way to use left-overs. My family calls them "cleaning-out-the-fridge-omelets." I just can't fool them.

3	(3)	scallions, finely chopped
½ cup	(125 mL)	mushrooms, fresh or canned
2	(2)	thin slices fresh ginger, finely minced
1 cup	(250 mL)	cooked shrimp, cut up into small pieces
2 tbs	(2 tbs)	cooking oil
2 tbs	(2 tbs)	soy sauce
		salt and pepper to taste
6	(6)	eggs

Heat oil in a skillet and stir-fry scallions, mushrooms, ginger and shrimp for about 5 minutes, then add soy sauce. Slightly beat eggs, add salt and pepper, then add to skillet, cover and cook slowly until set, like an omelette. Serve immediately.

For 4 or 5 people.

VARIATION:

Instead of shrimp, other ingredients may be used such as shredded chicken, shredded cooked steak, crab meat or lobster meat, crumbled cooked bacon, cooked green peas, or a combination of any of these.

China   **CANTONESE DUCK**

The most well-known way of preparing Chinese duck is Peking Duck. That is a very complicated and involved recipe, however, which takes several days of preparation and I have found that Cantonese duck is also a very good example of Chinese cuisine, and much easier to prepare.

1	(*1*)	duck, 4–5 lbs (2–2½ kg)
		salt to taste
2	(*2*)	cloves garlic, finely minced
2	(*2*)	scallions, finely chopped
2	(*2*)	thin slices fresh ginger, finely minced
		(or ¾ ts powdered ginger)
3 tbs	(*3 tbs*)	honey
¼ cup	(*60 mL*)	soy sauce
2 tbs	(*2 tbs*)	dry sherry
¼ ts	(*¼ ts*)	cinnamon
3 cups	(*750 mL*)	water
1 tbs	(*1 tbs*)	cider vinegar

Rub the duck inside and out with salt, then truss the body cavity securely, either by sewing it together or using skewers. In a small saucepan combine garlic, scallions, ginger, one tbs honey, 2 tbs soy sauce, sherry, cinnamon and 2 cups (500 mL) water and bring to a boil, then let cool for a few minutes. Place the duck in a bowl where it can stand as straight up as possible, then carefully pull away the skin at the neck cavity and pour the liquid inside the duck, then carefully truss together the opening so that no liquid will pour out during roasting.

Place the duck, breast up, on a rack in a roasting pan and roast for 15 minutes at 400° F (200° C) then turn down heat to 325° F (165° C). In the meantime mix together remaining honey, soy sauce, water and vinegar and baste the duck with this mixture every 15–20 minutes. The duck should roast altogether about 2–2½ hours. When ready, remove all strings, strain any liquid remaining in cavity and carve the duck into serving pieces, spooning the strained liquid over them.

Serves 4.

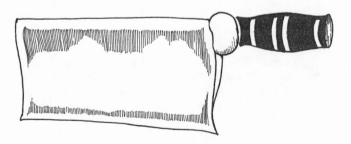

MIXED VEGETABLES

China

The secret for success in cooking vegetables the Chinese way is to undercook them slightly. In this way they keep their bright colors and are slightly crunchy to your bite.

1-2	(*1-2*)	stalks of broccoli (depending on size) or 1 package frozen broccoli
½ lb	(¼ *kg*)	fresh string beans or 1 package frozen string beans
1	(*1*)	medium size onion, sliced
2	(*2*)	carrots, sliced diagonally ⅛" (3 mm) thick
1	(*1*)	¼" thick (6 mm) slice of fresh ginger (or ¼ ts ground ginger)
2 tbs	(*2 tbs*)	cooking oil
1 ts	(*1 ts*)	salt
½ ts	(½ *ts*)	sugar
1 tbs	(*1 tbs*)	corn starch, mixed with 2 tbs water

Cut broccoli into small flowerets, slice stems diagonally very thin. Cut string beans diagonally into 1" (25 mm) pieces. Heat oil in wok or large skillet, using high flame, then add ginger and carrots and cook for about one minute, stirring constantly. Add string beans and cook about one more minute, then add broccoli and cook one minute. Turn down heat and cover pan and cook 3-4 minutes more, then add cornstarch mixture, sugar and salt. Boil one more minute.

Remove slice of fresh ginger, if this is used, and serve immediately. The vegetables will have nice bright colors and should be somewhat crisp in texture. Serves 5-6.

VARIATION:

The above vegetables are only one suggestion, many variations can be used, just use any vegetables you have on hand, such as mushrooms, red or green peppers, asparagus or whatever.

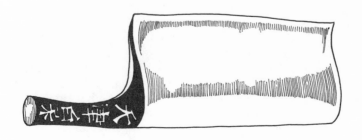

FRIED RICE

China

Another dish for left-overs. According to my Chinese cooking instructor it is rated as such a mundane dish that no Chinese housewife wants to prepare it for guests and it is mainly eaten just by the family. However, I feel it is good enough for anyone who wants to join me at my table.

3 cups	(750 mL)	cold, cooked rice
1	(1)	medium onion, chopped (¾ cup or 180 mL)
4 tbs	(4 tbs)	cooking oil
1	(1)	scallion, chopped fine (include green part)
1 ts	(1 ts)	finely minced fresh ginger (or ½ ts ground ginger)
3 tbs	(3 tbs)	soy sauce
		salt and pepper to taste
2	(2)	eggs, lightly beaten

In a wok or large skillet heat 3½ tbs oil, stir-fry onion, scallion, and fresh ginger, if this is used, for about 3 minutes. Push vegetables aside, then add cooked rice and stir to coat all the rice with oil. Mix with the vegetables, add soy sauce. In a small fry-pan heat remaining ½ tbs oil then add slightly beaten eggs and stir-fry quickly until eggs have coagulated. Cook only until set, then remove from heat and add this to rice mix-ture. Serve as a side dish, for 5–6.

VARIATION:

This recipe may be built up to a main dish by adding some other ingredi-ent—½ lb (¼ kg) cooked shrimp, cut into small pieces, one cup (250 mL) of diced ham, one cup (250 mL) of diced cooked chicken or one cup (250 mL) of cubed pork. If desired larger quan-tities of these "extras" may be used. It is a great way to use left-overs!

HONEY-DIPPED APPLE FRITTERS
China

3	(3)	crisp apples (about 1 lb or ½ kg)
2 tbs	(2 tbs)	corn starch
2 tbs	(2 tbs)	flour)
2	(2)	egg whites
⅓ cup	(80 mL)	honey
2 tbs	(2 tbs)	cooking oil
		oil for deep frying

Peel and core apples, then cut each into eight equal wedges. Mix together corn starch, flour and egg whites into a smooth batter. Dip apple pieces in batter and deep fry, a few at a time, in oil at 375° F (190° C) until golden in color. Drain on paper toweling. Heat oil and add honey and mix. Add apple pieces and stir until coated, spread out on a platter and serve. If desired, each piece may be dipped in ice-cold water just before eating.

Serves four.

ALMOND COOKIES
China

⅔ cup	(160 mL)	shortening
1 cup	(250 mL)	sugar
1	(1)	egg
2 cups	(500 mL)	rice flour or regular flour
½ ts	(½ ts)	baking powder
		pinch of salt
1 ts	(1 ts)	almond extract
For sprinkling:		⅓ cup (80 mL) chopped blanched almonds

Cream shortening and sugar until light and fluffy, add egg, chopped blanched almonds and almond extract and mix well. Sift together rice flour or flour with baking powder and salt and add to egg mixture, and mix well. Turn out of mixing bowl and knead until smooth.

Make balls about 1" (25 mm) in diameter and place on a greased baking sheet. Flatten cookies either with your floured knuckles or with a floured spoon or fork, then sprinkle with almonds. Bake in a 350° F (175° C) oven about 20 minutes until golden brown in color. Makes about 4 dozen cookies.

Czechoslovakia

THIS small country, situated in the middle of Eastern Europe, was created after the First World War to include people of several national backgrounds. Therefore, many of their dishes appear also in neighboring countries, and it is difficult to point to specific national dishes. One thing seems to stand out—their way of making dumplings of different kinds.

Their very special ham—Praguer Ham—has worldwide renown, and their city of Pilsen has lent its name to beer made all over the world.

BOUILLON WITH LIVER DUMPLINGS   *Knedlicky Jatrove*
PAPRIKA MEAT BALLS
SWEET ROLLS WITH FILLING   *Kolachi*
BOHEMIAN POPPY SEED CAKE

BOUILLON WITH LIVER DUMPLINGS

Czechoslovakia   *(Knedlicky Jatrove)*

Dumplings of a different kind make this soup a meal in itself.

½ lb	(¼ kg)	beef or calf's liver
1	(1)	egg
1 cup	(250 mL)	dry bread-crumbs
1	(1)	small onion
2 ts	(2 ts)	finely minced parsley
		pinch of thyme
		salt and pepper to taste
2 tbs	(2 tbs)	melted butter or margarine
4 cups	(1 L)	beef or chicken bouillon

Remove membranes from liver, cut into small pieces and grind in meat grinder or in an electric blender. Also grind or grate onion. Mix together liver, onion, egg, bread-crumbs, parsley and seasonings and blend well, then add melted butter and mix. Let rest in refrigerator at least 30 min-utes. Bring bouillon to a boil. Make balls the size of walnuts out of liver mixture, dusting hands with flour while shaping them, drop them into bouillon and bring it back to a boil. Then turn down heat and simmer about 10 minutes. Serve hot.

For 4–5.

PAPRIKA MEAT BALLS

Czechoslovakia

Meat balls are well liked in their many ways. Here is an Eastern European version that sure is good.

1 lb	(½ kg)	chopped chuck beef
1	(1)	small onion, finely chopped
		(about ½ cup or 125 mL)
½ cup	(125 mL)	dry bread crumbs
⅓ cup	(80 mL)	water
		salt and pepper to taste
2 tbs	(2 tbs)	butter or margarine
⅔ cup	(160 mL)	beef stock
1 tbs	(1 tbs)	tomato paste
1 tbs	(1 tbs)	paprika
1 cup	(250 mL)	sour cream

Mix chopped beef, onion, bread crumbs, water, salt and pepper in bowl and work mixture until well blended. Shape into meatballs about 1½″ (38 mm) in size and brown in a skillet in butter or margarine. Drain off excess fat and add beef stock, tomato paste and paprika and cook about 8–10 minutes. Add sour cream, mix well and heat thoroughly, but do not let it come to a boil, as it might then curdle. Serve with cooked noodles. Serves 4–5.

Czechoslovakia SWEET ROLLS WITH FILLING (*Kolachi*)

Kolachi pastries are sometimes made with a short pastry dough, and if you desire to use this instead, see Apple Tart recipe on page 39.

1 pkg	(*1 pkg*)	dry yeast
¼ cup	(*60 mL*)	sugar
⅓ cup	(*80 mL*)	water
3 tbs	(*3 tbs*)	butter or margarine
½ cup	(*125 mL*)	milk
½ ts	(*½ ts*)	salt
3 cups	(*750 mL*)	flour, approximately
2	(*2*)	eggs

Mix yeast with 1 tbs sugar and lukewarm water. Melt butter or margarine in a saucepan, add milk, and heat to lukewarm. Sift half amount of flour in a large mixing bowl, add salt, milk mixture, yeast mixture and eggs, and beat with an electric beater or by hand with a wooden spoon until a thick batter has been obtained.

Add more flour a bit at a time to make a soft dough and continue beating until the mixture gets too heavy for electric beating, then turn out on floured baking board and knead until dough is smooth and elastic, about 10 minutes, adding a bit more flour in case dough is too soft and sticky.

Place in greased bowl, turn over dough to get all sides greased then cover with plastic wrap and let rise in a warm place until double in bulk, about 1 hour. Punch down dough and roll out to ½″ (12 mm) thickness and cut 2–2½″ (50–60 mm) circles with a biscuit cutter, or if this size is not available, with a glass dipped in flour. Put rounds on a greased baking sheet, cover with a cloth and let rise again in warm place for 1 more hour. Press a deep indentation in the middle of each round with your fingers leaving just a narrow rim and put in one of the fillings below, or some other filling of your choice. Bake in a hot 400° F (205° C) oven for about 10 minutes, or until done. Remove from baking sheets and cool on wire rack. Sprinkle with confectioner's sugar.

Raisin Filling:

1½ cups	(*375 mL*)	seedless raisins
⅔ cup	(*160 mL*)	brown sugar
2 tbs	(*2 tbs*)	cornstarch
1 ts	(*1 ts*)	ground cinnamon
¼ ts	(*¼ ts*)	ground allspice
¼ ts	(*¼ ts*)	ground cloves
1 cup	(*250 mL*)	water
½ cup	(*125 mL*)	chopped walnuts

(*Continued on next page*)

Mix all ingredients, except nuts, in a saucepan, bring to a boil while stirring constantly, turn down heat and cook for about one more minute, still stirring, then remove from heat, stir in nuts and cool well before using.

Prune Filling:

The same ingredients and procedure as above except substitute one and a half cups (375 mL) finely chopped prunes for raisins.

BOHEMIAN POPPY SEED CAKE
Czechoslovakia

One of my favorite cakes—and especially handy when I find myself with too many egg whites on hand.

³⁄₄ cup	(*180 mL*)	poppy seeds
³⁄₄ cup	(*180 mL*)	milk
¹⁄₂ cup	(*125 mL*)	butter or margarine
1¹⁄₃ cup	(*330 mL*)	sugar
2 cups	(*500 mL*)	flour
3 ts	(*3 ts*)	baking powder
¹⁄₂ ts	(*¹⁄₂ ts*)	salt
¹⁄₂ cup	(*125 mL*)	milk
1 ts	(*1 ts*)	vanilla extract
3	(*3*)	egg whites (large)

Soak poppy seeds in milk 3–4 hours, or over-night, if desired. Cream sugar and butter until light and fluffy. Sift together flour, baking powder and salt and add to butter mixture alternately with poppy seed mixture and the plain milk. Add vanilla. Beat egg whites until stiff and carefully fold into batter. Put into two greased and floured 9″ (220 mm) round baking pans and bake in a 350° F (175° C) oven about 30 minutes. Cool in pans for about 10 minutes, then turn out onto wire racks. Frost with the following between layers and on top and sides of cake.

Chocolate Frosting:

¹⁄₂ cup	(*125 mL*)	butter or margarine
2	(*2*)	squares unsweetened chocolate (2 oz or 60 g)
3 cups	(*750 mL*)	confectioner's sugar
1	(*1*)	egg yolk
2 tbs	(*2 tbs*)	cream (or slightly more)
1 ts	(*1 ts*)	vanilla extract

Cream butter until light and fluffy. Melt chocolate in small dish over hot water and add to butter. Add sugar and continue beating, then egg yolk and cream, then vanilla, and beat until mixture is spreadable.

Denmark

AFTER a visit to Denmark, most people will remember *smørrebrod*, that is the open face sandwiches, heaped with a variety of foods, as the most outstanding feature of the Danish cuisine.

The most popular of the *smørre-brød* is the one with *pillede rejer*—cooked and peeled tiny shrimp, built up into a pyramid on the bread and decorated with lettuce, mayonnaise and dill. This shrimp is of that special Scandinavian variety that is cooked in sea water on board the fishing vessel as soon as it is caught and then cooled in this natural brine, giving a special flavor that cannot be duplicated with any kind of salt or spices. You can buy this type shrimp in cans, imported from the Scandinavian countries and also Iceland, but as with most canned goods, it is not the same in quality as when it is fresh.

There are many other good varieties of *smørre-brød*. They all have one thing in common—the artist in the one who prepares them has taken over, and has created little pieces of art which will make your gastric juices start flowing when you just look at them.

Of course, there are many other good things to eat in Denmark. It is a very richly agricultural country, with the best of raw materials for food. Its cheeses are among the best in the world. As their country is almost completely surrounded by the North Sea, they have over the ages developed many ways of cooking seafood in mouthwatering ways.

OPEN FACE SANDWICHES	Smørre-brød
DANISH SALAD (FOR SAND-WICHES)	Dansk Salat
OLD-FASHIONED SOUR RYEBREAD	Gammelsurbrod
ONION TART COPENHAGEN	Københavnvnsk Løkkpaj
FLOUNDER ROLLS IN LETTUCE LEAVES	Rødspøtte med Salat
STUFFED SPARERIBS	Fyldt Ribbensteg
SAILOR'S CASSEROLE	Sjømannens Køddkager
POTATO PUDDING	Kartoffelbudding
OLD-FASHIONED APPLE CAKE	Gammel Aeblekage
DANISH PASTRIES	Wienerbrød

OPEN FACE SANDWICHES

(*Smørrebrød*)

Anyone who has eaten a smørre-brød *with* pillede rejer *in Denmark will never forget the experience. And some other* smørre-brød *are not bad either.*

I wish to give a few general pointers for this type of sandwich. One of them is to keep in mind that you should never be stingy with what you put on top, because what makes them so outstanding is the fact that they are literally heaped with toppings. The bread should be of a firm quality, and the slices should not be too thick. They are eaten with knife and fork most of the time, but some of them can be picked up in the hand.

Use your best artistic ability to make them attractive, use anything you have on hand for decoration, such as olives, pearl onions, parsley, dill, pimiento etc. etc. Lettuce should almost always be used, either between the bread and the filling, if the topping is moist, (as when you use salads), or just for decorative purposes.

Here follow some suggestions:

Pumpernickel bread with slices of one small, boiled potato, about 3 pieces of herring of the canned Scandinavian type, decorated with a little mayonnaise and a dill sprig.

The same as the above but use sliced egg instead of potato.

White bread with sliced (or scrambled) egg and smoked salmon, decorated with a dill sprig.

White bread, covered with a lot of shrimp—preferably the small Scandinavian type—preferably laid out in a nice design and decorated with mayonnaise and dill sprigs.

Rye bread with several slices of salami or Taylor ham, decorated with dill pickle or sweet pickle, sliced or cut into strips.

Rye bread or white bread, slices of liver pate (see page 473) or liverwurst, decorated with several slices of cucumbers, plain or pickled, tomato slices or wedges, olives or pimiento strips.

Rye bread or white bread, several slices of smoked tongue with whipped cream, flavored to taste with a little prepared horseradish, and decorated with orange slices or mandarin orange sections.

White bread, with ham slices and apple slices. (Do not slice and add apple until just before serving, as the slices might otherwise turn brown.)

White bread, covered with lettuce leaf, then vegetable salad (see the following recipe) or lobster, crab or shrimp salad, piled into a mound.

Some type of hard bread, such as crisp-bread, covered with cheese and sliced or chopped radishes.

These are just a few samples of the many ways in which these sandwiches can be made.

Denmark	**DANISH SALAD** (for sandwiches)	(*Dansk Salat*)
1	(*1*)	medium size cooked potato, diced
1	(*1*)	medium size, cooked carrot, diced
1 cup	(*250 mL*)	cooked green peas
1	(*1*)	medium size cooked beet, diced
1	(*1*)	medium size apple, peeled, cored and diced
1 tbs	(*1 tbs*)	finely chopped sweet pickles, or, if preferred, dill pickles
		salt and pepper to taste
⅓-½ cup	(*80-125 mL*)	mayonnaise

Put all ingredients except mayonnaise in a bowl and mix well. Add mayonnaise, a little at a time and add only so much that the salad sticks together, as it should not be made so wet that it runs.

VARIATION:
Add ½-1 cup (125–250 mL) cubed cooked meat, be it chicken, beef, pork, veal or what-ever. Besides using the salad for *smørre-brød* it is then nice as a luncheon meal.

OLD-FASHIONED SOUR RYEBREAD

Denmark   (*Gammelsurbrød*)

Many people love sourdough bread but shy away from it as it is a bother to make, and to keep a starter for the next batch. This is a short-cut but it makes a very delicious bread, nevertheless.

1 pkg	(*1 pkg*)	dry yeast
4 cups	(*1 L*)	lukewarm water
6 cups	(*1-½ L*)	rye flour
1 tbs	(*1 tbs*)	salt
2 cups	(*500 mL*)	flour

For kneading: Mixture of half each of flour and rye
                         flour, about 1 cup (*250 mL*)

For brushing: 2 tbs melted butter or margarine

In a large bowl dissolve yeast in luke-warm water, add 4 cups (1 L) of the rye flour and salt and beat until well mixed, about 5 minutes, in an electric mixer or by hand. Cover bowl and put it in a warm place over-night. (By the next morning the dough will have risen and fallen. This prepares it for the next processing stage, in which the rest of the ingredients are used.)

Beat dough well, then add 2 cups (500 mL) of rye flour and 2 cups (500 mL) of flour and beat with a wooden spoon until well blended. Set aside again to rise in a warm place, until double in bulk, about 1½ hours. Remove from bowl and knead it on a floured baking board, using as much of the mixture of half of rye flour and half of flour as is necessary to make a firm dough. Make three loaves and put in baking pans (loaf pans about 5 x 9 x 3" (125 x 220 x 75 mm) and let rise for 45 minutes. Place loaf pans in a shallow pan filled with 1" (25 mm) water. Brush with melted butter and bake in a 325° F (165° C) oven for about 1 hour, or until done.

ONION TART COPENHAGEN

Denmark   (*Københavnsk Løkkpaj*)

Something similar to a quiche but provided with a definite Scandinavian flavor by the addition of anchovies.

Tart Shell:

1 cup	(*250 mL*)	flour
6 tbs	(*6 tbs*)	shortening
1	(*1*)	egg yolk
1-2 tbs	(*1-2 tbs*)	ice-cold water

(*Continued on next page*)

(Onion Tart Copenhagen, cont.)

Cut in shortening with a pastry-cutter until mixture resembles coarse crumbs. Mix in egg yolk and water and press together into a ball. Let dough rest 20 minutes, then roll out to fit into a 9″ (220 mm) pie pan.

Filling:

4	(4)	large onions, sliced
2 tbs	(2 tbs)	butter or margarine
4	(4)	anchovy fillets, preferably Scandinavian, otherwise one 2 oz (60 g) can of Portuguese type
3	(3)	eggs
1 cup	(250 mL)	light cream or half and half
		salt and pepper to taste
¾ cup	(180 mL)	grated cheese (just about any cheese that is not too strong-flavored)

Sauté onion in butter or margarine over low heat until onion is transparent. Chop and add anchovies, mix well, and cook a few more minutes. Put mixture in the pie shell. Beat eggs lightly, add cream, cheese and salt and pepper, mix well and pour over onion mixture. Bake in a 375° F (190° C) oven for 30–35 minutes or until eggs have coagulated. Test by inserting a knife in the middle, if it comes out clean, the tart is ready. Remove from oven and let rest 10 minutes before serving. Serves 6 as an appetizer and 4 as a main luncheon dish.

FLOUNDER ROLLS IN LETTUCE LEAVES

Denmark (*Rødspætte med Salat*)

One of many delicious Scandinavian ways of preparing fish.

6	(6)	fillets of flounder (about 1½ lb or ¾ kg)
		juice of 1 lemon
6	(6)	lettuce leaves

Sprinkle fish fillets with lemon juice. Dip lettuce leaves in boiling water for about 10 seconds to make them slightly wilted.

(Continued on next page)

(Flounder Rolls in Lettuce Leaves, cont.)

Filling:

½ lb	(¼ kg)	fresh mushrooms
½	(½)	medium onion, finely chopped (⅓ cup or 80 mL)
1 tbs	(1 tbs)	butter or margarine
½ cup	(125 mL)	heavy cream
		salt and pepper to taste

Sauté onion in butter or margarine until onion is translucent, add mushrooms and cook 5 minutes. Remove from heat, add cream, salt and pepper and mix well.

Divide filling among the six fillets and roll up. Put each roll inside a lettuce leaf, making a small "package" of each.

For poaching:

1 cup	(250 mL)	fish bouillon or water (or half water and half clambroth)
¾ cup	(180 mL)	dry white wine

Poach fish in the above for about 10 minutes.

Sauce:

2 tbs	(2 tbs)	butter or margarine
2 tbs	(2 tbs)	flour
1 cup	(250 mL)	broth from poaching of fish
½ cup	(125 mL)	heavy cream
		salt and pepper to taste

Melt butter or margarine in a saucepan, add flour and mix well. Add broth, a little at a time stirring constantly and cook for 5 minutes. Add salt, pepper, and heavy cream and mix well, do not let mixture come to a boil again as it would then curdle. Serve with fish to 4–6.

Denmark **STUFFED SPARERIBS** (*Fyldt Ribbensteg*)

about 4 lbs	(2 kg)	spareribs
		salt and pepper to taste
2	(2)	apples, peeled, cored and sliced
10	(10)	prunes
1 cup	(250 mL)	boiling water

(Continued on next page)

(Stuffed Spareribs, cont.)

Trim spareribs and sprinkle with salt and pepper. Pour boiling water over prunes and let stand for 10 minutes, then set aside the water and remove pits from prunes. Put half of the meat in a roasting pan, cover same with prunes and apples, then put remaining meat on top. Fasten edges with skewers or tie together with a string.

Bake uncovered in a 325° F (160° C) oven for about 45 minutes, then turn meat over and bake an additional 45 minutes. Remove meat. Add water in which prunes were soaked, to pan juices, stirring to loosen any hardened drippings.

Serve with this pan juice or make gravy by adding 1 tbs flour mixed with ¼ cup (60 ml) cold water and cook 5 minutes, then add ½ cup (125 mL) cream and heat but do not let it boil.   Serves 4–6.

SAILOR'S CASSEROLE

Denmark   (*Sjømannens Køddkager*)

A nice variety of hamburger—this time cooked in beer.

1 lb	(½ kg)	ground chuck
½ lb	(¼ kg)	ground pork (or use 1½ lbs or ¾ kg of either all ground beef or pork)
1	(1)	medium onion, finely chopped (¾ cup or 180 mL)
3 tbs	(3 tbs)	butter or margarine
½ cup	(125 mL)	dry bread crumbs
¼ cup	(60 mL)	water
1	(1)	egg
		salt and pepper to taste
½ ts	(½ ts)	ground allspice
4	(4)	medium size potatoes, peeled and thinly sliced
1	(1)	large onion, thinly sliced
1 tbs	(1 tbs)	flour
1½ cups	(375 mL)	beer

Sauté chopped onion in 1 tbs butter or margarine in a fry pan for 5 minutes. In a bowl, put water and bread crumbs, then add meat, sautéed onion, egg and seasonings and mix well. Form into small patties about 2″ (50 mm) in diameter and brown in remaining butter. Remove patties and slightly brown sliced onion. In a 2 qt (2 L) baking dish, put a layer of sliced potatoes on the bottom, sprinkle with a 1 ts flour, then some of the onion slices, a layer of meat patties, more potatoes, and sprinkle with 1 ts of flour. Repeat the layers once more, ending up with potatoes. Pour beer over and bake in a 350° F (175° C) oven for about 1 hour or until potatoes are tender.

Serves 4–6.

POTATO PUDDING

Denmark   *(Kartoffelbudding)*

A nice potato recipe if you are not too calorie conscious.

4 cups	*(1 L)*	grated raw potatoes (3–4 large ones, about 1½ lbs or ¾ kg)
3 tbs	*(3 tbs)*	melted butter
2 tbs	*(2 tbs)*	finely chopped onion
2	*(2)*	eggs, slightly beaten
		salt and pepper to taste
½ cup	*(125 mL)*	milk
½ cup	*(125 mL)*	grated sharp cheese, (cheddar)

Sauté onion in butter for 5 minutes, then add to grated potatoes and mix. Beat eggs, add salt and pepper, then milk and pour into potatoes and mix well.

Put in a well greased baking dish, or an 8″ (200 mm) pie plate and bake about 30 minutes, or until done. Remove from oven, sprinkle with cheese and return to oven and bake until cheese has melted, about 5 minutes.

Serves 5–6.

OLD-FASHIONED APPLE CAKE
Denmark   (*Gammel Aeblekage*)

This recipe, although I have credited it to Denmark, is an all-Scandanavia dessert. It was one of the most common of my Sunday-dinner desserts as a child in Sweden. Don't be stingy with the sauce, when you serve it—that is what makes this dessert so good. There are two ways of making it, each seems the best while you are eating it.

2 cups	(*500 mL*)	apple sauce
1 cup	(*250 mL*)	zwieback crumbs or graham cracker crumbs
3 tbs	(*3 tbs*)	butter or margarine
For sprinkling:		confectioners' sugar

Slightly brown bread crumbs in 3 tbs butter or margarine, stirring constantly so that they do not get too dark. Butter a 1½ qt (1½ L) baking dish and put ⅓ of the crumbs on the bottom of this, then half the apple sauce, then another ⅓ crumbs, then the rest of the apple sauce and finish with a layer of crumbs. Let stand for about 4 hours, sprinkle with confectioners' sugar and serve directly out of baking dish, with custard sauce.

Custard Sauce:

2	(*2*)	egg yolks
1½ cups	(*375 mL*)	light cream
2 ts	(*2 ts*)	corn starch
2 tbs	(*2 tbs*)	sugar
1 ts	(*1 ts*)	vanilla extract

Mix together all ingredients except the vanilla in a double boiler or a heavy-bottom saucepan. Simmer the mixture until it thickens, stirring continuously. Remove from heat, add vanilla, pour into a bowl and stir vigorously until slightly cooled. Chill and serve the sauce very cold.

VARIATION:

The ingredients are the same as in the above recipe but mixture is baked instead. Put half the crumbs on the bottom of a 1 qt (1 L) buttered baking dish, add the apple sauce and put remaining crumbs on top. Bake for 20 minutes in a 325° F (165° C) oven. Carefully unmold when it has cooled slightly and sprinkle with confectioners' sugar.

Chill well, then serve with Custard Sauce.

DANISH PASTRIES

Denmark (*Wienerbrød*)

Danish pastries take time to make, but are not too difficult if you go step by step, and they are so good when you eat them fresh out of the oven.

1¼ cup	(*310 mL*)	butter or margarine
4 cups	(*1 L*)	flour
1 pkg	(*1 pkg*)	dry yeast
¼ cup	(*60 mL*)	lukewarm water
3 tbs	(*3 tbs*)	sugar
1 cup	(*250 mL*)	milk, lukewarm
For brushing:		1 egg, slightly beaten

With a pastry cutter cut butter into ½ cup (125 mL) flour until mixture is like coarse crumbs, then cream together rapidly. Wrap in plastic wrap and put in refrigerator to harden.

Dissolve yeast in lukewarm water, add 1 tbs sugar and let rest for about 5 minutes. In a large bowl mix milk, remaining sugar and about half the flour. Beat vigorously, either by hand with a wooden spoon or in an electric mixer at medium speed. Add remaining flour, a little at a time and keep beating in the mixer until the dough gets too heavy for it to handle, then continue mixing by hand until a smooth dough has been obtained. Turn it onto a floured baking board and knead for about 10 minutes, or until the dough is smooth and shiny.

Roll out dough into a square about 15 x 15" (375 x 375 mm). Remove the butter mixture from the refrigerator and roll it out on a floured surface into a 10 x 15" (250 x 375 mm) rectangle and place on ⅔ of the dough square, towards one side. Fold the empty third of the dough over ½ of the covered dough, then fold remaining ⅓ on top of that. Squeeze the edges together with the rolling pin, then place the dough in refrigerator about 15 minutes.

Roll out into a 15 x 15" (375 x 375 mm) square again, then fold the dough in the same manner as above, again let rest in the refrigerator for 15 minutes. Repeat this procedure once more. (The dough should be rolled and folded three times. Do not forget to flour the board lightly each time it is rolled out.)

Before the final shaping, the dough should rest in a cold place once more for 15 minutes. This quantity will make about 32 pastries, which may be filled with one or the other of the following:

(*Continued on next page*)

(Danish Pastries, cont.)

Fillings:

1-1½ cup	(*250–375 mL*)	apricot or peach jam

Butter cream:

½ cup	(*125 mL*)	butter
1 cup	(*250 mL*)	confectioners' sugar

Cream together until light and fluffy.

Almond paste:

1 cup	(*250 mL*)	blanched almonds
1 cup	(*250 mL*)	confectioners' sugar
1	(*1*)	egg white

Grind almonds, add sugar and stir in sufficient egg white to make a smooth mixture.

Spandau shape:

Divide the dough into 2 portions, roll each portion into a square of about 12 x 12″ (300 x 300 mm), then cut into 16 squares of 3″ (75 mm) each. Put a little apricot or peach jam, or almond paste in the middle, then fold the four corners towards the center and press together firmly.

Snail shape:

Divide the dough into two portions, then roll each portion into an oblong strip, 8 x 12″ (20 x 30 mm). Spread top of each with butter cream filling or almond paste and roll each one together jelly-roll fashion. Cut them into approximately ¾″ (18 mm) slices and place into paper baking cups.

Let the pieces rise until double in bulk, about 45 minutes, brush with slightly beaten egg and bake in a 400° F (200° C) oven about 12–15 minutes, or until golden brown. If desired, brush with water icing (½ cup or 125 mL confectioners' sugar mixed with ½ ts water) when they have cooled.

England
and
Scotland

ENGLISH cuisine is much maligned, and I think, unfairly so. I often wonder why this has happened, as I have found so much good food in this part of the world. It may be based on the old rivalry between France and England, and as the French excelled in their cooking, they have liked to put down the English in this respect, as the English excelled in many other ways. Another thought is that it may have something to do with the American soldiers stationed in England during the war. They came from a country with an abundance of everything (even during the depression there was no great lack of food products in the U.S.) and there they were in England with great shortages of practically everything edible. The English had to make do with what they had. Many a soldier, spoiled with food from home, never realized the reason why the English food did not meet their standards was simply war shortages.

The English, living on an island surrounded by some of the greatest fishing waters in the world—at least they used to be, but alas, like in many other parts, they are getting over-fished—have found many wonderful ways of preparing fish. With the English interest in hunting they have also developed a great tradition in preparing game.

The English have developed sauces which have become standards on tables all over the world—I think mainly of ketchup (for better or for worse, as too many people have gotten into the habit of drenching everything in this)—and Worcestershire sauce. And the most English of all English dishes—roast beef—is also a favorite around the world.

The British sense of humor has also left its imprint on the names of some of their dishes—pigs in blankets, bubble and squeak, angels on horseback, toad in the hole, etc.

Many of the English dishes are greatly influenced by their colonial days. Indian cooking has left an especially firm imprint. They picked up the use of the spices in India. Thus curry powder which is a mixture of many spices, is said to have been developed by the English for convenience, to avoid measuring each spice individually.

Although the English have a habit of having a cup of tea, usually with sugar and milk, the moment they open their eyes in the morning, later on they may have a big breakfast consisting of juice, cooked or other cereals, eggs, bacon, sausages, kippers (smoked herring) and finnan haddies (smoked haddock), rolls or bread, butter and jams.

In the afternoons there is the High Tea, a very English institution, consisting not only of tea but is quite a substantial meal with sandwiches, rolls, buns, tarts, scones and butter and jam. However, today with so many people commuting to work, this custom has become something for the week-ends while daily they tend to follow the same pattern as we do in the U.S. with midday lunch, then dinner in the evening.

POTTED CHEESE WITH HERBS	STEAK AND KIDNEY PIE
SCOTCH BROTH	CURRIED KIDNEYS
(BARLEY SOUP)	TOAD IN THE HOLE
COCK-A-LEEKIE SOUP	BUBBLE AND SQUEAK
FISH PIE	CUMBERLAND SAUCE
FINNAN HADDIE	TRIFLE
BAKED FISH WITH CHEDDAR	PLAIN JANE PUDDING WITH
CHEESE	CHOCOLATE SAUCE
WEST COUNTRY CHICKEN	SYLLABUB
RIB ROAST OF BEEF	CREAM CROWDIE
YORKSHIRE PUDDING	QUEEN OF PUDDINGS
LANCASHIRE HOT POT	HOT CROSS BUNS
STUFFED BREAST OF LAMB	SCOTCH SHORTBREAD
POT HAGGIS	ROCK CAKES
CORNISH PASTY	RASPBERRY BUNS

POTTED CHEESE WITH HERBS

England

A flavorful cheese spread, speckled with green.

½ lb	(¼ kg)	strong cheddar, grated
¼ cup	(60 mL)	light cream
3 tbs	(3 tbs)	cream sherry
2 tbs	(2 tbs)	butter
1 ts	(1 ts)	finely chopped parsley
1 ts	(1 ts)	finely chopped chives
1 ts	(1 ts)	finely chopped sage (or ¼ ts dried)
1 ts	(1 ts)	finely chopped thyme (or ¼ ts dried)

Mix together all ingredients in a small saucepan and heat over low heat until cheese is melted, stirring often. Pour into small glass jars and let cheese mixture cool completely before using.

SCOTCH BROTH

Scotland (Barley Soup)

Barley is grown in Scotland not only for whiskey-making, but it is also used together with lamb meat in a nice and hearty highland soup.

2-3 lbs	(1-1½ kg)	stewing lamb (neck or ribs)
6 cups	(1½ L)	water
		salt and pepper to taste
1	(1)	small yellow turnip, diced into ¼″ (6 mm) cubes, about 3 cups (750 mL)
2	(2)	carrots, thinly sliced, about ⅔ cup (160 mL)
1	(1)	medium onion, chopped, about ¾ cup (180 mL)
¼ cup	(60 mL)	barley
1 tbs	(1 tbs)	chopped fresh parsley

Put meat and water in a soup kettle, add salt and pepper, bring to a boil, them skim off foam. Turn down heat and simmer until meat is loose on the bones, about 1-1½ hours. Remove bones and meat from stock, then chill it well in refrigerator so that you may be able to lift off cake of coagulated fat that will form on the top. Bring broth to a boil again, add barley and cook about 45 minutes, then add vegetables and cook until they are tender, about 20-25 minutes. Remove meat from bones, cut up and add to soup, and reheat. Check soup for seasonings, sprinkle with chopped parsley and serve piping hot.

For 4-6 portions.

COCK-A-LEEKIE SOUP

Scotland

Leeks are not only popular in France but also in England and it is the national plant of Wales.

1	*(1)*	stewing chicken 3½-4 lbs (1¾-2 kg), cut into serving pieces
3 qts	*(3 L)*	water
8	*(8)*	whole peppercorns
1 tbs	*(1 tbs)*	salt, or to taste
4	*(4)*	leeks, cut up, (about 3 cups or 750 mL)
¼ cup	*(60 mL)*	rice

Put chicken into a large pot with water and spices. Bring to a boil, skim foam off surface and turn heat down low, then simmer until chicken is tender 1½-2 hours for an older chicken, but only 35-40 minutes for a young one. Remove chicken pieces, then add leeks and rice and cook about 15 minutes, or until leeks and rice are tender. Serve chicken with the soup, or make a separate meal by serving the soup by itself and chicken with a sauce, made from part of the chicken stock. Serves 5-6.

Sauce:

2 tbs	*(2 tbs)*	butter or margarine
2 tbs	*(2 tbs)*	flour
1½-2 cups	*(375-500 mL)*	chicken stock
		salt and pepper to taste

Melt butter or margarine in a saucepan, add flour and mix well. Add stock, a little at a time stirring vigorously until sauce is thick and smooth. Add salt and pepper to taste.

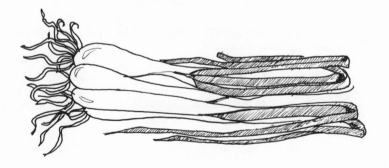

FISH PIE

England

Although the English refer to this dish as a pie, I guess we would think of it more as a casserole.

1½ lb	(¾ kg)	fish fillets, any kind of fish will do (or 2 lbs (1 kg) whole fish)
1	(1)	thick slice onion
1 ts	(1 ts)	lemon juice
1 ts	(1 ts)	salt
		water to cover

If whole fish is used, clean and cut into pieces. Place fish in a saucepan, add salt, lemon juice, onion and water to cover, then bring to a boil. Turn down heat to very low and poach fish until it is flaky, about 10 minutes. Immediately remove from heat and take out fish pieces so that they do not get over-cooked. When cool enough to handle, flake fish into bite-size pieces and set aside. Then prepare a sauce with the following ingredients:

Sauce:

1 tbs	(1 tbs)	butter or margarine
1 tbs	(1 tbs)	finely chopped onion
2 tbs	(2 tbs)	flour
1 cup	(250 mL)	milk, or milk and fish stock mixed salt and pepper to taste
¼ ts	(¼ ts)	dry mustard
½ cup	(125 mL)	grated cheese, preferably Cheddar
4	(4)	medium size potatoes
½ cup	(125 mL)	milk
1	(1)	egg, slightly beaten

Sauté onion in butter over slow heat until transparent, but make sure it does not get brown. Sprinkle with the flour and add milk, a little at a time, stirring vigorously to make a smooth sauce. Add seasonings and cheese and cook for about 3 minutes, then add fish and when all is thoroughly heated, pour mixture into a greased baking dish or pie pan.

Cut potatoes into pieces and boil, then mash them, adding milk. When mixture is smooth, add the slightly beaten egg. Place the mashed potatoes in a ring around the top of the fish, shaping into swirled tops. Bake in a 375° F (175° C) oven about 15 minutes, or until hot. If top has not browned nicely, put under broiler for about 30 seconds, but watch it, so it does not brown too much.

Serves 5–6.

FINNAN HADDIE

England

A simple-to-make dish which may not seem appealing to people not acquainted with smoked haddock, but it is really very good indeed.

1½–2 lbs	(¾–1 kg)	smoked haddock (or cod)
1 cup	(250 mL)	milk
½ cup	(125 mL)	water
		salt and pepper to taste
2 tbs	(2 tbs)	butter

Wash fish and cut into serving pieces. Simmer gently in milk mixed with water 5–10 minutes. Lift out carefully with a slotted spoon and put a pat of butter on each portion.

Serves 5–6.

BAKED FISH WITH CHEDDAR CHEESE

England

Fish with cheese seemed a strange combination but I adopted it happily after tasting this easily prepared dish.

1½ lb	(¾ kg)	cod or haddock fillets
1 tbs	(1 tbs)	lemon juice
		salt and pepper to taste
1 cup	(250 mL)	grated cheddar cheese
3	(3)	medium size tomatoes, peeled and sliced
1 tbs	(1 tbs)	butter or margarine

Put fish fillets in a buttered casserole, sprinkle with lemon juice, salt and pepper and half the cheese. Sauté tomato slices in butter or margarine about 5 minutes, then place on top of fish and sprinkle with remaining cheese. Bake in a 350° F (175° C) oven about 20–25 minutes, or until fish is flaky.

Serves 4–5.

WEST COUNTRY CHICKEN

England

Chicken with a difference, and if you like apple flavor you will like it here.

1	(*1*)	frying chicken, 3-3½ lb (1½-1¾ kg)
3 tbs	(*3 tbs*)	butter or margarine
1	(*1*)	medium onion, chopped (about ¾ cup or 180 mL)
1	(*1*)	carrot, thinly sliced
4	(*4*)	tart apples, peeled and thinly sliced
		salt and pepper to taste
1½ cups	(*375 mL*)	apple cider
1 tbs	(*1 tbs*)	flour, mixed with 3 tbs water
½ cup	(*125 mL*)	light cream

Cut chicken into serving pieces and brown in 2 tbs butter or margarine in a skillet, then put browned pieces into a baking dish. Add onion, carrot and half of the apples to the skillet and sauté until onion is transparent, then pour it all over chicken in the baking dish. Pour cider over and cover. Bake in 350° F (175° C) oven 45 minutes–1 hour, or until chicken is tender.

Strain pan juices into a saucepan, discarding solids, add flour and water mixture and bring to a boil, turn down heat and simmer about 5 minutes. In the meantime sauté remaining apple slices in 1 tbs butter until light brown and tender, 5–10 minutes. Add cream to sauce and mix well. Put chicken pieces on a serving dish, pour sauce over and place the fried apple slices around the chicken.

Serves 4–5.

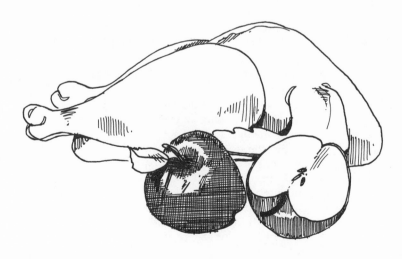

RIB ROAST OF BEEF

England

I assume that most people who read this book know how to roast beef but as the slow-roasting method is almost always used in the U.S., I thought it appropriate to show how the English generally cook their national dish. And I must admit that I prefer it that way, as you get a nice crusty surface. Do not get alarmed if you get some smoke out of the oven the first 15 minutes, it will not harm the roast at all. And, of course, the Yorkshire pudding is almost a must, to go with roast beef. It is quite common to place the roast high up in the oven with a baking dish underneath the rack to catch the drippings, and also to let the roast drip while the pudding bakes, but the difference in temperatures makes this a bit difficult.

1 rib roast of beef, 4–8 lbs (2–4 kg)

Preheat oven to 500° F (260° C) and put the rib roast on a rack with a pan below to catch dripping. Roast at this temperature for 15 minutes, then turn down heat to 325° F (160° C) and roast an additional 15 minutes per lb., for rare, 20–25 minutes per lb for medium and 25–30 for well done meat. If you have a meat thermometer, use this to guide you for doneness.

YORKSHIRE PUDDING

England

1 cup	(250 mL)	flour
½ ts	(½ ts)	salt
1 cup	(250 mL)	milk
2	(2)	eggs, slightly beaten
3 tbs	(3 tbs)	hot roast beef drippings

Sift together flour and salt into a bowl, add milk and mix well to make a smooth batter. Add eggs, one at a time and beat with an electric beater until smooth. Let rest for ½ hour.

Put the drippings in a low baking dish or pie plate, then add batter and bake in a 400° F (200° C) oven for 15 minutes, then turn down heat to 325° F (160° C) and bake an additional 10 minutes or until golden brown in color. Serve immediately.

England LANCASHIRE HOT POT

A *delicious lamb casserole.*

6	(6)	shoulder lamb chops
2	(2)	lamb kidneys, sliced
2 tbs	(2 tbs)	butter or margarine
		salt and pepper to taste
2	(2)	medium size onions, sliced
6	(6)	medium size potatoes, peeled and sliced
½ cup	(125 mL)	sliced mushrooms
1 tbs	(1 tbs)	flour
1½ cups	(375 mL)	beef stock or water

Brown chops and kidneys in butter or margarine, add salt and pepper and remove from pan. Sauté onion slices in remaining fat in pan for five minutes. In a large greased baking dish, arrange lamb chops on the bottom, then kidneys on top of them, then layers of onions, mushrooms and potatoes. Mix flour with stock and pour over casserole. Cover and bake in a 350° F (175° C) oven for 1½–2 hours, or until meat is tender. Remove cover and bake an additional 15 minutes to brown the potatoes on top. Serve immediately, directly from baking dish. Serves 5–6.

STUFFED BREAST OF LAMB (MARF ORGAN)

England

If you have read English novels about poor people you may have heard about a dish the cockneys call "marf organ." Well, here it is. If you are afraid of fatty meat, it may not be the dish for you, although you can trim away some excess fat to keep its content down.

4-5 lbs	(1-2½ kg)	breast of lamb, in either two or four pieces
4 oz	(125 g)	sausage meat
4	(4)	slices white bread, crust removed and cut into small cubes
1	(1)	medium onion, chopped (¾ cup or 180 mL)
		salt and pepper to taste
½ ts	(½ ts)	poultry seasoning
1 ts	(1 ts)	chopped parsley
1	(1)	egg
½ cup	(125 mL)	milk

(Continued on next page)

(Stuffed Breast of Lamb, cont.)

Trim as much excess fat off meat as possible and place one large or two smaller pieces in a roasting pan. Make a stuffing by mixing sausage meat, bread cubes, onion, seasonings, egg and milk thoroughly and place on top of meat. Place remaining one or two pieces on top of stuffing and fasten with skewers. Bake in a 325° F (165° C) about 2 hours or until meat is tender.

Serves 4–6.

POT HAGGIS

Scotland

If you have been to Scotland, you may have tasted haggis—that is if you are brave and adventurous when it comes to eating, but once they hear the ingredients are cooked inside a sheep's stomach, many people get prejudiced right there. This dish, however, is made in a pot instead, although the ingredients are similar to the real McCoy. . .

½ lb	(¼ kg)	liver (lamb or beef), sliced
1 cup	(250 mL)	water
¼ lb	(125 g)	beef suet
2	(2)	medium size onions chopped (1½ cup or 375 mL)
1 cup	(250 mL)	oatmeal
		salt and pepper to taste

Cook liver in water for 10 minutes, then add onions and cook another 10 minutes. Cool. Chop liver, onion and suet in food chopper, using fine blade. Toast oatmeal in a heavy skillet over medium heat until lightly browned, stirring off and on to prevent scorching. Using a large bowl, mix together liver, suet, onions, toasted oatmeal, and about 1 cup (250 mL) of the liquid in which liver was cooked. Turn mixture into a greased baking dish, cover with foil and steam (see below) for 2 hours. Serve immediately with vegetables.

Steaming:

Put baking dish on a trivet or support so that it does not rest on bottom of a 4–6 qt pot or Dutch oven with about ½" (12 mm) water on the bottom. Bring water to a boil, cover pot and turn down heat. Check off and on to see that pot does not boil dry, otherwise add more boiling water.

Serves 4–5.

CORNISH PASTY

England

Don't think the typesetter dropped the "R" in the title of this dish. Although it is made with pastry, the name refers to the filling.

Pastry:

2 cups	(500 mL)	flour
½ ts	(½ ts)	salt
		pepper to taste
⅓ cup	(80 mL)	bacon drippings, lard or shortening
¼ cup	(60 mL)	cold water

Sift together flour and seasonings, cut in bacon drippings, lard or shortening until crumbly, then add water and mix together to a stiff dough. Roll out about ⅛" (3 mm) thick and cut out circles 5–6" (120–150 mm) in diameter (use a small plate or a saucer as guide).

Filling:

½ lb	(¼ kg)	sirloin steak or other tender beef
½ cup	(125 mL)	finely diced raw peeled potato
½ cup	(125 mL)	finely diced raw peeled turnip
1	(1)	small onion, finely chopped (½ cup or 125 mL)
		salt and pepper to taste

Cut meat in fine cubes and mix with remaining ingredients until well blended.

Put about 2–3 tbs of filling in the center of each circle of dough then close by bringing all sides up and press edges together, fluting the seam with your fingers (as you do around the edge of a pie-crust). Bake them, standing up, in a 425° F (220° C) oven for 10 minutes, then turn heat down to 350° F (175° C) and bake an additional 40 minutes.

Serves 4–5.

STEAK AND KIDNEY PIE

England

This is an English classic, and I find it easy to prepare too.

2 lbs	(1 kg)	boneless top sirloin
1-2	(1-2)	veal kidneys (about ¾-1 lb
		(400-500 g)
3 tbs	(3 tbs)	butter or margarine
		salt and pepper to taste
1	(1)	small onion, finely minced
		(½ cup or 125 mL)
1 tbs	(1 tbs)	fresh chopped parsley
1 cup	(250 mL)	water
		crust for single pie,
		see page 54

Cut beef in 1″ (25 mm) cubes, brown in 2 tbs butter in a skillet, add salt and pepper to taste and cook for about 1 hour. Remove meat and sauté onion until transparent. Remove fat and membranes from kidneys and cut into thin slices, then brown in remaining butter. In a shallow baking dish make alternate layers of beef and kidney, sprinkling each layer with onion and parsley. Rinse out skillet with the water and pour over meat.

Make a single pie crust and roll out on floured board. Wet edges of baking dish and place pie crust on top, fitting it over the filling, and pressing it down well at the edges to seal the dish. Cut some gashes in the top to allow steam to escape. Bake in a 350° F (175° C) oven 1-1½ hours or until meat is tender. Serve immediately, preferably direct from the baking dish.

For 5-6 portions.

CURRIED KIDNEYS

England

England's involvement in India left pleasant traces in the English kitchens.

1½ lbs	(¾ kg)	veal kidneys
2 tbs	(2 tbs)	butter or margarine
1	(1)	small onion, finely chopped
		(½ cup or 125 mL)
1 ts	(1 ts)	curry powder
		salt and pepper to taste
½ cup	(125 mL)	water
1 tbs	(1 tbs)	flour, mixed with 2 tbs water
2 tbs	(2 tbs)	sherry

(Continued on next page)

Rinse kidneys in cold water, trim away membranes and any tubes. Cut into small cubes.

Sauté onion in 1 tbs butter in skillet until transparent, then remove from pan. Add remaining butter and kidneys, stirring to brown lightly. Add onions, curry powder, salt, pepper and water and bring to a boil, then turn down heat and cook for 10 minutes. Stir in flour mixed with water and sherry and cook 5 minutes more.

Serves 5-6.

England   **TOAD IN THE HOLE**

A perfect dish to prepare when you lack time and fancy ingredients.

1 lb	(½ kg)	small link pork sausages
2	(2)	eggs
1 cup	(250 mL)	milk
1 cup	(250 mL)	flour
1 ts	(1 ts)	baking powder
½ ts	(½ ts)	salt

Fry sausages in a frying pan until light brown, turning them frequently, about 10 minutes. Pour enough of the fat rendered into an 8 x 8" (200 x 200 mm) square baking dish to grease it liberally, then put in the sausages. Beat eggs until light and fluffy, add milk and flour, sifted together with baking powder and salt, alternately and beat until mixture is bubbly. Pour over the sausages and bake in a 375° F (190° C) oven for 30 minutes or until the batter has become light brown and puffed up.

Serves 4-5.

England   **BUBBLE AND SQUEAK**

An English idea to use left-over roast beef.

1 lb	(½ kg)	cooked roast beef, thinly sliced
2 tbs	(2 tbs)	butter or margarine
1	(1)	large onion, thinly sliced (1 cup or 250 mL)
1	(1)	small head of cabbage, shredded (4 cups or 1 L)
2 cups	(500 mL)	mashed potatoes
		salt and pepper to taste

Cook cabbage in slightly salted water until almost tender, about 5 minutes. Brown roast beef slices in one tbs butter on both sides, remove from skillet and keep warm. Sauté onion in remaining butter until transparent, then add drained cabbage, mashed potatoes and seasonings and mix well. Heat thoroughly. Place in serving dish, arrange beef slices on top and serve.

Four portions.

CUMBERLAND SAUCE

England

A classic among English sauces.

1	(*1*)	orange
½	(½)	lemon
3 tbs	(*3 tbs*)	red currant jelly
3 tbs	(*3 tbs*)	port wine, sherry or Madeira
¼ ts	(¼ *ts*)	ground ginger
		pinch of cayenne pepper

Cut orange and lemon rind into very thin shreds. Squeeze out juice and put into a small saucepan together with shredded rind. Simmer for 10 minutes. Strain, then add jelly, port wine and seasonings, and simmer an additional 10 minutes. Serve with cold ham, pork, or lamb.   4 servings

TRIFLE

England

One of the more popular desserts in England, but one which is often spoiled in our country by using pudding mixes in preparation. For a good trifle you simply have to have a good, creamy custard.

1	(*1*)	sponge layer (see page 36)
⅓ cup	(*80 mL*)	cream sherry
1-2 cups	(*250-500 mL*)	fresh raspberries (or frozen ones)
3	(*3*)	egg yolks
⅓ cup	(*80 mL*)	sugar
1½ cups	(*375 mL*)	light cream, scalded
1 ts	(*1 ts*)	vanilla extract
For decoration:		whipped cream and some fresh berries, if such are used

In a double boiler beat egg yolks until light and fluffy, add sugar and continue beating for a few minutes. Add scalded cream and vanilla, then cook over hot water, stirring often, until mixture will coat the spoon, then cool custard somewhat.

Slice the cake layer and line a glass bowl with the slices. Sprinkle with sherry. Spread a layer of raspberries (sweeten them first, if desired) over the cake slices and up against the sides, then pour custard on top. Cool until ready to use, then decorate with whipped cream, using a pastry tube for making rosettes, if desired. Place fresh berries, if used.

(*Continued on next page*)

(Trifle, cont.)

VARIATION:

Strawberries may be used instead of raspberries.
A fancier version of this dessert,

sometimes called Edwardian Trifle, can be made, using sliced sponge jelly roll with some berry filling, instead. In this case, the berries are omitted, but otherwise proceed as in the above recipe. Serves 5–6.

PLAIN JANE PUDDING
WITH CHOCOLATE SAUCE

England

Steamed puddings are almost a way of life in England. When ready to eat they look to us more like cake than pudding.

¼ cup	(60 mL)	butter or margarine
½ cup	(125 mL)	sugar
2	(2)	eggs, slightly beaten
1 ts	(1 ts)	vanilla flavoring
1½ cup	(375 mL)	flour
2 ts	(2 ts)	baking powder
¼ ts	(¼ ts)	salt
¼ cup	(60 mL)	milk

Cream butter and sugar until light and fluffy. Add beaten eggs and stir until smooth. Add flour alternately with milk, then vanilla, mixing well. Pour batter into a greased 1 qt (1 L) baking dish, cover with aluminum foil and close it tightly. Put baking dish on a trivet or support, so that it does not rest on bottom of a 4–6 qt (4– 6 L) pot with about ½″ (12 mm) water on the bottom. Bring water to a boil and cover pot, turning down heat. Check occasionally, and add boiling water if pot seems to be going dry. Steam for 1½ hours. Turn pudding (which is actually a cake by now) onto a plate and serve with chocolate sauce. Serves 4–6.

Chocolate Sauce

¼ cup	(60 mL)	cocoa
⅔ cup	(160 mL)	light brown sugar
1 cup	(250 mL)	milk
1 ts	(1 ts)	vanilla flavoring

Mix together all ingredients in a saucepan, stirring vigorously to remove all lumps and until sugar has been dissolved. Bring to a boil, cover, turn down heat and let boil for 2 minutes. If a thicker sauce is desired, cook a little bit longer, stirring continuously. Serve hot or cold.

SYLLABUB

England

Syllabub is a very old dessert said to go back to days of Henry VIII. And it is delicious and very easy to prepare.

1 cup	*(250 mL)*	heavy cream
¼ cup	*(60 mL)*	very fine sugar
1 tbs	*(1 tbs)*	fresh lemon juice
1 tbs	*(1 tbs)*	brandy
¼ cup	*(60 mL)*	sherry

Whip cream with sugar until firm, then pour in remaining ingredients and continue beating only until well blended (if beaten too long the cream may turn into butter). Serve with macaroons or fine cookies.

Serves 4–5.

CREAM CROWDIE

England

A simple but amazingly good dessert in which the toasting of the oatmeal gives an almost nut-like flavor.

1 cup	*(250 mL)*	oatmeal
1 cup	*(250 mL)*	heavy cream
¼ cup	*(60 mL)*	sugar
2 tbs	*(2 tbs)*	rum or sherry
2 cups	*(500 mL)*	fresh raspberries (or 1 pkg frozen, 10 oz or 300 g)

Toast oatmeal on a cookie sheet in a 350° F (175° C) oven for 10 minutes, stirring around once to make sure it does not scorch. Cool completely. Whip cream with sugar until stiff, then fold in rum or sherry, oatmeal and raspberries. (If frozen raspberries are used, they should first be drained). Chill at least two hours before serving to 5–6.

QUEEN OF PUDDINGS

England

A delightfully light and festive bread-pudding.

3-4	(3-4)	slices white bread, crusts removed, and cubed (about 2½ cups or 625 mL)
3 cups	(750 mL)	milk
		peel of 1 lemon
½ cup	(125 mL)	sugar
2 tbs	(2 tbs)	butter
3	(3)	eggs, separated
¼ cup	(60 mL)	raspberry jam

Peel the lemon very thinly, trying to avoid the white pith. Heat milk and lemon peel and let it simmer for at least 5 minutes, taking care not to let it boil. Remove peel and add ¼ cup (60 mL) sugar and the butter and simmer until butter is melted and sugar has dissolved. Remove from heat, add bread cubes and let mixture cool for a few minutes. Beat egg yolks and add to bread mixture, little by little and mix well.

Pour mixture into a greased pie pan or a low casserole and bake in a 350° F (175° C) oven for 20 minutes, or until the custard has set. Beat egg whites with remaining sugar until stiff. Carefully heat jam in a small saucepan to make it easy to spread. Remove custard from oven, spread with the jam, and top it with the beaten egg whites. Return to oven for about 5 minutes or until meringue is slightly brown. Serve warm.

Serves 5–6.

HOT CROSS BUNS

England

The buns of Lent and of our old nursery rhyme. But not one or two a penny any more . . .

1	*(1)*	pkg dry yeast
⅓ cup	*(80 mL)*	sugar
½ ts	*(½ ts)*	salt
1 ts	*(1 ts)*	cinnamon
1 cup	*(250 mL)*	milk
¼ cup	*(60 mL)*	butter or margarine
2	*(2)*	eggs
4 cups	*(1 L)*	flour (or slightly more)
¾ cup	*(180 mL)*	raisins

For brushing: ½ egg mixed with 1 tbs milk

Frosting: 4 tbs confectioners' sugar dissolved is 2 ts water

In a large bowl mix together yeast, sugar, salt, cinnamon and 1 cup (250 mL) flour. Melt butter or margarine, add milk and heat until warm, then add to flour mixture in bowl. Beat with an electric mixer or by hand until smooth, then add eggs and one more cup (250 mL) flour and continue beating until very smooth, scraping down sides of the bowls off and on. Add additional flour, while beating, until the mixer cannot handle it any longer, then continue to mix by hand, adding remaining flour, until a soft dough is formed.

Turn onto a floured baking board and knead until dough is elastic, about 10 minutes. Place in a greased bowl, turning dough over once to get the grease all around. Cover with a plastic wrap and let rise in a warm place until double in bulk, about 1 hour. Punch down dough and add raisins, kneading to get them distributed throughout the dough. Divide dough into two halves, then shape each half into an 8" (200 mm) square, then cut this into 9 pieces. Put these into a 9" (22 mm) square baking pan and let rise in a warm place for 1 hour.

Cut a cross on top of each bun with a sharp knife, then brush with egg mixture and bake in a 375° F (175° C) oven about 15–20 minutes, or until done. Remove from pan and cool on wire racks. Frost with confectioners' frosting while still slightly warm.

18 buns.

SCOTCH SHORTBREAD

Scotland

The traditional cookie of Scotland which is perfect for people who cannot eat very sweet things for one reason or another.

1 cup	*(250 mL)*	**butter**
½ cup	*(125 mL)*	**sugar**
2 cups	*(500 mL)*	**flour**
½ cup	*(125 mL)*	**rice flour (or, if unavailable use corn starch**

Cream together butter and sugar, either by hand or in an electric mixer, until light and fluffy. Mix together flour and rice flour, sift and add to butter mixture and work it until it is crumbly. Turn out onto a lightly floured baking board and work together into a solid ball, then divide into two balls. Flatten each one into a round cake, 6–8″ (150–180 mm) in diameter and about ½–¾″ (12–18 mm) thick.

Place each round on a greased baking sheet. Pinch edges for decoration as you would a pie crust. Pierce cake with a fork in many places. Preheat oven to 400° F (200° C), then turn it down to 300° F (150° C) as soon as cakes have been put into the oven. Bake for about 30 minutes or until shortbread is golden in color. Remove from oven and immediately cut each round in about 8 wedge-shaped pieces.

About 16 pieces.

ROCK CAKES

The name of these cookies does not refer to the consistency—or at least it should not—but rather to their shape. They are quite popular as part of an English tea, which does not refer to the drink only but is a meal in itself.

2 cups	(500 mL)	flour
1 ts	(1 ts)	baking powder
		pinch of salt
½ cup	(125 mL)	butter or margarine
½ cup	(125 mL)	sugar
1 cup	(250 mL)	seeded raisins (or currants)
1	(1)	egg
¼ cup	(60 mL)	milk

Sift together flour, baking powder and salt. Cut in butter or margarine with a pastry cutter until mixture is crumbly. Add sugar and raisins and mix well. Add egg and milk and stir together to make a rather stiff dough. Drop by large teaspoonfuls into "rocky" heaps on a greased baking sheet and bake in a 400° F (200° C) oven 12–15 minutes or until golden brown in color. Makes about 2 dozen.

VARIATION:

Add ¼ ts each of cinnamon and nutmeg to the above. Instead of currants, use the same amount of finely chopped mixed dried fruit and peel.

RASPBERRY BUNS
England

A nice "quicky" to bake if you get unexpected company for tea or coffee.

2 cups	*(500 mL)*	flour
2 ts	*(2 ts)*	baking powder
¼ ts	*(¼ ts)*	salt
½ cup	*(125 mL)*	sugar
6 tbs	*(6 tbs)*	butter or margarine
		grated rind of 1 lemon
1	*(1)*	egg
⅓ cup	*(80 mL)*	milk

For filling:

¼ cup	*(60 mL)*	raspberry jam
		1-2 tbs milk for brushing
		1-2 tbs sugar for sprinkling

Sift together flour, baking powder and salt, then mix in sugar. Cut butter or margarine into flour mixture with a pastry cutter until crumbly. Add lemon rind. Beat egg slightly and mix with milk then add to flour mixture and blend to form a soft dough.

On a floured baking board roll out dough by hand into a long cylinder, then divide into 12 portions. Form each one into a ball, flatten with hands and make an indentation in the middle. Place ½-¾ ts of jam in the centre of this. Pull over edges and press together to cover jam, then turn upside down and put on a greased baking sheet, allowing some space around each one. Brush with milk and sprinkle with sugar and bake in a 350° F (175° C) oven 15–20 minutes or until golden in color. Serve either warm or cold.

Finland

FINLAND was a part of Sweden for hundreds of years, while Sweden was still a great power in Europe. Since the early 1800's it was partly or wholly subject to Russia until it finally became independent after the first World War. Therefore, the eating habits and the cooking of Finland resemble both those of Sweden and of Russia. A Finnish buffet may thus contain the best of both countries.

Rye is the principal grain. At harvest time a special rye porridge is eaten by those who like to hold on to old traditions. Rye breads are popular, especially the dry crisp-breads (Finn-Crisp) which are exported to many countries, including the U.S.

As in many other places far to the North, the wild berries are of a very high quality because of the long daylight hours in the Summer, and they are used for many desserts and jams.

SUMMER SOUP	*Kesäkeitto*
LIVER PUDDING	*Maksalaatikko*
TURNIP LOAF	
CUCUMBER SALAD	*Kurkkusalaatti*
ALMOND BLUEBERRY CAKE	
FINNISH COOKIES	
RAISIN SPICE CAKE	

151

SUMMER SOUP

Finland   *(Kesäkeitto)*

This recipe is supposed to be made only with very freshly harvested vegetables.
These are available in Finland during the Summer—hence the name for this
soup.

1 cup	(250 mL)	sliced carrots
1 cup	(250 mL)	cubed potatoes (½ cm or 12 mm) cubes)
2 cups	(500 mL)	water
1 cup	(250 mL)	fresh green peas
1 cup	(250 mL)	cauliflower, cut into small flowerettes
½ cup	(125 mL)	finely chopped fresh spinach
		salt and pepper to taste
2 cups	(500 mL)	milk
2 tbs	(2 tbs)	flour

For garnish: 2 tbs chopped parsley

Cook carrots and potatoes in water for 10 minutes, then add peas, cauliflower, spinach and seasonings, and bring to a boil again, then turn down heat and simmer until all vegetables are tender. Mix together flour with ½ cup (125 mL) of the milk and add and stir well to mix. Add remaining milk, bring to a boil then turn down heat and simmer for five minutes. Serve hot sprinkled with parsley.

Serves 4–5.

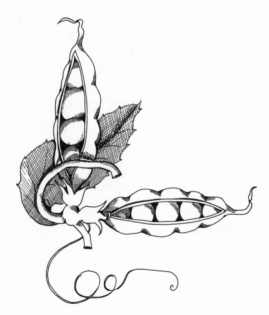

LIVER PUDDING

Finland   (*Maksalaatikko*)

A liver loaf from Finland with rice and raisins. Quite a nice combination!

1 lb	(½ kg)	beef liver
1	(*1*)	medium size onion, finely chopped (¾ cup or 180 mL)
2 tbs	(*2 tbs*)	butter or margarine
		salt and pepper to taste
2½ cups	(*625 mL*)	water
1 cup	(*250 mL*)	rice
2 cups	(*500 mL*)	milk
½ cup	(*125 mL*)	raisins
2 tbs	(*2 tbs*)	molasses
4 tbs	(*4 tbs*)	melted butter

Sauté onion in 1 tbs butter or margarine until transparent. Remove onion, add remaining butter and lightly brown liver on both sides, add onion and ½ cup (125 mL) water, bring to a boil, turn down heat and simmer for 10 minutes. Add salt and pepper.

Cool, then chop all in a meat grinder, using fine blade. In the meantime cook rice in 2 cups (500 mL) lightly salted water for 15 minutes, then add 2 cups (500 mL) milk, bring to a boil, turn off heat and let mixture cool.

Mix together liver, rice, raisins and molasses and taste mixture to see if additional seasonings are needed. Bake in a buttered baking dish in a 350° F (175° C) oven for 30 minutes. Serve with melted butter, to 5–6.

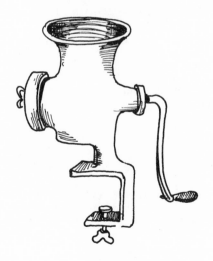

TURNIP LOAF

Finland

A tasty way to serve turnips.

1	(*1*)	medium size yellow turnip (about 2 lbs or 1 kg)
1 ts	(*1 ts*)	salt
1 tbs	(*1 tbs*)	butter or margarine
1	(*1*)	egg, slightly beaten
½ cup	(*125 mL*)	milk
1 tbs	(*1 tbs*)	brown sugar

Peel turnip and cut into thin slices. Cook in salted water until very tender. Drain off liquid and set aside. Mash turnip until smooth. Add butter, egg, milk, sugar and a little of the pot liquid to make a slightly loose mixture. Pour into a greased loaf pan and bake in a 325° F (165° C) oven about 1 hour.

Serves 5–6.

CUCUMBER SALAD

Finland   (*Kurkkusalaatti*)

A refreshingly cool salad.

2-4	(*2-4*)	cucumbers (depending on size)

Dressing:

½ cup	(*125 mL*)	sour cream
1 ts	(*1 ts*)	sugar
2 tbs	(*2 tbs*)	vinegar
½ cup	(*125 mL*)	salad oil
2 tbs	(*2 tbs*)	chopped fresh dill or 1 ts dry dillweed salt and pepper to taste

Clean cucumbers but do not peel them, then slice them into very thin slices with a potato peeler. Mix ingredients for the dressing and blend well, then pour over cucumbers. Chill for about 2 hours before using.

Serves 4–6.

ALMOND BLUEBERRY CAKE
Finland

A somewhat different dessert—it is not a pie and not a cake but something in between. But good (or better) just the same.

4 tbs	*(4 tbs)*	**butter or margarine**
⅓ cup	*(80 mL)*	**sugar**
1	*(1)*	**egg**
½ cup	*(125 mL)*	**flour**
1 tbs	*(1 tbs)*	**lemon juice**

Beat butter or margarine with sugar until light and fluffy, add egg and continue beating until smooth. Sift flour into batter, add lemon juice and mix well. Spread in a 9″ (220 mm) pie pan.

Filling:

2 cups	*(500 mL)*	**blueberries**
1 tbs	*(1 tbs)*	**flour**
¼ cup	*(60 mL)*	**sugar**
½ cup	*(125 mL)*	**heavy cream**
1	*(1)*	**egg**
¼ cup	*(60 mL)*	**chopped almonds**

For serving:

heavy cream (optional)

Spread blueberries on top of dough in pie pan. Mix together flour and sugar and sprinkle on top. Whip heavy cream until stiff, add egg and continue whipping until well incorporated. Spread on top of blueberries, then sprinkle with chopped almonds. Bake in a 350° F (175° C) oven about 30–35 minutes or until done. Serve warm either plain or with additional whipped cream. Serves 6.

VARIATION:

Use a similar quantity of frozen blueberries, but use less sugar if they are sweetened, also bake an additional 10–15 minutes.

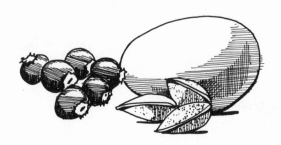

FINNISH COOKIES

Finland

A wonderful cookie that may have a name in Finland but as I got the recipe from a friend in Sweden who got it from Finland, they have become plain "Finnish cookies." I have not been able to find out more—but they sure are good.

1 cup	(250 mL)	butter
½ cup	(125 mL)	sugar
1 tbs	(1 tbs)	blanched, ground almonds
1½ cups	(375 mL)	flour (or up to ½ cup (125 mL) more)
1 ts	(1 ts)	baking powder

Beat sugar and butter until light and fluffy, add almonds, then 1½ cups (375 mL) flour sifted together with the baking powder. Work dough together into a ball. If it is too soft, add more flour to make it firmer. Cut pieces of dough the size of an orange and make them into rolls with your hands on a floured baking board.

Length should be about 6–8″ (150–200 mm). Place them on a greased baking sheet, then flatten them out to about 1½″ (38 mm) width, with your hand or with a floured rolling pin. Trim edges with a knife. If they are not completely flat and smooth, it does not matter as they are to be spread with the following topping:

Topping:

2	(2)	egg whites
½ cup	(125 mL)	sugar
⅔ cup	(160 mL)	blanched, ground almonds

Beat egg whites until stiff, add sugar, a little at a time and continue beating until well blended. Add almonds and mix well.

Spread the topping evenly over the strips and bake in a 350° F (175° C) oven 10–12 minutes or until the cookies are light golden in color. Let cool on the baking sheet for a few minutes, then cut them into bars about 1″ (25 mm) wide before they are completely cool. Makes about 80 cookies.

RAISIN SPICE CAKE

Finland

Most everyone loves a nice spice cake and Finland has a good one.

1 cup	(250 mL)	strong coffee
1 cup	(250 mL)	raisins
1½ ts	(1½ ts)	cinnamon
1½ ts	(1½ ts)	ground cloves
1 ts	(1 ts)	ground ginger
1 ts	(1 ts)	baking soda
1 cup	(250 mL)	butter or margarine (2 sticks)
2	(2)	eggs
1 cup	(250 mL)	sugar
2 cups	(500 mL)	flour

Bring coffee, raisins, spices and baking soda to a boil. Remove from heat and add butter or margarine and let it melt, then cool. Beat eggs and sugar until light and fluffy, then continue beating while adding spice mixture alternately with sifted flour. Pour into a 2 qt (2 L) greased and floured ring pan and bake in a 350° F (175° C) oven for about 45 minutes. Let stay in pan for ten minutes, then remove and let cool on wire rack.

France

THE culinary skill of France is well known around the world. Food preparation is considered to be a fine art, ranking in importance with literature, music, etc. among the French. They can go into deep discussions about the variations and compounding of a special sauce as seriously as if it were a subject of philosophy. Even such a prominent writer as Dumas, père, lent his hand in writing the "Grand dictionnaire de la Cuisine."

The history of cooking as an art in France dates back to the Rennaissance and is supposed to be connected with Italian princesses being married into the French court and bringing their own cooks along, so that many dishes therefore have Italian origins—something that is now forgotten by many who like to think their cuisine to be French through and through. And, of course, it has other origins also, and during several centuries it has developed its very own characteristics.

To select a few representative dishes from a cuisine that has so many wonderful treasures demands great self-control, because you want to include this—and this—and this, but after all, this is not just a French cookbook. I have, however, tried to select not only the popular dishes you come across in French restaurants, both in France and in our country, but also some that are less well known to us and are both fairly easy to make and have some special appeal. That the selection becomes somewhat prejudiced by the taste of the writer, just cannot be helped. I just hope that many people will agree with my taste, at least, to some extent.

A day of a typical Frenchman may start with café au lait, that is a cup of equal amounts of coffee and hot milk, and some fresh rolls, such as croissants, those delicious crescent shaped flaky rolls. At lunch one or more hors d'oeuvres are served, such as anchovies, sardines, sliced sausages, liver paté, olives and pickles. They seldom consist of any freshly prepared products. At dinner hors d'oeuvres are not supposed to be served, except for possibly oysters, and the soup is the important thing, together with the main dish and dessert. Among the country folks a hearty soup is the main meal at night and our word for the evening meal, supper, is derived from the French word "souper"—that is, to eat soup. These soups may be based on fish (among which bouillabaisse is the best known), chicken, or meat with vegetables.

One important thing in French cookery is the emphasis that is placed on the quality of the ingredients. Most French housewives expect to do daily shopping for fresh vegetables, which are chosen with utmost care. This painstaking care shows in the superb results. She is typically very economical and can do much with lower priced cuts of meat. Herbs and spices are used with great precision and never in such quantities as to overwhelm other ingredients. They have subtle sauces to make many varieties of one cut of meat, but here also the rule is that they should not be used in excess but to enhance the meat itself.

After a French meal one should be happy and content, but not overloaded as gluttony is much frowned upon. But it is easy to overeat when you have French foods only occasionally, and the taste calls so much for a little bit more of this or that.

GARLIC SAUCE	*Aioli*
BRANDADE DE MORUE	
SCALLOPS SAINT-JACQUES	*Coquilles Saint-Jacques*
ONION SOUP	*Soupe a l'Oignon*
LEEK AND POTATO SOUP	
(VICHYSSOISE)	*Potage Parmentier*
TOMATO SOUP	*Potage de Tomates*
CREAM OF CARROT SOUP	*Potage Crécy*
FISH SOUP	*Bouillabaisse*
FISH ORLY	*Poisson Orly*
PEPPER STEAK	*Steak au Poivre à la Crème*
BEEF BURGUNDY	*Boef Bourguignon*

RAGOUT OF VEAL	*Blanquette de Veau*
CHICKEN MARENGO	*Poulet Marengo*
CHICKEN TARRAGON	*Poulet à l'Estragon*
CHICKEN IN WINE	*Coq au Vin*
DUCK WITH ORANGE	*Canard à l'Orange*
VEGETABLE MEDLEY	*Ratatouille*
ZUCCHINI GRATIN	*Gratin de Courgettes*
BACON AND CHEESE TARTE	*Quiche Lorraine*
ONION TARTE	*Tarte à l'Oignon*
SALAD FROM NICE	*Salade Niçoise*
RED RICE SALAD	*Salade de Riz Rouge*
HARD CRUST FRENCH BREAD	
CRESCENTS	*Croissants*
CRÊPES SUZETTES	
CREAM PUFF CAKE	*Gâteau Saint Honoré*
APPLE CAKE	*Géneron*
CHOCOLATE MOUSE	*Mousse au Chocolat*
LEMON RICE PUDDING	*Riz au Citron*

GARLIC SAUCE

France   (***Aioli***)

This sauce is like a mayonnaise and if you like garlic, you may add as many as six cloves. It goes very well with bite size pieces of raw vegetables such as cucumbers, broccoli, cauliflower, zucchini, etc.

2-4	(*2-4*)	cloves of garlic, finely minced
2	(*2*)	egg yolks
½ ts	(*½ ts*)	salt
		pepper to taste
¾ cup	(*180 mL*)	vegetable oil
½ cup	(*125 mL*)	olive oil
1 tbs	(*1 tbs*)	lemon juice

Warm the bowl, in which sauce is to be mixed, with hot water. Dry well and put in garlic, egg yolks and seasonings. Beat with a wire whisk, egg beater, or an electric mixer until thick and lemon colored. Add oil, first drop by drop, continuously beating, then in a thin stream. Add lemon juice and mix well. Serve with cold fish, cold fresh or raw vegetables or hard-boiled eggs.

Makes about 1½ cup (375 mL).

France   **BRANDADE DE MORUE**

An unusual and delicious appetizer and a wonderful addition to a buffet in the French style. But I could not think of an English word to name it.

1 lb	(½ kg)	salted dried cod
¼ cup	(60 mL)	milk
1	(1)	slice onion
1	(1)	boiled hot potato, medium size
2	(2)	cloves garlic, finely minced
⅔ cup	(160 mL)	heavy cream
¼ cup	(60 mL)	olive oil
½ cup	(125 mL)	salad oil
		pepper to taste
5	(5)	slices of toast, crusts removed and cut into four triangles each

Soak the fish in cold water for about 24 hours, changing the water at least once. Cut the fish into a couple of pieces, then add milk and onion slice plus enough water to cover, and bring to a boil. Turn down heat to very low and simmer fish 15–20 minutes, or until very tender. Drain off liquid, cool the fish until it can be handled, then flake it with your fingers.

Heat a mixing bowl with hot water, wipe dry and add fish, hot potato and garlic, and beat for a few minutes.

Heat cream and oil in two separate pans, without letting them come to a boil, then add to the mixture, each a little at a time while beating vigorously until all oil and cream have been used up. Add pepper to taste.

Mound the mixture in the center of a serving dish, then place toasted and buttered bread triangles around it. Brandade de morue may be served slightly warm or cold as an appetizer, or as a part of a buffet.

Makes 6–8 appetizer servings.

SCALLOPS SAINT-JACQUES

France   *(Coquilles Saint-Jacques)*

A lot of visitors to France have eaten scallops under the name Coquilles Saint-Jacques. However, like so many popular dishes in a country, it has many versions, some with garlic, some with tomato sauce etc. I have chosen this version because it leaves the fine flavor of scallops more or less intact and appeals to me most as a scallop lover.

1 lb	(½ kg)	bay or sea scallops
⅓ cup	(80 mL)	water
⅓ cup	(80 mL)	dry white wine

(Continued on next page)

(Scallops Saint-Jacques, cont.)

½ cup	(*125 mL*)	fresh mushrooms, sliced
4 tbs	(*4 tbs*)	butter
2 tbs	(*2 tbs*)	flour
1	(*1*)	yolk from a large egg
½ ts	(*½ ts*)	fresh lemon juice
		salt and pepper to taste
		grated Swiss cheese or Parmesan cheese

If sea scallops are used, cut each one into four pieces. Put scallops together with water and wine in a small saucepan, bring to a boil, then immediately remove from heat and let cool. In the meantime sauté mushrooms in 2 tbs butter over low heat for 5 minutes. Make sure they do not brown.

In another saucepan melt butter, and add flour while stirring, then add scallop liquid and beat well, either with a wire whisk or an electric beater. When sauce is smooth, add egg yolk, lemon juice, salt, and pepper and stir. When sauce is cool, add scallops and mushrooms and fill into scallop shells, either small or large.

Sprinkle with cheese and bake in a 350° F (175° C) oven until sauce bubbles slightly, it may take from 5–10 minutes. Serve immediately as an appetizer. Serves 4–5.

ONION SOUP

(Soupe a l'Oignon)

One of the most beloved and popular French soups, in France as well as over here.

3	(*3*)	large onions, thinly sliced
1	(*1*)	clove garlic, finely minced
3 tbs	(*3 tbs*)	butter or margarine
5 cups	(*1250 mL*)	beef stock or chicken stock
1 tbs	(*1 tbs*)	flour
		salt and pepper to taste
		thick slices of French or Italian bread
¼ cup	(*60 mL*)	grated Parmesan cheese
¼ cup	(*60 mL*)	grated Swiss cheese

Sauté onions and garlic in butter or margarine until onions are golden brown in color. Add flour and mix well, then add beef stock, salt and pepper and bring to a boil, turn down heat and simmer for about 30 minutes. Toast bread slices in a very hot oven 500° F (260° C) until golden

(*Continued on next page*)

(Onion Soup, cont.)

brown in color, turning them once.
Pour soup into individual oven-
proof bowls, almost full, float toasted
bread on top and sprinkle with
cheese. Put bowls under the broiler
for a few minutes, until cheese is
melted. Serve at once.

4 to 6 portions.

LEEK AND POTATO SOUP (Vichyssoise)

France   (*Potage Parmentier*)

*The Vichyssoise soup is said to have been made up by an American chef, but as
the French leek and potato soup is most well-known under this name in the
U.S., I have left it. The soup is equally good served hot or cold.*

4	(*4*)	leeks, thinly sliced
1	(*1*)	medium onion, sliced
2 tbs	(*2 tbs*)	butter or margarine
4	(*4*)	medium size potatoes, cubed (about 4 cups or 1 L)
3 cups	(*750 mL*)	chicken stock
1½ cup	(*375 mL*)	milk
1 cup	(*250 mL*)	cream
		salt to taste

For serving:

finely chopped chives
a dusting of paprika

Sauté leeks and onion in butter until
soft, then add potatoes and chicken
stock and bring to a boil. Turn down
heat and let it simmer for about 30
minutes, or until vegetables are very
soft. Purée mixture in a blender, or
pass it through a sieve, then return to
pot. Add milk, cream and salt, and
heat till thoroughly warm if you plan
to serve the soup hot. Serve either hot
or very cold, sprinkled with a dusting
of paprika and finely chopped chives.

Serves 5–6.

France   **TOMATO SOUP**   (*Potage de Tomates*)

*For home gardeners who find themselves with an over-supply of tomatoes I
think the French have the answer for a flavorful soup with "real tomato" flavor.
And the taste is really different from canned soup.*

1	(*1*)	medium size onion, finely chopped (¾ cup or 180 mL)
1	(*1*)	clove garlic, finely minced

(*Continued on next page*)

2 tbs	(*2 tbs*)	butter or margarine
5-6	(*5-6*)	medium size well ripened tomatoes (2 lbs or 1 kg)
3 cups	(*750 mL*)	chicken stock
2 tbs	(*2 tbs*)	tomato paste
1 tbs	(*1 tbs*)	finely chopped, fresh basil or ½ ts dried basil
1	(*1*)	bay leaf
1 tbs	(*1 tbs*)	fresh lemon juice salt and pepper to taste
For sprinkling:		2 tbs finely chopped parsley

In a saucepan sauté onion and garlic over low heat in butter or margarine until onion is transparent. Cut tomatoes into wedges and add to saucepan together with chicken stock, tomato paste, bay leaf and basil. Bring to a boil, turn down heat and simmer under cover for 20 minutes.

Remove bay leaf, and purée soup in a blender, or pass it through a sieve. After the blender, it should be strained through a sieve to remove pits and other solids. Add lemon juice to soup, season with salt and pepper and re-heat but do not let soup come to a full boil. Serve hot sprinkled with chopped parsley.

Serves 4–5.

France **CREAM OF CARROT SOUP** (*Potage Crécy*)

A simple but tasty soup, using the common carrot.

1 lb	(½ *kg*)	carrots, peeled and cut up into pieces
2	(*2*)	ribs of celery, chopped
1 tbs	(*1 tbs*)	chopped onion
1	(*1*)	bay leaf
3 cups	(*750 mL*)	chicken stock or consommé salt and pepper to taste
½ cup	(*125 mL*)	cream
1	(*1*)	egg yolk, slightly beaten

Combine carrots, celery, onion, bay leaf and chicken stock in a saucepan and bring to a boil, then turn down heat and simmer until vegetables are tender. Remove bay leaf and add salt and pepper.

Either mash mixture well or purée in an electric blender. Return it to the pot and slowly bring to a boil, carefully stirring, as the purée has a tendency to splatter at this point. Remove from heat. Mix cream with egg yolk, add a little purée, then add this mixture into pot and heat, but do not let it boil. Serve immediately.

Serves 5–6.

FISH SOUP

France   *(Bouillabaisse)*

The classical fish soup of France. It is not cheap to make, as it has so many different kinds of fish and shellfish, but it is really worth it as the flavor is "fresh-out-of-the-sea."

1 lb	(½ kg)	fish fillets (striped bass or other white fish), cut into serving pieces
1 lb	(½ kg)	mussels
2 doz	(2 doz)	clams
½ lb	(¼ kg)	raw shrimp, shelled and deveined
1	(1)	fresh lobster (about 1½ lb or ¾ kg) or 2–3 rock lobster tails
1	(1)	large onion, finely chopped (1 cup or 250 mL)
1	(1)	clove garlic, finely minced
1 cup	(250 mL)	chopped leeks
2 tbs	(2 tbs)	olive oil
2 cups	(500 mL)	peeled and chopped tomatoes (fresh or canned)
½ ts	(½ ts)	dried thyme
1	(1)	bay leaf
2–3	(2–3)	sprigs of parsley salt and pepper to taste
4 cups	(1 L)	fish broth (or 2 cups or 500 mL each of bottled clam broth and water)
1 cup	(250 mL)	dry white wine
For serving:		4 pieces of toast made from French bread, which have been rubbed with a piece of garlic

Sauté onion, garlic and leeks in olive oil in a heavy bottom saucepan until vegetables are soft, but watch out so that they do not get brown. Add tomatoes, herbs, salt, pepper, fish broth and wine, and simmer about 15 minutes. If fresh lobster is used, steam same by plunging into boiling water about 1″ (25 mm) deep in a big covered kettle for about 10 minutes, then remove shells and cut into bite-size pieces, as soon as it is cool enough to handle. Carefully crack claws in one place only and remove meat, putting aside shells for decoration. Remove liver and coral from head and set aside.

Steam mussels and clams in 1″ (25 mm) of water in kettle until they open, then remove meat from shells and set aside. Add fish, shellfish, liver

(Continued on next page)

and coral from lobster to soup and bring to a boil, then simmer about 15 minutes. Serve in deep soup plates on the bottom of which has been placed a piece of toasted French bread, rubbed with garlic.   Serves 4–6.

France   **FISH ORLY**   *(Poisson Orly)*

Batter-fried fish with a light tomato base sauce.

1½ lb	(¾ kg)	fish fillets (sole, flounder or other flat fish)
1 tbs	(1 tbs)	lemon juice
		salt and pepper to taste
½ cup	(125 mL)	flour
		pinch of nutmeg
1	(1)	egg, separated
⅓ cup	(80 mL)	milk
		oil for deep frying

Cut fish into bite size pieces and sprinkle with lemon juice, salt and pepper. Mix together flour, nutmeg, egg yolk, milk, salt and pepper and blend well. Beat the egg-white until stiff and fold into batter. Dip fish pieces into batter and deep-fry in oil, a few at a time until golden brown on one side, then turn over and fry the other side. Drain on paper toweling. If possible, serve immediately, otherwise keep hot in oven. However, fish loses its crispness very rapidly, so do not keep in oven more than 5–7 minutes.

Serves 4–5.

Orly sauce:

1 tbs	(1 tbs)	olive oil
2 tbs	(2 tbs)	butter or margarine
1	(1)	medium size onion, finely chopped (¾ cup or 180 mL)
1	(1)	clove garlic, finely minced
¼ ts	(¼ ts)	thyme
1	(1)	bay leaf
1 ts	(1 ts)	sugar
1 cup	(250 mL)	fresh tomatoes, peeled and chopped (or canned plum tomatoes)
		salt and pepper to taste

Sauté onion and garlic in olive oil until onion is transparent. Add remaining ingredients except butter and simmer about 15–20 minutes. Remove bay leaf and strain sauce through a food mill or purée it in a blender. Heat sauce again, add butter and stir until melted. Serve with deep-fried fish.

PEPPER STEAK

France   *(Steak au Poivre à la Crème)*

You have to appreciate a strong pepper flavor in order to like this dish, as it is made with whole peppercorns that are only coarsely crushed. You cannot avoid biting into them while eating, and I know not everybody likes this. But there are many who just love it.

About 3 lbs	(*about 1½ kg*)	boneless sirloin steak
1-2 tbs	(*1-2 tbs*)	whole black peppercorns
		salt to taste
3 tbs	(*3 tbs*)	butter or margarine
2 tbs	(*2 tbs*)	finely chopped onion
¼ cup	(*60 mL*)	cognac
1 cup	(*250 mL*)	heavy cream
2 ts	(*2 ts*)	mustard (preferably Dijon)

Crush peppercorns coarsely, either by using a mortar and pestle or by rolling them with a rolling pin on waxed paper. Sprinkle crushed pepper evenly over the surface of both sides of the steaks, pressing particles into the steak with hand, then sprinkle with salt. Heat 2 tbs butter or margarine until very hot in a large skillet, add steak or steaks and brown on both sides, either all at once or one at a time, if smaller steaks are used. Then cook them in the skillet together, turning them off and on, until desired degree of doneness, 30–40 minutes.

Remove steaks from pan and keep hot. Add remaining butter and onions and cook, stirring continuously about 5 minutes. Add cognac and ignite it, put on cover to extinguish flame, then add cream and cook for about 5 minutes. Remove from heat, stir in mustard. Pour sauce over steaks and serve immediately.

Serves 4–5.

BEEF BURGUNDY

France   (*Boeuf Bourguignon*)

A French beef-stew using wine for both flavoring and tenderizing.

2 lbs	(*1 kg*)	lean beef of tender cut, cut into 1½″ or 38 mm cubes
3 tbs	(*3 tbs*)	flour
3 tbs	(*3 tbs*)	butter or margarine
1	(*1*)	clove garlic, finely minced
		salt and pepper to taste
1	(*1*)	carrot, thinly sliced
2 tbs	(*2 tbs*)	chopped parsley
1	(*1*)	bay leaf
½ lb	(¼ *kg*)	small white onions
½ lb	(¼ *kg*)	sliced fresh mushrooms
1 cup	(*250 mL*)	red Burgundy
For sprinkling:		chopped fresh parsley

Dredge beef in flour, mixed with salt and pepper, then brown well in 2 tbs butter in a skillet, a few pieces at a time. Remove to a heavy saucepan. Brown garlic, then rinse out skillet with a little water and add to meat. Add carrot, chopped parsley, bay leaf, salt, pepper and wine and bring to a boil, then turn down heat very low and simmer meat about 1½ hours. Add peeled onions and cook about 20 minutes. In the meantime, sauté mushrooms in 1 tbs butter for 5 minutes. When onions are tender, add mushrooms to pot and cook 5 more minutes. Serve with rice or noodles.

Serves 4–6.

RAGOUT OF VEAL

France   *(Blanquette de Veau)*

Veal does not have the well-deserved popularity in this country that it has in Europe. This is a nice, tasty stew of veal, fit for a king or just about anybody.

3 lbs	(1½ kg)	boneless stewing veal cut into 1″ (25 mm) cubes
2 tbs	(2 tbs)	butter or margarine
		salt and pepper to taste
12	(12)	small white onions, about ¾ lb or ⅓ kg
1	(1)	large carrot, sliced
1	(1)	clove garlic, finely minced
1	(1)	sprig of parsley
3 tbs	(3 tbs)	flour
½ cup	(125 mL)	white wine
		hot water
½ lb	(¼ kg)	fresh mushrooms, sliced
1	(1)	egg yolk
2 ts	(2 ts)	lemon juice
½ cup	(125 mL)	heavy cream

Sauté veal slightly in butter or margarine in a large pot or Dutch oven, add salt and pepper to taste. But make sure meat does not get brown. Remove meat, then sauté the onions. Return meat to pot, add carrot, garlic and parsley. Sprinkle the flour over the mixture, then stir gently to get most of the ingredients in the pot covered with it. Add white wine and enough water to reach almost to the surface of the meat. Bring to a boil, then turn down heat to very low and simmer for 1½ hours. Add sliced mushrooms and cook for 10 minutes. Beat together egg yolk and lemon juice, then add some of the pot liquid to bowl and mix well, then add it all to the pot and heat, but do not let it boil, as it might then curdle. Stir in cream and mix well and heat again without boiling. Serve at once with rice.

Serves 6.

France   **CHICKEN MARENGO**   *(Poulet Marengo)*

Chicken Marengo is first supposed to have been made by a chef to Napoleon while he was out doing battles somewhere, and with not too many ingredients at hand. He surely did all right and it is now popular all over Europe.

1	*(1)*	frying chicken, 3-3½ lbs (1½-1¾ kg), cut into serving pieces
2 tbs	*(2 tbs)*	butter or margarine
		salt and pepper to taste
15-20	*(15-20)*	small white onions
½ lb	*(¼ kg)*	fresh mushrooms, preferably whole small ones
¼ cup	*(60 mL)*	sherry or white wine
¼ cup	*(60 mL)*	cream (optional)

Brown chicken in butter in a skillet, add salt and pepper to taste then put into a heavy pan or Dutch oven. Add onions, mushrooms and wine and bring to a boil. Turn heat very low and simmer about 40–45 minutes, or until tender. Serve chicken in sauce, as it is, or if a thicker sauce is desired, stir in the cream just before serving. For 4–5 portions.

France   **CHICKEN TARRAGON**   *(Poulet à l'Estragon)*

1	*(1)*	frying chicken (3-3½ lbs or 1½-1¾ kg, cut into serving pieces
2 tbs	*(2 tbs)*	butter or margarine
1	*(1)*	large onion, finely chopped (1 cup or 250 mL)
1	*(1)*	clove garlic, finely minced
1	*(1)*	bay leaf
3 tbs	*(3 tbs)*	chopped fresh tarragon, or 1½ ts dried
4-5	*(4-5)*	tarragon stems, if available
½ cup	*(125 mL)*	white wine
2 tbs	*(2 tbs)*	flour
¼ cup	*(60 mL)*	water
1 tbs	*(1 tbs)*	fresh lemon juice
1	*(1)*	egg yolk, slightly beaten
		salt and pepper to taste
For sprinkling:		chopped parsley

(Continued on next page)

(Chicken Tarragon, cont.)

Sauté onion and garlic in butter in a heavy bottom pan or chicken fryer until onion is transparent. Add chicken, bay leaf, salt, pepper, tarragon (and tarragon stems if used) and wine and bring to a boil, then turn down heat to very low and simmer until chicken is tender, about 40–45 minutes. Remove chicken and keep warm. Also remove bay leaf.

Mix flour with water and lemon juice and add to pan, stirring to make a smooth sauce. Add about ½ cup (125 mL) sauce to egg yolk and stir together, then return to pan but do not let it come to a boil, as the sauce might then curdle. Test for seasonings and add more salt and pepper if needed. Serve, sprinkled with parsley, with rice. Serves 4–5.

CHICKEN IN WINE

France   *(Coq au Vin)*

1	*(1)*	frying chicken, 3–3½ lbs or 1½–1¾ kg, cut into serving pieces
6	*(6)*	slices bacon
1	*(1)*	medium size onion, finely chopped (¾ cup or 180 mL)
1	*(1)*	clove garlic, finely minced
		salt and pepper to taste
		a few sprigs of parsley
1	*(1)*	bay leaf
½ lb	*(¼ kg)*	small white onions
1 cup	*(250 mL)*	red wine
½ lb	*(¼ kg)*	small ("button") mushrooms
2 tbs	*(2 tbs)*	flour, mixed with ¼ cup (60 mL) water

Fry bacon until crisp in a large frying pan, then remove and set aside. Brown chicken pieces in bacon fat until golden brown and sprinkle with salt and pepper, then remove. Sauté onion and garlic in the same fat for about 5 minutes, then put chicken back into frying pan together with parsley and bay leaf. Pour wine over and bring to a boil, then turn down heat to very low and simmer 40 minutes. Turn chicken pieces over a couple of times if they are not covered with liquid. Add mushrooms, and flour mixed with water, and cook an additional 10 minutes. Serves 4–6.

DUCK WITH ORANGE

France   *(Canard à l'Orange)*

One of the most popular French dishes in our country.

1	(1)	duck (5-6 lbs or 2½-3 kg)
		juice of half a lemon
		salt and pepper to taste
3	(3)	oranges

Rub the duck inside and outside with the lemon juice, then sprinkle with salt and pepper. Peel one of the oranges and put in the stomach cavity, then either sew it together or use skewers to seal. Roast in a 450° F (230° C) oven for 15 minutes, turning the duck several times to make it evenly brown. Turn down heat to 350° F (175° C) and continue roasting until duck is tender, about 1 hour.

Gravy:

		thinly pared skin of 2 oranges
		(make sure no white pith is included)
1½ cups	(375 mL)	water
½ cup	(125 mL)	red wine
2 tbs	(2 tbs)	flour, mixed with ¼ cup (60 mL)
		cold water
		giblets
		salt and pepper to taste

Cook giblets in ¾ cup (180 mL) of the water for 30 minutes or until tender. Save cooking water. Cook orange peel in ¾ cup (180 mL) water for 10 minutes. Chop both giblets and orange peel. When duck is roasted, remove from roasting pan and skim off fat. Add water in which giblets were cooked to roasting pan, stirring vigorously to loosen brown particles. Strain into a saucepan, add flour mixed with water, wine, orange peel and giblets and cook until gravy has thickened, about 5 minutes. Cut duck into serving pieces, discard orange from stomach cavity, divide the two remaining oranges into segments and serve with the duck. Serve gravy from a separate bowl.

Serves 4.

France   **VEGETABLE MEDLEY**   *(Ratatouille)*

A wonderful hot vegetable dish in the Summer when vegetables are plentiful and at their best. It is also good cold as an appetizer, and calorie counters love it, as so many appetizers are no-nos for them.

1	(1)	medium size eggplant
2	(2)	medium size onions, coarsely chopped (1½ cups or 375 mL)
2	(2)	cloves garlic, finely minced
3 tbs	(3 tbs)	olive oil, salad oil, or half of each
2	(2)	green peppers, cored, seeded and cut into small pieces
3	(3)	medium size zucchinis, cut into ¼″ (6 mm) slices
2	(2)	medium size tomatoes, peeled and cut into ¾″ (18 mm) cubes
		salt and pepper to taste
½ ts	(½ ts)	thyme
1 ts	(1 ts)	dried basil
¼ cup	(60 mL)	finely chopped parsley

Cut the eggplant into 1″ (25 mm) cubes, and if so desired, sprinkle with salt and let stand for 30 minutes, then drain off liquid that has accumulated. Sauté onion and garlic in oil for 5 minutes, then add peppers and cook an additional 3 minutes. Add remaining vegetables and seasonings, bring to a boil then simmer without cover for 30–40 minutes, or until vegetables are tender. Serve hot, with meat, or cold as an appetizer. Serves 5–6, more if used as an appetizer.

France   **ZUCCHINI GRATIN**   *(Gratin de Courgettes)*

1½ lbs	(¾ kg)	small size zucchinis, sliced very thin, (⅛″ or 3 mm)
2	(2)	slices white bread, crusts removed and cubed
1½ cups	(375 mL)	milk
¼ cup	(60 mL)	olive oil
3	(3)	eggs, slightly beaten
½ cup	(125 mL)	cooked rice
1 cup	(250 mL)	grated Swiss or Parmesan cheese (or half of each)
		salt and pepper to taste

(Continued on next page)

(Zucchini Gratin, cont.)

Soak bread cubes in half the amount of milk for five minutes, then add olive oil and mix well. Add eggs and beat until mixture is batter-like, then add remaining milk, rice, zucchini, salt and pepper and stir until well mixed. Spread mixture in a 9 x 9" (220 x 220 mm) or a 7½ x 11½" (19 x 29 mm) baking dish, sprinkle with remaining cheese and bake in a 375° F (190° C) oven for about one hour, until golden in color and firm in texture.

Serves 5–6.

BACON AND CHEESE TARTE

France *(Quiche Lorraine)*

A nice luncheon dish that hardly needs an introduction as in the last couple of years it has become very popular here in the U.S.

Pastry:

1 cup	*(250 mL)*	**flour**
½ ts	*(½ ts)*	**salt**
⅓ cup	*(80 mL)*	**shortening**
2–3 tbs	*(2–3 tbs)*	**ice water**

Mix together flour and salt, cut in shortening with a pastry blender until mixture is crumbly. Add ice water and shape into a ball, scraping up loose crumbs with the ball. Chill for about ½ hour, then roll out on a floured baking board and fit into a 9" (220 mm) pie plate.

Filling:

½ lb	*(¼ kg)*	**bacon**
¼ lb	*(125 g)*	**Swiss cheese, grated**
3	*(3)*	**eggs**
1½ cup	*(375 mL)*	**milk, or half milk and half cream**
		salt and pepper to taste
		pinch of nutmeg

Fry bacon until crisp and crumble on the pie crust. Add grated cheese. Mix together eggs, milk and seasonings and blend thoroughly with an egg beater or a wire whisk. Pour mixture into pie crust and bake in a 375° F (190° C) oven about 30–40 minutes or until a knife, inserted in center, comes out clean. Serve hot or cold.

Serves 4–6.

ONION TARTE

France   *(Tarte à l'Oignon)*

A Quiche with a difference—onions, that is, and if you like them, you'll love this.

Pastry:

Same as for Quiche Lorraine, see preceding recipe

Filling:

6	*(6)*	medium onions, cut into thin slices (about 4 cups or 1 L)
3 tbs	*(3 tbs)*	butter or margarine
		salt and pepper to taste
		pinch of nutmeg
3	*(3)*	eggs
1¼ cup	*(310 mL)*	light cream, or half cream and half milk

Place pastry in a 9″ (220 mm) pie plate. Sauté onions in butter over low heat until tender, about 20 minutes, stirring often to prevent browning. Season with salt, pepper and nutmeg, then put into pie shell. Beat together eggs and cream and pour over onions. Bake in a 375° F (190° C) oven about 30 minutes, or until knife inserted in center comes out clean. Serve immediately.

Serves 4–6.

SALAD FROM NICE

France   (*Salade Niçoise*)

*A nice salad for a Summer luncheon or light supper. It can be made more
substantial by using two cans of tuna instead of one. Sometimes small new,
sliced potatoes are added also—they make a nice addition.*

1 (or 2)	(*1 or 2*)	cans tuna (7 oz or 200 g size), drained and broken into chunks
1	(*1*)	2 oz (60 g) can anchovy fillets, chopped
1	(*1*)	clove garlic, finely minced
1	(*1*)	small onion, finely chopped (about ⅓ cup or 80 mL)
¼ cup	(*60 mL*)	green pepper, finely chopped
½ cup	(*125 mL*)	celery, finely chopped
1 cup	(*250 mL*)	cooked green beans, cut into 1″ (25 mm) pieces
3	(*3*)	medium size tomatoes, cut into wedges
10	(*10*)	stuffed green olives
10	(*10*)	black olives, pitted
3	(*3*)	hard boiled eggs, quartered
1	(*1*)	medium size red onion, cut into thin slices

Dressing:

2 tbs	(*2 tbs*)	wine vinegar
½ cup	(*125 mL*)	salad oil (partly olive oil, if desired)
2 ts	(*2 ts*)	prepared mustard, preferably Dijon
¼ ts	(*¼ ts*)	dried thyme
		salt and pepper to taste

Combine the first seven ingredients in
a salad bowl and mix gently. Mix
together all the ingredients for the
dressing and stir vigorously then add
to the salad bowl, tossing gently.
Carefully fold in tomatoes, olives and
eggs and chill well in refrigerator.
Just before serving add sliced red
onion as garnish on top.

Serves 5–6.

RED RICE SALAD

France   *(Salade de Riz Rouge)*

A nice Summer salad or just a nice colorful addition to a buffet table. And it does not hurt that it tastes so good too.

3 cups	*(750 mL)*	cooked cold rice
2	*(2)*	scallions, cut into thin slices
2 cups	*(500 mL)*	cooked beets, cut into julienne strips
¾ cup	*(180 mL)*	French dressing
		salt and pepper to taste
⅓ cup	*(80 mL)*	sour cream
⅓ cup	*(80 mL)*	mayonnaise
1	*(1)*	medium size cucumber, peeled, seeded and coarsely chopped
1	*(1)*	medium size onion, thinly sliced

Combine rice with scallions and beets, add salt and pepper and ½ cup (125 mL) French dressing and let the mixture rest in refrigerator for 8 hours or more. Shortly before serving, combine remaining dressing with sour cream and mayonnaise and blend into rice mixture together with cucumbers. Chill salad well again. Arrange on lettuce leaves and garnish with sliced onion.

Serves 6–8.

HARD CRUST FRENCH BREAD

France

When bakeries make French bread they use special ovens that are filled with steam during the whole baking process, which makes the familiar hard, glossy crust of the bread. You just cannot duplicate this at home but you can make something similar by putting a large, low baking dish with boiling water up to about 1″ (25 mm) deep on a low shelf of the oven for 30 minutes before the loaves go into the oven and leave it there during baking. This will create steam, but work quickly when you open the oven door to put the bread in there, so the steam does not escape.

1	(*1*)	pkg dry yeast
2 cups	(*500 mm*)	luke-warm water
1 tbs	(*1 tbs*)	sugar
5 cups	(*1250 mL*)	flour, sifted
1 ts	(*1 ts*)	salt

For brushing: ½ egg white mixed with 2 ts water

Soften yeast in lukewarm water with sugar in a large bowl. Sift together flour and salt and add to yeast mixture, a little at a time, beating with an electric mixer at medium speed until well blended and until the dough gets too heavy for the mixer to handle, then add remaining flour and beat by hand with a wooden spoon until dough is shiny and leaves the sides of the bowl.

Make dough into a ball, place in a greased bowl, turn over once, then let rise in a warm place for 1 hour, or until double in bulk. Punch down dough, which will be rather sticky, then knead it on a floured baking board until smooth, dusting hands off and on with flour. Divide dough into two pieces, then form two loaves, about 12″ (300 mm) long and let rise in a warm place for 45 minutes. Place on a greased baking sheet, then bake in a steam-filled 375° F (190° C) oven (see discussion above) for 30 minutes.

Remove loaves and quickly brush with a little bit of egg white, mixed with water, then return to oven for an additional 10 minutes. When ready, remove and let loaves cool on a wire rack.

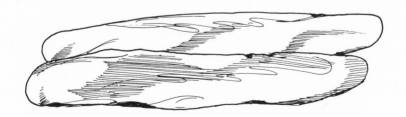

CRESCENTS

France   (*Croissants*)

Croissants are what most French eat for breakfast and it is a nice way to start the day with these light and flaky baked products. They are also appreciated as dinner rolls here in the U.S. They are a bit tedious to make but are worth the effort.

6½ cups	(*1625 mL*)	flour, approximately
1 tsp	(*1 ts*)	salt
1 pkg	(*1 pkg*)	dry yeast
1 tbs	(*1 tbs*)	sugar
2 cups	(*500 mL*)	milk
⅔ cup	(*160 mL*)	butter or margarine
For brushing:		1 egg mixed with 1 tbs milk

Mix salt into 5 cups (1250 ml) flour and put into a large bowl. Heat milk to lukewarm and mix yeast with ½ cup (125 mL) of the milk and sugar until yeast has dissolved. Add remaining milk to flour and mix in an electric mixer for a few minutes, then add yeast-milk mixture and continue beating for about 5 minutes. Add 1 cup (250 mL) of flour, a little at a time to the mixer and beat until mixture gets too heavy for it, then beat by hand.

Then spread ½ cup (125 mL) flour on baking board, add dough and knead for a while, adding a little additional flour if necessary and continue kneading until dough is smooth and elastic, at least 10 minutes. Brush a big bowl with salad oil, put dough into this and brush top with oil, then cover with plastic wrap and put in a warm place to rise, for about 1 hour.

Roll out dough on lightly floured baking board into a square about ⅛″ (3 mm) thick. Cut all butter into thin slices and place all over the surface of dough, then fold in sides toward the center and seal in butter by turning over the ends. Turn dough over and roll it out again into a square, again folding the sides towards the center.

This rolling and folding sequence should be repeated altogether four times, then let dough rest in refrigerator for 15 minutes. Roll out dough again into a long rectangle ⅛″ (3 mm) thick. Cut strips 4″ (100 mm) wide lengthwise, then cut each strip into 4″ (100 mm) squares. Divide these squares into triangles by cutting them in half. Roll them with your hands, starting at the wide base, towards the point, then place on a greased baking sheet, point sides under. Turn the ends of the rolls somewhat to form a crescent. Let the croissants rise in a warm place under a clean cloth for 30 minutes. Brush croissants with egg-milk mixture and bake in a 375° F (190° C) oven for 15 minutes or until golden brown.

Makes about 30.

CRÊPES SUZETTES

France

Crepes have lately caught on in our country in a big way and some stores specializing in kitchen utensils are even offering special crepe pans. However, these special pans are not at all necessary, and a simple small Teflon frying pan will do very well.

1 cup	(250 mL)	milk
¼ cup	(60 mL)	sugar
¼ ts	(¼ ts)	salt
1 cup	(250 mL)	flour
2 tbs	(2 tbs)	melted butter
2	(2)	eggs
2 tbs	(2 tbs)	melted butter for frying

Mix together milk, sugar, salt and flour and stir until all lumps have disappeared. Add melted butter and eggs and mix well. Let batter rest in refrigerator for 1–2 hours. Fry crepes, either in a crepe pan or a small 6–7″ (150–170 mm) fry pan, preferably Teflon. First brush pan with melted butter, then pour in a little of the batter, swirling it around the pan to cover bottom thinly. Cook over medium heat until little bubbles appear on the surface, then turn pancake over with a pancake turner and cook on the other side until lightly brown. Stack crepes on a platter and keep warm until they are all made.

Sauce:

3 tbs	(3 tbs)	butter
¼ cup	(60 mL)	sugar
		juice of two oranges
		grated rind of one orange
2 tbs	(2 tbs)	Grand Marnier, Cointreau or other orange liqueur (or use cognac or bourbon whisky instead)

Melt butter in a skillet, add remaining ingredients and cook until the sauce is slightly thickened.

To serve, fold pancakes into halves twice, then place in skillet, pour sauce all over and turn them around once to get sauce to cover them.

If desired, serve them flambé by heating ¼ cup cognac (60 mL) and pouring over the pancakes just before serving and then igniting it at the table, while serving.

For 4–5 people.

CREAM PUFF CAKE

France   (*Gâteu Saint Honoré*)

Cream puffs have always been a popular dessert in this country, in France they put them together and make a cake out of them. Quite impressive looking that way. And of course, tasty.

¾ cup	(*180 mL*)	water
3 tbs	(*3 tbs*)	butter or margarine
		pinch of salt
2 tbs	(*2 tbs*)	sugar
¾ cup	(*180 mL*)	flour
3	(*3*)	eggs

Bring water, butter, salt and sugar to a boil, remove from heat and add flour, all at once, stirring vigorously to make a smooth ball, that separates from the walls of the pot. Add one egg at a time, beating vigorously to blend in with the flour mix before the next one is added. When mixture is very smooth, grease and flour a baking sheet, then draw a 9″ (220 mm) circle in the flour. With the aid of two spoons drop balls of the mixture in this circle, touching each other. The dough should not be smooth but stand up in peaks here and there.

Bake at 375° F (190° C) until dry, 40–45 minutes. Cool and cut in half horizontally, then fill.

Filling:

1 cup	(*250 mL*)	heavy cream
¼ cup	(*60 mL*)	confectioners' sugar
1 ts	(*1 ts*)	vanilla extract

Whip cream, add sugar and vanilla, beat again until thick. Toast almonds in a 350° F (175° C) oven for 5 minutes, then cool.

Topping:

⅓ cup	(*80 mL*)	apricot preserves
⅓ cup	(*80 mL*)	blanched and slivered almonds

Heat apricot preserves and strain to remove lumps. Put cream between the two layers of cake, then spread the warm apricot preserve on top with a pastry brush, add almonds.

(*Continued on next page*)

(Cream Puff Cake, cont.)

For dusting:

2 tbs   (*2 tbs*)   **confectioners' sugar**

Dust entire cake with sugar, and
serve.   Serves 4–6.

APPLE CAKE

France   (*Géneron*)

*Every country has its own version of apple cake and this French one is as good
as any.*

5	(*5*)	**medium size tart apples**
³⁄₄ cup	(*180 mL*)	**sugar**
¹⁄₂ ts	(*¹⁄₂ ts*)	**cinnamon**
2 tbs	(*2 tbs*)	**brandy**
¹⁄₂ cup	(*125 mL*)	**butter or margarine**
3	(*3*)	**eggs**
1¹⁄₄ cups	(*310 mL*)	**flour**
1 ts (scant)	(*1 ts*)	**baking powder**
1 ts	(*1 ts*)	**vanilla extract**

For sprinkling: **confectioners' sugar**

For topping: **whipped cream or
                                        ice cream (optional)**

Peel, core and slice apples (there should be about 3 cups) and put in a 1¹⁄₂ qt (1¹⁄₂ L) baking dish. Sprinkle with ¹⁄₄ cup (60 mL) sugar, cinnamon and brandy and let mixture stand for about 1 hour. Beat butter and remaining sugar until light and fluffy, then add eggs, one at a time and keep beating until very light. Sift together flour and baking powder then add to egg mixture and mix carefully. Add vanilla, and stir until well mixed.

Spoon batter on top of apples and bake in a 375° F (190° C) oven 30–35 minutes, or until top is golden in color. Serve warm, sprinkled with confectioners' sugar, and with whipped cream or ice cream if desired.

Serves 5.

CHOCOLATE MOUSSE

France   (*Mousse au chocolat*)

Chocolate lovers' favorite dessert. And so easy to make.

4 oz	(*125 g*)	semi-sweet chocolate
1 tbs	(*1 tbs*)	water
1 tbs	(*1 tbs*)	rum
3	(*3*)	eggs, separated
⅓ cup	(*80 mL*)	heavy cream, whipped

Melt chocolate together with water in a bowl set in hot water, or in a double boiler. Add rum. Beat egg yolks until thick and lemon-colored, then gradually add melted chocolate. Fold in whipped cream. Beat egg-whites until stiff and carefully fold into chocolate mixture. Spoon into sherbet glasses and chill until ready to serve. If desired, serve additional whipped cream on top.

Serves 5–6.

LEMON RICE PUDDING

France

(Riz au Citron)

¼ cup	*(60 mL)*	rice
2 cups	*(500 mL)*	milk
2	*(2)*	eggs, separated
2 tbs	*(2 tbs)*	butter or margarine
½ cup	*(125 mL)*	sugar
1 tbs	*(1 tbs)*	lemon juice
		grated rind of one lemon
¼ ts	*(¼ ts)*	nutmeg (optional)
½ cup	*(125 mL)*	heavy cream

Cook rice in milk over very low heat, stirring often to avoid scorching, for about 35–40 minutes, or until rice is very tender. Beat egg yolks slightly in a bowl, then stir in some of the hot rice mixture and put all of it back into the rice pot and mix well. Cook for 2 minutes, while stirring, then remove from heat. Cream butter with sugar, add lemon juice, grated rind and nutmeg then combine with rice mixture, stirring well, and let it cool.

Whip cream until stiff and stir into cooled rice, then beat egg whites until stiff and carefully fold into rice mixture. Put it in a buttered 1 qt (1 L) baking dish and bake in a 325° F (160° C) oven for 30 minutes or until rice custard is set and the top is golden in color. Cool slightly, but serve warm. If desired, additional whipped cream may be provided.

Serves 4–5.

Germany

GERMAN cooking leans toward the heavy side. Germans like to eat, and many of them like to eat in quantity. This may be because the Germans are energetic and hard workers and need the extra nutrition to keep them going. This does not mean that quality is lacking, they have many very tasty dishes.

Of course, there are many facets to their cooking—from the almost Scandinavian ways of preparing herring and other fish dishes in the North, to the typical Middle European ways with many kinds of dumplings and noodles in the South. Potatoes are almost a must every day. The Germans like cabbage in many forms, but that is no reason to sneer at their culinary arts, because so do the French. They like smoked meats and one of their most popular dishes when they entertain is smoked loin of pork—*Kasseler*—and their sausages are excellent and of great variety.

Soups are popular, often as a main meal, and are a substantial part of the German cuisine.

Their breads are delicious—like pumpernickel and other kinds of rye bread. At holiday time they go all out for baking their specialties, which have spread to many countries both because of their excellence and their keeping qualities. All over Germany are small *"Konditoreien,"* which offer rich, delicious little pastries and cookies for the daily coffee break—*Kaffee Klatsch*—an idea that has been adopted by the American way of life and vocabulary.

Among the fruits, apples are one of the most popular, and they even use apple soup—and also other fruit soups—as a course for dinner. This is not entirely German, however, as other middle European countries have the same custom.

187

CARAWAY STICKS	*Kümmelstangen*
SAUERBRATEN	
SMOKED PORK LOIN WITH SAUERKRAUT	*Kasseler mit Sauerkraut*
MEAT AND CABBAGE CASSEROLE	*Rothenburger Krautbraten*
LIVER WITH APPLES	*Berliner Leber*
KONIGSBERG MEATBALLS	*Königsberger Klops*
POTATO PANCAKES	*Kartoffelpuffer*
BAVARIAN POTATO DUMPLINGS	*Bayrische Kartoffelklösse*
HOT POTATO SALAD	*Warmer Kartoffelsalat*
SWEET AND SOUR LENTILS	
SAUSAGE SALAD	*Wurstsalat*
HOMEMADE NOODLES	*Spätzle*
SAUERKRAUT WITH APPLES	*Sauerkraut mit Äpfeln*
PUMPERNICKEL BREAD	
APPLE RICE PUDDING	*Apfelreis*
APPLE STRUDEL	*Apfelstrudel*
RHUBARB CAKE	
BERLINER JELLY DOUGHNUTS	*Berliner Pfannkuchen*
BLACK FOREST CAKE	*Schwarzwaldtorte*
APPLE NUT CAKE	
SPICE COOKIES	*Pfeffernüsse*
CHRISTMAS BREAD	*Stollen*

CARAWAY STICKS

Germany *(Kümmelstangen)*

A nice snack with cocktails or beer.

1 cup	*(250 mL)*	rye flour
1 cup	*(250 mL)*	flour
1 ts	*(1 ts)*	baking powder
1 ts	*(1 ts)*	salt
½ cup	*(125 mL)*	butter or margarine
1	*(1)*	egg, well beaten

For brushing: one egg yolk mixed with 1 tbs milk

For sprinkling: coarse salt and caraway seeds

(Continued on next page)

(Caraway Sticks, cont.)

Sift together dry ingredients and mix well, then cut in butter or margarine with a pastry cutter until mixture resembles coarse crumbs. Add well beaten egg and mix into a soft dough. If dough should not be moist enough, add 1 tbs water. Let dough rest in refrigerator for about 30 minutes.

Roll out dough on floured baking board to about ¼″ (6 mm) thickness, then cut into bars, 1 x 2″ (25 x 50 mm). Brush with egg yolk mixture and sprinkle with coarse salt and caraway seeds to taste. Bake in a 400° F (200° C) oven 10–12 minutes or until golden brown.

Makes 40–50.

SAUERBRATEN

Germany

Sauerbraten is the classic dish of Germany, well worth the extra effort and early preparation it demands. It is almost always served with red cabbage, and potatoes which are often in the form of dumplings or pancakes. Because of the long marinating the meat gets to be fork-tender, and if there are left-overs, they seem even more tender.

4–5 lbs	(2–2½ kg)	bottom round of beef
Marinade:		
8	(8)	whole cloves
1 ts	(1 ts)	whole peppercorns
2	(2)	bay leaves
		pinch of thyme
3	(3)	large onions, thinly sliced (about 3 cups or 750 mL)
2	(2)	cloves garlic, finely minced
2 ts	(2 ts)	salt
		vinegar and water in equal amounts to cover roast

Place meat in a deep earthen ware or china bowl. Mix together all the ingredients for the marinade and pour over. Cover the dish and let stand for 3–4 days in refrigerator. Turn the meat twice a day.

When marinated enough to cook, remove meat from marinade, dry it well and brown in 2 tbs butter or margarine in a Dutch oven. In the meantime, boil down the marinade until liquid has been reduced to half, then add to the meat. Also add the following:

(Continued on next page)

(Sauerbraten, cont.)

1 tbs	(*1 tbs*)	brown sugar
1 tbs	(*1 tbs*)	lemon juice
1 cup	(*250 mL*)	red wine
5-6	(*5-6*)	ginger snaps, crumbled
3 tbs	(*3 tbs*)	tomato paste

Bring to a boil, then turn down heat to very low and simmer 3½-4 hours, or until meat is tender. Turn meat several times during cooking. When ready, remove meat from pot and slice. Strain the gravy, pour some around sliced meat and put the remainder in a gravy bowl.

Serves 8–10.

SMOKED PORK LOIN WITH SAUERKRAUT
Germany (*Kasseler mit Sauerkraut*)

The German name for this meat is Kasseler. It originated in a small town in West Germany named Kassel and has become popular not only all over Germany but in other European countries as well. Smoked pork loins are available from butchers with customers of a German background. Once in a while some supermarkets also feature it.

1	(*1*)	smoked loin of pork, about 3-4 lbs (1½-2 kg)
1	(*1*)	1 lb (500 g) can of sauerkraut
1	(*1*)	medium onion, chopped (¾ cup or 180 mL)
1 tbs	(*1 tbs*)	butter or margarine
1	(*1*)	medium apple, peeled, cored and chopped
1-2 tbs	(*1-2 tbs*)	caraway seeds (optional)

Cut pork loin into chops. Drain and rinse sauerkraut in cold water, precook for 15 minutes in a little fresh water then drain it and spread it in a large (wide) baking dish. Sauté onion in butter or margarine until wilted, then mix with apple and spread on top of sauerkraut. If caraway seeds are used, sprinkle these on top. Cover the whole mixture with chops, overlapping each other, if necessary, cover with aluminum foil and bake in a 350° F (175° C) oven for 45 minutes. Serve immediately with boiled potatoes.

Serves 5–6.

MEAT AND CABBAGE CASSEROLE

Germany   (*Rothenburger Krautbraten*)

The Germans do have a way with cabbage and here is an easy casserole for cabbage lovers.

1	(*1*)	medium head of white cabbage (1½ lbs or ¾ kg)
½ lb	(*¼ kg*)	sliced bacon
5–6	(*5–6*)	medium size potatoes, thinly sliced
1 lb	(*½ kg*)	ground chuck beef
¾ cup	(*180 mL*)	hard bread crumbs
		salt and pepper to taste
½ ts	(*½ ts*)	paprika
1 ts	(*1 ts*)	caraway seeds
⅔ cup	(*160 mL*)	light cream or half and half
2 tbs	(*2 tbs*)	flour
1	(*1*)	egg yolk

Remove core from cabbage as far in as is possible, then boil whole head in salted water about 5 minutes, or until outside leaves are softened and easy to remove. Lift and drain. Strip off 5–6 leaves, then shred remaining cabbage.

Line a large greased baking dish with bacon slices, then arrange cabbage leaves on top of these and spread half the sliced potatoes over leaves. Mix together ground beef, bread crumbs and seasonings and arrange alternate layers of meat and shredded cabbage, then cover with remaining potatoes. Mix together cream, flour and egg yolk and pour over potatoes.

Cover and bake in a 350° F (175° C) oven about 1 hour, or until potatoes are tender. Serve hot.

For 5–6 portions.

LIVER WITH APPLES

Germany   (*Berliner Leber*)

Liver, being both nutritious and economical to serve, comes here dressed up with apples.

1½ lb	(*¾ kg*)	beef liver (or calves liver), sliced
		salt and pepper to taste
3 tbs	(*3 tbs*)	butter or margarine
1	(*1*)	large onion, sliced
2	(*2*)	large apples, peeled, cored and cut into slices

(*Continued on next page*)

(Liver with Apples, cont.)

Brown liver in 2 tbs butter or margarine in a skillet, and season with salt and pepper. Cook about 4 minutes on each side, then remove slices and keep warm. Sauté onion in remaining butter for about 10 minutes, then add apple slices and sauté together with the onions about five minutes. Serve liver slices with onions and apples piled on top.   Serves 5.

KONIGSBERG MEATBALLS

Germany   (*Königsberger Klops*)

1 lb	(½ kg)	ground chuck (or half each of chuck and ground pork)
½ cup	(125 mL)	dry bread crumbs
½ cup	(125 mL)	milk
1	(1)	small onion, finely chopped (½ cup or 125 mL)
2 tbs	(2 tbs)	butter or margarine
1	(1)	egg
		salt and pepper to taste
1 ts	(1 ts)	grated lemon rind

Soak bread crumbs in milk for 10 minutes. Sauté onion in 1 tbs butter or margarine until onion is transparent. Mix together all ingredients in a bowl and work until well blended. Shape into 1½″ (40 mm) meatballs and brown slightly in butter, shaking the pan to keep the meatballs round and evenly brown.

Sauce:

1 cup	(250 mL)	beef stock (or water plus 2 cubes beef bouillon)
2 tbs	(2 tbs)	lemon juice
3	(3)	anchovies, chopped
1 ts	(1 ts)	capers
2 tbs	(2 tbs)	flour mixed with ¼ cup (60 mL) water

Mix together stock, lemon juice, chopped anchovies and capers and bring to a boil, add flour and water and cook until thickened, about 5 minutes. Pour over meatballs and simmer together for 10 minutes.

Serves 4–6.

POTATO PANCAKES

Germany *(Kartoffelpuffer)*

Potato pancakes may be served with meat as a vegetable, or just by themselves.

4	(4)	medium size potatoes
1	(1)	small onion, grated
2 tbs	(2 tbs)	flour
1	(1)	egg, slightly beaten
		salt and pepper to taste
3 tbs	(3 tbs)	butter or margarine

Peel potatoes and shred into a mixing bowl. Add onion, flour, egg and seasonings, and mix well. Shape into thin patties and fry in butter in a large skillet over medium heat. Turn over once after five minutes and fry on other side for five more minutes. Serve immediately.   Serves 5–6.

BAVARIAN POTATO DUMPLINGS

Germany *(Bayrische Kartoffelklösse)*

Here are some good dumplings that go well with sauerbraten (page 189).

6–8	(6–8)	medium size potatoes
		(about 2 lbs–1 kg)
¼ cup	(60 mL)	butter or margarine
		salt and pepper to taste
1	(1)	egg yolk, slightly beaten
¾–1 cup	(180–250 mL)	flour

Peel and boil potatoes, then drain water and mash them, adding butter and seasonings. Add slightly beaten egg yolk and enough flour to make the mixture easy to handle. Make balls of about 2″ (50 mm) size and drop into a large pot of boiling water. Bring it all back to a boil, then turn down heat and simmer for 20 minutes, or until the dumplings float on top. Drain in a colander and serve immediately with Sauerbraten or roast.

Serves 5–6.

HOT POTATO SALAD

Germany   (*Warmer Kartoffelsalat*)

2 lbs	(*1 kg*)	potatoes (about 6 medium size)
5	(*5*)	slices bacon
1	(*1*)	medium onion, finely chopped (³/₄ cup or 180 mL)
1 tbs	(*1 tbs*)	flour
¼ cup	(*60 mL*)	vinegar
¼ cup	(*60 mL*)	water
2–3 tbs	(*2–3 tbs*)	sugar
		salt and pepper to taste

Cook potatoes in their jackets. When done, peel and slice and keep hot. Fry bacon until crisp, remove and drain, then crumble into pieces. Add flour, onion, sugar, salt and pepper to bacon fat and mix well. Add vinegar and water and stir till well mixed, cook until slightly thickened, then pour over hot potatoes. Sprinkle with bacon and serve immediately.

Serves 4–6.

SWEET AND SOUR LENTILS

Germany

In parts of Germany, an old superstition promises good luck and prosperity through the New Year in which the first food eaten is lentils. So I like to include them in my New Year midnight buffet—it can't hurt, and with this recipe, they are very good.

1 lb	(*½ kg*)	lentils
4–5	(*4–5*)	slices bacon (about ¼ lb or 100 g), finely chopped
1	(*1*)	large onion, chopped (about 1 cup or 250 mL)
1	(*1*)	clove garlic, finely chopped
4 cups	(*1 L*)	water (approximately)
		salt to taste
3 tbs	(*3 tbs*)	vinegar
1 tbs	(*1 tbs*)	sugar

Soak lentils in cold water for two hours. Fry bacon in a large saucepan over medium heat for 5 minutes, add onion and garlic and continue frying over low heat for 10 minutes. Add lentils, water, salt, vinegar and sugar and bring to a boil, turn down heat to low and simmer until lentils are tender, about 30–45 minutes. If they should be too dry by then, add a little bit more water.   Serves 5–6.

SAUSAGE SALAD

Germany   (*Wurstsalat*)

A nice summer salad, substantial enough to make a main meal on a hot day.

1 lb	(½ *kg*)	potatoes
½ lb	(*150 g*)	salami (or some German sausage of the Jagdwurst type)
1	(*1*)	small cucumber
2	(*2*)	medium size apples
1 tbs	(*1 tbs*)	chives

Boil potatoes in their jackets, then peel them while still warm and cut into ½″ (12 mm) cubes. Cut sausage in similar size cubes, and unpeeled cucumber and apples somewhat smaller. Mix all together in a large bowl, pour dressing over and mix well. Sprinkle with chives and chill until thoroughly cool.

Serves 4–5.

Dressing:

¼ cup	(*60 mL*)	mayonnaise
¼ cup	(*60 mL*)	sour cream
2 ts	(*2 ts*)	prepared mustard, preferably of Dusseldorf or Dinjon type
1 tbs	(*1 tbs*)	lemon juice
1 ts	(*1 ts*)	sugar
		salt and pepper to taste

Beat together all ingredients until a smooth mixture has been obtained.

HOMEMADE NOODLES

Germany   (*Spätzle*)

Spaetzle (or spätzle), a home-made type of noodle, is widely popular, not only in Germany but in the surrounding countries of middle to Eastern Europe as well.

2	(*2*)	eggs
2 cups	(*500 mL*)	flour
		salt to taste
¼ ts	(*¼ ts*)	nutmeg
⅔ cup	(*160 mL*)	milk
3 tbs	(*3 tbs*)	butter or margarine

(*Continued on next page*)

(Homemade Noodles, cont.)

Beat eggs in bowl of electric mixer until light and fluffy. Sift together flour, salt and nutmeg and add to eggs gradually while beating, then add milk a little at a time, and blend thoroughly.

Boil 3–4 quarts of water with 1 tbs salt added. In Germany and Eastern Europe many households have a special spaetzle-maker, but in lack of this, put the above mixture in a coarse colander and with a wooden spoon force the mixture through into the boiling water. The spaetzle will float to the top as they are done. Remove them from the water and drain. Melt the butter in a saucepan, add the cooked spaetzle and toss lightly to cover. Serve immediately. If desired, chopped parsley may be added at this stage.

The spaetzle may be prepared in advance, then be coated with the butter and carefully heated just before serving.

Serves 4–6.

SAUERKRAUT WITH APPLES

Germany   (*Sauerkraut mit Äpfeln*)

Sauerkraut is always a popular addition to the menu in Germany and here is a variation of same, where apples are added to make a nice flavor combination.

2 cups	(*500 mL*)	sauerkraut (1 lb or 500 g can)
1 tbs	(*1 tbs*)	bacon fat
1	(*1*)	medium size onion, finely chopped (³⁄₄ cup) (180 mL)
4	(*4*)	medium size apples, peeled, cored and sliced
1–2 tbs	(*1–2 tbs*)	brown sugar
½ ts	(*½ ts*)	caraway seeds
		salt and pepper to taste

Sauté onion in bacon fat until transparent, add sauerkraut and apples and cook over slow heat until sauerkraut is tender, about 30 minutes. Add 1–2 tbs brown sugar (according to taste) caraway seeds and salt and pepper.

Serves 5–6.

PUMPERNICKEL BREAD

Germany

According to legend the first pumpernickel bread was not made in Germany but by a Swiss baker with this name. However, the Germans have sort of adopted it and made it their own. This recipe makes a somewhat heavy bread but it has a lot of flavor.

2 pkgs	(*2 pkgs*)	dry yeast
1 tbs	(*1 tbs*)	sugar
3 cups	(*750 mL*)	lukewarm water
3 cups	(*750 mL*)	rye flour, unsifted
4 cups	(*1 L*)	white flour, approximately
1 cup	(*250 mL*)	yellow corn meal
1 cup	(*250 mL*)	whole bran
3 tbs	(*3 tbs*)	salt
⅓ cup	(*80 mL*)	cocoa
¼ cup	(*60 mL*)	butter or margarine
¼ cup	(*60 mL*)	molasses
2 ts	(*2 ts*)	caraway seeds (optional)
For brushing:		**1 egg yolk mixed with 1 tbs milk**

Dissolve dry yeast in ½ cup (125 mL) lukewarm water and sugar. In a large bowl of an electric mixer, blend together rye flour, 2 cups (500 mL) white flour, corn meal, whole bran, salt and cocoa. Melt butter in a small saucepan, add molasses and remaining water and mix, then add to flour mixture and beat at medium speed until a smooth mixture has been obtained, about 3–5 minutes, scraping dry particles off the sides of the bowl off and on. Add more white flour and continue beating until the mixture gets too heavy for the mixer to handle, then beat in most of the remaining flour with a wooden spoon, setting aside about ½ cup (125 mL) of the flour to work into dough while kneading.

Turn out onto a floured baking board and knead for at least 10 minutes, or until dough is shiny and elastic. Place dough in a greased bowl, turning over once to get top greased also. Cover and let rise in a warm place until double in bulk, about 1½ hours. Punch down dough and divide into two parts, shape into round balls and place in 8″ (200 mm) round baking pans, or shape into oblong loaves. Cover and let rise again for 45 minutes, brush with egg yolk mixture, and bake in a 350° F (175° C) oven about 45–50 minutes or until done. Remove and let cool on wire rack.

APPLE RICE PUDDING

Germany   *(Apfelreis)*

⅓ cup	*(80 mL)*	rice
1½ cups	*(375 mL)*	milk
		grated rind of ½ lemon
½ cup	*(125 mL)*	sugar
6	*(6)*	apples, peeled, cored and sliced
½ cup	*(125 mL)*	cider or apple juice

Meringue:

2	*(2)*	egg whites
2 tbs	*(2)*	confectioners' sugar

Cook rice with milk, lemon rind and sugar until rice is tender and milk completely absorbed. Spread half of rice in a buttered 1½ qt (1½ L) baking dish, spread with half the apples, then repeat layers. Pour apple cider or juice over mixture and bake in a 350° F (175° C) oven for 45 minutes. In the meantime make meringue by beating egg whites until stiff, adding confectioners' sugar little by little.

Spread this on top of pudding and continue baking for an additional 10 minutes or until meringue is golden in color. Serve slightly warm, plain, or with heavy or medium cream.

Serves 4–6.

APPLE STRUDEL

Germany   (*Apfelstrudel*)

In Germany, as well as in other middle European countries, most people will buy the dough to make a strudel. It can be done at home, but it is not an easy thing and may be quite frustrating, as the dough has a tendency to tear once you get it thin enough. But if you wish to try, here is a recipe.

1½ cup	(*375 mL*)	flour
¾ cup	(*180 mL*)	instantized flour ("Wondra")
1 cup	(*250 mL*)	lukewarm water
1	(*1*)	egg, slightly beaten
1 ts	(*1 ts*)	vinegar
¼ ts	(*¼ ts*)	salt
¼ cup	(*60 mL*)	butter, melted

Sift together both kinds of flour into a bowl, add water, egg, vinegar and salt and work together into a ball. Turn onto a slightly floured baking board and knead and beat dough with hands for at least 10 minutes or until it is smooth, then cover and let it rest for 30 minutes. Cover a large table with a clean cloth and sprinkle it with flour. Place dough on cloth, and carefully roll and stretch it into an oblong shape, continuously working it but taking care not to tear it. Sprinkle with lukewarm water and knead into a loaf again, cover and let rest for another 30 minutes. Divide the dough into two parts, then stretch and roll each one into a sheet, as large and thin as possible. Brush with melted butter.

Filling:

6	(*6*)	medium size crisp apples (about 2 lbs or 1 kg)
¼ cup	(*60 mL*)	raisins
¼ cup	(*60 mL*)	chopped walnuts
⅔ cup	(*160 mL*)	sugar
2 ts	(*2 ts*)	ground cinnamon
½ cup	(*125 mL*)	melted butter
¼ cup	(*60 mL*)	fine cake crumbs, or, if unavailable, fine dry breadcrumbs

Peel and core apples, then grate them coarsely. Mix with raisins, walnuts, sugar and cinnamon, then blend in half of the melted butter. Sprinkle the crumbs on each buttered strudel sheet and spread apple filling over crumbs, leaving a 1″ (25 mm) margin all around the sheet. Roll it together, jelly-roll fashion, carefully closing the edges. Brush outside with remaining melted butter and bake in a 375° F (190° C) oven 35–40 minutes.

RHUBARB CAKE

Germany

A nice and light dessert for rhubarb lovers. And if you do not like rhubarb, I guess it can be replaced by other fruits, such as apples, pears or peaches.

Bottom layer:

2 tbs	(*2 tbs*)	butter or margarine
4 tbs	(*4 tbs*)	sugar
½ cup	(*125 mL*)	filbert nuts, finely chopped

Melt butter and add sugar and nuts, stirring vigorously, then spread in a greased 8 x 8″ (200 x 200 mm) baking dish.

Rhubarb layer:

2 cups	(*500 mL*)	rhubarb, cut into small pieces

Spread rhubarb on top of nut mixture in baking dish.

Top layer:

½ cup	(*125 mL*)	butter or margarine
¾ cup	(*180 mL*)	sugar
2	(*2*)	eggs
1 ts	(*1 ts*)	vanilla flavoring
⅓ cup	(*80 mL*)	corn starch
1 cup	(*250 mL*)	flour
1 ts	(*1 ts*)	baking powder
For sprinkling:		confectioners' sugar
For serving:		whipped cream

Beat butter or margarine with sugar until light and fluffy, add eggs, one at a time and continue beating until well blended. Add vanilla flavoring. Sift together corn starch, flour and baking powder and add to batter, a little at a time and mix until smooth. Spread batter on top of rhubarb and bake in a 350° F (175° C) oven for about 35 minutes, or until cake tests done and is golden in color. Sprinkle with confectioners' sugar before serving. Serve either warm or cold with whipped cream.

BERLINER JELLY DOUGHNUTS
Germany   (*Berliner Pfannkuchen*)

3½ cups	(*875 mL*)	flour
⅓ cup	(*80 mL*)	sugar
1 ts	(*1 ts*)	salt
1 pkg	(*1 pkg*)	dry yeast
1 cup	(*250 mL*)	warm milk
2 tbs	(*2 tbs*)	salad oil
1	(*1*)	egg, slightly beaten
1 tbs	(*1 tbs*)	rum
		flour for dusting of baking board
½ cup	(*125 mL*)	grape jelly for filling
1	(*1*)	egg white, slightly beaten, for brushing
		oil for deep frying
For sprinkling		confectioners' sugar

In a large mixing bowl sift together 2 cups (500 mL) flour, sugar and salt, then add dry yeast and warm (but not hot) milk. Beat with medium speed of electric mixer for a few minutes, then add oil and egg and continue beating. Add flour a little at a time and beat until mixture gets too heavy for mixer, then beat by hand with a wooden spoon until a soft dough is obtained. Roll into a ball, place in a greased bowl, turn over once to get all sides greased and cover with plastic wrap. Put in a warm place to rise for 1 hour.

Remove from bowl and punch down dough, then roll out to ½" (12 mm) thickness on a floured baking board. Cut into 5" (125 mm) rounds (using a large glass or a knife if a cutter of this size is not available). Place 1 ts of jelly in center of each round. Brush edges with egg white, bring them together over the jelly, and pinch together to seal. Place, sealed side down, on a floured surface until all are ready for frying and let rise for 15–20 minutes.

Heat oil to 360° F (180° C) in a deepfryer and fry a few doughnuts at a time, turning them after about 4 minutes, to make them evenly brown on both sides. Second side should fry about 3 minutes. Remove from oil with a slotted spoon, then drain on paper towels. When cool, sprinkle with confectioners' sugar.

Makes 16–18 doughnuts.

BLACK FOREST CAKE

Germany   *(Schwarzwaldtorte)*

I have come across so many versions of Black Forest Cake that I have a feeling that just about any cake baked in this region of Germany may be called by that name. They are popular not only in Germany, but all over Europe, and in the last few years also in the U.S. This version containing cherries seems to be the one most commonly used here.

Chocolate layers:

4	(4)	eggs
⅔ cup	(160 mL)	sugar
¼ cup	(60 mL)	cocoa
1 ts	(1 ts)	baking powder
1 cup	(250 mL)	flour
½ cup	(125 mL)	butter or margarine (1 stick) melted

Beat eggs until very light and fluffy, at least 10 minutes, then add sugar gradually and continue beating until sugar has melted. Sift together cocoa, baking powder and flour and add to batter, alternately with the melted butter. Bake in two 9″ (22 cm) greased and floured baking pans in a 350° F (175° C) oven about 20 minutes, or until done. Let cakes cool in pans for a few minutes, then turn them out onto wire racks to cool.

Nut layer:

¾ cup	(180 mL)	shelled filberts, finely ground (measure before grinding)
2	(2)	egg whites
⅔ cup	(160 mL)	confectioners' sugar, sifted

Beat egg whites until very stiff, then fold in confectioners' sugar and nuts. Grease a baking sheet, put wax paper on top, grease and flour this and draw a 9″ (22 cm) circle on it. Spread nut mixture as evenly as possible inside circle and bake in a 350° F (175° C) oven for 10 minutes. Remove from oven and carefully peel off wax paper and let cake layer cool on wire rack.

Filling:

2 oz	(60 g)	unsweetened chocolate (two squares)
1 tbs	(1 tbs)	butter
1	(1)	egg yolk
3 tbs	(3 tbs)	milk

(Continued on next page)

(Black Forest Cake, cont.)

| ½ cup | (125 mL) | confectioners' sugar, sifted |
| ½ ts | (½ ts) | vanilla extract |

Melt chocolate together with butter over hot water, then mix with remaining ingredients, stirring until smooth in texture.

Assembly:

1	(1)	1 lb (500 g) can Bing cherries, or other sweet cherries
1 cup	(250 mL)	heavy cream
¼ cup	(60 mL)	confectioners' sugar, sifted
		flaked semisweet chocolate

Put one of the chocolate layers on the bottom, then cover this with the drained Bing cherries. Add second chocolate layer and spread with the filling. Put nut layer on top, then cover whole cake with the cream, whipped until stiff with the confectioners' sugar. Decorate with flaked semisweet chocolate in any desired quantity.

APPLE NUT CAKE
Germany

A simple but sophisticated little cake which you can get done in a jiffy.

1	(1)	egg
⅔ cup	(160 mL)	sugar
½ cup	(125 mL)	flour
1 ts	(1 ts)	baking powder
¼ ts	(¼ ts)	salt
1 cup	(250 mL)	chopped apples (peeled and cored)
½ cup	(125 mL)	chopped walnuts
1 ts	(1 ts)	vanilla extract
For serving:		whipped cream

Beat egg in electric mixer until light and fluffy, gradually add sugar and continue beating until well mixed. Sift together flour, baking powder and salt and fold into egg mixture. Add apples, nuts and vanilla and stir only until well blended. Pour batter into a greased and floured 8″ (200 mm) square or round baking pan and bake 30–35 minutes. Serve cake warm with whipped cream.

Serves 4–5.

SPICE COOKIES

Germany   *(Pfeffernüsse)*

The Christmas cookie of Germany.

½ cup	*(125 mL)*	honey
½ cup	*(125 mL)*	molasses
¼ cup	*(60 mL)*	shortening
1	*(1)*	egg
3½ cups	*(875 mL)*	flour
1 ts	*(1 ts)*	salt
1 ts	*(1 ts)*	baking soda
1 ts	*(1 ts)*	baking powder
½ ts	*(½ ts)*	ground nutmeg
½ ts	*(½ ts)*	cinnamon
1 ts	*(1 ts)*	ground allspice
¼ ts	*(¼ ts)*	ground anise seeds

Heat honey and molasses in a saucepan but do not allow to boil. Add shortening and mix. Cool mixture, then beat in egg. Sift together all dry ingredients and gradually stir into honey mixture. Turn onto floured baking board and smooth out dough with hands. Put in refrigerator for about 30 minutes. Shape dough into ¾" (18 mm) balls and bake on greased cookie sheet in a 350° F (175° C) oven about 12–15 minutes. Let cookies cool, then frost with the following mixture.

Frosting:

1	*(1)*	egg white
½ tbs	*(½ tbs)*	corn syrup
1½ cups	*(375 mL)*	confectioners' sugar, sifted

In an electric mixer beat egg white and corn syrup until soft peaks form, then gradually add confectioners' sugar and beat until smooth. Dip cookies in this mixture until lightly covered and put on a wire rack to harden. Put waxed paper underneath to catch the drippings.

Makes about 4 dozen cookies.

CHRISTMAS BREAD

Germany   *(Stollen)*

The classical Christmas bread of Germany. It has a wonderful keeping quality because of the high fat content. I remember some years ago a friend of mine with relatives in East Germany had received some stollen for Christmas from there which had been in transit for 5 or 6 weeks. To my amazement it tasted as if it had been just baked!

1 pkg	*(1 pkg)*	dry yeast
¼ cup	*(125 mL)*	lukewarm water
⅔ cup	*(160 mL)*	butter or margarine
1 cup	*(250 mL)*	milk
3	*(3)*	eggs, at room temperature
½ cup	*(125 mL)*	sugar
5-6 cups	*(1250-1500 mL)*	flour
1 ts	*(1 ts)*	salt
½ cup	*(125 mL)*	chopped blanched almonds
¾ cup	*(180 mL)*	or other nuts
½ cup	*(125 mL)*	mixed candied fruits, cut small
½ cup	*(125 mL)*	raisins

Dissolve yeast in water with 2 ts sugar. Melt butter then add milk, heat to warm, then combine with 2 cups (500 mL) flour, sugar and salt in bowl of an electric mixer. Beat for a couple of minutes at medium speed, then add yeast mixture and mix well. Add additional flour to make a thick batter and continue beating, scraping the bowl off and on. Add more flour until the mixer cannot handle the beating, then stir in enough flour to make a soft dough.

Turn out onto a floured board and knead about 5 minutes, then add nuts, candied fruits and raisins and knead into the dough. Place in a greased bowl, turning over once to get both sides of dough greased. Cover and let rise in a warm place until double in bulk, about 1½ hours. Punch down dough and divide into three pieces.

Roll out each piece into a 8 x 12" (200 x 300 mm) oval, fold in half lengthwise and place on a greased baking sheet. Cover and let rise again in a warm place until double in bulk, about 40 minutes. Bake in a 350° F (175° C) oven about 25–30 minutes, or until done. Remove from baking sheet and cool on wire racks. Ice with confectioners' sugar frosting while still warm and, if desired, decorate with almonds and candied fruit.

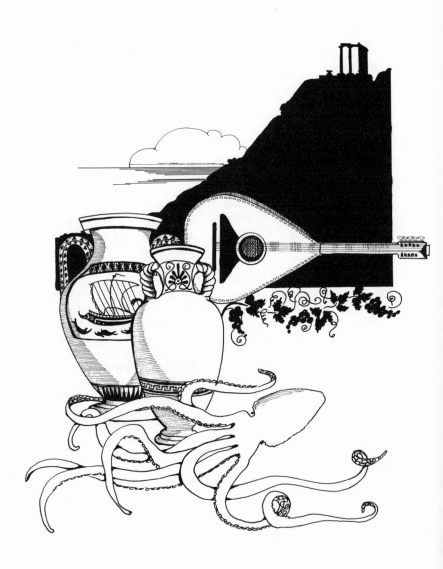

Greece

EVEN in ancient times the Greeks devoted much interest and effort to the culinary arts, to such an extent that Socrates is supposed to have felt that too much time was taken away by this from more serious and important subjects, such as astrology, geometry, medicine, etc.

As they were a nation of seafarers they came in contact with food from many other countries, and situated as they were geographically, they were greatly influenced by the Middle East. As Alexander the Great spread the Greek power and trade even further East, the influence of the ways of eating in these countries were brought back to the Greeks who came to adopt many of them, including the use of the spices of India. Therefore, many of the dishes in Greece are very similar to those eaten in other Balkan countries as well as in Turkey and the Middle East as a whole.

They use locally grown high quality vegetables, mainly tomatoes, eggplant, onions and olives, in their cooking, as in other Mediterranean countries, and also garlic, saffron and basil for seasonings.

Because the geography of the country lends itself to sheep raising, lamb and mutton are the most common and popular meats. Every visitor to Greece will remember the smell of roasting spits of lamb chunks in small stalls and restaurants along the streets. Goats are raised for their milk and a product of goat milk—feta—is the favorite among cheeses. It is used in cooking, in salads, and eaten plain with bread.

Another memory that lingers on after a visit to Greece is that of the delicate, laminated phyllo pastries, used not only for desserts, including their favorite baklava (see page 384) but also for main dishes that they call "pies," filled with spinach, cheese, meats or other things. In Greece of today the old art of making phyllo pastry dough at home is practically gone, at least in the larger cities, as it is usually bought ready made.

RED CAVIAR DIP	*Taramasalata*
SPICY FINGER SAUSAGES	*Soutzokakia*
STUFFED GRAPE LEAVES	*Dolmas or Dolmathes*
EGG AND LEMON SOUP	*Avgolomeno Soupa*
SHRIMP SARANIKOS	
RAGOUT OF VEAL	
EGGPLANT CASSEROLE	*Moussaka*
MACARONI CASSEROLE	*Pastitsio*
PORK STEW	*Afelia*
SPINACH PIE	*Spanakopita*
MARINATED MUSHROOMS	
GREEK SALAD	
WEDDING COOKIES	*Kourabiedis*
HONEY DIPPED COOKIES	*Fenikias*
RAISIN WALNUT CAKE	
WALNUT SESAME CHEWS FROM ANDROS	*Pasteli me Karydia*

RED CAVIAR DIP

Greece   *(Taramasalata)*

So many surprises come your way when you delve into different countries'
recipes! I had never imagined that the creamy, smooth mixture of taramasalata
had a base of bread crumbs.

4 oz	*(125 g)*	tarama (a paste made of red fish roe eggs) (available in specialty stores and some super-markets)
2 cups	*(500 mL)*	soft bread crumbs (crust removed)
¼ cup	*(60 mL)*	water
		juice of one lemon
½	*(½)*	small onion, chopped (about 2 tbs)
¾ cup	*(180 mL)*	olive oil

Blend all ingredients into a smooth paste in an electric blender, or use an electric mixer. Chill thoroughly and use as a dip for fresh, raw vegetables, such as cherry tomatoes, green pepper strips, celery sticks, flowerets of broccoli or cauliflower, or serve it as a spread on crackers.

SPICY FINGER SAUSAGES

Greece   *(Soutzokakia)*

These sausages may not really be sausages as they do not have any casings, but
rather sausage shaped patties. No matter, they are really tasty, and are great as
appetizers.

1 lb	*(½ kg)*	coarsely ground lamb or beef
1 cup	*(250 mL)*	bread crumbs
1	*(1)*	medium size onion, finely chopped (¾ cup or 180 mL)
2	*(2)*	cloves garlic, finely minced
1 ts	*(1 ts)*	cumin
1 ts	*(1 ts)*	coriander
2 tbs	*(2 tbs)*	fresh chopped parsley (or 2 ts dried flakes)
1	*(1)*	egg
		salt and pepper to taste
½ cup	*(125 mL)*	tomato sauce (home made or canned)
1 cup	*(250 mL)*	flour
½–¾ cup	*(125–180 mL)*	salad oil

(Continued on next page)

(Spicy Finger Sausages, cont.)

Mix together all ingredients except flour and oil and work until well blended. Form sausage shaped lengths of the meat mixture, using about 1 ts for each and making them the size of a little finger, about 1½″ (38 mm) long. Heat some of the oil in a skillet, then roll the "sausages" in flour and fry in the hot oil, turning them to make them evenly brown, about 10 minutes. Shake the pan frequently while frying, so that some of the sausages do not get too brown while the others are being made. Drain on paper toweling and serve them plain, either hot or cold, as an appetizer; or with tomato sauce for a main meal. Serves 4–6 as a main meal, more when used as appetizers.

VARIATION:

After the sausages have been fried, cool them, then wrap around each one a ¼ x 3″ (12 x 75 mm) strip of pie crust (see page 54) and bake in a 400° F (200° C) oven for 10 minutes.

STUFFED GRAPE LEAVES

Greece   **(*Dolmas or Dolmathes*)**

No matter where I turned, I got the impression that only preserved grape leaves were used in this traditional dish of the Balkan area. But through somebody fresh out of Greece I happily found that fresh young, tender grape leaves are used just as often over there by people who have gardens, and as grape vines grow in so many places here in the U.S., why not make use of them?

| 1 | (*1*) | 8 oz (500 g) jar of grape leaves, or about 25 freshly cut young leaves from grape vines |

Filling:

1 lb	(½ *kg*)	ground lamb
2	(*2*)	medium size onions, finely chopped (about 1½ cups or 375 mL)
1	(*1*)	clove garlic, finely minced
1 tbs	(*1 tbs*)	olive oil
2 cups	(*500 mL*)	cooked rice
1 ts	(*1 ts*)	mint leaves, finely minced (or ½ ts dried)
1 ts	(*1 ts*)	fresh parsley, finely minced (or ½ ts dried)
		salt and pepper to taste
¼ ts	(¼ *ts*)	cinnamon

(*Continued on next page*)

(Stuffed Grape Leaves, cont.)

| 2 tbs | (*2 tbs*) | pine nuts (*pignoli*) or finely chopped walnuts |

For cooking:

| 2 cups | (*500 mL*) | water |
| ½ cup | (*125 mL*) | fresh lemon juice |

Sauté onion and garlic in olive oil in a skillet until onion is transparent. Add meat, rice, spices and nuts, and mix well. If fresh grape leaves are used, place in a bowl and cover with boiling water, then drain immediately.

Spread each leaf with stem side up and put one tbs of filling in the center, then roll up into a tight little "package" and place with the open edges tucked under in a skillet or electric frying pan. Pack them all tightly together in a single layer, then put a heavy plate or baking dish on top as a weight to prevent them from opening during cooking. (If a square electric frying pan is used, a 9″ (220 mm) square glass baking dish placed bottom-down is suitable). Add water mixed with lemon juice and bring to a boil, cover and reduce heat and simmer for 30–35 minutes. Can be served as an appetizer, either hot with Egg and Lemon Sauce, or chilled, with lemon wedges.

Serves 8–10.

Egg and Lemon Sauce:

3	(*3*)	eggs
		juice of 2 lemons
1 cup	(*250 mL*)	chicken broth, hot

Beat eggs until very thick and creamy. Strain lemon juice and add little by little while beating the whole time. Add hot broth and stir quickly so that the hot broth will not curdle the eggs. Serve immediately. (If there is left-over sauce, re-heat very carefully without boiling as the sauce would then curdle).

EGG AND LEMON SOUP

Greece   (*Avgolomeno Soupa*)

4 cups	(*1 L*)	chicken broth
		salt to taste
2	(*2*)	eggs
		juice of one lemon

Heat chicken broth in a saucepan, and remove from heat. Beat eggs in a bowl, add lemon juice a little at a time while continuously beating to prevent curdling. Add hot, but not boiling, broth and stir vigorously, then pour it all into the saucepan and stir to blend well. Heat soup, but do not let it come to a boil, as it may then curdle. Season with salt and serve hot, with lemon wedges if desired.   Serves 4–5.

VARIATION:

Add ¼–½ cup (60–125 mL) cooked rice to soup before reheating.

SHRIMP SARANIKOS

Greece

A quick way to fix delectable shrimp. But watch out so you do not overcook them as they can become tough and stringy very quickly.

1½ lb	(*¾ kg*)	raw shrimp
1 tbs	(*1 tbs*)	butter or margarine
1 tbs	(*1 tbs*)	olive oil
1	(*1*)	medium onion, finely chopped (¾ cup or 180 mL)
1	(*1*)	clove garlic, finely minced
2 tbs	(*2 tbs*)	finely chopped fresh parsley
2	(*2*)	medium tomatoes, peeled and chopped (1 cup or 250 mL) or same amount canned chopped tomatoes
1 tbs	(*1 tbs*)	red wine
1 tbs	(*1 tbs*)	cognac
¼ lb	(*125 g*)	Feta cheese (or, if not obtainable, Mozzarella cheese)

Peel and devein shrimp. Sauté onion and garlic in olive oil and butter until onion is transparent, then add parsley and tomatoes and bring to a boil. Turn down heat and simmer at least 30 minutes. Add shrimp, bring to a

(*Continued on next page*)

(Shrimp Saranikos, cont.)

boil and cook 3 minutes, add wine and brandy and blend well. Pour into a 1½ qt (1½ L) baking dish, sprinkle with crumbled Feta cheese (or place sliced Mozzarella on top) and put under broiler about 2 minutes, or until cheese is melted. Serve immediately. Serves 5–6.

RAGOUT OF VEAL

Greece

1½ lbs	(¾ kg)	veal stew, cut into 1″ (25 mm) pieces
2 tbs	(2 tbs)	olive oil
		salt and pepper to taste
3	(3)	large onions, finely chopped (3 cups or 750 mL)
2	(2)	cloves garlic, finely minced
3	(3)	medium size tomatoes, peeled, seeded and chopped
½ cup	(125 mL)	dry white wine
1 cup	(250 mL)	chicken broth

Brown veal lightly, a few pieces at a time, in olive oil in a large frying pan, add salt and pepper to taste, then remove and put into a heavy-bottom saucepan. Sauté onion and garlic until onion is transparent, then add to meat. Add tomatoes, white wine and chicken broth and bring to a boil, then turn down heat to very low, cover and simmer for 2–2½ hours or until meat is very tender. Check at 2 hours and if mixture is too thin, leave cover off the last 30 minutes. Accompany with rice or potatoes.

Serves 4–5.

EGGPLANT CASSEROLE

(*Moussaka*)

The best way ever to prepare eggplant, I believe. No wonder it is so popular in Greece as well as other Balkan and Middle East countries.

1	(*1*)	large eggplant salad oil for frying

Cut eggplant into ⅓″ (8 mm) thick slices. (If desired, sprinkle with salt and let stand for 20 minutes, then drain off liquid that has formed and rinse under cool water and pat dry with paper toweling. This procedure is recommended for people who do not like the slightly bitter flavor of eggplant prepared without this step). Fry a few slices at a time in salad oil in a large skillet on both sides until golden in color and tender. The eggplant absorbs a lot of oil so more may have to be added during frying.

Filling:

2	(2)	medium size onions, chopped (1½ cups or 375 mL)
1	(*1*)	clove garlic, finely minced
2 tbs	(*2 tbs*)	butter or margarine
1 lb	(*½ kg*)	ground lamb (or ground beef)
1	(*1*)	can tomato paste (6 oz or 180 mL)
½ cup	(*125 mL*)	water
½ cup	(*125 mL*)	red wine
⅓ cup	(*80 mL*)	finely minced parsley
½ ts	(*½ ts*)	paprika
¼ ts	(*¼ ts*)	cinnamon
		salt and pepper to taste

Sauté onion and garlic in butter or margarine for about 5 minutes, add meat and cook until its red color disappears, separating lumps with a fork. Pour off excess fat, then add tomato paste, water, wine, parsley and seasonings and cook under cover about 10 minutes.

Topping:

3 tbs	(*3 tbs*)	butter or margarine
3 tbs	(*3 tbs*)	flour
2 cups	(*500 mL*)	milk
2	(*2*)	eggs
⅔ cups	(*160 mL*)	grated Parmesan cheese salt and pepper to taste

(*Continued on next page*)

(Eggplant Casserole, cont.)

In a saucepan melt butter, then add flour stirring constantly, add milk, a little at a time and make a white sauce, cooking until mixture has thickened, about 5 minutes. Add ½ cup (125 mL) grated cheese and season with salt and pepper. Remove from heat. Beat eggs slightly, add to sauce and mix well.

Assembly:

Arrange eggplant slices to cover bottom of a 2 qt (2 L) greased casserole, spread with a layer of meat, then alternate with eggplant slices and meat until it is all used up, ending with eggplant slices on top. Carefully pour topping over, then sprinkle with remaining Parmesan cheese (from topping ingredients) and bake in a 350° F (175° C) oven for 30 minutes. Serves 5–6.

MACARONI CASSEROLE

Greece   (*Pastitsio*)

If you have visited public beaches in Greece, you will have noticed stalls selling squares or rectangles of something that is not quite pizza, but what? Pastitsio is what it is, and here is the recipe.

1 lb	(½ kg)	elbow macaroni
		salted water

Cook macaroni in salted water according to instructions on package, about 8 minutes. (however, do not cook thoroughly, as macaroni will be baked also). Drain in colander and rinse under warm, running water and set aside.

Filling (Meat sauce):

1 lb	(½ kg)	ground lamb or beef
2	(2)	medium size onions, finely chopped (1½ cup or 375 mL)
1	(1)	clove garlic, finely minced
2 tbs	(2 tbs)	butter or margarine
½ cup	(125 mL)	tomato paste
½ cup	(125 mL)	red wine (optional)
		salt and pepper to taste
¼ ts	(¼ ts)	cinnamon
¼ ts	(¼ ts)	oregano
½ cup	(125 mL)	hot water

(*Continued on next page*)

(Macaroni Casserole, cont.)

Sauté onions and garlic in butter in skillet for about 5 minutes, add meat and cook, breaking up with a fork, about 10 minutes. Add tomato paste, wine, hot water and seasonings and mix well.

Topping:

2 tbs	(*2 tbs*)	**butter or margarine**
2 tbs	(*2 tbs*)	**flour**
2 cups	(*500 mL*)	**milk**
		salt and pepper to taste
3	(*3*)	**eggs, slightly beaten**
²⁄₃ cup	(*160 mL*)	**grated Parmesan cheese**

Melt butter in a saucepan, add flour, stirring continuously, add 1½ cup (375 mL) milk, a little at a time while stirring, and cook until mixture is smooth. Add half the cheese and mix well. Beat eggs, add ½ cup (125 mL) milk, and add to sauce, stirring until smooth, but do not let it boil.

Assembly:

In a square 9 x 9″ (220 x 220 mm) greased baking dish put a layer of half of the macaroni, add half the meat sauce, then repeat layers. Carefully spread the topping and sprinkle with remaining cheese (from topping ingredients). Bake in a 350° F (175° C) oven 40–45 minutes and let cool somewhat before serving. Slice into squares and serve to 6–8.

Greece   **PORK STEW**   (*Afelia*)

A nice "make ahead of company" casserole for pork lovers.

2 lbs	(*1 kg*)	**boneless pork tenderloin**
1 cup	(*250 mL*)	**dry red wine**
2 tbs	(*2 tbs*)	**butter or margarine**
6	(*6*)	**medium size potatoes, cut into strips**
		(¼″ x 1″ or 6 x 25 mm)
		salt and pepper to taste
2 ts	(*2 ts*)	**coriander**
1 cup	(*250 mL*)	**water**

Cut meat into 1″ (25 mm) cubes and marinate in wine, at least overnight but preferably 3–4 days, then remove and pat dry. Reserve marinade.

Brown meat in a heavy saucepan or Dutch oven, then remove it. Brown potatoes, then remove them. Return meat to the bottom of pan, place potatoes on top, add spices and water and bring to a boil. Turn down

(*Continued on next page*)

(Pork Stew, cont.)

heat very low and simmer for one hour, or until meat is tender. Check once or twice to make sure it has not boiled dry, if so, add a bit more water. When meat is well done, remove from heat, add wine marinade and let it all stand for 15 minutes before serving.   For 4–5 portions.

Greece   **SPINACH PIE**   *(Spanakopitta)*

Raw phyllo (or filo) pastry is available in many specialty shops in a frozen state, rolled up in oblong packages, and also many supermarkets now keep it on hand in their frozen section. However, if not available, try to make your own. A similar recipe (strudel dough) is on page 199, but it is not easy to match the paper-thin sheets made by machine. The spinach pie is a heavenly concoction either way, however, and is welcome either as a luncheon or light supper dish by itself, or as part of a buffet.

¾ lb	*(400 g)*	phyllo pastry
1 cup	*(250 mL)*	butter or margarine

Filling:

2 lbs	*(1 kg)*	fresh spinach, or 2 pkgs (10 oz or 300 g size) frozen spinach
1	*(1)*	small onion, finely chopped (½ cup or 125 mL)
½ lb	*(¼ kg)*	feta cheese
½ lb	*(¼ kg)*	cottage cheese
¼ cup	*(60 mL)*	parsley, finely minced
5	*(5)*	eggs, slightly beaten salt and pepper to taste

If frozen phyllo pastry is used, let it defrost slowly. In the meantime prepare the filling. Wash spinach, steam for a few minutes until it wilts, then drain, chop finely and squeeze out excess moisture. Sauté onion in one tbs of the butter or margarine until transparent, then mix in with spinach. Crumble feta cheese and cottage cheese and add to spinach together with parsley. Finally add beaten eggs and mix well.

Grease a 7 x 12″ (180 x 300 mm) baking dish. Melt butter or margarine. Add one phyllo sheet and let part of it hang over the sides of the baking dish. Brush sheet with melted butter or margarine and repeat with six more layers of phyllo sheets. Add spinach and cheese mixture, then cover with remaining phyllo sheets, each one well brushed with butter. Tuck in and under the overlapping parts of the sheets, then brush top and edges with butter or margarine. Bake in a 350° F (175° C) for 45 minutes. Serve pastry hot, cut into squares or rectangles.   For 6–8 people.

Greece   MARINATED MUSHROOMS

Mushrooms à la Grecque is what this dish is called in most restaurants. It is a delicious way to serve mushrooms.

1 lb	(½ kg)	mushrooms
½ cup	(125 mL)	olive oil
		juice of one lemon
¼ ts	(¼ ts)	oregano
¼ ts	(¼ ts)	thyme
		salt and pepper to taste

Preferably use small mushrooms, either whole or sliced. Clean them and put them in a bowl, mix together with remaining ingredients and refrigerate for 24 hours. Stir mushrooms carefully now and then to make sure marinade covers them all—if not, mix a little more marinade and add. Serve as an appetizer to 6–8.

Greece   GREEK SALAD

A real Greek-tasting salad to go with a Greek meal.

1	(1)	head lettuce (Iceberg, or any other kinds, or a mixture of them), about 3-4 cups (750-1,000 mL) coarsely shredded
2	(2)	medium size tomatoes, cut into wedges or a corresponding amount of cherry tomatoes
1	(1)	medium size cucumber, peeled and sliced
½	(½)	green pepper, cored, seeded and cut into strips
5	(5)	radishes, sliced
1	(1)	small red onion, thinly sliced
1	(1)	stalk celery, thinly sliced
2 tbs	(2 tbs)	parsley, chopped
6-8	(6-8)	black Greek olives
6	(6)	flat anchovy fillets, cut into pieces
½ cup	(125 mL)	cubed Feta cheese (¼″ or 6 mm cubes)

Mix together all ingredients just before serving and add the following dressing, then toss and serve to 5–6.

(*Continued on next page*)

(Greek Salad, cont.)

Dressing:

¼ cup	*(60 mL)*	olive oil
2 tbs	*(2 tbs)*	fresh lemon juice
1 ts	*(1 ts)*	oregano
		salt and pepper to taste

Mix together all ingredients and stir to blend well. Pour over the above salad.

WEDDING COOKIES

Greece   *(Kourabiedis)*

The traditional cookies in Greece for festive occasions, and they are even called "wedding cookies." They literally melt in your mouth.

1 lb	*(½ kg)*	unsalted butter
½ cup	*(125 mL)*	sugar
1	*(1)*	egg yolk
2 tbs	*(2 tbs)*	ouzo (a Greek liquor), brandy or whiskey
½ cup	*(125 mL)*	corn starch
3½ cups	*(875 mL)*	flour, approximately
½ ts	*(½ ts)*	baking powder

For sprinkling:	1-2 cups *(250-500 mL)* confectioners' sugar

Let the butter soften to room temperature and then beat in an electric beater or by hand until very light and fluffy, 10–15 minutes. Add sugar and continue beating until smooth, about 5 minutes more. Add egg yolk and liquor, beating until well blended. Sift together corn starch, flour and baking powder and add to batter, a little at a time, giving up the electric mixer when mixture gets too thick, then continue mixing by hand. Add only sufficient flour to make a very soft dough, then pinch off pieces of dough, rolling into crescent shapes, finger shapes or tiny rounds. Dust hands lightly with flour before making each cookie.

Place on an ungreased cookie sheet about 1" (25 mm) apart and bake in a 350° F (175° C) oven 15–20 minutes or until lightly golden in color. Allow to cool slightly on baking sheet, then remove cookies carefully and place on a wax paper which has been heavily sprinkled with confectioners' sugar. Sprinkle the tops of the cookies with more sugar and let cool. Makes 7–8 dozen cookies.

HONEY DIPPED COOKIES

Greece   (*Fenikias*)

Another delicious cookie, this one dipped in a honey syrup.

½ cup	(125 mL)	butter or margarine
½ cup	(125 mL)	salad oil
½ cup	(125 mL)	sugar
1	(1)	egg
⅓ cup	(80 mL)	milk
2 tbs	(2 tbs)	brandy or sherry
½ ts	(½ ts)	cinnamon
½ ts	(½ ts)	cloves
2½ cups	(625 mL)	flour (plus flour for dusting your hands)
½ ts	(½ ts)	baking soda
1 ts	(1 ts)	baking powder

Cream butter, oil and sugar until very light and fluffy, add egg, milk, brandy or sherry and spices and mix well. Sift together flour with baking soda and baking powder and mix into a soft dough. Dust your hands with flour and using about 1 ts dough for each, roll into small ovals and put on a greased baking sheet. (The dough will be a bit sticky, so make sure you dust your hands for each cookie). Bake in a 350° F (175° C) oven for 15–20 minutes or until golden brown. Let cool on a rack, then dip each cookie for a few seconds in the following:

Syrup:

1 cup	(250 mL)	honey
1 cup	(250 mL)	sugar
1 cup	(250 mL)	water

Bring all the ingredients to a boil in a small saucepan, then simmer for 5 minutes. Use the syrup while it is still boiling hot, using a slotted spoon to dip the cookies into it. Let cookies drip off and cool on a wire rack. If desired, they may be sprinkled with chopped walnuts immediately after they have been dipped into syrup.

Makes about 5 dozen.

RAISIN WALNUT CAKE

Greece

¾ cup	(*180 mL*)	butter or margarine (1½ stick)
1 cup	(*250 mL*)	sugar
3	(*3*)	eggs, separated
⅓ cup	(*80 mL*)	hot milk
1 ts	(*1 ts*)	vanilla extract
2 cups	(*500 mL*)	flour
2 ts	(*2 ts*)	baking powder
⅓ cup	(*80 mL*)	golden raisins
⅓ cup	(*80 mL*)	chopped walnuts

Cream butter and sugar until light and fluffy, add egg yolks and continue beating until well blended. Add hot milk and vanilla. Beat egg whites until stiff. Sift together flour and baking powder and mix into batter, then fold in egg whites, raisins and walnuts. Pour batter into a buttered and floured ring cake pan and bake in a 325° F (160° C) oven about 45 minutes, or until cake tests done.

WALNUT-SESAME CHEWS FROM ANDROS

Greece   (*Pasteli me Karydia*)

These chews are more like candy than cookies, but are tasty whatever you call them.

⅔ cup	(*160 mL*)	honey
⅓ cup	(*80 mL*)	sugar
1½ cups	(*375 mL*)	chopped walnuts
¼ cup	(*60 mL*)	zwieback crumbs or dry bread crumbs
½ cup	(*125 mL*)	toasted sesame seeds

Cook honey and sugar over medium heat until the soft-ball stage, or the mixture registers 250–256° F (120–125° C) on a candy thermometer. Remove from heat. Mix nuts and bread crumbs then add to honey mixture and stir with a wooden spoon. On a marble slab—or a cutting board—sprinkle half the sesame seeds, then spread the nut mixture on top to about ½″ (12 mm) thickness, then sprinkle remaining seeds on top. Cool overnight in refrigerator, then cut into diamond shapes or squares. Store in a covered tin cannister. Makes about 40 1″ (25 mm) squares.

Holland

DUTCH cooking is down to earth cooking. The country is very fertile and has a large rural population. Being a major cheese producer has also influenced their cooking strongly.

Holland's proximity to the sea shows itself in its many ways of preparing fish, and the Dutch have been very prominent in developing tasty ways of curing, smoking and serving the herring they fish in the North Sea. The word Maatjes, which today is almost a synonym for herring, actually means "virgin"; and the reason for this name is that only young, immature herring are used. They love their salt herring to the extent that they eat *Groene Haring*—lightly salted young herring—raw, bones and all, by holding on to the tail and starting with the head.

Another influence on the Dutch cuisine has been Holland's many colonies, especially those in the Far East, so that they use exotic spices extensively in their cooking.

Rice is also used. Many restaurants feature *Rijstafel* (rice table), which is a buffet style meal, featuring rice with many side dishes, most of them of Eastern origin, such as curries, etc.

One Dutch specialty is a cinnamon sauce which is used with cooked cereals or rice pudding.

HERRING SALAD	*Haringsla*
CHEESE BALLS	*Kaasbolletjes*
CHEESE STICKS	*Kaasstokjes*

(*Continued on next page*)

OSTENDE FISH SOUP	*Ostende Vissoep*
BEAN SOUP	*Bruine Bonensoep*
POACHED FISH WITH MUSTARD SAUCE	*Vis met Mostersaus*
BRAISED STEAKS	*Runderlappen*
BEAN CASSEROLE	*Vijfschaft*
PAN-FRIED POTATOES WITH CHEESE	*Gebacken Aardappelen met Kaas*
LEMON CHIFFON PUDDING	*Citroenvla*
CINNAMON SAUCE	*Kanelsaus*
DATE CAKE	*Dadelkoek*

HERRING SALAD

Holland   *(Haringsla)*

In countries near the North Sea in Europe herring salad is very popular. The Dutch have a very nice version of same.

2	(2)	salt herrings (or 4 fillets)
3	(3)	medium size boiled potatoes, cut into $\frac{1}{4}''$ (6 mm) cubes (about $1\frac{1}{2}$ cups or 375 mL)
1 cup	(250 mL)	cubed pickled beets
1 cup	(250 mL)	peeled and cubed tart apples
1	(1)	small onion, finely chopped ($\frac{1}{2}$ cup or 125 mL)
$\frac{1}{2}$ cup	(125 mL)	chopped sweet pickles
2	(2)	hard boiled eggs
$\frac{1}{2}$ ts	($\frac{1}{2}$ ts)	dry mustard
		pepper and salt to taste
2 tbs	(2 tbs)	vinegar
1 cup	(250 mL)	mayonnaise

If whole salt herrings are used, clean fish, remove heads and soak overnight in cold water. Drain off water and cut herring into small pieces. Mix well with potatoes, beets, apples, onion, pickles and 1 chopped hard boiled egg. Add seasonings and vinegar. Mix mayonnaise with mustard and blend into the herring mixture.

Chill for at least 4–5 hours in refrigerator, then either put salad into a serving bowl, or build it up into a mound, on a platter, smoothing the surface with extra mayonnaise, if necessary. Decorate with the remaining egg, either sliced, or the yolk and white chopped separately and added to the salad in stripes. Garnish with parsley.

Serves 4–6.

CHEESE BALLS
Holland   *(Kaasbolletjes)*

Delicious appetizers in which the grated pumpernickel crumbs make the difference from other cheese balls.

½ cup	*(125 mL)*	butter, softened to room temperature or 8 oz (¼ kg) cream cheese, soft
1 cup	*(250 mL)*	grated Gouda or Edam cheese salt and pepper to taste
1 ts	*(1 ts)*	Worcestershire sauce
½ cup	*(125 mL)*	finely grated stale pumpernickel (about 2 slices)

In a mixing bowl work together butter or cream cheese, cheese, seasonings and Worcestershire sauce to a smooth paste. (Use an electric mixer, if desired). Roll into balls the size of hazelnuts and roll them in pumpernickel crumbs. Refrigerate for 2–3 hours, or until firm. Serve as an appetizer.

For 6–8 people.

CHEESE STICKS
Holland   *(Kaasstokjes)*

Another nice and cheesy appetizer.

½ cup	*(125 mL)*	butter or margarine
1	*(1)*	egg yolk
1 cup	*(250 mL)*	grated Gouda cheese
¼ ts	*(¼ ts)*	salt
1 ts	*(1 ts)*	Worcestershire sauce
1 cup	*(250 mL)*	flour

For brushing: 1 lightly beaten egg white

Stir butter until light and fluffy, add egg yolk, half the cheese and seasonings, and mix well. Work flour and mixture together into a ball, scraping up loose pieces on the side of the bowl. Wrap the dough in plastic wrap and let rest in refrigerator for at least 2 hours.

Roll out dough into ¼″ (6 mm) thickness and cut into strips ½ x 2″ (12 x 50 mm). Brush top with egg white then dip in remaining cheese to coat the top and put on a well greased baking sheet. Bake in a 375° F (190° C) oven 12–15 minutes, or until golden in color. Makes about 2 dozen.

OSTENDE FISH SOUP

Holland   (*Ostende Vissoep*)

A light and flavorful soup which provides a really nice way to eat fish. Fish soup is not as common in the U.S. as in Europe, but perhaps some day it will be.

2 lbs	(*1 kg*)	fish fillets (any salt water fish)
1	(*1*)	8 oz (250 mL) bottle clam juice
5 cups	(*1¼ L*)	water
1	(*1*)	small onion, sliced
		a few sprigs of parsley
1	(*1*)	medium size carrot, peeled and sliced
1	(*1*)	slice lemon
1 ts	(*1 ts*)	salt
6	(*6*)	whole peppercorns
3 tbs	(*3 tbs*)	butter
3 tbs	(*3 tbs*)	flour
1 cup	(*250 mL*)	cooked shrimp (7 oz or 225 mL) can
1 tbs	(*1 tbs*)	tomato ketchup
½ cup	(*125 mL*)	light cream
For sprinkling:		1 tbs chopped fresh parsley

Cut fish fillets into bite size pieces and put together with water, onion, parsley, carrot, lemon, salt and peppercorns in a large saucepan. Bring to a boil, turn down heat and simmer under cover for 15 minutes. Remove fish, strain the broth and discard vegetables. In a small saucepan melt butter and add flour, stirring to make a smooth paste, then add fish stock, a little at a time to get a smooth mixture. Purée half the shrimp in a blender together with ketchup and a little of the cream, then add this to the soup and heat, but do not let mixture boil. Just before serving, stir in remaining shrimp and cream and sprinkle with parsley.   Serves 5–6.

BEAN SOUP

Holland   (*Bruine Bonensoep*)

A "sticks to your ribs" type of soup, which makes a meal in itself and is perfect if you adhere to the one-day-a-week-without-meat policy.

1½ cups	(*375 mL*)	dried kidney beans
5–6 cups	(*1250–1500 mL*)	water
1	(*1*)	bay leaf
3	(*3*)	medium size potatoes, peeled and cubed

(*Continued on next page*)

(Bean Soup, cont.)

1	(1)	medium onion, finely chopped ($\frac{3}{4}$ cup or 180 mL)
2 tbs	(2 tbs)	butter or margarine
2 ts	(2 ts)	curry powder
		salt and pepper to taste

Soak beans in water over-night. Drain water in which beans were soaked, then add 5 cups (1250 mL) fresh water and bay leaf and bring to a boil. Turn down heat to very low, then simmer beans for 2 hours. Add potatoes and cook for 30 minutes more.

In the meantime sauté onion in butter, add curry powder, and continue sautéing until onion is transparent. Purée beans and potatoes in an electric blender, or press mixture through a sieve. Return to pot, add onion mixture and simmer for 20 minutes over low heat, stirring off and on to prevent sticking. Season with salt and pepper and add a bit more water if soup tends to get too thick.

If desired, serve with sliced frankfurters or smoked sausages, sliced or whole, depending upon size.

Serves 5–6.

POACHED FISH WITH MUSTARD SAUCE

Holland (*Vis met Mostersaus*)

I believe that poached fish is more common in Europe than in the U.S. With a good sauce, in this case Mustard Sauce, it is very nice, indeed.

2 lbs	(1 kg)	fish fillets (haddock, hake or cod)
1½ cup	(375 mL)	water
		juice of one lemon
1	(1)	small onion, sliced
1	(1)	small carrot, sliced
6	(6)	whole peppercorns
1	(1)	bay leaf
		salt to taste

For serving: 2 tbs chopped fresh parsley

Put fish fillets in a heavy saucepan and pour water mixed with lemon juice over them. Add onion, carrots, peppercorns, bay leaf and salt and bring to a boil. Cover pot, turn heat down to very low and simmer until fish is flaky, about 10 minutes. Remove fish and keep hot. Strain broth to be used for sauce.

(Continued on next page)

(Poached Fish with Mustard Sauce, cont.)

Mustard Sauce:

2 tbs	(*2 tbs*)	**butter or margarine**
2 tbs	(*2 tbs*)	**flour**
1½ cup	(*375 mL*)	**fish broth**
		salt and pepper to taste
⅓ cup	(*80 mL*)	**white wine (optional)**
2 tbs	(*2 tbs*)	**prepared mustard (Dijon type)**
¼ cup	(*60 mL*)	**cream**

Melt butter in a saucepan, add flour while stirring, then gradually add fish broth, a little at a time, stirring continuously. Season with salt and pepper and simmer sauce for about 5 minutes, then add wine and bring to a boil, turn down heat and cook over low heat about 3 minutes. Remove from heat and stir in mustard and cream. Place fish on a platter, sprinkle with chopped parsley and serve mustard sauce from a sauce bowl.

Serves 5–6.

BRAISED STEAKS

Holland   (*Runderlappen*)

This is a tasty way to prepare steaks which are under suspicion of being too tough for broiling.

3 lbs	(*1½ kg*)	**boneless steaks, such as top round or similar**
		salt and pepper to taste
2 tbs	(*2 tbs*)	**butter or margarine**
1½ cups	(*375 mL*)	**water**
4 tbs	(*4 tbs*)	**vinegar**
8	(*8*)	**peppercorns**
2	(*2*)	**bay leaves**
½ ts	(*½ ts*)	**whole cloves**
¼ ts	(*¼ ts*)	**nutmeg**

Cut steaks into pieces, suitable for individual servings, sprinkle with salt and pepper and brown well in butter or margarine on both sides. Bring water to a boil, then pour over steaks together with vinegar and spices and simmer until steaks are very tender, about one hour or more, turning them over several times during simmering period. Serve with potatoes cooked in any style.

Serves 5–6.

BEAN CASSEROLE

Holland

(*Vijfschaft*)

An economical and good meal.

½ lb	(¼ kg)	kidney or pinto beans
3½ cups	(875 mL)	water
2 ts	(2 ts)	salt
1 lb	(½ kg)	carrots, peeled and cut into ½″ (12 mm) slices
4	(4)	medium size onions, peeled and quartered
2	(2)	firm, tart apples, peeled, cored and cut into wedges
5	(5)	medium size potatoes, peeled and cut into ½″ (12 mm) slices
½ lb	(¼ kg)	sliced bacon, crisply fried
1 lb	(½ kg)	smoked sausage or frankfurters

Soak beans overnight, or for several hours, drain, then bring to a boil with 3½ cups (750 mL) water in a flameproof casserole or heavy bottom pot. Lower heat and cook beans for about 1½ hour. Add carrots, onions and apples, bring to a boil, turn down heat and simmer for 15 minutes, then add potatoes and continue cooking until potatoes and other vegetables are tender, about 15 minutes. Heat sausage or frankfurters thoroughly on top of vegetables in pot. Serve directly from pot with fried bacon crumbled on top.

For 5–6 people.

PAN-FRIED POTATOES WITH CHEESE

Holland   (*Gebacken Aardappelen met Kaas*)

A potato dish which is delicious with steak or roasts.

5	(5)	medium size potatoes, peeled and thinly sliced
4 tbs	(*4 tbs*)	butter or margarine
1 ts	(*1 ts*)	salt
¼ lb	(*125 g*)	Gouda cheese, sliced

In a large skillet melt butter, add sliced potatoes and salt. Cook over low heat under cover, pressing down now and then with spatula until potatoes are golden brown on the bottom. Turn over potatoes carefully and cook until golden brown on other side. When potatoes are tender, add cheese slices and continue cooking until cheese has melted. Serve piping hot.

Serves 4–5.

LEMON CHIFFON PUDDING

Holland   (*Citroenvla*)

A perfect dessert for a very hot day—light in texture and cool in flavor.

3	(3)	eggs, separated
½ cup	(*125 mL*)	sugar
¼ cup	(*60 mL*)	fresh lemon juice
		grated rind of one lemon
⅓ cup	(*80 mL*)	white wine

Beat egg yolks and sugar until light and fluffy, add remaining ingredients except egg whites, and stir to mix. Transfer into a double boiler and cook until mixture has thickened, stirring off and on, then let it cool somewhat. Beat egg whites until stiff and fold into lemon mixture, put it in a bowl and chill until serving. Serve with fancy cookies.

Serves 4–6.

CINNAMON SAUCE

Holland   (*Kanelsaus*)

2 cups	(*500 mL*)	milk
3 tbs	(*3 tbs*)	flour
3 tbs	(*3 tbs*)	sugar
1	(*1*)	cinnamon stick

Mix together flour and sugar and add
½ cup (125 mL) milk and stir till well
mixed. Bring remaining milk and cinnamon stick to boil, turn down heat
and simmer until milk is well flavored
by the cinnamon. Stir in flour mixture
and mix well, then simmer for 5 minutes or until thickened. Remove cinnamon stick. Serve with rice or other
cooked cereals.   Serves 4–5.

DATE CAKE

Holland   (*Dadelkoek*)

½ cup	(*125 mL*)	butter or margarine
½ cup	(*125 mL*)	brown sugar
2	(*2*)	eggs
1 cup	(*250 mL*)	flour
1½ ts	(*1½ ts*)	baking powder
1 cup	(*250 mL*)	oatmeal
¾ lb	(*350 g*)	pitted dates

For serving: whipped cream

Beat butter until light and fluffy, add
brown sugar and eggs and continue
beating until a smooth batter is obtained. Sift together flour and baking
powder and add to batter, then add
oatmeal. Set aside 8–10 dates for decoration, then chop remaining dates
finely.

Put half the dough into a 9"
(220 mm) pie plate or cake pan with
removable bottom, add chopped
dates, then cover with remaining
dough and press remaining whole
dates into dough as decoration. Bake
in a 375° F (190° C) oven 30 minutes.
Let cake cool before turning it out of
the plate or pan. Serve with whipped
cream, plain or flavored with either
vanilla or 1 tbs sherry.

Hungary

THE cuisines of Hungary and Austria seem closely related, at least to an outsider. What we find most striking in the Hungarian cooking is the heavy use of paprika, a powder made from certain red peppers. This is not a hot condiment, but very distinct in flavor, and it also gives a nice colorful touch. The Hungarian name for paprika—*nemes edes*—means in direct translation "noble and sweet" and that is how it is regarded in Hungary. Sour cream is also used to a large extent, as it is in many other eastern European countries.

Also in Hungary there are wonderful baked goods and pastries, but the most famous of them all—*Dobo's Torte*—I have not included as it is quite intricate and tedious to make. You have probably seen it—a rectangular cake with many thin layers of sponge cake with chocolate cream filling in between.

LIPTAUER CHEESE SPREAD	
GOULASH SOUP	*Gulyásleves*
CHICKEN PAPRIKA	*Csirke Paprikás*
PORK GOULASH	*Gulyás*
BEEF GOULASH	*Gulyás*
POPPY SEED ROLL	*Mákos és Dioś Kalács*
APRICOT MERINGUE TORTE	
WITCHES' FROTH	*Boszorkányhab*
CREAM CHEESE PASTRIES	*Ragalach*

233

Hungary　　　　　　**LIPTAUER CHEESE SPREAD**

This is not a last minute thing you can whip up for an appetizer as it takes a whole week to "ripen" after it has been mixed. But it is worth waiting for. In Hungary the cheese in it is made from sheep's milk, but this is just about impossible to get in the U.S. Our cottage cheese does very well.

½ lb	(¼ kg)	sheep's-milk cheese, or cottage cheese
½ lb	(¼ kg)	cream cheese, softened (8 oz or 250 g package)
½ cup	(125 mL)	butter
1½ tbs	(1½ tbs)	paprika
½ ts	(½ ts)	dry mustard
1 tbs	(1 tbs)	caraway seeds, pounded
½ ts	(½ ts)	salt
¼ ts	(¼ ts)	pepper
½ ts	(½ ts)	anchovy paste
1	(1)	small onion, grated
2 tbs	(2 tbs)	gin (optional)

Either sieve the cottage cheese, or work it in an electric blender until smooth, then turn into a mixing bowl and add the remaining ingredients and work mixture until well blended. Refrigerate and let it rest for at least one week to let the spread "mellow." Serve with crackers or good, crusty bread as an appetizer. Makes about 2 cups (500 mL).

Hungary　　　　　　**GOULASH SOUP**　　　　　　(*Gulyásleves*)

A "stick to the ribs" soup that is popular in Hungary. It is often served in restaurants along the Auto-Bahns (super-highways) for a quick and satisfying meal.

1½ lbs	(¾ kg)	boneless chuck or other stewing beef, cut in 1″ (25 mm) cubes
2 tbs	(2 tbs)	lard or bacon grease
3	(3)	medium size onions, chopped (about 2 cups or 500 mL)
2	(2)	red or green sweet peppers, chopped
5 cups	(1250 mL)	water
2 tbs	(2 tbs)	paprika (preferably imported Hungarian) salt to taste
3	(3)	medium size potatoes, cubed (1″ or 25 mm)

(*Continued on next page*)

(Goulash Soup, cont.)

Sauté onion in butter or margarine for 10 minutes, but do not allow to get brown. Add meat and peppers and cook for 30 minutes, stirring often then add water and seasonings and bring to a boil, turn down heat and simmer very gently for about 1 hour. Add potatoes and continue cooking until both meat and potatoes are thoroughly tender.   Serves 4–6.

VARIATION:

About ¼–½ lb (125 g–¼ kg) smoked sausages may be sliced and added to soup about 10 minutes before serving.

This soup is just as popular in Austria but there they add about 2 tbs of caraway seeds to the above recipe.

CHICKEN PAPRIKA

Hungary   *(Gsirke Paprikás)*

A wonderful way to prepare chicken.

1	*(1)*	**frying chicken, 3-3½ lbs (1½-1¾ kg)**
1	*(1)*	**small onion, finely chopped (½ cup or 125 mL)**
3 tbs	*(3 tbs)*	**butter or margarine**
		salt and pepper to taste
1 cup	*(250 mL)*	**chicken stock or hot water**
3 tbs	*(3 tbs)*	**paprika**
1 cup	*(250 mL)*	**sour cream**

Cut chicken into serving pieces, then brown well on all sides in a chicken fryer or electric fry pan. Sprinkle with salt and pepper. Remove from frying pan, then sauté onions until transparent. Return chicken to frying pan, add chicken stock or water and bring to a boil. Turn down heat to very low and simmer until chicken is almost done, about 30 minutes. Add paprika and make sure all chicken pieces are covered, then turn them over. Cook an additional 20 minutes. Put chicken pieces in a serving dish and keep hot. Add sour cream to pan drippings and mix well over low heat. Make sure mixture does not boil, as it might then curdle. Pour sauce over chicken and serve immediately with noodles or Spaetzle (see page 195).

Serves 4–5.

PORK GOULASH

Hungary *(Gulyás)*

The goulash can be made with different kinds of meat—veal, pork and beef. Here follow two recipes, one with pork and the other with beef, each good in its own way—similar but different.

2 lbs	*(1 kg)*	pork tenderloin, cut into 1″ (25 mm) cubes
2 tbs	*(2 tbs)*	butter or margarine
1	*(1)*	large onion, chopped (1 cup or 250 mL)
1	*(1)*	green pepper, chopped
		salt and pepper to taste
1 tbs	*(1 tbs)*	paprika
½ cup	*(125 mL)*	water
½ cup	*(125 mL)*	sour cream

In a skillet, brown meat in butter or margarine, then put it into a heavy saucepan. Sauté onions for a few minutes, then add to meat. Add green pepper, seasonings and water and bring to a boil, then turn heat down to very low and simmer, under cover, until meat is tender, 1–1½ hours. Just before serving, stir in sour cream. Serve with noodles. Serves 5–6.

BEEF GOULASH

Hungary *(Gulyás)*

2 lbs	*(1 kg)*	stew beef, cut into 1″ (25 mm) cubes
2	*(2)*	large onions, thinly sliced
2 tbs	*(2 tbs)*	butter or margarine
1	*(1)*	clove garlic, finely minced
		salt and pepper to taste
2 tbs	*(2 tbs)*	paprika
2 tbs	*(2 tbs)*	tomato paste
1	*(1)*	bay leaf
1 cup	*(250 mL)*	beef stock or water

Brown meat in butter or margarine in a skillet, then transfer into a heavy bottom stew pot. Brown onions and garlic slightly and add to pot. Rinse out skillet with the stock or water, scraping the bottom with a spoon, and pour it over meat. Add salt, pepper, paprika, tomato paste and bay leaf and stir it into beef and onion mixture to get them evenly distributed.

Bring to a boil, then turn down heat very low and let mixture simmer for about 1½ hours, or until meat is fork-tender. Discard bay leaf. Serve over noodles. Serves 4–6.

POPPY SEED ROLL

Hungary (*Makos es Dios Kalacs*)

This is a Christmas cake in Hungary. It makes use of poppy seeds, which are often used in baking throughout Eastern Europe.

½ package	(½ *package*)	dry yeast
3 cups	(*750 mL*)	flour
½ cup	(*125 mL*)	sugar
½ ts	(*½ ts*)	salt
½ cup	(*125 mL*)	butter or shortening
		grated rind of 1 lemon
½ cup	(*125 mL*)	lukewarm milk

For brushing:

½ egg
1 tbs milk

Sift together 2 cups (500 mL) flour, sugar and salt, then add yeast in a large bowl. Cut in butter or shortening with a pastry cutter until mixture is crumbly, then add lukewarm milk and mix well. Add ¾ cup (180 mL) more flour a little at a time. When dough is smooth, turn out onto floured baking board, using remaining flour, and knead for about 10 minutes. Place in a clean, greased bowl and let rise in a warm place for 1 hour.

Filling:

⅓ cup	(*80 mL*)	milk
½ cup	(*125 mL*)	sugar
1½ cup	(*375 mL*)	poppy seeds
¾ cup	(*180 mL*)	raisins

Mix all the ingredients together in a heavy saucepan, bring to a boil, turn down heat to very low and simmer until a thick spread has been obtained, stirring off and on.

Assembly:
Divide dough into two pieces and roll each one out to about ⅓″ (8 mm) thickness, spread evenly with the filling, leaving about 1″ (25 mm) bare all around. Roll up each piece jelly roll fashion, and place rolls seam down on a greased baking sheet, and let rise for another 45 minutes. Brush with beaten egg and milk and bake in a 350° F (175° C) oven about 25–30 minutes or until golden brown.

APRICOT MERINGUE TORTE

Hungary

Another light and delectable dessert.

Pastry:

1 cup	*(250 mL)*	flour
1 ts	*(1 ts)*	baking powder
½ cup	*(125 mL)*	butter (or half butter and half margarine)
2	*(2)*	egg yolks
1 ts	*(1 ts)*	vanilla extract *or* grated rind of 1 lemon

Sift together flour and baking powder, cut in butter with a pastry cutter until mixture resembles coarse crumbs. Add egg yolks and flavoring and mix together into a ball, scraping loose particles from the sides of the mixing bowl, then work together with your hands for a minute or so. Wrap in plastic and let rest in refrigerator for 30 minutes. Roll out to fit bottom and sides of a 9″ (220 mm) spring-pan, or, if such is not available, in a pie pan of the same size.

Filling:

⅓ cup	*(80 mL)*	apricot purée

If ready-made purée is not on hand, soak ⅓ cup (80 mL) dried apricots in the same amount of water for 30 minutes, then cook until fruit is tender. Purée in a blender.

Topping:

2	*(2)*	egg whites
⅓ cup	*(80 mL)*	veri-fine sugar
2 tbs	*(2 tbs)*	chopped, blanched almonds

Beat egg whites until stiff, add sugar a little at a time and continue beating until sugar is well incorporated.

Assembly:

Spread apricot purée over pastry, then spread with meringue. Sprinkle with nuts and bake in a 350° F (175° C) oven for 30 minutes. Serve slightly warm, or cold, to 4–6.

WITCHES' FROTH

Hungary   *(Boszorkanyhab)*

A nice light dessert to be used for those egg whites that accumulate now and then in the refrigerator.

4	*(4)*	medium size apples
1 tbs	*(1 tbs)*	lemon juice
2	*(2)*	egg whites
¼ cup	*(60 mL)*	verifine sugar
For serving:		whipped cream, sliced fresh fruit

Bake apples in a 350° F (175° C) oven until very soft, 30–60 minutes, depending on variety. Remove core, scoop out pulp and pass through a sieve. Add lemon juice and chill. Beat egg whites, adding sugar a little at a time, and continue beating until very stiff. Fold in apple pulp and put in a serving dish. Decorate with some whipped cream and sliced fresh fruit. Serves 4–5.

CREAM CHEESE PASTRIES

Hungary   *(Ragalach)*

These pastries should be served very fresh as they do not taste as well after they have been stored. But they are so good that they go very fast.

½ cup	*(125 mL)*	butter or margarine
1	*(1)*	3 oz (85 g) pkg cream cheese
1 cup	*(250 mL)*	flour
⅓ cup	*(80 mL)*	chopped walnuts
3 tbs	*(3 tbs)*	sugar
1½ ts	*(1½ ts)*	cinnamon

Cream butter or margarine with cream cheese until light and fluffy, stir in flour and mix well. Shape into a ball and refrigerate for at least 8 hours or over-night.

Mix together nuts, sugar and cinnamon. Divide pastry into eight equal size balls, flatten each one slightly with your hand then roll it out into a 6″ (150 mm) circle (if it is not evenly round, it does not matter). Cut each one into four pieces, then place about 1 ts of nut filling on each, towards the wide side of the wedge, then roll the pastry over the filling toward the point, pinch edges of dough together to enclose the filling, then shape into a crescent. Place on an un-greased baking sheet and bake in a 350° F (175° C) oven for 12–15 minutes or until golden brown. Cool on wire-rack and serve very fresh. Makes 2 dozen.

India

LIKE many other people, I used to think that in India people mainly ate curried chicken or meat, and that curry was one spice. It is, of course, true that curried dishes are important in the Indian cuisine but to me it was quite a revelation to find out how many other things they have to offer besides a great variety of curries, not only in regard to the main ingredients but also the degree of spiciness.

Curry is not one spice but a mixture of different ones. The curry powder we use in the western world is something of a shortcut, probably invented by the British, during their colonial days there, when combining the different spices and what the Indian call aromatics. In India no cook with self-esteem would use a commercial, ready-made curry powder, and every curried dish they make is therefore not quite the same each time, as they use the method of "a pinch of this and a pinch of that."

An Indian curry may contain any one or ones of the following seasonings and aromatics: garlic, fresh ginger, turmeric, sesame seeds, cardamom seeds, cloves (whole and/or ground), coriander seeds and leaves, cumin, black pepper, anise, caraway seeds, coconut, dillweed and seed, lemon, mustard seed and rose-water. It is practically impossible to have them all in one powder. However, for convenience sake many households make their own mixes, and I have given a couple of different suggestions.

As more than 80% of the Indian population is of the Hindu faith, and therefore cannot eat beef, and since many are also vegetarians, the Indians lean heavily towards eating vegetables. They use their "lentils" (some of them we call beans) of all shapes and kinds to supply the necessary protein, and prepare them in such a variety of ways that one

241

really does not seem to miss eating meat. But there are also millions of both Moslems and Christians in India who eat meats and there are therefore plenty of Indian ways to prepare these.

We tend to think that all Indian food is quite spicy but this is not agreed to in India. On my visit there I was told that "here in the North (the state of Kashmir) we do not use very spicy foods, that is mainly done in the South of India." Still, their "mild" flavoring was just about at the tolerance level of my apparently bland westernized taste buds.

Another misconception I had about Indian cooking was that the frying had to be done in *ghee*, that is clarified butter, a somewhat tedious thing to make. This is far from so, however, as butter is expensive and therefore oil is used to a great extent, especially in the South, and a vegetable shortening, *Vanospati*, similar to our Crisco and Spry, is used everywhere. *Ghee* is, however, used when special occasions call for it.

As far as regional eating habits are concerned, there is more rice eaten in the South, and other grains in the North. All over the country yogurt is eaten with practically everything, sometimes used as an ingredient, and practically always as an accompaniment to spicy foods with which it gives a nice cooling effect.

I would like to mention that when you come across Indian names for foods (these are, by the way, spelled in many different ways in English as they are translated phonetically) the word *korma* means made with yogurt, *molee* made with coconut milk and *vindaloo* made with vinegar as ingredients.

To have the opportunity to have meals in an Indian home is an unforgettable experience. Foremost, there is a natural hospitality that shines through everything, as they are such a gracious people.

Their meals are not set up like ours with different courses following each other. Usually there is a tray or a cleared space in the middle of the table, and all of the meal, from appetizers to desserts, are placed there at the same time. After different foods have been placed on your plate, the food is eaten with the fingers.

When you just hear it, it sounds as if it would be a messy affair, but they are so fastidious about it, for example using torn off pieces of their breads to scoop up tiny morsels of food, and the whole procedure is quite neat. However, like everything else, it takes practice to do it the right way, and I am afraid our first attempts to do it this way would be quite clumsy.

VEGETABLE FRITTERS	*Pakoras*
SHRIMP FRITTERS	*Shrimp Bhajia*
LENTIL SOUP	
MULLIGATAWNY SOUP	
CHICKEN TANDOORI	*Tandoori Murgh*
CHICKEN WITH APRICOTS	
MEAT WITH RICE	*Biriani*
CURRIED BEEF	*Beef Vindaloo*
GROUND BEEF CURRY	*Kheema*
PLAIN RICE PILAF	*Sadah Pilau*
LENTIL STEW	*Urd Dhal*
CABBAGE CURRY	*Bandhgobi Turrcarri*
PUFFED FRIED BREAD	*Puri*
GRIDDLE CAKES	*Chapatis and Parathas*
CURRY POWDERS	*Masalah*
TOMATO CHUTNEY	*Tamattar Chutney*
MINT CHUTNEY	*Pudiina Chutney*
YOGURT	*Dhai*
CUCUMBERS WITH YOGURT	*Raita*
HALVA (Semolina Pudding)	*Suji Halva*
CARROT HALVA	*Gajjar Halva*
ROYAL SWEET DESSERT	*Shahi Tokri*
FRIED MILK BALLS	*Gulab Jamun*
CARDAMOM PUFFS	*Suji Karkarias*
CARDAMOM COOKIES	*Lurka Logs*

India   **VEGETABLE FRITTERS**   (*Pakoras*)

These tasty morsels are often served in Indian restaurants as an appetizer and in India they may be provided as a snack.

1 cup	(*250 mL*)	chick pea flour (*besam*)
		salt to taste
¼ ts	(*¼ ts*)	turmeric
¼ ts	(*¼ ts*)	ground cumin
		pinch of cayenne
		pinch of pepper
¼ ts	(*¼ ts*)	baking powder
¾ cup	(*180 mL*)	water
		raw vegetables, cut into bite-size pieces, such as carrots, eggplant, cauliflower flowerets, cucumber, green or red pepper, potatoes, onions, celery etc.
		oil for deep-frying

Stir together all the ingredients except vegetables into a batter and mix well. Dip vegetable pieces and cook in 375° F (190° C) oil until golden brown in color. (If preferable, they may be partly cooked ahead of time, cooled until ready to serve then plunged into hot oil again for 20–30 seconds.) Serve immediately as an appetizer or snack, to 4–5.

VARIATION:

If chick pea flour is unavailable, ordinary pancake-mix may be used with the addition of the seasonings. There will be a difference however, as the chick pea flour does not let the oil penetrate into the vegetable, as it might with any mix containing ordinary flour.

SHRIMP FRITTERS

India   (*Shrimp Bhajia*)

A slightly spicy dish, suitable for an appetizer, or part of a whole Indian meal.

½ lb	(*¼ kg*)	shrimp, peeled and de-veined
2 cups	(*500 mL*)	flour
1 ts	(*1 ts*)	turmeric
		pinch of cayenne
		salt to taste
1	(*1*)	small onion, finely chopped (½ cup or 125 mL)

(*Continued on next page*)

(Shrimp Fritters, cont.)

1	(*1*)	small clove of garlic, finely minced
1 ts	(*1 ts*)	finely chopped fresh mint leaves
		(or ½ ts dried)
2	(*2*)	eggs, slightly beaten
		oil for deep-frying

Cut shrimp into small pieces. Sift together flour, turmeric, cayenne, salt, then mix with onion, garlic, mint and eggs. Mix into a thick batter. If the batter should be too stiff, add a tablespoon or two of milk. Add shrimp and mix well. Drop by teaspoonfuls into 375° F (190° C) hot oil and cook until golden brown in color.

Serves 5–6.

India   **LENTIL SOUP**

Lentils are very popular in India. It is said that there are more than 50 varieties—green, yellow, black and white in addition to the round brown ones that we in the U.S. are most used to. They can be eaten in many ways; as a vegetable with meat dishes, as cakes and croquettes. Here is a lentil soup that is tasty and substantial enough to make a main dish.

1 cup	(*250 mL*)	dry lentils
2	(*2*)	slices salt pork (or bacon)
5 cups	(*1250 mL*)	water
		salt and pepper to taste
1	(*1*)	small onion, finely chopped
		(½ cup or 125 mL)
½ cup	(*125 mL*)	celery, finely chopped
1	(*1*)	bay leaf
¼ ts	(*¼ ts*)	thyme
½ ts	(*½ ts*)	sugar
		juice of half a lemon
For garnish:		**thin slices of lemon**

Soak lentils in cold water overnight. Drain and put them in a saucepan together with water, salt pork, salt and pepper and bring to a boil, then turn down heat and simmer for 2 hours. Add onion, celery, thyme, bay leaf and sugar.

Bring to a boil again, then turn down heat and simmer for another 30 minutes or until lentils, onion and celery are tender. Remove pork, then purée soup in an electric blender or pass it through a sieve, return to pan and heat thoroughly. Add lemon juice, and more salt and pepper if desired. Serve hot and garnish each portion with a thin slice of lemon.

Serves 4–5.

India   MULLIGATAWNY SOUP

It is questioned whether this soup is really an authentic Indian dish or actually concocted by or for the British during their reign in India, as it is so popular in England. No matter what, it is a very good soup and the actual translation means "pepper water." Being of the breed of cook who wants to utilize every last bit of the Thanksgiving turkey, I have found that its carcass lends itself beautifully to this soup, as the flavor does not make you think of left-over turkey.

1	(1)	frying chicken, 3-3½ lbs (1½-1¾ kg)
8 cups	(2 L)	water
1	(1)	medium size onion
4-5	(4-5)	celery tops or 2 ribs with tops
1	(1)	carrot
		a few parsley sprigs
¼ ts	(¼ ts)	whole black pepper
		salt to taste
2 tbs	(2 tbs)	curry powder
¼ cup	(60 mL)	flour
		pinch of cayenne
2 cups	(500 mL)	cooked rice
1 cup	(250 mL)	heavy cream or light cream
		lemon slices for garnish (optional)

Cut chicken into serving pieces then bring to a boil with water, onion, celery, carrot, parsley, pepper and salt, skim foam off surface, turn down heat and simmer until chicken is tender, 45 minutes–1 hour. Remove chicken pieces, skin them and cut the meat into bite-size pieces and set aside. Strain the broth and discard the solids.

Skim 4 tbs of the chicken-fat off the top and put into the pot together with the curry powder and fry for 2 minutes, add flour and cayenne and stir to mix, then add chicken broth, a little at a time, stirring constantly to obtain a smooth mixture. Add rice and chicken pieces and cook for 10 minutes. Just before serving, add heavy cream, but do not let it

come to a boil again, as it might then curdle. Serve with lemon slices, if desired, to 6.

VARIATION:

Vegetables, such as diced carrots, peas, onions etc. may be added. 1–2 cups (250–500 mL) of coconut milk (see page 70) may be substituted for the same quantity of water for a different flavor.

Instead of using the chicken, a big turkey carcass with some meat sticking to it may be disjointed and cooked. Otherwise remove meat from bones etc. as from chicken. Stewing lamb—about 3–4 lbs (1½–2 kg) may be used instead of chicken or turkey. Vegetables may be passed through a sieve, instead of being served diced.

CHICKEN TANDOORI

India   *(Tandoori Murgh)*

The word "tandoori" in this recipe refers to the clay ovens ("tandoor") that are used all over India and which may be man-high in some instances. There is, of course, a special flavor from these ovens which we can not duplicate but a closed rotisserie is a good substitute, or else, use the oven as this recipe recommends. The flavorings are different enough to make this a special dish anyway.

3	(3)	broilers, about $2\frac{1}{2}$ lbs ($1\frac{1}{4}$ kg) ea
1 ts	(1 ts)	paprika
$\frac{1}{4}$ ts	($\frac{1}{4}$ ts)	cayenne
1 ts	(1 ts)	finely diced fresh ginger (or $\frac{1}{2}$ ts powder)
1	(1)	clove garlic, finely minced
1	(1)	medium onion, finely chopped ($\frac{3}{4}$ cup or 180 mL)
4 tbs	(4 tbs)	wine vinegar
		juice of one lemon
$\frac{1}{2}$ ts	($\frac{1}{2}$ ts)	salt
2 tbs	(2 tbs)	butter, melted

Split chickens in half, clean and then pat dry. Mix together all the remaining ingredients, except butter, into a paste, rub into chicken and refrigerate for 1 hour. Place in a large baking dish and bake in a 350° F (175° C) oven (brushing several times with the melted butter) for about 30 minutes, then turn heat up to 425° F (220° C) and bake an additional 5 minutes. Serve with rice.

Makes 5–6 portions.

India   **CHICKEN WITH APRICOTS**

As mildly flavored—but still exotic—a chicken preparation as anyone would wish.

1	*(1)*	frying chicken, 3-3½ lbs (1½-1¾ kg)
1	*(1)*	large onion, finely chopped
1	*(1)*	clove garlic, finely chopped
2 tbs	*(2 tbs)*	salad oil or shortening
2	*(2)*	medium size tomatoes, peeled and chopped
1	*(1)*	cinnamon stick
½ ts	*(½ ts)*	ground ginger
½ ts	*(½ ts)*	ground cardamom
		salt to taste
1 cup	*(250 mL)*	water
1 cup	*(250 mL)*	dried apricots
¼ cup	*(60 mL)*	light cream

Cut chicken into serving pieces. Sauté onion and garlic in oil or shortening in a large skillet for 5 minutes, then add chicken pieces and sauté for 10 minutes or more, turning chicken pieces over once. Add tomatoes, cinnamon, ginger, cardamom, salt and water. Bring to a boil, cover, turn down heat to very low and simmer for 30 minutes. Add apricots and continue simmering until they are tender but not soft and mushy, 15–20 minutes. Add cream and mix well.

Serve to 4–6.

MEAT WITH RICE

India   *(Biriani)*

*If a somewhat more bland mixture is desired, use a little less of the chili. This
dish is only moderately hot, though.*

2 lbs	*(1 kg)*	boneless beef, lamb or pork, cut into 1″ (25 mm) pieces
2 cups	*(500 mL)*	water
		a few sprigs of parsley or coriander leaves
1	*(1)*	slice of fresh ginger, 1/2″ (12 mm) thick, finely chopped
2	*(2)*	pieces stick cinnamon
1	*(1)*	small chili, seeded and finely minced or 1/4 ts dried chili
5	*(5)*	cardamoms, crushed
6	*(6)*	whole cloves
		salt to taste
2 cups	*(500 mL)*	rice
1/2 cup	*(125 mL)*	butter
1 tbs	*(1 tbs)*	ground coriander seeds
1 ts	*(1 ts)*	cumin
1 ts	*(1 ts)*	turmeric
1/4 ts	*(1/4 ts)*	cayenne pepper
4	*(4)*	cloves garlic, finely minced
1 cup	*(250 mL)*	raisins, rinsed
4	*(4)*	medium size onions, thickly sliced
1/4 cup	*(60 mL)*	blanched and slivered almonds

Rinse meat and cook in water together with parsley, ginger, 1 cinnamon stick, chili and salt until meat is thoroughly tender, 1–2 hours, depending on the cut. Drain off liquid and set aside meat.

Put remaining cinnamon stick, cardamoms and cloves in a small piece of cheesecloth and tie it. Melt half of the butter in a large saucepan and add rice and cook until translucent, then add turmeric, ground coriander seeds, cumin, cayenne, the cheesecloth bag, garlic, raisins, and water to reach 1½″ (38 mm) above the rice, bring to a boil, then turn down heat and simmer until rice is tender.

In the meantime, fry onions in remaining butter for about 5 minutes, but they should still be crisp, then add meat and heat thoroughly, then combine this with rice mixture together with slivered almonds, and cook it all together for about 5 minutes, then serve.   For 5–6 people.

VARIATION:

Biriani may also be made with chicken. For the above, use a fryer of about 3 lbs (1½ kg), otherwise proceed as above.

CURRIED BEEF

India   *(Beef Vindaloo)*

This is a quite spicy dish and be sure to have a glass of cold water on hand to drink when you taste it, in case it is too hot for you.

2 lbs	*(1 kg)*	lean beef, cut into ¾″ (18 mm) cubes
1	*(1)*	large onion, chopped (1 cup or 250 mL)
1	*(1)*	clove garlic, finely minced
2 tbs	*(2 tbs)*	butter or margarine
1½ tbs	*(1½ tbs)*	curry powder (see pages 254 and 255)
½ ts	*(½ ts)*	ground ginger
2 tbs	*(2 tbs)*	vinegar
2 cups	*(500 mL)*	beef stock or water
		salt to taste
2 tbs	*(2 tbs)*	lemon juice

Sauté onion and garlic in butter or margarine until onion is transparent, then add spices and vinegar and stir until well blended. Add beef and cook for about 10 minutes, stirring off and on and turning meat cubes on all sides. Add the stock or water and bring to a boil, turn down heat and simmer, covered, about 45 minutes– 1 hour, or until meat is tender. Add salt and lemon juice just before serving with boiled rice.

For 5–6 portions.

GROUND BEEF CURRY

India   *(Kheema)*

An easy chopped meat dish, fairly hot.

2	*(2)*	medium onions, chopped (1½ cups or 375 mL)
4	*(4)*	cloves garlic, coarsely chopped
1 tbs	*(1 tbs)*	fresh ginger, coarsely chopped
¼ cup	*(60 mL)*	water
¼ cup	*(60 mL)*	cooking oil
4	*(4)*	whole peppercorns
4	*(4)*	whole cloves
1	*(1)*	stick cinnamon
1	*(1)*	bay leaf
1–2	*(1–2)*	chilies, seeded and chopped
1 tbs	*(1 tbs)*	ground coriander

(Continued on next page)

(Ground Beef Curry, cont.)

1 ts	(*1 ts*)	**cumin, crushed**
½ ts	(*½ ts*)	**turmeric**
1	(*1*)	**large tomato, peeled and chopped**
1½ lbs	(*¾ kg*)	**ground chuck beef**
		salt to taste
½ cup	(*125 mL*)	**water**
1 tbs	(*1 tbs*)	**lemon juice**

Put onion, garlic and ginger in blender together with water and blend to a purée. In a large fry pan heat oil, add peppercorns, cloves, cinnamon, bay leaf and peppers and fry for 10 seconds. Add purée from blender and fry while stirring off and on for five minutes. Add coriander, cumin, turmeric and fry an additional five minutes, then add tomatoes, meat and salt. Fry over high heat to brown meat, breaking up lumps with a fork, add water and simmer for about one hour. Just before serving, add lemon juice. Serve with rice, or chapatis (see page 254). For 5–6 portions.

PLAIN RICE PILAF

India (*Sadah Polau*)

Plain pilafs are used instead of plain rice and are served with curried meat-dishes, or curried lentils.

2	(*2*)	**medium size onions, thinly sliced**
2 tbs	(*2 tbs*)	**butter or margarine**
1 cup	(*250 mL*)	**rice**
½ ts	(*½ ts*)	**salt**
2 cups	(*500 mL*)	**hot water, approximately**
⅓ cup	(*80 mL*)	**blanched, slivered almonds**
½ cup	(*125 mL*)	**seedless raisins**
1 cup	(*250 mL*)	**cooked green peas**

In a large skillet sauté onion in 1 tbs butter until lightly browned, remove onion and set aside. Rinse rice in several waters, draining each time. Melt remaining butter in a skillet, add rice and cook over medium heat while stirring until rice becomes translucent. This should take about 8–10 minutes. Add water, a little at a time at first, and let it get absorbed by the rice, then remaining water and bring to a boil. Add salt, almonds, raisins and cook over low heat until rice is tender, then add peas and a bit more water if rice mixture should be too dry. Just before serving, warm up the onions and sprinkle them on top. For 5–6 people.

India　　　　　　　　　　**LENTIL STEW**　　　　　　　　*(Urd Dhal)*

The "urd" lentils that are supposed to be used for this dish are almost impossible to get in this country. I have used the lentils you can find in most super-markets instead and the dish still tastes good with these. But nothing will quite equal the Urd Dhal I first tasted in Kashmir, made with urd lentils by a lovely lady in a sari.

1½ cups	*(375 mL)*	lentils
½ cup	*(125 mL)*	red beans or kidney beans
1	*(1)*	thin slice fresh ginger, finely minced, or ½ ts powdered ginger
2	*(2)*	cloves garlic, finely minced
2 tbs	*(2 tbs)*	tomato paste
		salt to taste
¼ ts	*(¼ ts)*	cayenne, or slightly more if desired

Soak beans only in cold water over-night. Cook beans and lentils in slightly salted water until almost tender. This should be done in two pots, as the lentils get soft sooner than the beans and they get mushy if over-cooked. Combine lentils and beans with remaining ingredients and cook until well done, stirring off and on to prevent scorching. Check for season-ings and add a little bit more cayenne if a spicy dish is desired.

Serves 5–6.

CABBAGE CURRY

India　　　　　　　　　　　　　　*(Bandhgobi Turrcarri)*

In India not only meats are curried but vegetables too. Cabbage lends itself nicely to this way of cooking.

1	*(1)*	medium head of cabbage (about 2 lbs or 1 kg) finely shredded
2	*(2)*	medium size onions, finely chopped (1½ cups or 375 mL)
3 tbs	*(3 tbs)*	butter
2 tbs	*(2 tbs)*	finely minced pimento
1½ ts	*(1½ ts)*	turmeric
¼ ts	*(¼ ts)*	cayenne pepper
¼ ts	*(¼ ts)*	coriander
		salt to taste
		juice of ½ lemon

(Continued on next page)

(Cabbage Curry, cont.)

Sauté onion in butter for a few minutes, then add shredded cabbage and cook while stirring off and on for about 10 minutes. Add remaining ingredients, mix well, cover pot and simmer until cabbage is tender. The time will depend upon how fresh the cabbage is. Start checking after 10 minutes.

Serves 5–6.

PUFFED FRIED BREAD

India   (*Puri*)

It seems like a miracle when you make these bread puffs. There is no baking powder or yeast, but still they puff out like balloons and then taste like real bread. They are fun to make and good to eat.

2½ cups	(*625 mL*)	whole wheat flour
¼ ts	(¼ *ts*)	salt
½ cup	(*125 mL*)	warm water
1 tbs	(*1 tbs*)	melted butter
		oil for deep-frying

Mix salt with flour, add water and mix into a soft dough. Add melted butter and work dough until smooth and elastic, either by kneading on a floured board or by working it in your hands, about 10 minutes altogether. Let dough rest for a half hour.

Heat oil to 350° F (175° C). Break off pieces of dough, the size of walnuts, then flatten into about 4″ (100 mm) circles, either with a rolling pin or with your hands. Carefully put dough rounds into the hot oil, a few at a time, and cook until they puff up and are golden in color, about 30 seconds, then turn over and cook about 10 seconds on the other side.

A more even puffing is achieved if you use a spatula to hold the dough rounds just below the surface of the oil, when the cooking first takes place.

Remove with a slotted spoon and drain on paper toweling. Serve warm.

Serves 4–6.

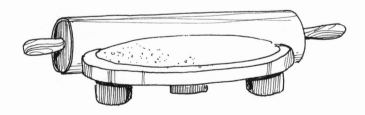

GRIDDLE CAKES

India
(Chapatis and *Parathas)*

Do not get confused by the name "griddle cakes." They are not soft like our griddle cakes but are solid in texture and are eaten as bread. They are usually torn into bite-size pieces and used to scoop up whatever you have on your plate, be it meat, vegetables or rice.

2 cups	(500 mL)	whole wheat flour
³/₄ ts	(³/₄ ts)	salt
1 cup	(250 mL)	water (approximate)

Mix together flour and salt and add water and stir well until mixture is smooth. If mixture is too stiff, add a bit more water, if too loose add a bit more flour. Knead well on a floured baking board until dough is shiny, then cover it with a cloth and let it rest for about 1 hour.

Knead the dough again for a minute or so, then pinch off pieces the size of a walnut, flatten with the palms of your hands then roll out as thin as possible, (paper-thin if you can do it). Cut into rounds, 6–8" (150–200 mm) in diameter, and cook on an un-greased griddle with medium heat. When slight bubbles appear on top, turn over the cake and cook on the other side. Keep them hot by placing them in a thick napkin. Serve hot, either plain or with butter.

VARIATION: PARATHAS

Proceed as above but use 2 tbs of melted butter for brushing. After the griddle cake has been rolled out the first time, brush with melted butter, then turn over the sides to hide the butter, then roll out the cake again into a round shape. For these the griddle should be slightly buttered when they are cooked.

CURRY POWDER, fairly mild

India
(Masalah)

If you like to have some of your own curry powder ready to use, here follow two versions—one mild and one hot.

3 tbs	(3 tbs)	ground coriander
1 tbs	(1 tbs)	ground cumin
2 tbs	(2 tbs)	ground turmeric
1 tbs	(1 tbs)	ground ginger

Mix well and store in an airtight jar.

CURRY POWDER, more pungent
India   (*Masalah*)

3 tbs	(*3 tbs*)	coriander seeds
2 tbs	(*2 tbs*)	caraway seeds
1 tbs	(*1 tbs*)	crushed red pepper
1 tbs	(*1 tbs*)	whole cloves
2	(*2*)	cardamon pods, shell removed and only seeds retained
2 tbs	(*2 tbs*)	ground turmeric
1 tbs	(*1 tbs*)	ground cinnamon
¼ ts	(*¼ ts*)	cayenne pepper

Bake the five first ingredients in a 250° F (120° C) oven for 15 minutes, then grind while still hot in an electric blender or pound to a powder with a mortar and pestle. When a smooth powder has been obtained, mix with the three remaining spices. When cool, store in an airtight container.

TOMATO CHUTNEY
India   (*Tamattar Chutney*)

Chutneys may be made part of something served at practically every meal and go nicely with curries.

6–8	(*6–8*)	cloves of garlic, coarsely chopped
2 tbs	(*2 tbs*)	coarsely chopped fresh ginger
1½ cups	(*375 mL*)	wine vinegar
6	(*6*)	medium size tomatoes, peeled and chopped
1 ts	(*1 ts*)	salt
1½ cups	(*375 mL*)	sugar
2 tbs	(*2 tbs*)	golden raisins

Put garlic, ginger and ½ cup (125 mL) of the vinegar in a blender and make a purée. Put tomatoes, sugar, salt and remaining vinegar in a pot, then add purée and mix well. Bring to a boil, turn down heat to very low and simmer 1½–2 hours or until mixture has thickened. Add raisins and cook an additional 10 minutes. Makes 2–2½ cups (500–625 mL) of chutney.

MINT CHUTNEY

India   (*Pudiina Chutney*)

1 cup	(*250 mL*)	fresh mint leaves, firmly packed
1	(*1*)	large onion, finely chopped (1 cup or 250 mL)
1	(*1*)	medium size tomato, finely chopped (½ cup or 125 mL)
¼ cup	(*60 mL*)	lemon juice
		salt to taste

Wash mint leaves and pat them dry with paper toweling, then chop them finely. Mix with remaining ingredients and let stand for at least a couple of hours to blend the flavors before using. Serve as an accompaniment to curry dishes.

Makes 1½–2 cups (375–500 mL).

YOGURT

India   (*Dhai*)

Yogurt is used in many dishes, and eaten with almost every meal in India, so that if commercial yogurt were used entirely, it would get much too expensive. It is easy to make, however, and you do not need any special yogurt makers for it.

4 cups	(*1 L*)	milk
2 tbs	(*2 tbs*)	plain yogurt

Bring milk to boiling point, remove from heat and cool until luke-warm (test by putting a few drops on the inside of your wrist, as you do when you test the temperature of a baby's bottle), then stir in yogurt and mix well. Pour into a glass bowl, cover, wrap some cloth around the bowl and put near a warm place, such as a radiator, on top of a heater in the basement, or something like that. Let it stand for at least 8 hours, by which time the yogurt should have formed (it is then jelly-like in consistency). If not, let it stand a couple more hours.

If you wish to have mild flavored yogurt, use the shortest time possible (sometimes it will form in about 5–6 hours), and if a more tart version is desired, let it stand for 10–12 hours. Before you use it, let it stand at least 2 hours in the refrigerator. Remember to save 2 tbs of this yogurt to be used for the next batch you will make. Some sugar, vanilla or other sweetener or flavor may be used, if desired.

CUCUMBERS WITH YOGURT

India *(Raita)*

*Yogurt is used in many ways and in many dishes. Here is a recipe for a
cool-tasting dish that goes well with spicy meats.*

1	*(1)*	medium size cucumber, peeled and coarsely grated
½ ts	*(½ ts)*	ground cumin
		salt and pepper to taste
1 cup	*(250 mL)*	yogurt (natural flavor)
1 tbs	*(1 tbs)*	chopped fresh coriander, or if not available, chopped parsley

Mix together all the ingredients, except parsley, and chill for several hours in refrigerator. Just before serving, add chopped parsley. Serve as an accompaniment to meat.

Serves 5–6.

HALVA (SEMOLINA PUDDING)

India *(Sugi Halva)*

*Halva is a dish that is popular not only in India but all over the Middle East as
well. In India it is eaten not only as a dessert, but also as a breakfast cereal.*

½ cup	*(125 mL)*	butter or margarine
1 cup	*(250 mL)*	semolina or farina
1 cup	*(250 mL)*	sugar
1½ cups	*(375 mL)*	water
¼ cup	*(60 mL)*	chopped walnuts or almonds (or more, if desired)
¼ cup	*(60 mL)*	golden raisins

In a large frying pan heat butter or margarine, add semolina or farina and cook while stirring off and on until golden brown in color, about 15 minutes.

In the meantime make a syrup of sugar and water and cook for 15 minutes, then add syrup to frying pan and mix well. Add nuts and raisins and cook an additional 15 minutes, stirring off and on. It should have the consistency of a thick porridge. It may be eaten either very hot or after chilling in refrigerator.

Serves 4–6.

CARROT HALVA

India   *(Gajjar Halva)*

It seems strange to us here to have carrots in a dessert, but a sweet and rich dessert it is.

1 lb	(½ kg)	carrots
½ cup	(125 mL)	butter or *ghee* (clarified butter)
1 cup	(250 mL)	sugar
1 tbs	(1 tbs)	cream
½ cup	(125 mL)	raisins
½ cup	(125 mL)	nuts or almonds, chopped

Peel and grate carrots finely and put into a heavy bottom saucepan. Cook over very slow heat until carrots begin to stick to bottom, then add butter and keep cooking while stirring off and on for 15 minutes. Add sugar and continue cooking for an additional 15–20 minutes, then add cream, raisins and nuts. Cook an additional 15 minutes and serve warm. It may also be chilled and served cool, with cream, if desired.

Serves 4–5.

Ghee:

To make ghee, which is the same as clarified butter (also called drawn butter), melt butter over low heat, remove from heat and let it stand for a few minutes to allow the milk solids to sink to the bottom, then just skim the butter fat off the top, putting it into a container, and discard the solids on the bottom. This clarified butter will keep quite well for further use.

ROYAL SWEET DESSERT

India   *(Shahi Tokri)*

I would have guessed that the bread squares would have been soggy after being left in a syrup for 30 minutes, but this is not the case, as you will find out. It is quite a good dessert.

1 cup	(250 mL)	sugar
1 cup	(250 mL)	water
4	(4)	slices white bread (they should be ¾″ (20 mm) thick, so unsliced bread is necessary for this)
⅓ cup	(80 mL)	salad oil or ghee

(Continued on next page)

(Royal Sweet Dessert, cont.)

Make a syrup by boiling sugar and water together until sugar is melted. Trim crusts off bread slices and cut into four squares. Heat oil or ghee in a skillet and fry bread squares on both sides until golden brown, about one minute on each side. Add bread squares to syrup and leave them in this for about 30 minutes. Remove bread from syrup and put it in a single layer in a serving dish. Cover with *khoya* and serve either slightly warm, or chilled.

Khoya

4 cups   (*1 L*)   milk

This is an Indian name for milk that has been boiled down to such an extent that it is only $\frac{1}{3}$ or $\frac{1}{2}$ of its original quantity. To do this bring the milk to an "almost" boil, that is, it is supposed to bubble but not so hard that it boils over. It has to be stirred off and on during the whole process which may take a long time, up to one hour. Make sure it does not stick to bottom and then get scorched.

I have found this procedure goes a little faster if I do it in an electric frying pan, preferably with a teflon bottom which reduces sticking and scorching, and keeping it at a temperature of 225°. It still has to be stirred off and on, and the sides need to be scraped free of the slightly hardened milk that sticks there.

VARIATION:

If you do not have the patience to wait for the milk to reduce as described above, you may use dry milk powder—1 cup (250 mL) to $\frac{1}{4}$ cup (60 mL) of water. As most milk powders are without fat content you will have to add about 2 tbs of heavy cream to the above. You will have a usable thick milk this way, but it does not taste as good as when it is done the real way.

You may use whipped cream instead of *khoya*, but you will lose the Indian touch.

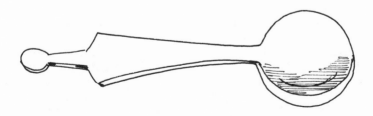

FRIED MILK BALLS

India   (*Gulab Jamun*)

Many desserts from both the Middle and the Far East contain heavy syrups. This makes them, of course, very sweet but tasty just the same.

1 cup	(*250 mL*)	milk powder
¼ cup	(*60 mL*)	flour
¼ ts	(*¼ ts*)	baking powder
3 tbs	(*3 tbs*)	heavy cream
¼ cup	(*60 mL*)	milk
1 cup	(*250 mL*)	sugar
1 cup	(*250 mL*)	water
		oil for deep frying

Make a syrup by boiling sugar and water until all sugar has melted. Make a soft dough by mixing milk powder, flour, baking powder, cream and milk and working it into a ball. Shape into smooth balls, about ¾" (20 mm) in diameter and fry in oil 5–6 at a time, at about 325° F (160° C) until balls are reddish brown in color.

It is important that the heat is not too high, in which case they would brown too quickly and the insides would remain raw. When ready, put them into the syrup and bring to a boil and let the balls simmer in the syrup for about 5 minutes. Cover the pot and leave them in syrup for about one hour. They can be eaten slightly warmed up, at room temperature, or chilled. Serve the balls only, not the syrup.

CARDAMOM PUFFS

India   (*Suji Karkarias*)

These puffs are nice to serve with tea or coffee.

1 cup	(*250 mL*)	milk
¼ cup	(*60 mL*)	sugar
⅓ cup	(*80 mL*)	farina
1 tbs	(*1 tbs*)	butter
1	(*1*)	egg
½ ts	(*½ ts*)	ground cardamom
1 tbs	(*1 tbs*)	ground almonds
		oil for deep-frying

(*Continued on next page*)

(Cardamon Puffs, cont.)

Cook farina with milk and sugar until thick, about 3 minutes, remove from heat and add butter and stir to mix. Allow to cool. Beat egg until light and fluffy, then add farina and cardamom and mix well. Drop by tea-spoonfuls into hot oil (375° F) (190° C) and turn them while frying so that they get evenly golden brown. Drain on paper toweling. Serve as a snack.

Serves 4–5.

CARDAMOM COOKIES

India   (*Lurka Logs*)

A mild-flavored cookie which does not mean "logs" as we would think but rather in translation from an Indian dialect would mean "boys." Anyway, I think boys, young and old, will like them.

½ cup	(*125 mL*)	butter
⅔ cup	(*160 mL*)	sugar
1	(*1*)	egg
1½ cup	(*375 mL*)	flour
1 ts	(*1 ts*)	baking powder
¼ ts	(*¼ ts*)	ground cardamom
¼ ts	(*¼ ts*)	salt

For sprinkling: sugar
                                         grated coconut

Stir butter and sugar until light and fluffy, add egg and continue stirring until well blended. Sift together flour, baking powder, cardamom and salt and add gradually to butter mixture. Drop ½ ts portions onto a greased cookie sheet about 2″ apart. Flatten to about ⅛″ (2 mm) thickness with the back of a wooden spoon, dipped in flour. Sprinkle with sugar and grated coconut and bake in a 375° F (190° C) oven 8–10 minutes, or until cookies are golden brown around the edges. Cool on baking sheet for a minute, then put on wire rack to cool. Store in air-tight container.

Makes about 4 dozen.

Ireland

THIS name, when related to cuisine, immediately brings to mind potatoes and cabbage. These staple foods do play an important part in Ireland, but there is of course much more to it than that.

Ireland is a poor country as far as agriculture is concerned, the soil in most places is meagre and there is not enough sunshine to bring bumper crops. But they have learned to do with what they have, and some of their dishes (lamb stew for example) have become well known everywhere; down to earth, wholesome and good as they are.

They use their favorite Irish whiskey in making one of the easiest desserts there is to prepare—Irish coffee—that is, if you want to *drink* your dessert. Otherwise, tea is the most common daily drink.

BAKED COD IN CIDER
WEXFORD MACKEREL
IRISH STEW
DONEGAL PIE
TRIPE WITH ONIONS
POTATOES WITH CABBAGE   *Colcannon*
BOXTY
KERRY APPLE CAKE
IRISH SODA BREAD
IRISH SCONES
SYRUP TART   *Treacle Tart*
IRISH COFFEE

BAKED COD IN CIDER

Ireland

A refreshing lemon flavor lingers with this dish. Therefore it is excellent if your fish has been in the freezer, as it causes that "frozen flavor" to disappear.

1½ lbs	(¾ kg)	cod slices or fillets
1	(1)	medium onion, sliced thin
½	(½)	lemon, sliced very thin
		salt and pepper to taste
⅓ cup	(80 mL)	dry bread crumbs
1 tbs	(1 tbs)	butter
⅓ cup	(80 mL)	apple cider
2 tbs	(2 tbs)	vinegar
For sprinkling		chopped parsley (optional)

Put fish in a buttered baking dish, put onion and lemon slices on top, add salt and pepper to taste, then sprinkle with bread crumbs, and dot with butter. Mix together cider and vinegar and add to baking dish. Bake in a 350° F (175° C) oven for 35 minutes. Serve immediately, sprinkled with chopped parsley, if desired.

Serves 4–6.

WEXFORD MACKEREL

Ireland

This recipe is for those only who have access to clean, unpolluted ocean water. In the fishing town of Wexford (and maybe also in other fishing towns) the fishermen cook mackerel in sea water, without any other ingredients. It gives a wonderful flavor to mackerel and to other salt water fish and shellfish. I tried it out with enthusiasm, as I had never eaten shrimp that was not cooked in sea water before I came to the U.S., as boiling in sea water is the common way of preparing shrimp on the west coast of Sweden.

1½–2 lbs	(¾–1 kg)	mackerel
		sea water

Cut fish into serving pieces, barely cover with fresh, clean sea water and poach gently until mackerel is cooked and flaky, about 15 minutes. No other seasonings are needed.

IRISH STEW

Ireland

One of the most well-known Irish contributions to cooking everywhere.

3–4 lbs	*(1½–2 kg)*	stewing lamb, cut into serving pieces
1 cup	*(250 mL)*	water
1	*(1)*	bay leaf
2	*(2)*	sprigs of parsley
8–10	*(8–10)*	peppercorns
		salt to taste
1	*(1)*	small yellow turnip, about 1 lb (½ kg) cut into ½″ (12 mm) cubes
2	*(2)*	medium size onions, quartered
4	*(4)*	medium size carrots, cut into ½″ (12 mm) cubes
3	*(3)*	medium size potatoes, cut into ½″ (12 mm) cubes
2 tbs	*(2 tbs)*	flour, mixed with ¼ cup (60 mL) water (optional)

Bring meat and water, bay leaf, parsley, peppercorns and salt to a boil. Skim off foam, then turn down heat and simmer about 1–1½ hours. If desired, let meat cool and put it in the refrigerator together with the broth for a couple of hours until the fat has coagulated and can be lifted off the top. Heat meat and broth again and add the vegetables and cook until they are tender. If desired, thicken with flour mixed with water and cook for 5 minutes, otherwise put stew on table as it is.   Serves 5–6.

DONEGAL PIE

Ireland

2 lbs	(*1 kg*)	potatoes, cooked and mashed with milk and butter
		salt and pepper to taste
3	(*3*)	hard-boiled eggs
3	(*3*)	slices bacon
		pastry for top (see single pastry on page 54)

Fry bacon until crisp, then remove and crumble it. Put half the amount of mashed potatoes into a greased 8″ (200 mm) pie pan. Slice hard-boiled eggs and put on top of potatoes, then sprinkle with crumbled bacon pieces and bacon fat. Add remaining pota-toes on top. Roll out pastry to fit top of pie pan, then seal around the edges. Make a few slits on top to let steam escape. Bake in a 400° F (200° C) oven for about 20 minutes or until pie crust is golden brown.
Serves 4–5.

TRIPE WITH ONIONS

Ireland

Tripe is a food that most people like to leave well enough alone. But some like it and Ireland has a good way of preparing it.

1 lb	(½ *kg*)	honeycomb tripe
2	(*2*)	medium size onions, finely sliced
2	(*2*)	whole cloves
2 tbs	(*2 tbs*)	butter or margarine
1½ cups	(*375 mL*)	milk, or cream and milk mixed
2 tbs	(*2 tbs*)	flour
		salt and pepper to taste

Wash tripe well in cold water, then cook in water to cover for two hours, or longer if tripe is not tender at that time. Drain and cut into small pieces. Sauté onion in butter or margarine for five minutes, but do not let it get brown, then add cloves, 1 cup (250 mL) milk and the tripe pieces, bring to a boil, turn down heat and cook over low heat until onions are tender. Mix remaining milk with flour and stir in to thicken mixture, season with salt and pepper and serve with either mashed potatoes or on toast.
Serves 4–5.

POTATOES WITH CABBAGE

Ireland   *(Colcannon)*

A nice combination of cabbage and potatoes in this traditional Irish dish.

3	(3)	medium size potatoes, about 1 lb (½ kg)
½ cup	(125 mL)	milk (approximately)
3 cups	(750 mL)	green cabbage, finely shredded
		salt and pepper to taste
3	(3)	slices bacon
1	(1)	medium size onion, finely chopped (¾ cup or 180 mL)
2 tbs	(2 tbs)	butter or margarine

Peel and cut potatoes into small pieces and cook until tender in salted water. Drain and mash them, adding milk a little at a time. Cook cabbage in salted water until tender, about 10 minutes. Fry bacon until crisp and set aside. Sauté onion in bacon fat until transparent, then mix together with mashed potatoes and cabbage and add salt and pepper.

Put into a baking dish, dot with butter and bake in a 375° F (190° C) oven about 10–15 minutes, or until golden in color. Crumble fried bacon on top and serve immediately.

Serves 4–5.

BOXTY

Ireland

A specialty of Ireland that makes a nice snack with coffee or tea.

2 cups	(500 mL)	peeled grated raw potatoes
1 cup	(250 mL)	flour
1 ts	(1 ts)	baking powder
1 ts	(1 ts)	salt
½ cup	(125 mL)	milk
1	(1)	egg, slightly beaten
3 tbs	(3 tbs)	butter or margarine, melted

Put grated potatoes in a cheesecloth or clean towel and squeeze out as much moisture as is possible. Sift together flour, baking powder and salt and add to potatoes together with milk and beaten egg and mix well. Brush a hot griddle with melted butter and drop by tablespoonfuls for each cake and cook about 2–3 minutes on each side, until golden brown and the raw potato is cooked. Serve warm, with butter and sprinkled with sugar, with tea or coffee.

Makes about 18.

KERRY APPLE CAKE

Ireland

Ireland's special apple dessert.

1½ cup	(375 mL)	flour
½ cup	(125 mL)	sugar
1 ts	(1 ts)	baking powder
½ ts	(½ ts)	cinnamon
¼ ts	(¼ ts)	ground cloves
¼ ts	(¼ ts)	salt
½ cup	(125 mL)	butter or margarine
1	(1)	egg, slightly beaten
⅓ cup	(80 mL)	milk
3	(3)	medium size apples, peeled and thinly sliced, (about 2½ cups or 625 mL)

For sprinkling: ¼ cup (60 mL) brown sugar

Sift together flour, sugar, baking powder and spices. Cut in butter or margarine with a pastry blender until mixture is coarse crumbs. Add egg and milk and blend well to a stiff batter. Mix in apple slices and spread in a greased 9″ (220 mm) square baking pan. Sprinkle top with brown sugar, bake in a 375° F (190° C) oven 25 minutes. Serve warm, with whipped cream if desired.

Serves 6–8.

IRISH SODA BREAD

Ireland

4 cups	(1 L)	flour
2 ts	(2 ts)	baking soda
1 ts	(1 ts)	baking powder
1 ts	(1 ts)	salt
2 tbs	(2 tbs)	sugar
1½ cup	(375 mL)	buttermilk (if not available, add 1½ tbs lemon juice or vinegar to 1½ cup (375 mL) fresh milk and let it stand for a few minutes)
1 cup	(250 mL)	raisins

For brushing: 1 tbs melted butter or margarine

(Continued on next page)

(Irish Soda Bread, cont.)

Sift together dry ingredients and mix well. Stir in buttermilk, using a fork, until mixture is moist but still lumpy. Add raisins and mix in. Turn out dough on a baking board, dusted with flour, knead lightly, then shape into a round ball. Place on a greased baking sheet and flatten ball into an 8″ (200 mm) circle. With a sharp knife, cut a cross on top, about ¼″ (6 mm) deep. Bake in a 375° F (190° C) oven 35–40 minutes, or until bread is golden in color and has a hollow sound when you tap it on the bottom. Brush with melted butter as soon as it is removed from oven, then cool on wire rack.

VARIATION:

If desired, 1 tbs of caraway seeds may be added with the dry ingredients.

IRISH SCONES

Ireland

2 cups	(500 mL)	flour
2 ts	(2 ts)	baking powder
½ ts	(½ ts)	baking soda
2 ts	(2 ts)	sugar
1 ts	(1 ts)	salt
¼ cup	(60 mL)	shortening
¾ cup	(180 mL)	buttermilk (if unavailable, add 2 ts vinegar to the same amount of fresh milk and let it stand for 5 minutes)

Sift together flour, baking powder, baking soda, sugar and salt, then cut in shortening with a pastry cutter until mixture resembles coarse crumbs. Add milk and mix well into a ball, scraping the sides of the bowl to get all the crumbs. Knead on floured board for about 10 seconds then divide dough into two parts. Flatten each one into a round cake, about ¾″ (18 mm) thick, cut into six pie-shaped wedges and bake in a 450° F (230° C) oven 8–10 minutes. Serve them split open with butter and jam while still warm. (If used later when cold, they may be split and toasted.)

Makes 12 scones.

SYRUP TART

Ireland   *(Treacle Tart)*

If you are afriad that a tart made with so much syrup will be overly sweet, rest assured that the lemon juice makes it amazingly refreshing instead.

1	*(1)*	tart shell (see page 39)
Filling:		
1-½ cups	*(375 mL)*	Irish golden syrup (imported) or if unavailable use ½ cup (125 mL) molasses and 1 cup (250 mL) light corn syrup)
¼ cup	*(60 mL)*	lemon juice
		grated rind of one lemon
2	*(2)*	slices white bread, crusts removed and finely crumbled
2	*(2)*	eggs, slightly beaten

In order to protect the tart shell from scorching during baking, park it in the freezer for at least one hour before filling.

FILLING:

Beat syrup with lemon juice and rind until well mixed, add eggs and bread crumbs and continue beating until a smooth mixture has been obtained. Poor into tart shell and bake in a 400° F (200° C) oven for 15 minutes, then turn down heat to 350° F (175° C) and bake an additional 25 minutes. Remove from oven and let cool before serving.   Serves 6–8.

IRISH COFFEE

Ireland

Heat stemmed goblets. In each, pour one jigger (3 tbs) of Irish whiskey, add 1 ts sugar and fill with strong black coffee up to about 1″ (25 mm) from the top. Fill to the top with whipped cream and serve without stirring.

Israel

Squeezed in among several Middle Eastern countries as it is, I feel Israel ought to have a little write-up by itself, not for political reasons but because it is such a new country with a mixture of the very old and very modern. It is such a melting pot of people who have arrived from every corner of the world, and who have brought with them their own ways of cooking from the countries they came from, which were not always directed by the dietary laws of Judaism. Israel is also striving for an identity of its own as a country, and tries to encourage foods that it feels are its very own.

With their accomplishments in making the deserts bloom with citrus and other fruits, there is a great enthusiasm for these. At formal dinners appetizers in the American fashion, with fruit cocktails, or avocados stuffed with either fruit or seafood, are very popular.

In many ways the modern Israelites eat very similar foods to those in the U.S. and Europe. Of course, there is a segment of the population who keep to the Kosher diets, and as in many other religions, around the holidays almost everyone uses the traditional foods regardless of how seriously they take their religious aspect.

Among the Arabs in Israel you will find that the foods they eat are very much the same as in other Middle East countries. (One of these foods has become popular to such an extent that it is almost a national Israeli dish—I am referring to *"falafel"*—a spicy chickpea mixture that is eaten with *pitta*, the Arabian flat bread, and often sold from push-carts by street vendors.)

CHICKPEA CROQUETTES   *Falafel*
FISH COCKTAIL
ESAU'S POTTAGE (LENTIL SOUP)   *Mujadarrah*
FISH SOUFFLE
BARBECUED CHICKEN
CARROT PUDDING
CARROT CAKE
ORANGE CHEESE CAKE
CHALLAH

CHICKPEA CROQUETTES

Israel   (*Falafel*)

2 cups	(*500 mL*)	cooked chickpeas (about 1 lb or 500 g can)
2–3	(*2–3*)	cloves garlic, finely minced
½ cup	(*125 mL*)	flour
1 ts	(*1 ts*)	baking powder
		salt to taste
¼ ts	(*¼ ts*)	cayenne pepper
1	(*1*)	egg
		oil for deep-frying

Grind chickpeas either in a food-mill or a blender, then mix well with remaining ingredients. Shape into small croquettes and deep-fry in hot oil, 375° F (190° C) until golden in color, about one minute. Remove and drain on paper towels. Makes about 2 dozen. Serve as appetizer or snack.

FISH COCKTAIL

Israel

A very nice appetizer which uses humble ingredients to a sophisticated end.

1 lb	(½ kg)	fish fillets (haddock, bass or cod)
1	(1)	slice lemon
1	(1)	small onion, sliced
1	(1)	carrot, sliced
		salt and pepper to taste
1½ cups	(375 mL)	water
¼ cup	(60 mL)	finely chopped dill pickles
		(or sweet pickles, if preferred)
1 tbs	(1 tbs)	capers

Cook onion and carrots with salt and pepper in water for 10 minutes, add fish and lemon slice, and poach gently until fish is flaky but still firm, about 15 minutes. Remove fish from broth and cool, then either cut into ½" (12 mm) pieces or flake it with a fork. Add pickles and capers and mix carefully so that fish pieces do not break up. Divide into small serving bowls and put the following dressing on top.

Dressing:

½ cup	(125 mL)	mayonnaise
2 tbs	(2 tbs)	lemon juice, freshly squeezed
½ cup	(125 mL)	ketchup
2 tbs	(2 tbs)	brandy

Decoration:		lemon, cut into wedges

Serves 4–5.

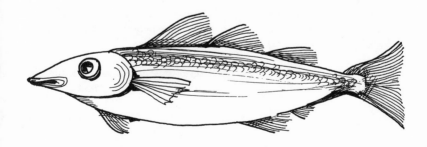

ESAU'S POTTAGE (LENTIL SOUP)

Israel   (*Mujadarrah*)

Lentils may have been one of the earliest food staples of mankind. They are mentioned in Genesis XXV:34—"Then Jacob gave Esau bread and pottage of lentils. . . ." Whether this soup actually originated in Israel proper, I am not sure of as the name Mujadarrah gives me no clue, but anyway it must be from that general region.

1	(*1*)	small onion, chopped
1	(*1*)	clove garlic, finely minced
2 tbs	(*2 tbs*)	olive oil
1 cup	(*250 mL*)	lentils
4 cups	(*1 L*)	water (or beef broth)
¼ cup	(*60 mL*)	rice
1	(*1*)	bay leaf
		salt and pepper to taste

Sauté onion and garlic in olive oil for five minutes then add lentils and stir. Add water, rice and seasonings, bring to a boil, then turn down heat and simmer until lentils are tender: about 45 minutes. The soup may be eaten as it is, or may also be partly puréed in a food mill or a blender. In such a case, set aside about 1 cup (250 mL) and leave that as it is and mix it into the purée before re-heating and serving. Serves 4–5.

FISH SOUFFLÉ

Israel

A light and delectable way to serve fish.

1½ lbs	(*¾ kg*)	fish fillets (just about any fish will do, according to taste)
3	(*3*)	eggs, separated
1½ cups	(*375 mL*)	sour cream
3 tbs	(*3 tbs*)	cracker crumbs
		salt and pepper to taste
¼ ts	(*¼ ts*)	paprika
		pinch of nutmeg
		dash of Worcestershire sauce
¼ cup	(*60 mL*)	grated cheese (Parmesan)

(*Continued on next page*)

(Fish Soufflé, cont.)

Cut the fish into small pieces, $\frac{1}{4}''$ (6 mm) cubes. Mix together egg yolks, sour cream, crumbs and seasonings, then add fish and blend well. Beat egg whites with a pinch of salt until stiff, then gently fold into fish mixture. Place in a greased soufflé dish, or other baking dish with straight sides, sprinkle with grated cheese and bake in a 350° F (175° C) oven about 45 minutes.

Serves 5–6.

BARBECUED CHICKEN

Israel

A barbecue sauce with coffee, it sounds weird, but it sure tastes good.

1	(*1*)	3–3½ lbs (1½–1¾ kg) frying chicken cut into serving pieces
1 ts	(*1 ts*)	paprika
		salt to taste
2 tbs	(*2 tbs*)	margarine

Barbecue Sauce:

⅓ cup	(*80 mL*)	ketchup
⅓ cup	(*80 mL*)	vinegar
¾ cup	(*180 mL*)	coffee
½ ts	(*½ ts*)	dry mustard
1	(*1*)	clove garlic, finely minced
2 tbs	(*2 tbs*)	soy sauce
⅓ cup	(*80 mL*)	brown sugar
2 tbs	(*2 tbs*)	lemon or lime juice

Brown chicken pieces in margarine, and season with paprika and salt. Put all the ingredients for the sauce into a small saucepan and bring to a boil, then turn down heat and simmer over low heat for 5 minutes. Place chicken pieces in a baking dish, pour barbecue sauce over and bake in a 350° F (175° C) oven 45–50 minutes, or until chicken is tender, basting off and on with the sauce.

Serves 4–5.

CARROT PUDDING

Israel

A nice substantial non-dessert pudding to go with any kind of meat, or good just by itself.

4	*(4)*	slices white bread
1 lb	*(½ kg)*	carrots
½ cup	*(125 mL)*	walnuts or pecans, coarsely chopped
2 tbs	*(2 tbs)*	raisins
1 tbs	*(1 tbs)*	butter or margarine, softened
¼ cup	*(60 mL)*	orange marmalade
2 ts	*(2 ts)*	lemon juice
1 ts	*(1 ts)*	brown sugar
2 tbs	*(2 tbs)*	rum
2	*(2)*	eggs, separated
		salt to taste

Soak bread in water, then squeeze it dry. Grate carrots finely, then mix thoroughly with bread, add nuts, raisins, butter and marmalade. Season mixture with lemon juice, brown sugar, salt and rum. Beat egg yolks slightly and add. Beat egg whites until stiff, then carefully fold into carrot mixture. Pour into a greased baking dish and bake in a 350° F (175° C) oven for 1 hour.

Serves 5–6.

CARROT CAKE

Israel

A cake that is moist in texture and good in flavor, which keeps very well.

4	*(4)*	eggs, separated
½ cup	*(125 mL)*	brown sugar
½ cup	*(125 mL)*	seedless raisins
½ cup	*(125 mL)*	hot water
½ cup	*(125 mL)*	salad oil
1½ cups	*(375 mL)*	flour
1 ts	*(1 ts)*	baking powder
½ ts	*(½ ts)*	baking soda
½ ts	*(½ ts)*	salt
1 ts	*(1 ts)*	cinnamon
1 cup	*(250 mL)*	coarsely grated carrots
		grated peel of one lemon

(Continued on next page)

(Carrot Cake, cont.)

Beat egg whites until stiff, set aside. Soak raisins in hot water for 5 minutes. Beat egg yolks and sugar in a large bowl until light in texture, then add salad oil and continue beating until light and fluffy. Sift together flour, baking powder, baking soda, salt and cinnamon and add part of this to bowl. Add water, in which raisins were soaked, then remaining flour and mix well. Add carrots, lemon peel and raisins and stir till well blended. Finally fold in beaten egg whites. Put batter into a greased and floured 2 quart (2 L) ring pan and bake in a 350° F (175° C) oven for 30 minutes, or until it tests done. Let pan rest on wire rack for 10 minutes, then turn out cake on wire rack to cool.

ORANGE CHEESE CAKE
Israel

Cheese cake with a difference.

Crust:

1 cup	*(250 mL)*	**flour**
¼ cup	*(60 mL)*	**sugar**
6 tbs	*(6 tbs)*	**butter or margarine**
1	*(1)*	**egg yolk**
2–3 tbs	*(2–3 tbs)*	**cold water**

Mix together flour and sugar, then cut in butter or margarine with a pastry cutter until mixture is like coarse crumbs in texture. Add egg yolk and water and work mixture together into a ball. Let it cool in refrigerator for about 20 minutes, then roll out and fit into a 8" (200 mm) spring pan or pie pan, crimping the edges to make it attractive.

Filling:

1 cup	*(250 mL)*	**ricotta or cottage cheese**
1 cup	*(250 mL)*	**sugar**
2	*(2)*	**eggs, lightly beaten**
½ cup	*(125 mL)*	**orange juice**
1 tbs	*(1 tbs)*	**lime or lemon juice**

Put cottage cheese through a sieve, then mix with sugar and remaining ingredients. Beat thoroughly until mixture is smooth, then spoon into pie shell and bake in a 350° F (175° C) oven about 40 minutes or until golden in color. Remove from oven and cool before adding topping.

(*Continued on next page*)

(Orange Cheese Cake, cont.)

Topping:

¾ cup	(*180 mL*)	orange juice
½ cup	(*125 mL*)	sugar
1 tbs	(*1 tbs*)	orange marmalade
1 ts	(*1 ts*)	brandy (optional)
1 ts	(*1 ts*)	finely grated coconut

For decoration: **fresh orange sections, if desired**

Put orange juice, sugar, marmalade and brandy in a small saucepan, bring to a boil and continue cooking, stirring constantly, until mixture thickens and gets the consistency of molasses or honey. Add coconut, and spread over cooled tart. If desired, garnish with fresh orange sections.

Serves 6.

CHALLAH

Israel

Challah is a traditional Sabbath bread, usually served two braids at a time on a silver platter with a special fringed silk cover, in remembrance of the Jewish forefathers who wandered in the desert for 40 years and lived on a lean ration of bread from heaven, with a double portion every seventh day.

1 pkg	(*1 pkg*)	dry yeast
1 cup	(*250 mL*)	luke-warm water
2 tbs	(*2 tbs*)	sugar
About 5 cups	(*1250 mL*)	flour
1 ts	(*1 ts*)	salt
½ cup	(*125 mL*)	butter or margarine, melted
3	(*3*)	eggs, slightly beaten
2 ts	(*2 ts*)	cold water
¼ ts	(*¼ ts*)	poppy seeds

Dissolve yeast in ¼ cup (60 mL) lukewarm water and 1 ts of the sugar. In a bowl of an electric mixer put 2 cups (500 mL) flour, sugar, salt, melted butter, and remaining water then mix at high speed until well blended.

Add the yeast mixture and beat until blended. Put aside about 1 tbs of the beaten eggs to be brushed on top, then add eggs to dough and additional flour, a little at a time, continuing beating until the mixture gets too heavy for the mixer. Then beat in with a wooden spoon enough additional flour to make a soft dough. Turn onto a floured baking board and knead until smooth and elastic, about

10 minutes. Place in a greased bowl, turn dough over once to get all sides greased.

Cover it, and let rise in a warm place, until double in bulk, about 1–1½ hour. Punch down dough, then turn out on floured board. Divide dough in halves, then divide each half into three pieces, roll out to about 15″ (38 cm) long rolls and make two braids, sealing each end securely. Put on a greased baking sheet and let rise in warm place for 1 hour. Just before baking, mix egg yolk with cold water and brush on braids, then sprinkle with poppy seeds. Bake in a 375° F (190° C) oven for about 30 minutes, or until done. Remove from baking sheet and cool on wire rack.

Italy

THE glories of Italian cuisine are too well known in our country to need many words. Of all foreign cooking in the U.S., I believe that the Italian is the most popular. Quite a few of its dishes have become part of the American cuisine, so much that one often hears Wednesdays referred to as "spaghetti days." Among restaurants for foreign foods, Italian was way up front for many years. With today's greater interest, other countries seem to be catching up—but the gap is still quite wide.

However, when we think of Italian food, it is mainly the food of a part of Italy we refer to—that is the South and Sicily, where tomato sauce reigns supreme in most dishes. And when you like it, there is nothing wrong with this.

But Italy has many other types of interesting foods. Their regional origins often show up in the Italian names of the dishes—*alla Milanese, Bolognese, Romana* etc.

The people of northern Italy feel that their eating habits have very little in common with those of the South. In parts of the North more rice is eaten, and from them we get the *risottos*. In the poorer mountain regions in the middle of Italy beans are a main food staple and meat is a luxury.

All over Italy, south, north and central, pasta is important—all the different kinds such as spaghetti, vermicelli, macaroni, lasagne, ravioli etc. etc. in all manner, shapes and sizes that make a difference in the looks and texture of the meal, if not so much in the flavor. In formal eating, pasta is eaten as a separate course, as often mixed with just butter or olive oil and cheese as with a special sauce. One thing that may strike you on your first visit to Italy is that the tables in restaurants (possibly also in the homes, I did not get to visit any while there) are higher than we are used to. That is to facilitate pasta eating by shortening the road from the plate to the mouth to reduce spilling. It is fun to watch with what agility these experts manage to eat it. And how serious they look! But then, eating *is* a serious business with most Italians, and enjoyable too, thanks to all the good stuff they know how to prepare.

As in other Mediterranean countries the flavoring leans heavily towards garlic, oregano, anise and basil, but marjoram, bay leaves, saffron and capers are also used to a great extent. Their cheeses are so well known and used so extensively in American kitchens that they hardly need an introduction—but here are some of them—Mozzarella, Romano, Parmesan, Provolone and Ricotta.

They are fond of fish and prepare it in many fine ways. Among the meats veal and chicken seem to have high priority but lamb is also popular. Desserts include some outstanding successes—the rich and delicious *zabaglione,* and the *granitas* which are sold even on street-corners in New York as "Italian Ices."

Although I have given quite a few Italian recipes, there are many more that I would have liked to have included if space allowed. But I hope what I have chosen will inspire readers to go on to other recipes in the many good Italian cookbooks around.

HORS D'OEUVRES	*Antipasto*
FRIED PEPPERS	*Pepperoni Fritti*
STUFFED CLAMS	*Vongole Imbottite*
SQUID SALAD	*Insalata di Calamari*
STUFFED MUSHROOMS	*Funghi Ripieni*
EGGS WITH PARSLEY SAUCE	*Uova con Salsa Verde*
CHEESE PIE	*Pizza Rustica*
SICILIAN EGGPLANT RELISH	*Caponatina alla Siciliana*
VEGETABLE SOUP	*Minestrone*
SQUID IN TOMATO SAUCE	*Calamari con Salsa Pomodori*
SHRIMP SCAMPI	*Scampi*

(*Continued on next page*)

MACKEREL IN TOMATO SAUCE	*Scombro con Salsa Pomodori*
CHICKEN CACCIATORE	*Pollo alla Cacciatora*
CHICKEN TETRAZZINI	*Pollo Tetrazzini*
BEEF ROLLS	*Braciole*
SICILIAN MEAT ROLL	*Polpettone Imbottite*
VEAL WITH TUNA SAUCE	*Vitello Tonnato*
VEAL WITH MARSALA WINE	*Scaloppine alla Marsala*
STUFFED BREAST OF VEAL	*Vitello Imbottito*
CABBAGE WITH SAUSAGES	*Verzada*
GREEN BEANS WITH PARMESAN CHEESE	*Fagiolini alla Parmegiana*
BAKED ZUCCHINI WITH HAM	*Zucchini con Prosciutto*
RICE WITH MUSHROOMS	*Risotto con Funghi*
CORNMEAL MUSH	*Polenta*
EGGPLANT PARMESAN	*Melanzane alla Parmegiana*
SPAGHETTI SAUCE (MARINARA TYPE)	*Salsa di Pomodori*
SAUSAGE AND EGGPLANT SAUCE	*Salsa di Salsiccia e Melanzane*
BASIL SAUCE	*Pesto Genovese*
WHITE CLAM SAUCE	*Salsa di Vongole Bianca*
RED CLAM SAUCE	*Salsa di Vongole Rossa*
SPAGHETTI WITH CHICKEN LIVERS	*Fegato di Pollo con Salsa Pomodori*
LASAGNE	*Lasagne al Forno*
MANICOTTI	*Manicotti Imbottiti*
CANELLONI WITH CHEESE FILLING	*Canelloni con Formaggio*
BAKED ZITI	*Ziti al Forno*
ZABAGLIONE	
ST. JOSEPH'S CREAM PUFFS	*Sfinge di San Giuseppe*
RICOTTA PIE	*Torta di Ricotta*
BISCUIT TORTONI	*Biscotti Tortoni*
RUM COOKIES	*Favette*
ANISE COOKIES	*Biscotti all'Anice*
COFFEE CAKE	*Panettone*

HORS D'OEUVRES

Italy   *(Antipasto)*

Antipasto is the traditional appetizer for the formal Italian meal. Translated it means "before the pasta." It can be very elaborate or contain just a few simple tidbits. Usually it is served on a large platter in a way that is pleasing to the eye as well as the stomach. Below are a few things that may be used for such a platter besides the regular recipes for antipasto I have given below:

Artichoke hearts, olives, radishes, pickled beets, cherry tomatoes, celery, pimiento, hardboiled eggs (sliced or quartered), cheese cut into strips, anchovies, tuna, salami, pepperoni, prosciutto, melon and salad greens.

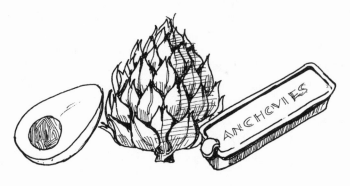

FRIED PEPPERS

Italy   *(Pepperoni Fritti)*

Peppers are sometimes roasted over a hot charcoal grill, then peeled and cut into strips. I have found this procedure somewhat difficult as the peppers too often get either burnt to a crisp or are almost raw. I therefore prefer them fried in this manner, a shortcut also taken by many Italian cooks.

6	(6)	large peppers (green, red or yellow or any combination of colors)
¼ cup	(60 mL)	olive oil
1	(1)	clove garlic, finely minced salt and pepper to taste

Cut peppers length-wise into ¾–1" (20–30 mm) wide strips and remove any seeds and white membranes. Heat oil in a large skillet, add garlic and cook for about 2 minutes, stirring, then add peppers and cook over medium heat for 5 minutes. Add salt and pepper, cover pan and cook an additional 15–20 minutes until peppers are tender, but not mushy. Serve either hot or cold as an antipasto.

STUFFED CLAMS

Italy   (*Vongole Imbottite*)

A delicious appetizer, by itself, or part of an antipasto platter.

3 dozen	(*3 dozen*)	hard-shell clams (about half this amount if very large clams are used)
1 cup	(*250 mL*)	dry bread crumbs
⅓ cup	(*80 mL*)	grated Parmesan cheese
2	(*2*)	cloves garlic, finely minced
2 tbs	(*2 tbs*)	finely minced parsley
½ ts	(*½ ts*)	oregano
		salt and pepper to taste
1–2 tbs	(*1–2 tbs*)	olive oil
½ cup	(*125 mL*)	tomato sauce (see page 304, or use canned sauce)

Put clams in a small kettle with about 12 mm water in the bottom. Cover and bring to a boil and cook for about 5 minutes, or until the clams have opened and given up their juice. Remove meat. Set aside half the shells for stuffing, or use scallop shells.

Strain broth in kettle through double layers of cheese cloth to remove any sand the clams might have given out while steaming. Chop the clams and combine with bread crumbs, cheese, garlic, parsley, oregano, salt and pepper and add enough clam broth to moisten.

Stuff half-shells with mixture and sprinkle olive oil and tomato sauce on top. Bake in a 350° F (175° C) oven about 15–20 minutes, or until clams are thoroughly hot. Serve immediately as an appetizer.

Serves 5–6.

SQUID SALAD

Italy   (*Insalata di Calamari*)

A mention of squid seems to bring a shudder to most Americans. However, only one visit to one of the Mediterranean countries will make converts of many of them to this delicious seafood, as it is served there in just about every little bar or restaurant as an appetizer, a snack or a main meal.

1 lb	(½ kg)	**small squid**
1 cup	(250 mL)	**lightly salted water**

Clean squid (see page 293). Cut in 1″ (25 mm) strips. Simmer in lightly salted water for 1 hour, or until squid is tender. Drain squid and immedi-ately pour the following sauce over them. Let stand at room temperature for 1 hour, then chill in refrigerator for several hours.

Sauce:

3 tbs	(*3 tbs*)	**olive oil**
2 tbs	(*2 tbs*)	**wine vinegar**
3	(*3*)	**anchovy fillets, finely chopped**
		juice of one lemon
1	(*1*)	**clove garlic, finely chopped**
1 tbs	(*1 tbs*)	**finely chopped fresh parsley**
		salt and pepper to taste
1	(*1*)	**medium size red onion, sliced**

Garnish: **strips of green pepper and tomato wedges**

Combine all ingredients and mix well, before pouring over hot squid. Just before serving, decorate with pepper strips and tomato wedges.
Serves 4–6.

STUFFED MUSHROOMS

Italy   (*Funghi Ripieni*)

12	(*12*)	**large mushrooms (or 18 medium size)**
1	(*1*)	**medium size onion, finely chopped**
		(¾ cup or 180 mL)
1	(*1*)	**clove garlic, finely minced**
1 tbs	(*1 tbs*)	**chopped parsley**

(*Continued on next page*)

(Stuffed Mushrooms, cont.)

2 tbs	(*2 tbs*)	olive oil or butter (or half of each)
½ cup	(*125 mL*)	dry bread crumbs
½ cup	(*125 mL*)	grated Parmesan cheese
1	(*1*)	egg, slightly beaten
		salt and pepper to taste

Clean and wash mushrooms, drain on paper toweling. Carefully remove stems and chop them finely. In a skillet sauté onion in olive oil or butter until transparent, add parsley and mushroom stems and sauté over slow heat for about 5 minutes. Remove from heat and cool, then add bread crumbs, cheese, egg and seasonings, and mix thoroughly.

Stuff this mixture into mushroom caps and arrange in a baking dish. Add a thin layer of water to bottom to prevent sticking to pan and bake in a 350° F (175° C) oven for 20 minutes, basting off and on. Serve as an appetizer. Serves 5–6.

EGGS WITH PARSLEY SAUCE

Italy (*Uova con Salse Verde*)

An appetizer possibility around Easter time, when you have all those hard-boiled Easter eggs on hand.

6	(*6*)	hard-boiled eggs

Sauce:

1	(*1*)	hard-boiled egg yolk
		juice of one lemon
½ cup	(*125 mL*)	olive oil
¾ cup	(*180 mL*)	finely chopped parsley
3	(*3*)	canned anchovy fillets, finely chopped
1 tbs	(*1 tbs*)	finely chopped capers
		pepper to taste
		shredded lettuce (optional)

Mash egg yolk until very smooth in a mixing bowl, add lemon juice and mix well. Add oil, little by little, stir until a smooth sauce has been obtained, then add remaining ingredients and mix well. Leave in refrigerator for a couple of hours, to improve flavor.

To serve, cut eggs in half lengthwise and put them, cut side down, in a serving dish. (If desired, shredded lettuce may be spread underneath the eggs). Pour the sauce over the eggs. Serve to 6 as an appetizer.

CHEESE PIE

Italy   (*Pizza Rustica*)

This is Italy's answer to France's Quiche Lorraine. And what a tasty dish indeed! What surprises me is that it is so little known in our country, even among Italians who know a lot about the food of "the old country." The reason for this might be that this dish originates in the Abruzzi region of Italy which is on the east coast and consists of a narrow strip of land between very high mountains and the sea. It may therefore be more isolated than many other regions in Italy.

Pie Crust:

2 cups	(*500 mL*)	flour
½ ts	(½ *ts*)	each of salt and pepper
¼ cup	(½ *dl*)	butter or margarine (half stick)
½ cup	(*125 mL*)	lard
1	(*1*)	egg, slightly beaten

Mix flour and salt, then cut in butter and lard with a pastry cutter until mixture is crumbly. Add egg and mix together into a ball, cover with plastic wrap and keep in refrigerator for 1 hour.

Filling:

½ stick	(½ *stick*)	pepperoni (about 3 oz or 85 g), sliced thin and cut into quarters
⅓ lb	(*150 g*)	prosciutto, cut in thin slices and diced
4 oz	(*125 g*)	Swiss cheese, cut in small cubes
4 oz	(*125 g*)	mozzarella, cut in small cubes
4 oz	(*125 g*)	provolone, cut in small cubes
6	(*6*)	eggs
1 lb	(½ *kg*)	ricotta
		salt and pepper to taste

Mix together pepperoni, prosciutto, Swiss cheese, mozzarella and provolone. Beat eggs until light and lemon-colored, add ricotta (if ricotta should look lumpy, pass it through a sieve) and continue beating until a smooth mixture has been obtained. Add meat-cheese mixture, mix well.

Assembly:

Roll out half the pastry to fit a 10" (250 mm) pie plate. Add filling then roll out remaining pastry and place on top, pinching edges together to close. Bake in a 350° F (175° C) oven for 15 minutes, reduce heat to 325° F (165° C) and continue baking for 45 minutes to one hour, or until pie is ready. (Test by inserting a knife in the middle, if it comes out clean, the pie is done). This is a very rich pie and will serve 12 as an appetizer and 6 as a luncheon or supper dish.

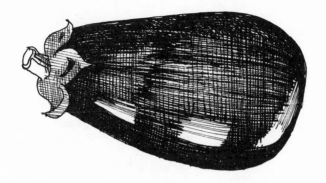

SICILIAN EGGPLANT RELISH

Italy   (*Caponatina alla Siciliana*)

1	(*1*)	large eggplant, peeled and cut into $\frac{1}{2}''$ (12 mm) cubes (about 4 cups or one L)
1 cup	(*250 mL*)	celery, finely chopped
$\frac{1}{3}$ cup	(*80 mL*)	olive oil
1	(*1*)	large onion, finely chopped (1 cup or 250 mL)
3 tbs	(*3 tbs*)	wine vinegar
2 ts	(*2 ts*)	sugar
1 tbs	(*1 tbs*)	tomato paste
$\frac{1}{2}$ cup	(*125 mL*)	water
$\frac{1}{2}$ tbs	(*$\frac{1}{2}$ tbs*)	capers
6	(*6*)	large green olives, pitted and chopped
1 tbs	(*1 tbs*)	parsley, finely minced
		salt and pepper to taste

Sauté celery in $\frac{1}{4}$ cup (60 mL) olive oil, stirring off and on for about 5 minutes. Remove celery, add eggplant and sauté for 8–10 minutes, stirring often so that it does not get too brown but attains a nice golden color. Remove eggplant to a plate and pat it with paper toweling to remove excess fat.

Sauté onion in remaining olive oil until transparent, stirring so that it does not get brown. Add vinegar, sugar, tomato paste and water and simmer 10 minutes. Add celery, eggplant, parsley, olives, capers, salt and pepper and simmer 15 minutes. Let mixture cool. Serve as antipasto, or with roast meat or fowl. (It will keep for 1 week to 10 days in refrigerator.)

Serves 5–6.

VEGETABLE SOUP

Italy   (*Minestroni*)

Minestrone can be made in so many ways that every cook may have his own version (or versions) of it. This sample recipe makes a good hearty soup and is perfect on a cold day.

1	(*1*)	large onion, chopped (1 cup or 250 mL)
1	(*1*)	clove garlic, finely chopped
2 tbs	(*2 tbs*)	olive oil
2 qts	(*2 L*)	soup stock (preferably made from marrow bones)
2	(*2*)	carrots, diced
1	(*1*)	celery stalk, diced
1 cup	(*250 mL*)	fresh or frozen peas, or the same quantity of fresh or frozen string beans, cut into ½″ (12 mm) long pieces
2 cups	(*500 mL*)	fresh tomatoes, peeled and chopped, or canned ones (one cup or 250 mL)
2 cups	(*500 mL*)	cooked kidney or navy beans
2 cups	(*500 mL*)	finely shredded cabbage
1 cup	(*250 mL*)	elbow macaroni, or spaghetti broken up into small pieces
		salt to taste
For serving:		2 tbs chopped fresh parsley grated parmesan cheese

Sauté onion and garlic in olive oil for about 5 minutes, add soup stock, carrots, celery, and tomatoes and bring to a boil. Turn down heat and simmer for 20 minutes. Add peas or beans and cook for 10 minutes, then add kidney or navy beans, cabbage, macaroni or spaghetti, salt and bring to a boil again. Turn down heat and simmer for 10–15 minutes or until pasta is ready. Serve piping hot sprinkled with parsley and grated cheese.

Serves 6.

SQUID IN TOMATO SAUCE

Italy   (*Calamari con Salsa Pomodoro*)

2 lbs	(*1 kg*)	squid
2 tbs	(*2 tbs*)	olive oil
1	(*1*)	medium size onion, chopped (¾ cup or 180 mL)

(*Continued on next page*)

(Squid in Tomato Sauce, cont.)

1	(1)	clove garlic, finely minced
2 tbs	(2 tbs)	chopped parsley
¼ cup	(60 mL)	tomato paste
⅓ cup	(80 mL)	water

Clean squid, cutting off head and removing the translucent spiny part of the body, then remove the dark skin-like covering and the ink-sac at the base of the head. Cut the tentacles off near the head and cut them into bite-size pieces, then cut the body into pieces of about 1" (25 mm), which will be in the shape of tubes or rings.

Heat olive oil in frying pan and sauté onion and garlic until onion is transparent, then add parsley, tomato paste and water and cook together about 5 minutes. Add squid and bring to a boil, turn heat down to low and simmer about 30–40 minutes, or until squid is tender. Cooking time depends upon the size of the squid. Small squid are tender and may cook faster than 30 minutes, but larger ones may take even longer. Serve immediately with rice or spaghetti. For 5–6 people.

SHRIMP SCAMPI

Italy   (*Scampi*)

I am afraid I have fallen for the temptation of misnaming this dish. The reason is that this is how it appears on the menu in many Italian restaurants in this country, and as it is very popular, I wanted it to be easily identified. The fact is that shrimp and scampi are two different varieties of crustaceans—shrimp being the one we fish in our waters and scampi a different variety that abound in European waters. But the word scampi in the U.S. now represents a way of cooking shrimp rather than the animals themselves.

2 lbs	(1 kg)	large shrimp
3 tbs	(3 tbs)	butter
3 tbs	(3 tbs)	olive oil
2	(2)	cloves garlic, finely minced
		salt to taste
3 tbs	(3 tbs)	finely chopped parsley
		lemon wedges for garnish and flavoring

Peel shrimp but let the tail remain, then de-vein. Heat oil and butter in a large skillet, add garlic and shrimp and cook over medium heat, while stirring, only until shrimp turn pink, about 5 minutes. (Cooking longer than necessary will make shrimp tough.) Add salt to taste, sprinkle with parsley, garnish with lemon wedges, and serve at once to 4.

MACKEREL IN TOMATO SAUCE

Italy   (*Scombro con Salsa di Pomodoro*)

1½ lbs	(¾ kg)	mackerel fillets
2 tbs	(2 tbs)	olive oil
1	(1)	large onion, thinly sliced
1	(1)	clove garlic, finely chopped
1 tbs	(1 tbs)	chopped fresh parsley
1	(1)	(16 oz or 500 g) can of tomatoes
2 tbs	(2 tbs)	water
¼ ts	(¼ ts)	oregano
		salt and pepper to taste

Sauté onion and garlic in olive oil until onion is transparent, add parsley, tomatoes, water and seasonings and bring to a boil. Turn down heat and simmer about 15 minutes. Put mixture in a baking dish, add mackerel and bake in a 350° F (175° C) oven about 15–20 minutes, or until fish is flaky.

Serves 4–5.

CHICKEN CACCIATORE

Italy   (*Pollo alla Cacciatora*)

1	(1)	frying chicken, 3–3½ lbs or 1½–1¾ kg
3 tbs	(3 tbs)	olive oil, butter or margarine
1	(1)	small onion, finely chopped (½ cup or 125 mL)
1	(1)	clove garlic, finely minced
½ cup	(125 mL)	chopped green pepper
1	(1)	can tomatoes (one lb or 500 g), about 2 cups (500 mL)
⅓ cup	(80 mL)	red wine
1 tbs	(1 tbs)	vinegar
1 ts	(1 ts)	oregano
		salt and pepper to taste

Cut chicken into serving pieces. Brown in a skillet in olive oil, butter or margarine, then remove and put into a large heavy-bottom saucepan. Brown onion and garlic slightly and add to pan. Add all the remaining ingredients and mix well. Bring to a boil, turn down heat to very low and simmer, covered, about 40–45 minutes, or until chicken is tender. If sauce is not thick enough, let it simmer for 5–10 minutes without cover. Serve with rice or spaghetti.

For 4–5 people.

CHICKEN TETRAZZINI

Italy   *(Pollo Tetrazzini)*

I have been to several Italian weddings, and each time Chicken Tetrazzini has been served. I guess it can be said to be the Italian version of Chicken à la King. It is really a pleasing and efficient dish when you have lots of people to feed. It is handy because you can make most of the preparations way ahead of time. As it freezes well, all ready and prepared, it only has to be put into the oven a while before serving time.

Cooking of chicken:

1	(*1*)	stewing chicken (about 4 lbs or 2 kg) or a large fryer (about 3½ lbs or 1¾ kg)
1-2	(*1-2*)	celery tops
1	(*1*)	small onion, quartered
1	(*1*)	small carrot, peeled and sliced salt to taste
10	(*10*)	whole peppercorns
4-6 cups	(*1-1½ L*)	water

Cut chicken into large pieces and put in a big pot or Dutch oven. Add remaining ingredients, bring to a boil, skim surface, turn down heat and simmer slowly 1½-3 hours, depending upon the toughness of the chicken. When meat is tender and easily removed from the bones, take up chicken from stock, free meat from skin and bones, cut into cubes and set aside. Strain stock.

Assembly:

½ lb	(*¼ kg*)	fettucini or other broad egg noodles (however, spaghetti is sometimes used instead)
1	(*1*)	large onion, finely chopped (1 cup or 250 mL)
1	(*1*)	green pepper, chopped
3 tbs	(*3 tbs*)	butter or margarine
½ lb	(*¼ kg*)	fresh mushrooms, sliced
½ cup	(*125 mL*)	heavy cream
1½ cups	(*375 mL*)	grated Parmesan cheese
3 tbs	(*3 tbs*)	chopped parsley

(Continued on next page)

(Chicken Tetrazzini, cont.)

Cook noodles in 2–2½ cups (500–600 mL) chicken stock until tender, about 8–10 minutes. If any stock has not been absorbed by the noodles, strain them.

Sauté onion and pepper in butter 10–15 minutes, add mushrooms and cook five minutes more. Add chicken, cream, noodles and one cup (250 mL) cheese and mix well and cook until thoroughly hot. (If mixture should be too dry, add a bit more stock.) Just before serving, add parsley and mix. Serve with remaining cheese sprinkled on top, to 5–6.

BEEF ROLLS

Italy   *(Braciole)*

This dish is not as common as many of the other Italian dishes in this book, but in my opinion it should rate almost on top.

1½ lb	(¾ kg)	round steak, cut into ¼″ (6 mm) thick slices
⅓ cup	(80 mL)	bread crumbs
¼ cup	(60 mL)	finely minced ham or salami
1 tbs	(1 tbs)	chopped green pepper
2 tbs	(2 tbs)	grated Parmesan cheese
2 tbs	(2 tbs)	finely chopped parsley
1	(1)	clove garlic, finely minced
		salt and pepper to taste
3 tbs	(3 tbs)	olive oil
2 cups	(500 mL)	tomato sauce (see page 304)
¼ cup	(60 mL)	red wine

Spread out meat and pound with a mallet to make it as flat as possible without making holes in it. Sprinkle with salt and pepper. Mix together remaining ingredients, except olive oil, tomato sauce and wine and divide mixture up evenly and place on the beef slices. Roll up tightly and tie with a cotton string. Brown rolls well in olive oil, add tomato sauce and bring to a boil. Turn down heat to very low and simmer 1½–2 hours, or until meat is tender. Remove strings, and serve with sauce and additional grated parmesan cheese. Accompany with pasta, rice or *Polenta*.

Serves 4–5.

SICILIAN MEAT ROLL

Italy   *(Polpettone Imbottite)*

A meatloaf with a difference, in the true South Italian manner.

1½ lbs	(¾ kg)	ground chuck
1 cup	(250 mL)	dry breadcrumbs
2	(2)	eggs, lightly beaten
½ cup	(125 mL)	tomato juice
2 tbs	(2 tbs)	chopped fresh parsley
1	(1)	clove garlic, finely minced
½ ts	(½ ts)	oregano
		pepper and salt to taste
½ lb	(¼ kg)	thinly sliced ham (preferably proscuitto)
½ lb	(¼ kg)	chunk mozzarella cheese (cut off three slices and coarsely grate the remainder)

Combine meat, breadcrumbs, eggs, tomato juice, parsley, garlic, oregano, salt and pepper in a bowl and mix until well blended. Place mixture on a sheet of waxed paper or aluminum foil and pat it into a rectangle, about 10 x 12″ (250 x 300 mm). Place a layer of sliced ham on top, then sprinkle with a layer of the grated cheese.

With the aid of the wax paper or foil for a guide, roll the rectangle into a roll, jelly-roll fashion, and pinch to seal the edges. Place roll, seam side down, in a roasting pan and bake in a 350° F (175° C) oven for 45 minutes. Cut reserved cheese slices into strips and place on top of roll, then return to oven and bake until cheese is melted, about 5 minutes. Remove from oven and let stand about 10 minutes before cutting into slices. Serve with noodles or rice.
Serves 5–6.

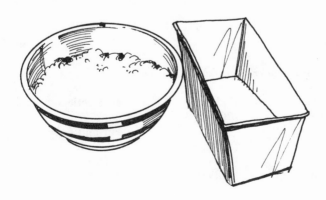

Italy   **VEAL WITH TUNA SAUCE**   (*Vitello Tonnato*)

This is one of my favorites for Summer entertainment. It can be prepared completely ahead of time, it is elegant to look at and seems to be liked by everyone who tries it.

3-3½ lbs	(1½-1¾ kg)	veal roast, either rolled and boned breast of veal or a boneless piece from the leg
1	(1)	can tuna fish (8 oz or 250 g)
1	(1)	medium size onion, finely chopped (¾ cup or 180 mL)
1	(1)	2 oz can (60 g) of anchovies
2 cups	(500 mL)	dry white wine
⅓ cup	(80 mL)	olive oil
		juice from 2 lemons
2 tbs	(2 tbs)	pickles, finely chopped
		salt and pepper to taste
For garnish:		lemon wedges and parsley

The meat should be tied so that it will keep its shape during cooking. Put it in a heavy saucepan together with broken-up tuna pieces, onion, anchovies, salt, pepper and wine. Cover and bring to a boil. Skim and let simmer over very low heat 1½ hours, or until meat is tender when pierced with a fork. Remove meat and put it in a deep bowl.

Purée the remaining broth mixture from the pot in a blender, or press it through a sieve. Pour this sauce over meat and keep in refrigerator for at least 2 days. Serve meat at room temperature, cut into very thin slices, together with the sauce which should be re-mixed. (If desired, it may be mixed with ½-1 cup (125-250 mL) mayonnaise, before serving). Garnish with lemon wedges and parsley.

Serves 6-8.

VEAL WITH MARSALA WINE

Italy   (*Scaloppine alla Marsala*)

If you get nice tender veal, few things will beat this simple-to-prepare dish.

1½ lbs	(¾ kg)	veal cutlets
¼ cup	(60 mL)	flour
		salt and pepper to taste
2 tbs	(2 tbs)	olive oil
2 tbs	(2 tbs)	butter
½ cup	(125 mL)	Marsala or sweet sherry

(*Continued on next page*)

(Veal with Marsala Wine, cont.)

Mix together flour and salt and pepper. Pound veal cutlets until ¼″ (6 mm) thick, then dredge in flour. Heat olive oil and butter in a frying pan, then brown meat lightly on both sides, about 5 minutes in all. Remove and keep hot.

Add wine to the frying pan and scrape brown pieces from bottom and mix well. Cook for about 3 minutes then pour sauce over meat and serve immediately.

For 4–5 people.

STUFFED BREAST OF VEAL

Italy   (*Vitello Imbottito*)

For an economical meal this recipe rates far up on the list. This cut of meat is quite often very reasonable, and prepared this way it does not appear to be a penny-pinching meal at all.

1	(*1*)	breast of veal, 3–4 lbs (1½–2 kg)
½ lb	(¼ *kg*)	Italian sausages, hot or sweet, or a mixture of both, according to taste
1	(*1*)	small onion, finely chopped (½ cup or 125 mL)
1	(*1*)	clove garlic, finely minced
2	(*2*)	slices white bread, cubed
½ ts	(½ *ts*)	powdered sage
		salt and pepper to taste
1	(*1*)	egg, slightly beaten

Have butcher cut a pocket in veal breast for stuffing. (Some supermarkets have the meat already thus prepared). Cut open and crumble sausages, and fry mixed together with onion and garlic about 10 minutes. Pour off excess fat then add bread cubes, seasonings and egg and mix well. Stuff pocket with this mixture and seal with skewers or by sewing it together.

Roast in covered pan in a 350° F (175° C) oven for about 2½ hours, or until meat is tender. Turn over once during roasting. Cut into slices (between ribs) and serve hot.

For 4–6 people.

VARIATION:

After 2 hours of roasting time add 2 cups (500 mL) tomato sauce (see page 304) and cook an additional 30 minutes or until meat is tender.

CABBAGE WITH SAUSAGES
Italy   (*Verzada*)

Not only Germans are cabbage lovers. Every country seems to have a special dish or two for this mundane vegetable, which can taste so differently in different cooking traditions.

1	(*1*)	small head of cabbage, about 2 lbs (1 kg)
2 tbs	(*2 tbs*)	butter or margarine
½ cup	(*125 mL*)	salt pork or fat bacon, finely diced
1	(*1*)	medium size onion, thinly sliced
2 tbs	(*2 tbs*)	wine vinegar
		salt and pepper to taste
1 lb	(½ *kg*)	Italian pork sausages, sweet, hot, or both, according to taste

Discard outer leaves of cabbage, then cut the head into coarse shreds. In a large pot or Dutch oven, heat butter and fry salt pork or bacon cubes for about 5 minutes, then add onion and sauté until onion is transparent, but do not let it get brown. Add cabbage, stirring it so it will be all covered with some of the fat. Cook over moderate heat until cabbage begins to brown slightly. Sprinkle with vinegar, add salt and pepper to taste. Arrange the sausages on top of the cabbage, prick them with a fork, cover the pan, bring to a boil, then turn down heat and simmer for one hour. Serve immediately.

For 4–5 people.

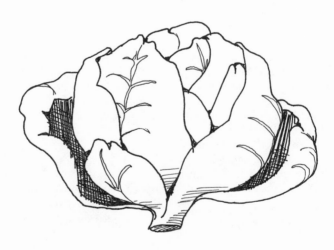

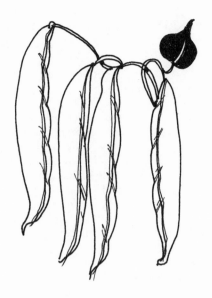

GREEN BEANS WITH PARMESAN CHEESE

Italy (*Fagiolini alla Parmegiana*)

Make string or wax beans more exciting, this easy Italian way.

1 lb	(½ kg)	fresh green beans (or wax beans) (one lb or 500 g can)
3 tbs	(3 tbs)	olive oil
1 tbs	(1 tbs)	chopped onion
1	(1)	clove garlic, finely minced
½ cup	(125 mL)	green pepper, coarsely chopped
¼ cup	(60 mL)	boiling water
½ ts	(½ ts)	salt, or to taste
1 ts	(1 ts)	fresh basil leaves, finely minced or ½ ts dried ones
⅓ cup	(80 mL)	grated parmesan cheese

If fresh beans are used, wash them, cut off tips and cut into 1″ (25 mm) lengths. Heat oil in saucepan, add garlic, onion and green pepper and sauté for about 5 minutes. Add beans, water, salt and basil leaves. Cover saucepan and cook over low heat about 10 minutes, or until beans are tender. Check that there is enough liquid in pan, and add hot water if needed. Otherwise beans might burn. Just before serving, stir in half the cheese and mix with the beans, then pour into a serving dish and sprinkle with remaining cheese. Serve immediately. Serves 5–6.

BAKED ZUCCHINI WITH HAM

Italy   (*Zucchini con Prosciutto*)

For home gardeners there is often a super-abundance of zucchini in the summer, and so it is nice to find a new way to prepare them.

2 lbs	(*1 kg*)	small zucchini
4	(*4*)	slices prosciutto (or Smithfield ham), finely diced, about ¼ lb (125 g)
4	(*4*)	slices bacon, finely chopped
3 tbs	(*3 tbs*)	minced fresh parsley
1	(*1*)	small onion, finely chopped (½ cup or 125 mL)
		salt and pepper to taste
3 tbs	(*3 tbs*)	melted butter

Clean zucchini and cook in salted water about 3–4 minutes. Drain, then slice them in half lengthwise and put in a single layer in a buttered baking dish. Mix together prosciutto, bacon, parsley and onion and spread on top of zucchini. Sprinkle with melted butter and bake in a 350° F (175° C) oven 30–40 minutes, or until zucchini is tender. Serves 5–6.

RICE WITH MUSHROOMS

Italy   (*Risotto con Funghi*)

In Northern Italy pasta is not as popular as in the South and rice seems to have preference. And they sure have a way with it!

½ lb	(¼ *kg*)	fresh mushrooms, thinly sliced
2 tbs	(*2 tbs*)	olive oil
1	(*1*)	clove garlic
¼ cup	(*60 mL*)	minced parsley
2 tbs	(*2 tbs*)	butter or margarine
1	(*1*)	small onion, finely chopped (½ cup or 125 mL)
1 cup	(*250 mL*)	long grain rice
		salt and pepper to taste
3 cups	(*750 mL*)	chicken stock (canned stock or bouillon cubes with water may be used instead of home-made stock)
½ cup	(*125 mL*)	white wine
½ cup	(*125 mL*)	grated parmesan cheese

(*Continued on next page*)

(Rice with Mushrooms, cont.)

In a heavy bottom saucepan sauté mushrooms in olive oil with garlic and parsley, about 5 minutes. Set aside mushrooms and discard garlic clove. Heat butter in pan and sauté onion until transparent, then add rice and cook over medium heat, stirring continuously for a couple of minutes. Heat chicken stock and add, a little at a time, as the rice absorbs it. When rice is almost done and has reached a creamy consistency, add wine and mushrooms and cook about 5 more minutes, or until both rice and mushrooms are tender. Stir in parmesan cheese and serve immediately.

Serves 4–5.

CORN MEAL MUSH

Italy   *(Polenta)*

Polenta is served instead of pasta or rice with meat dishes and is popular in the north of Italy. If there are left-overs, the pudding is then often sliced and fried in butter the next day, as it slices nicely when cold.

1 cup	(250 mL)	yellow corn meal
1–2 ts	(1–2 ts)	salt
4 cups	(1 L)	water

Bring water and salt to a rapid boil in a heavy saucepan, then slowly pour in corn meal while stirring constantly with a wire whisk until well moistened. Turn down heat to very low and simmer without cover for 20–30 minutes. Check pan often and stir off and on to prevent scorching. When ready the corn meal seems to shrink from the sides of the pan. Serve hot, either directly from pan or from a serving dish to 5–6.

VARIATION:

Stir in ½ cup (125 mL) grated parmesan cheese just before the *polenta* is ready and sprinkle with an additional ½ cup (125 mL) when it is served.

EGGPLANT PARMESAN

Italy   *(Melanzane alla Parmegiana)*

If you want to have a meatless dish and not miss the meat, I think this dish is the answer, especially for eggplant lovers.

1	(1)	medium size eggplant (about 1½ lbs or ¾ kg)
		salt
½–¾ cup	(125–180 mL)	olive oil
2 cups	(500 mL)	tomato sauce (see recipe below)
1	(1)	clove garlic, finely minced
2 ts	(2 ts)	finely minced fresh basil
1 tbs	(1 tbs)	finely minced fresh parsley
1 cup	(250 mL)	grated parmesan cheese
½ lb	(¼ kg)	thinly sliced mozzarella cheese

Peel eggplant and cut into ⅓″ (8 mm) slices. (If desired, sprinkle with salt and let stand for about 20 minutes to draw out any bitter juice. Rinse under cold water and pat dry.) Heat half the olive oil in a skillet and cook the egg plant slices, a few at a time until golden brown on both sides, adding more oil as it gets absorbed.

In the meantime simmer tomato sauce together with garlic, basil and parsley for about 15 minutes. Put a layer of sauce in bottom of a baking dish (9 x 9″ or 220 x 220 mm), then a layer of eggplant, a layer of half of the mozzarella slices and ⅓ of grated parmesan, then a layer of sauce. Repeat layers and end with sauce then sprinkle with the remaining ⅓ cup parmesan. Bake in a 350° F (175° C) oven for 20–30 minutes or until it is very hot and cheese is thoroughly melted. Serve piping hot.

For 5–6.

SPAGHETTI SAUCE (Marinara Type)

Italy   *(Salsa di Pomodore)*

Again, there must be as many ways to prepare pasta sauce as there are cooks. This one is so easy that it seems to make it quite unnecessary to buy ready-made brands, no matter how well advertised they are.

2 tbs	(2 tbs)	olive oil
1	(1)	large onion, finely chopped (1 cup or 250 mL)
1	(1)	clove garlic, finely minced

(Continued on next page)

(Spaghetti Sauce, cont.)

1	(*1*)	can tomatoes (about 3 cups or 750 mL) or about 10 medium fresh tomatoes, peeled and chopped
1	(*1*)	can tomato paste (6 oz or 200 mL) salt and pepper to taste
1 ts	(*1 ts*)	oregano
1 tbs	(*1 tbs*)	fresh minced parsley (or 1 ts dried flakes)
1 tbs	(*1 tbs*)	fresh minced basil leaves (or 1 ts dried)

Sauté onion and garlic in olive oil until onion is transparent. Add remaining ingredients and bring to a boil, then turn down heat and simmer first with cover for about 1½ hours then without cover for an additional 1 hour. Stir the sauce off and on.
Makes 4–5 cups.

SAUSAGE AND EGGPLANT SAUCE
Italy   (*Salsa di Salsiccia e Melanzane*)

1 lb	(½ *kg*)	Italian sweet sausage (or half sweet and half hot, if preferred)
1	(*1*)	large onion, finely chopped (1 cup or 250 mL)
1	(*1*)	clove garlic, finely minced
2 tbs	(*2 tbs*)	olive oil
1	(*1*)	green pepper, chopped
2 tbs	(*2 tbs*)	finely minced fresh parsley
1	(*1*)	medium size eggplant (about 1½ lbs or ¾ kg)
2 cups	(*500 mL*)	canned plum tomatoes, cut up
1	(*1*)	can tomato paste (6 oz or 200 mL) salt and pepper to taste
For serving:		parmesan cheese

Sauté onion and garlic in olive oil for five minutes. Peel off casings around the sausages and cut the meat into small pieces, add to onions together with green pepper and cook for a few minutes. Remove stem end from eggplant and discard. Cut the rest, unpeeled, into ½″ (12 mm) cubes, add to onion mixture and cook for 5 minutes, then add tomatoes, tomato paste, salt and pepper. Mix well, then cook for about 45 minutes. Serve with spaghetti and sprinkle with cheese.
Serves 5–6.

BASIL SAUCE

Italy   (*Pesto Genovese*)

This is the utmost in sauce for pasta, according to many aficionados. It definitely is different from the common tomato sauces which are usually served in the U.S. with pasta.

1½ cup	(*375 mL*)	fresh basil leaves, loosely packed
2	(*2*)	cloves garlic, coarsely chopped
½ cup	(*125 mL*)	*pignoli* (pine nuts) or chopped walnuts
⅔ cup	(*180 mL*)	grated parmesan cheese
½ cup	(*125 mL*)	olive oil
1 lb	(*½ kg*)	thin spaghetti

Put basil leaves, *pignoli* and garlic in an electric blender, or crush to a paste with mortar and pestle and blend thoroughly, scraping down sides when necessary. Add cheese and olive oil, and mix well. Cook spaghetti in accordance with package directions, then drain it and mix with the above sauce and serve. If desired, the sauce may be served separately, in which case the spaghetti should be stirred with 2–3 tbs butter.

Serves 4–5.

WHITE CLAM SAUCE

Italy   (*Salsa di Vongole Bianca*)

Another pasta sauce, without tomatoes, and as most people like clams, they should like this sauce too.

2 cups	(*500 mL*)	minced clams (about 6 dz clams in shell or two 8 oz or 250 g cans)
3 tbs	(*3 tbs*)	olive oil
3 tbs	(*3 tbs*)	butter or margarine
2	(*2*)	cloves garlic, finely minced
2 tbs	(*2 tbs*)	finely chopped parsley
		salt and pepper to taste

If fresh clams are used, steam in a large pot with about 1″ (25 mm) of water for about 5 minutes or until they open, then remove meat from shells and chop finely. Strain liquid through several layers of cheese cloth and set aside.

(*Continued on next page*)

(White Clam Sauce, cont.)

Heat olive oil and butter in a skillet, add garlic and sauté over low heat until golden in color, about 5 minutes.

Add clam juice (either from can or water set aside after steaming) to skillet, then add parsley, salt and pepper and bring to a boil. Reduce heat to very low and simmer without cover about 10 minutes. Add clams and simmer until clams are heated through. Serve immediately over spaghetti.   For 4–5 people.

RED CLAM SAUCE

Italy   (*Salsa di Vongole Rosso*)

But if you feel you cannot do without red color in sauce, here is a clam sauce with tomatoes.

2	(2)	**cans minced clams (about 8 oz or 250 g size)**
		(or 6 dozen clams in shell)
3 tbs	(*3 tbs*)	**olive oil**
2	(2)	**cloves garlic, finely minced**
¼ cup	(*60 mL*)	**finely minced fresh parsley**
		salt and pepper to taste
2 cups	(*500 mL*)	**tomato sauce (see page 304)**

If you have fresh clams, cook and prepare as in the previous recipe. If canned, drain and reserve juice.

Sauté the garlic in oil for 5 minutes, but do not let it get brown, add clam juice (either from can or what was set aside after steaming) then add parsley and tomato sauce and simmer for a few minutes. Add salt and pepper. A few minutes before serving, add clams and heat only until it starts to boil, then serve immediately with spaghetti.

For 5–6.

SPAGHETTI WITH CHICKEN LIVERS

Italy   (*Fegato di Pollo con Salsa Pomodoro*)

1 lb	(½ kg)	chicken livers
2 tbs	(2 tbs)	butter or margarine
		salt and pepper to taste
3 cups	(750 mL)	tomato sauce (see page 304)
½ lb	(¼ kg)	spaghetti
2 tbs	(2 tbs)	butter or margarine
½ cup	(125 mL)	grated parmesan cheese

Brown chicken livers in butter or margarine, sprinkle with salt and pepper to taste. While browning cut up into small pieces. Add tomato sauce and bring to a boil, turn down heat and simmer about 5 minutes.

Cook spaghetti in accordance with directions on package, drain and toss with butter, then put in a serving dish. Serve sauce either separately or poured on top of the spaghetti. Sprinkle with cheese.

For 4–5 people.

LASAGNE

Italy   (*Lasagne al Forno*)

This type of Italian dish takes extra work but is well worth the effort, as practically everyone likes it. There are many different versions. I think this is a rather nice one, and it is one of the most popular in the U.S.

1 lb	(½ kg)	lasagne noodles (very wide)
		salt
3 tbs	(3 tbs)	salad oil
6 cups	(1,500 mL)	tomato sauce (see page 304)
1 lb	(½ kg)	ground chuck
½ lb	(¼ kg)	sweet Italian sausages
½ lb	(¼ kg)	hot Italian sausages (or all sweet sausages if preferred)
¼ cup	(60 mL)	chopped parsley
		salt and pepper to taste
1 lb	(½ kg)	ricotta cheese
1 lb	(½ kg)	mozzarella cheese
1 cup	(250 mL)	grated parmesan cheese

Cook noodles in salted water to which 2 tbs salad oil has been added. (The oil will help to prevent noodles from sticking together). Cook according to directions on package, but not fully as they will be baked further in the oven. Drain in a colander.

Brown meat in remaining oil in a frying pan, breaking up pieces with a fork. Add sausages and cook until well done, then remove skins and cut them into slices.

Add meat and sausages to tomato sauce and heat. Butter a large baking dish (9 x 13 or 220 x 320 mm) then pour some meat and tomato sauce on the bottom. Cover with one layer of lasagne noodles, overlapping each other. Spread a thin layer of ricotta cheese, a layer of sliced mozzarella and a light sprinkling of parmesan cheese, then more sauce. Repeat layers until noodles are used up. The top layer should be sauce, sprinkled with parmesan cheese. Bake uncovered in a 350° F (175° C) oven 20 minutes or until bubbling hot.

Serve immediately, cut into portions, to 6–8.

MANICOTTI

Italy (*Manicotti Imbottiti*)

Manicotti seems to bring a happy smile to most Italians, at least those I have met in this country, and it seems that when they want to give you a real nice treat for dinner, manicotti is probably on the menu. They may seem a bit tedious to make, but are well worth the effort. Instead of these thin pancakes, the large tubular shaped pasta may be used. (Sometimes they are called canneloni—sometimes manicotti).

4	(*4*)	eggs
1 cup	(*250 mL*)	water
1 cup	(*250 mL*)	flour
¼ ts	(¼ *ts*)	salt
For frying:		salad oil

Beat eggs slightly in a mixing bowl, add water and mix well. Gradually add flour mixed with salt, beating after each addition. Heat a small frying pan, or teflon pan, and brush with oil. Add about 2 tbs batter and cook only on one side, about one minute. Make sure pancake does not burn. Stack them on a plate, separated by pieces of wax paper.   Makes 18–20 manicotti.

Filling:

¼ lb	(*125 g*)	mozzarella cheese, coarsely grated or chopped
½ lb	(¼ *kg*)	ricotta cheese
2	(*2*)	eggs, slightly beaten
2 tbs	(*2 tbs*)	finely minced parsley
		salt and pepper to taste

Stir together all ingredients and mix well.

Assembly:

2 cups	(*500 mL*)	tomato sauce

Put 1–2 tbs filling on the uncooked side of each pancake, then roll them up and arrange them close together in a low baking dish. Spoon tomato sauce over the manicotti and bake 15–20 minutes in a 350° F (175° C) oven until they are piping hot right through.   Serves 5–6.

CANELLONI WITH CHEESE FILLING
Italy *(Canelloni con Formaggio)*

This is a similar preparation to the previous recipe but pasta shells are used instead of pancakes. If you feel it is too much trouble to make your own shells, they can be bought already made, and filled after being boiled according to directions on package.

Shells:

2 cups	(500 mL)	flour, approximately
½ ts	(½ ts)	salt
2	(2)	eggs
1	(1)	egg yolk
1 tbs	(1 tbs)	salad oil
1-2 tbs	(1-2 tbs)	water, if necessary

Sift together flour and salt into a bowl, make a well in the center, put in eggs, egg yolk and oil and work in flour, a little at a time, until a ball of dough has been formed. If dough is too stiff, add a little water, ½ tbs at a time, or if it is too loose, add a little flour.

Knead dough on a floured surface until elastic, about 10 minutes. Cover with a floured towel and let it rest for 20 minutes. Divide dough into three parts and roll each one out as thin as possible and cut into 4" (100 mm) squares.

Drop a few at a time into boiling, salted water, cook about 3 minutes, remove with a slotted spoon and drop into cold water. Keep them there until ready to use, then drain off water, pat squares dry and fill with following mixture:

Cheese Filling:

2 cups	(500 mL)	grated mozzarella cheese
½ cup	(125 mL)	grated parmesan cheese
½ cup	(125 mL)	butter, melted

Assembly:

2 cups	(500 mL)	tomato sauce

Mix together cheese and melted butter. Place 1 tbs of cheese mixture on each noodle square, roll up and arrange in a square baking pan, seams down. Cover with tomato sauce, and bake in a 325° F (165° C) oven for 20–25 minutes.

Serve piping hot to 4–5.

BAKED ZITI

Italy   *(Ziti al Forno)*

A hearty pasta dish combining those good Italian sausages with tomato sauce and cheese.

1 lb	(½ kg)	ziti (a specially shaped pasta)
½ lb	(¼ kg)	sweet Italian sausages
½ lb	(¼ kg)	hot Italian sausages
		(or all sweet sausages, if preferred)
1	(1)	clove garlic, finely minced
2	(2)	medium onions, finely chopped
		(1½ cups or 375 mL)
1 ts	(1 ts)	oregano
1 ts	(1 ts)	dried basil
		salt and pepper to taste
2	(2)	cans tomatoes (about 6 cups
		or 1½ L), chopped
½ lb	(¼ kg)	sliced fresh mushrooms, or one 4 oz
		(125 mL) can of mushrooms
½ lb	(¼ kg)	mozzarella cheese, cut into ¼″
		or 6 mm cubes
½ cup	(125 mL)	grated parmesan cheese

Cook ziti in salted water in accordance with instructions on package. In a skillet cook sausages for about 25 minutes, then peel off skins and cut them into ¼″ (6 mm) slices and set aside. Sauté onion and garlic in remaining sausage fat until onion is transparent.

Transfer into a 6 qt (6 L) saucepan, add tomatoes and seasonings and bring to a boil. Turn down heat and simmer for about 2 hours. Add mushrooms and cook about 5 minutes, then add sausage slices and heat thoroughly. Add ziti and cubed mozzarella cheese and mix well. Put it all in a large baking dish, sprinkle top with grated parmesan cheese and bake in a 350° F (175° C) oven for 30 minutes. Serve piping hot.   For 5–6 people.

ZABAGLIONE

Italy

A very rich dessert, but simple to prepare.

4	(4)	egg yolks, at room temperature
¼ cup	(60 mL)	sugar (preferably "verifine" granulated)
¾ cup	(180 mL)	Marsala, or sweet sherry

Beat egg yolks until light and fluffy. Add sugar, a little at a time while continuing beating. Place pan over hot, but not boiling water, and add wine, a little at a time, while beating, and continue beating until mixture is smooth and as thick as sour cream. Serve warm in dessert glasses, plain or sprinkled with cinnamon; or chill it and serve with fruit.

5–6 portions

ST. JOSEPH'S CREAM PUFFS

Italy   *(Sfinge di San Giuseppe)*

Cream puffs the Italian way! Mmm, good and rich, as most desserts, alas.

6 tbs	(6 tbs)	butter or margarine
¾ cup	(180 mL)	water
¾ cup	(180 mL)	flour
		pinch of salt
3	(3)	eggs

Bring butter and water to a boil in a saucepan, then add flour and salt all at once and stir vigorously until you obtain a smooth compact mass. Remove from heat and add the eggs, one at a time, beating thoroughly after each addition. Drop by tablespoonfuls on a greased baking sheet and bake in a 400° F (200° C) oven for 35–40 minutes or until golden brown in color. Cool, then make a slit in each puff towards the bottom and fill with the following mixture.

Filling:

1½ cups	(375 mL)	ricotta cheese (¾ lb or 400 g)
⅓ cup	(80 mL)	sugar
2 tbs	(2 tbs)	semi-sweet chocolate, coarsely chopped
1 ts	(1 ts)	grated orange rind

Combine all ingredients and mix thoroughly until well blended.

RICOTTA PIE

Italy   *(Torta di Ricotta)*

Ricotta Pie is the Italian equivalent of our cheese cakes. They are very popular and almost every family claims to have a recipe of their own. I have tried many of them, but when it comes to flavor as well as texture I find this one hard to equal.

Crust:

2 cups	(*500 mL*)	flour
½ ts	(*½ ts*)	salt
1 cup	(*250 mL*)	soft shortening
2	(*2*)	egg yolks
2 tbs	(*2 tbs*)	sherry approximately
		(or, if preferred, use water instead)

Sift together flour and salt, then cut in shortening with a pastry-cutter until mixture resembles coarse crumbs. Add egg yolks and enough sherry or water to hold dough together. Make into a ball and scrape up all crumbs along the sides of the bowl. Roll out to fit either a 9″ (220 mm) square pan, a 9″ (220 mm) spring pan or a 10″ (250 mm) pie pan. Pour in the following filling and bake in a 350° F (175° C) oven for about one hour, or until firm. Check towards the end of baking time to see if the pie is getting too dark on top, in such a case cover with aluminum foil. If desired, sprinkle with confectioners' sugar just before serving.

Filling:

3 cups	(*750 mL*)	ricotta cheese
¼ cup	(*60 mL*)	flour
2 tbs	(*2 tbs*)	grated orange rind
2 tbs	(*2 tbs*)	grated lemon rind
2 tbs	(*2 tbs*)	vanilla
½ ts	(*½ ts*)	salt
4	(*4*)	eggs, well beaten
1 cup	(*250 mL*)	sugar

For sprinkling: confectioners' sugar (optional)

Combine ricotta, flour, orange and lemon rinds, vanilla and salt and mix well. Add beaten eggs and blend, then add sugar gradually and stir until well mixed.

BISCUIT TORTONI

Italy   (*Biscotti Tortoni*)

A quite easily prepared frozen dessert which looks more complicated when served.

1 cup	(*250 mL*)	heavy cream
⅓ cup	(*80 mL*)	confectioners' sugar
2 tbs	(*2 tbs*)	cognac, Marsala or sweet sherry
1	(*1*)	egg white, beaten stiff
⅓ cup	(*80 mL*)	almonds, toasted and finely ground
⅓ cup	(*80 mL*)	crumbled macaroons (or chopped toasted almonds, if desired)

Whip cream until thick, then add sugar gradually while beating until cream is stiff. Stir in cognac or wine, then fold in egg white and ground almonds. Put mixture into paper muffin cups and sprinkle top with crumbled macaroons or toasted almonds. Freeze for about 4 hours. Remove from freezer about 10 minutes before serving.   For 5–6 people.

RUM COOKIES

Italy   (*Favette*)

These are like tiny doughnuts and taste best when eaten quite fresh.

2 cups	(*500 mL*)	flour
2½ ts	(*2½ ts*)	baking powder
½ cup	(*125 mL*)	sugar
4 tbs	(*4 tbs*)	butter, softened
2	(*2*)	eggs, slightly beaten
3 tbs	(*3 tbs*)	rum
		oil for deep-frying
		confectioners' sugar for dusting

Sift together flour, baking powder and sugar, then cut in butter with a pastry blender. Add eggs and rum and mix well. Knead dough until light and workable, about 10 minutes, then shape pieces of dough into small lengths, about the size of your little finger, (1½″ or 40 mm). Deep-fry these in hot oil, 375° F (190° C), a few at a time. When golden brown in color, lift out and drain on paper towels. When cool, dust with confectioners' sugar.

Makes about 3 dozen.

ANISE COOKIES

Italy   *(Biscotti all'Anice)*

Holiday cookies in the Italian fashion. They are not crisp like most American cookies but have a soft consistency.

4 cups	(1 L)	flour
3 ts	(3 ts)	baking powder
¾ cup	(180 mL)	sugar
4 tbs	(4 tbs)	butter, melted
6	(6)	eggs, unbeaten
1½ ts	(1½ ts)	anise extract

Sift together flour, baking powder and sugar and mix well in a large mixing bowl. Make a well in center then put eggs and melted butter into this and mix by gradually pushing flour off the sides into the center. Mix until well blended into a soft dough. Turn onto a floured baking board and knead for a few minutes.

Divide dough into three parts and form into long rolls. Cut off a small piece, then roll it in your hands or on the board, dusting with flour off and on, into a 4″ (100 mm) strip, ⅓″ (8 mm) in diameter. Tie into a knot and place on a greased baking sheet. Repeat until dough is used.

Bake in a 350° F (175° C) oven 10–12 minutes or until golden in color. Remove from baking sheet and cool, then dip top of cookies in the following icing and sprinkle with colored sugar bits.

Icing:

2½ cups	(625 mL)	confectioners' sugar
½ ts	(½ ts)	anise extract
2–3 tbs	(2–3 tbs)	warm water

Sift sugar, then add anise extract and sufficient water to make a smooth mixture that will not run.

Makes 7–8 dozen.

COFFEE CAKE

Italy   *(Panettone)*

That good, sweet Italian yeast bread, especially welcome around holiday time.

1 pkg	(*1 pkg*)	dry yeast
¼ cup	(*60 mL*)	lukewarm water
½ cup	(*125 mL*)	butter or margarine, melted
¾ cup	(*180 mL*)	milk
½ cup	(*125 mL*)	sugar
1 ts	(*1 ts*)	salt
2	(*2*)	eggs
		grated rind of 1 lemon
4 cups	(*1 L*)	flour
½ cup	(*125 mL*)	raisins
½ cup	(*125 mL*)	mixed candied fruit, diced

For kneading: ¼-½ cup (60-125 mL) flour

For brushing: 1 egg mixed with 1 tbs milk

Dissolve yeast in lukewarm water with 1 ts of the sugar. Melt butter and add milk, heating it until lukewarm. In the bowl of electric mixer or other bowl, combine milk, butter, sugar, salt, eggs and lemon rind, then add yeast mixture and about 1 cup (250 mL) flour. Beat until well blended, then add remaining flour, a little at a time, beating continuously until the electric beater cannot handle the dough any longer, then continue with a wooden spoon.

Add raisins and candied fruit and mix well, then turn dough onto a floured baking board and knead about 10 minutes or until smooth and elastic. Place dough in a greased bowl, turn over to get grease on all sides, cover and let rise in a warm place for 1½ hours. Punch down dough and divide in half, then shape into loaves to fit into 5 x 9″ (120 x 200 mm) greased loaf pans, or shape into round loaves directly on a greased baking sheet. Let rise for 1 hour, brush with egg and milk mixture and bake in a 350° F (175° C) oven about 35–40 minutes.

Japan

ONE vision that comes to mind when I think of Japan is a print of some beautiful Japanese garden with a pond and a bridge, and Mount Fuji hovering in the background. Every detail is drawn with beauty in mind, just as the landscaping itself was created by an artist in his trade.

And when it comes to the Japanese cuisine the same type of impression is created. They do not just get the food together and put it on serving platters in a haphazard way, it is done with utmost attention to both design and details, so that it will be most pleasing to the eye—as well as to the palate—so successfully that you may feel it is a pity to ruin its beauty by eating it.

Japan of today has so many people for the food that is available that they must make do with smaller portions of meat and fish than we are used to. But they do so well with what they have, and they fix the food in such a way, that you actually do not realize this.

One of their meat products is quite incredible, the *shimofuri* also called *Kobe beef*, well-marbled and tender beef, which comes from cattle that must be the most pampered beasts in the world. When they are young they get fed on rice, beans and bran but from about their third year on they also get large quantities of *beer*. But this is not all, for in order to get the meat really tenderized, the cattle are massaged daily by human hands. This type of beef is naturally very expensive and when you order it in a restaurant you only get thin slices of it—but it tastes delicious.

Another thing that comes to mind when you mention Japanese food is raw fish (*sashimi*), seaweeds and such things. And people are apt to make a face at this. Oh, yes, these things do exist, but when you eat them you cannot imagine why you ever wrinkled your nose. The fish used in this fashion is very, very fresh, it is sliced paper thin and usually served with a vinegared rice, mixed with tiny specks of chopped vegetables, and all of a sudden you cannot help realizing how very good it is.

The soups, eaten in the beginning of a meal, are usually just a thin broth, made with a base of dried fish flakes (bonito flakes) and sometimes also a sheet of seaweed (*yamadashi*) and in this broth just a few pieces of vegetables or slivers of chicken are floated, with the color and the shape of the vegetables selected to make the soup attractive to the eye. But there is also a hearty soup with spaghetti type noodles that is commonly sold by vendors on street corners in Japan on chilly days. You do not get spoons, so the soup is taken in with a lot of slurping noises—and in Japan this is not considered bad manners at all.

Desserts at the end of the meal as we know it have not been generally used in Japan, but the strong Western influence of today on life in Japan in general carries on into eating habits, so dessert is getting more and more common. Sweets are otherwise usually served in the form of snacks or part of buffet style meals.

CLAMS IN SOY SAUCE	
BUTTERFLY SHRIMP	
SOUP BROTH & SOUP	*Dashi*
BATTER-FRIED FISH OR VEGETABLES	*Tempura*
SLICED RAW FISH	*Sashimi*
VINEGARED RICE	*Sushi*
FRIED FISH PATTIES	
PORK MEATBALLS	
BEEF (OR PORK) SUKIYAKI	
BEEF (OR CHICKEN) TERIYAKI	
FRIED PORK WITH RICE NOODLES	*Sanmi Yaki*
SAUTÉED CELERY	
SNOW SPONGE WITH MANDARIN ORANGES	

Japan   CLAMS IN SOY SAUCE

A good appetizer which may be served with crackers in this country.

2 dozen	(*2 dozen*)	clams
¼ cup	(*60 mL*)	soy sauce
1 tbs	(*1 tbs*)	sherry
1 tbs	(*1 tbs*)	sugar
4	(*4*)	thin slices fresh ginger or ½ ts dry ginger

Put clams in a large kettle with about ½″ (12 mm) water, and steam until they open. Remove from shells then put in a saucepan with remaining ingredients. Bring to a boil, then turn down heat to very low and simmer for not more than 5 minutes. Serve warm or cold as an appetizer.

Japan   BUTTERFLY SHRIMP

1-1½ lbs	(½-¾ *kg*)	large shrimp
½ cup	(*125 mL*)	flour
1 tbs	(*1 tbs*)	corn starch
1 ts	(*1 ts*)	salt
1 ts	(*1 ts*)	baking powder
1-2 tbs	(*1-2 tbs*)	water
1	(*1*)	egg, well beaten
		oil for deep frying

Clean shrimp, remove shells and devein. Split shrimp down the back to about ⅓″ (8 mm) of its tail, then flatten into a butterfly shape. Make a batter by sifting together flour, corn starch, salt and baking powder into a bowl, then add beaten egg and 1 tbs water and mix well. If the batter is too stiff, add one more tbs water. Dip shrimp into this batter and cook in hot fat (375° F or 190° C) until golden brown. Serve immediately with the following sauce, as an appetizer.

Sauce:

⅓ cup	(*80 mL*)	soy sauce
½ ts	(½ *ts*)	sugar
⅛ ts	(⅛ *ts*)	ginger (powdered)
⅔ cup	(*160 mL*)	water
2 tbs	(*2 tbs*)	dry sherry

Mix together all the ingredients and let stand for 1 hour before serving to mix the flavors.   Serves 4–6.

SOUP BROTH

Japan   (*Dashi*)

6 cups	(*1,500 mL*)	water
1 cup	(*250 mL*)	bonito flakes
1 sheet	(*1 sheet*)	black seaweed (*yamadashi*), optional

Bring water to a boil, add bonito
flakes and seaweed and simmer for
5 minutes. Remove from heat and let
stand for an additional 5 minutes,
then strain the broth and discard the
fish flakes.

VARIATION: SOUP

Use the above broth and just add a
few very thin slivers or flakes of vegetables, such as carrots, scallions etc.
and cook for only one minute. Add
1 ts soy sauce, salt to taste and serve.

BATTER-FRIED FISH OR VEGETABLES

Japan   (*Tempura*)

*Tempura is often served as an appetizer but with larger quantities of fish and or
vegetables it is eaten as a main course.*

Batter:

1½ cups	(*375 mL*)	flour
⅓ cup	(*80 mL*)	corn starch
2 ts	(*2 ts*)	baking powder
1 ts	(*1 ts*)	salt
2	(*2*)	eggs, slightly beaten
1 cup	(*250 mL*)	water
		oil for deep frying

Sift together flour, corn starch, baking
powder and salt, add eggs and water
and mix. The batter is supposed to be
somewhat lumpy so do not mix it
too well.

(*Continued on next page*)

(Batter-Fried Fish or Vegetables, cont.)

Fish or vegetables:

1½ lb	(¾ kg)	raw shrimp, fish, or crab legs
		Vegetables such as carrots, onions, potatoes, broccoli, green peppers, egg plant, string beans etc. in quantities to serve 5–6 people. Clean and prepare vegetables by cutting them into 1½" (40 mm) lengths, and not thicker than ⅓" (8 mm) for heavier stuff such as potatoes and carrots.

Shrimp should be shelled and deveined, and fish and crab legs cut into bite-size pieces. Dip fish and vegetables in batter then deep-fry in 375° F (190° C) oil. Do only about 5–6 pieces at a time, otherwise oil would cool off too much and the result would be soggy instead of crisp. Fry until golden brown, turning over once for even color. Remove and drain on paper towels.

Tempura sauce:

½ cup	(125 mL)	soy sauce
2	(2)	thin slices fresh ginger
½ cup	(125 mL)	water
1 tbs	(1 tbs)	lime juice
1 tbs	(1 tbs)	sugar
2 tbs	(2 tbs)	sake or dry sherry

Mix together all ingredients and let stand in refrigerator at least 6 hours or overnight.

When tempura is ready to be served, pour sauce into 5–6 individual small bowls. Pieces are dipped as they are eaten.

Serves 5–6.

Japan   **SLICED RAW FISH**   *(Sashimi)*

This title may turn some people off as they cannot imagine eating raw fish. However, after using very fresh fish of top quality and any of the dipping sauces, they may easily change their minds.

1 lb	(½ kg)	**very fresh fish, such as salmon, fresh tuna, or really any kind at all with bones removed**

Cut fish diagonally into very thin slices. Often more than one kind of fish is used. Put on a serving platter together with cucumbers, carrots, white radishes, all cut into thin strips and added in an attractive way on the platter. Serve with either one of the following sauces, poured into small individual bowls.

Sashimi Sauce 1:

½ cup	*(125 mL)*	**soy sauce**
		hot mustard to taste (use dry mustard mixed with water)

Sashimi Sauce 2:

3 tbs	*(3 tbs)*	**soy sauce**
2 tbs	*(2 tbs)*	**vinegar**
1½ ts	*(1½ ts)*	**sugar**
1	*(1)*	**small clove garlic, finely minced**
2 tbs	*(2 tbs)*	**finely chopped scallions**
¼ ts	*(¼ ts)*	**crushed red pepper (or more if a really hot sauce is desired)**
½ ts	*(½ ts)*	**toasted sesame seeds**

Mix well and let stand for at least 1 hour for flavors to blend.

Japan   **VINEGARED RICE**   *(Sushi)*

1½ cups	*(375 mL)*	**rice**
3 cups	*(750 mL)*	**water**
3	*(3)*	**dried mushrooms (Chinese type)**
½ cup	*(125 mL)*	**chopped carrots**
½ cup	*(125 mL)*	**chopped string beans**

(Continued on next page)

(Vinegared Rice, cont.)

1 cup	(250 mL)	water
1 tbs	(1 tbs)	sugar
1 tbs	(1 tbs)	soy sauce
		salt to taste

Boil rice for 15 minutes, until cooked but not dry. Leave cover on during the whole cooking process. Soak mushrooms in a bowl with cold water for 30 minutes, then drain and cut into small pieces. Cook vegetables with water, sugar, soy sauce and salt until they are tender. It will take only a few minutes. Drain off water, and combine with rice and mix well.

Sauce:

3 tbs	(3 tbs)	vinegar
1½ tbs	(1½ tbs)	sugar
1 ts	(1 ts)	salt

Cook all ingredients in small saucepan until sugar and salt have dissolved. Pour over rice mixture and stir to get all grains coated. Press mixture into square or round pan, cover with plastic wrap then put a weight on top (a similar shaped dish filled with water will do) and let it remain thus for 4–6 hours.

Cut into squares or wedges and serve cold.

6	(6)	eggs
½ ts	(½ ts)	salt
1 ts	(1 ts)	corn starch
2 tbs	(2 tbs)	sugar
		oil for frying

Beat eggs with salt, corn starch and sugar only until well blended. Then add oil to a 6–7" (120–150 mm) frying pan, swirling it around to cover the bottom. Add a thin layer of egg mixture and cook over low heat, turning over once to cook both sides, then remove. Repeat until egg mixture is used up. Stack them until ready to use.

VARIATIONS:

Decorate squares before weight is added with small shrimp, slices of raw fish, lemon peel etc., *or* place rice mixture on a sheet of *nori* (seaweed) and roll into a cylinder and cut into 1" (25 mm) pieces.

The same basic vinegared rice is also sometimes served wrapped in a small "pouch" made of eggs cooked like a pancake, as follows:

Put rice mixture in the middle of each "pancake," gather together and tie with a string, letting some flaps of pancake hang over string and the rice mixture showing through. Decorate with small shrimp, parsley or just a few peas for color contrast.

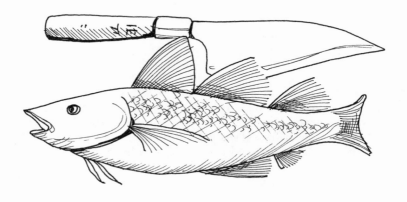

FRIED FISH PATTIES

Japan

1½ lbs	(¾ kg)	fish fillets (flounder, sole, cod or haddock)
1	(1)	small onion, finely chopped (½ cup or 125 mL)
1 tbs	(1 tbs)	coarsely grated carrot
1 ts	(1 ts)	finely minced fresh ginger (or ½ ts powder)
2 tbs	(2 tbs)	corn starch
1	(1)	egg white
		salt to taste
2 tbs	(2 tbs)	salad oil

Grind fish or chop very finely, then mix together with onion, carrot, ginger, corn starch, salt and egg white and blend well. Shape into small patties and fry in oil in a skillet until lightly brown on both sides. Turn down heat and cover skillet and cook for five more minutes.

Sauce:

2 tbs	(2 tbs)	ketchup
1 tbs	(1 tbs)	Worcestershire sauce
1 tbs	(1 tbs)	sherry

Mix together and heat and serve with above fish patties.

PORK MEATBALLS

Japan

1 lb	(½ kg)	ground pork
1	(1)	small onion, finely chopped
1 ts	(1 ts)	finely minced ginger
1 cup	(250 mL)	soft bread crumbs, soaked in water
⅓ cup	(80 mL)	flour
		salt to taste
¼ cup	(60 mL)	soy sauce
3 tbs	(3 tbs)	sugar

For sprinkling: chopped parsley

Mix meat, onion, ginger, flour, salt and soaked bread crumbs until a smooth mixture is obtained. Shape into small meatballs, ¾"–1" (18–25 mm) in diameter. Steam them in ¼ cup (60 mL) water in a covered fry pan over medium heat, shaking pan off and on to prevent sticking. Add a little bit more water if pan should dry out. Remove meatballs.

Add soy sauce and sugar to pan and heat, add meatballs, turn up heat to high and cook for a couple of minutes, shaking and rolling to coat them evenly with the soy sauce mixture. Serve meatballs, sprinkled with chopped parsley, as an appetizer, on small bamboo skewers or toothpicks.

Serves 5–6.

BEEF SUKIYAKI

Japan

This dish is best cooked right at the table. Make a show of it while you are cooking. When its aromas rise out of the pan, they will get the gastric juices flowing, and you can build up a nice appetite in your guests.

1 lb	(½ kg)	very thinly sliced beef (tenderloin or sirloin)
2 tbs	(2 tbs)	salad oil
2	(2)	medium size onions, thinly sliced
8–10	(8–10)	scallions, cut into 1″ (25 mm) lengths
2	(2)	stalks celery, thinly sliced diagonally
¼ lb	(125 g)	fresh mushrooms, thinly sliced
2 cups	(500 mL)	Chinese cabbage, thinly sliced diagonally
1	(1)	small can bamboo shoots, drained and thinly sliced
2	(2)	cakes of bean curd (optional)
1–1½ oz	(30–45 g)	vermicelli noodles (rice noodles)
½ lb	(¼ kg)	fresh spinach
½ cup	(125 mL)	soy sauce
½ cup	(125 mL)	beef broth (canned or made with bouillon cube)
2 tbs	(2 tbs)	sugar

Mix together soy sauce, beef broth and sugar and set aside. On a platter arrange all the vegetables, meat and noodles in neat piles. Put the salad oil into a skillet over a hibachi stove, or in an electric skillet heated to 375° F (190° C), add onions, scallions and celery, stirring off and on while cooking, about 5 minutes. Add mushrooms and Chinese cabbage and cook for 3 minutes, still stirring.

Push vegetables on the side, then add meat, moving it around to get evenly heated. Add soy-sauce mixture, bamboo shoots, bean curd and spinach and mix it lightly all together with other contents of skillet and cook about 3 minutes, or until spinach is slightly wilted. Serve immediately with hot rice.

For 5–6 people.

VARIATION:

Thinly sliced pork may be used instead of beef.

BEEF TERIYAKI

Japan

1½ lb	(¾ kg)	lean tender cut of beef (tenderloin or sirloin)
½ cup	(125 mL)	dry sherry
½ cup	(125 mL)	soy sauce
⅓ cup	(80 mL)	sugar
1 ts	(1 ts)	grated fresh ginger (or ½ ts ground ginger)
1 tbs	(1 tbs)	salad oil

Make a marinade of sherry, soy sauce, sugar and ginger and stir until sugar is dissolved. Cut the meat into thin strips, ½″ x ¼″ x 1″ (12 x 6 x 25 mm) and marinate for about 30 minutes.

Drain and pat meat dry with paper toweling. Heat oil in skillet and then cook meat briefly (about 1 minute) on each side. The beef should be slightly rare. Serve with rice.

For 4–6 people.

VARIATION:

Chicken Teriyaki

1-1½ lbs	(½-¾ kg)	boned chicken breast

Cut meat into strips as for the Beef Teriyaki and proceed as in beef recipe.

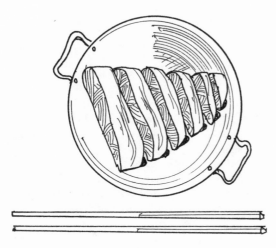

FRIED PORK WITH RICE NOODLES

Japan   *(Sanmi Yaki)*

1	*(1)*	small red chili, seeds removed and cut into small pieces, or $\frac{1}{4}$ ts red pepper flakes
1 tbs	*(1 tbs)*	chopped scallions
1 tbs	*(1 tbs)*	ground sesame seeds (whole seeds may be pounded with a mortar and pestle)
2 tbs	*(2 tbs)*	soy sauce
2 tbs	*(2 tbs)*	dry sherry
1 lb	*($\frac{1}{2}$ kg)*	boneless pork, cut into serving pieces about $\frac{1}{4}''$ (6 mm) thick
2 tbs	*(2 tbs)*	salad oil
2 oz	*(60 g)*	rice noodles (vermicelli)
4 cups	*(1 L)*	water
$\frac{1}{2}$	*($\frac{1}{2}$)*	medium size cucumber
1	*(1)*	small tomato, seeded
2 tbs	*(2 tbs)*	vinegar
1 tbs	*(1 tbs)*	sugar
$\frac{1}{2}$ ts	*($\frac{1}{2}$ ts)*	coarsely ground black pepper

Make a marinade of soy sauce, wine, pepper, scallions and sesame seeds. Add pork and marinate for 1–1$\frac{1}{2}$ hours. Heat oil in an electric frying pan or large skillet and brown pork well on both sides. Soak rice noodles in water for 10 minutes then boil in water until tender, about 5 minutes. Cut cucumbers and tomatoes into paper-thin strips and mix in with noodles. Place noodles and pork slices, side by side, on a serving platter. Add vinegar, sugar and pepper to frying pan, stir vigorously, then pour on top of pork.

Serves 4–5.

SAUTÉED CELERY

Japan

4 cups	*(1 L)*	diagonally sliced ($\frac{1}{4}''$ or 6 mm thick) celery (about 6–8 stalks)
$\frac{1}{3}$ cup	*(80 mL)*	salad oil
3 tbs	*(3 tbs)*	soy sauce
1 ts	*(1 ts)*	sugar
1 ts	*(1 ts)*	grated fresh ginger (or $\frac{1}{2}$ ts ground ginger)

Sauté celery slices in hot oil for 5 minutes, stirring continuously, or until almost tender. Add soy sauce, sugar and grated ginger, stirring to blend. Cook for about 2 more minutes and serve.

Serves 4–6.

SNOW SPONGE WITH MANDARIN ORANGES
Japan

*Although the Japanese do not have the custom of eating dessert after a meal,
they do have food stuffs which do very well as desserts. This one, for example.*

1	(1)	small can mandarin oranges (11 oz or 300 g)
1 tbs	(1 tbs)	gelatin
⅔ cup	(160 mL)	sugar
2	(2)	egg whites
1 ts	(1 ts)	vanilla extract

Soften gelatin in ½ cup (125 mL) cold water. Drain juice from can of oranges, then add enough water to juice to make 1½ cups (375 mL). Combine this with softened gelatin and sugar in a small saucepan and bring to a boil, turn down heat and simmer for a couple of minutes. Cool until mixture becomes syrupy in consistency. Beat egg whites until stiff and dry, then pour syrup over egg whites, stirring continuously but lightly. Stir in vanilla.

Pour into a square pan (9 x 9″ or 220 x 220 mm) and put orange pieces on top in a nice pattern. Press them slightly into the surface. Refrigerate for about 3–4 hours, then cut into 16 squares and serve as a dessert.

Serves 6–8.

Mexico

THROUGHOUT large areas of the U.S., Mexican cooking is the most familiar of all foreign cuisines. I am, of course, referring to the southwest and California. But no wonder, these places were once part of Mexico and the cooking habits lingered on after they became part of the United States. But even in the rest of the country, there has been an upsurge of interest in Mexican food in the last ten years, but it mainly centers around a few items such as tacos, tostadas, chili-beans etc. And there is much, much more to Mexican cooking than that.

The cuisine is really ancient in history, as many of the ingredients used were not known outside this area when the conquistadores arrived in the 16th century. They found the Aztecs eating tortillas, tamales and other varieties of corn products—and most of these are still used and eaten in Mexico. Furthermore, corn, chilies, beans, tomatoes, peanuts, chocolate, vanilla, sweet potatoes, papayas and many other things were grown and used so extensively that they traveled back to Europe where some were greeted enthusiastically and others apprehensively.

The food products of old are still used to such an extent today because they are not only good, but also nutritious, and often economical too. Many tourists who have traveled off the main roads in Mexico have marvelled at the way that every little plot of land is utilized and planted with something, most often corn, and sometimes the corn patches seem to be practically climbing vertically up a steep mountain side. This sight makes you wonder how Mexican peasants can ever be joked about as being lazy, and the importance of corn in the diet becomes very obvious.

A group of recipes, sometimes referred to as the *corn-kitchen*, is indeed what makes the Mexican cooking different. It is made up of a surprising variety of dishes and textures from the same source.

Another thing you connect with Mexican cooking is their liking for hot spicy dishes. I thought I liked them—until I came to Mexico and in a restaurant recklessly asked for "a real hot Mexican dish." And I got it—my first mouthful made me feel as if my eyes would come out of their sockets. I saw some cool-looking green sauce in a little dish on the table and took a spoonful to cool my mouth a little. Wow! That was even hotter. No water or anything to drink, so there I sat trying not to make an absolute spectacle of myself, while my eyes and nose both started to run. So I learned the hard way to be careful about putting strange things into my mouth, especially before the drinkables arrive. So if you are not used to hot food, go easy on the chilies you add, and learn to accept them in stages. Once you get to like them, however, they become almost addictive.

But there are many things in Mexican cooking that are just good without being too spicy, as you will find.

Spain had a great influence on the cooking and many dishes in Mexico are the same or similar to those of Spain. An example is the most popular of desserts, *flan*. You will find a recipe for it under SPAIN.

CHILIES	*Chiles*
PICKLED FISH	*Ceviche*
BEAN DIP	*Frijoles para Sopear*
AVOCADO DIP	*Guacamole*
CHEESE DIP	*Chile con Queso*
MEATBALL SOUP	*Sopa de Albondigas*
CORN SOUP	*Sopa de Elote*
RED SNAPPER VERA CRUZ	*Huachinango à la Veracruzana*
CHICKEN WITH CHILIES	*Chicken Mole Poblano*
PORK CHOPS	*Chuletas de Cerdo*
PORK STEW WITH RED CHILI SAUCE	*Puerco en Adobo Rojo*
STUFFED PEPPERS	*Chiles Rellenos*
CHILI CON CARNE	*Chiles con Carne*
TORTILLAS	
WHEAT FLOUR TORTILLAS	*Tortillas de Harina de Trigo*

TACOS	
TOSTADAS	
QUESADILLAS	
PICADILLO	
ENCHILADAS	
TORTILLA AND CHEESE CASSEROLE	*Chilaquiles*
TAMALES	
TAMALE CASSEROLE	*Tamal de Casuela*
BEANS	*Frijoles*
FRIED BEANS	*Frijoles Refritos*
YELLOW RICE	*Arroz Amarillo*
SCRAMBLED EGGS	*Huevos Revueltos*
TOMATO SAUCE	*Salsa di Jitomate*
CHRISTMAS EVE SALAD	*Ensalada de Noche Buena*
ROYAL EGGS	*Huevos Royales*
"PILLOW" FRITTERS	*Sopaipillas*
ANISE-SESAME COOKIES	*Pastelitos con Anis y Sesamo*
RICE PUDDING WITH ALMONDS	*Budin de Arroz con Almendra*
WEDDING COOKIES (OR BRIDE'S COOKIES)	*Polverones de Boda*
SWEET ROLLS	*Pan Dulce*
SANGRIA	

CHILIES

In the southwestern parts of the U.S. and in California chilies are fairly well known, but in most other parts of our country many of us do not know more than that they are hot peppers. As chilies are used in so many Mexican recipes and they often are referred to by name, I feel I should give a list of the most common kinds used and indicate the degree of hotness. This will enable the cook in some instances to exchange one variety for another without risk of ruining the recipe by using the same amount of extremely hot chilies instead of some milder variety, or vice versa.

Chile guero is pale, yellowish green, medium in size and tapered, and is a sweet, green pepper.

Chile valenciano is slightly larger and deeper green and also a sweet pepper.

Red bell pepper or *green bell peppers* are the mild ones that are most well-known to all of us.

Pimiento is a mild red pepper, most often used canned.

Chile poblano is about the same size as a bell pepper and is usually mild in flavor, but sometimes is hot. It is available in cans, also.

Chile ancho is a dried, wrinkled, red chile, 2–3″ (5–7 cm) long, very flavorful, but on the mild side.

Chile mulato is a dried, wrinkled, reddish-brown chile, more pungent in flavor than *chile ancho*.

Chile pasilla is a very long (about 7″ or 18 cm) dark-reddish, wrinkled, dried chile, stronger in flavor than *mulato* and *ancho* (said to be more "picante.")

Chile serrano is a small (about 1½″ or 4 cm) green chile which is hot. It is often canned.

Chile jalapeño is larger than *serrano* and is hot. It is available canned, sometimes in a milder version with the cans marked "Mild Jalapeno," in which the chilies have been seeded and membranes removed.

Chile chipotle is a dried, wrinkled brick-red chile, which is extremely hot. Sometimes available in cans.

Chile morita is a darker color than *chipotle* and is also extremely hot. Also available in cans.

Chile cascabel is a large round, red chile which is very hot.

Chile pequin or *tepin* is a very tiny red chile which is very hot.

Chile largo is a long, thin yellowish green chile, also available in cans, which is extremely hot.

When dried chilies are used, wash them in cold water, remove membranes, seeds and stems. Tear the remaining chile into pieces, cover with hot water and soak for one hour. They are then ready to be used by chopping, puréeing or whatever. Be careful not to touch your eyes or your mouth while handling the chilies. Wash your hands well afterwards.

If you use canned chilies and wish them to be slightly less hot, just rinse them in cold water, as much of the strong flavor is in the liquid of the can.

In some specialty stores you can buy powdered chilies by the name of the chile from which it originated. Most of the time you can figure on one tablespoon of such powder to equal one chile. The powder, called Chili Powder, found on spice shelves in super-markets all over, does not consist of chilies only, but has other flavorings as well, such as oregano, garlic, cumin, etc. If nothing else is available, it, of course, will have to take the place of real or powdered chilies.

PICKLED FISH

Mexico   *(Ceviche)*

For fish lovers, this is a wonderful delicacy. And the fact that the fish is not cooked should not worry you, as the lime juice does the equivalent of cooking and makes the fish meat firm to the bite.

1 lb	(½ kg)	fillets of red snapper, mackerel, or ocean perch
		juice of 4–5 limes (1 cup or 250 mL)
1	(1)	large tomato, peeled, seeded and cut into small pieces
1	(1)	small onion, finely chopped (½ cup or 125 mL)
1	(1)	Jalapeño chile, seeded and cut into thin strips
2 tbs	(2 tbs)	olive oil
1 tbs	(1 tbs)	vinegar
2 tbs	(2 tbs)	fresh parsley, finely minced
¼ ts	(¼ ts)	oregano
		salt and pepper to taste
		green olives for garnish

Cut fish into bite size pieces and put into a bowl. Cover with lime juice and refrigerate for at least 6 hours, or overnight. Drain the fish, and mix the juice together with remaining ingredients except olives. Place fish in a serving dish and pour the sauce over, mixing it gently. Just before serving, garnish with the olives.

Serves 6 as an appetizer.

BEAN DIP

Mexico   (*Frijoles para Sopear*)

An easy-to-make dip which is both flavorsome and wholesome.

1 cup	(*250 mL*)	dried kidney beans, or 1 can (1 lb or 500 g) of cooked ones
1	(*1*)	large onion, chopped
1	(*1*)	clove of garlic, finely minced
3 tbs	(*3 tbs*)	lard
1	(*1*)	large tomato, peeled, seeded and chopped
2 ts	(*2 ts*)	chili powder
2 ts	(*2 ts*)	prepared mustard
		salt and pepper to taste
⅓ cup	(*80 mL*)	sour cream

If dried beans are used, soak them overnight or for at least 4 hours, cook them until tender, 1–2 hours, depending upon the beans, then drain off excess water. Cook onion and garlic in lard until onion is translucent, add tomato, mix and cook for 5 minutes. Add kidney beans, chili powder, mustard, salt and pepper and cook for an additional 10 minutes. Either mash mixture and put through a sieve, or blend until smooth, a little at a time, in an electric blender. Add sour cream and mix thoroughly. Chill and serve as a dip for fried tortillas, corn chips or vegetables, or use it as a spread on crackers.   Serves 5–8

AVOCADO DIP

Mexico   (*Guacamole*

A smooth, creamy, spicy delicacy from South of the Border, which is also pretty to look at with its soft green color. Heed my advice about putting the pit in the mixture, until ready to serve, as it really does prevent it from turning brown

2	(2)	very ripe avocados, medium size, peeled and pitted
1	(1)	small onion, finely chopped (½ cup or 125 mL)
2	(2)	*chiles serranos* (or other hot chilies, seeded and finely chopped
1	(1)	small tomato, peeled, seeded and finely chopped
		juice of ½ lemon
		salt and pepper to taste
		chopped fresh coriander leaves (also called cilantro or Chinese parsley), if available

(*Continued on next page*

(Avocado Dip, cont.)

Mash avocados with a fork, add onion, peppers and lemon juice, and mix well. Add salt and pepper to taste and stir mixture until creamy. Add chopped tomato and mix gently. Put into a bowl and keep the avocado pit in the center until ready to serve, as this should prevent the *guacamole* from turning dark. Makes about 2–2½ cups (500–600 mL). Serve as an appetizer, or a salad, with *tostadas*. (See page 350.)   For 6–8 people.

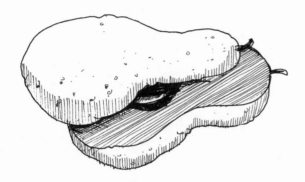

CHEESE DIP

Mexico   (*Chile con Queso*)

A snappy cheese dip or spread, which can be made more or less hot depending upon the amount of chilies you add.

1	(*1*)	medium size onion, finely chopped (¾ cup or 180 mL)
2 tbs	(*2 tbs*)	butter or margarine
2 cups	(*500 mL*)	canned tomatoes, drained and chopped
4-8	(*4-8*)	canned chilies, seeds and membranes removed, drained and chopped (quantity depends upon type of chilies and how spicy you wish to have this)
½ lb	(*¼ kg*)	Monterey Jack, Muenster or mild cheddar cheese, diced
		salt to taste

In a small saucepan sauté onion in butter or margarine until onion is translucent, add the chopped tomatoes and chilies, cheese and salt. Cook over low heat, stirring often, until cheese has melted. Transfer to a fondue pot or some heatproof earthenware dish, put on a heating tray or similar, to keep the cheese melted. Serve with cornchips or tostadas.

Serves 4–6.

MEATBALL SOUP

Mexico   *(Sopa de Albondigas)*

A version of the well-known meatball soup, make it as bland or as spicy as you like it.

Meatballs:

½ lb	(¼ kg)	ground pork
½ lb	(¼ kg)	ground beef
½ cup	(125 mL)	yellow cornmeal
1	(1)	egg, slightly beaten
		salt and pepper to taste
½ ts	(½ ts)	ground cumin seeds
½ ts	(½ ts)	ground coriander seeds
2 tbs	(2 tbs)	butter or margarine or salad oil

Mix all the ingredients except butter together and form into balls, the size of walnuts. Brown well on all sides in butter, margarine or oil, shaking the pan off and on to keep the meatballs evenly round.

Soup:

1	(1)	small onion, chopped (½ cup or 125 mL)
1	(1)	clove garlic, finely minced
2 tbs	(2 tbs)	salad oil
4 cups	(1 L)	soup stock or beef broth
1½ cup	(375 mL)	tomato juice
2 ts	(2 ts)	chili powder (or more, if desired)

Sauté onion and garlic in oil for about 5 minutes, add soup stock, tomato juice and chili powder and bring to a boil. Turn down heat and simmer for 10 minutes, add meatballs and cook an additional 10 minutes.

Serves 4–6.

CORN SOUP

Mexico

(Sopa de Elote)

A wonderful cheesy type of soup.

6	*(6)*	ears of fresh corn
3 tbs	*(3 tbs)*	butter or margarine
1	*(1)*	small onion, chopped (½ cup or 125 mL)
1 tbs	*(1 tbs)*	flour
4 cups	*(1 L)*	chicken broth
		salt and pepper to taste
½ ts	*(½ ts)*	ground cumin
¼ lb	*(125 g)*	grated cheese (Monterey Jack or plain American)
1 cup	*(250 mL)*	light cream

Sauté onion in butter or margarine in a saucepan until transparent. With a sharp knife, scrape corn off the cobs and add to pan. Cook slowly about 5 minutes over low heat, then add flour while stirring to prevent sticking. Add chicken broth and seasonings and mix well, bring to a boil, turn down heat and cook slowly about 15 minutes. Add a little water or more stock, if soup should be too thick. Just before serving, add cream and grated cheese and heat only until cheese has melted. Serves 5–6.

RED SNAPPER VERA CRUZ

Mexico (*Huachinango à la Veracruzana*)

This dish is not for anyone who is afraid of hot food, but is a typical Mexican way of preparing fish.

2 lbs	(*1 kg*)	red snapper fillets (or haddock or ocean perch)
3 tbs	(*3 tbs*)	lemon juice
¼ cup	(*60 mL*)	flour
		salt and pepper to taste
4 tbs	(*4 tbs*)	salad oil
2	(*2*)	large onions, sliced (about 2 cups or 500 mL)
2	(*2*)	cloves garlic, finely minced
2 cups	(*500 mL*)	canned tomatoes (1 lb or 500 g can)
3 tbs	(*3 tbs*)	chopped black olives
2 tbs	(*2 tbs*)	capers
2	(*2*)	canned *Jalapeño chiles*, seeded and cut into strips
		pinch of cinnamon

Cut fish into serving pieces and sprinkle with lemon juice. Mix flour with salt and pepper and dredge fish pieces in this, then sauté until golden in 2 tbs oil in a frying pan, about 5 minutes on each side. Remove from pan, then add remaining oil and sauté onion and garlic until onion is transparent. Add remaining ingredients, except fish, and bring to a boil. Turn down heat very low and simmer sauce for 15 minutes, then add fish and cook until fish is tender and flaky, about 10 minutes, then serve immediately.

Serves 6.

CHICKEN WITH CHILIES

Mexico (*Chicken Mole Poblano*)

One of my favorite Mexican dishes. Maybe not exactly easy, but not hard either. I got a bit apprehensive when I saw all those ingredients but it was not nearly as hard to prepare as I had expected. The beautiful part of making this dish is that it actually improves in flavor by being refrigerated for a day before serving, and then reheated, so it is perfect for a buffet or a party when you like to have as many things as possible made well in advance.

(Continued on next page)

(Chicken with Chilies, cont.)

1	(1)	roasting or stewing chicken, about 5 lbs (2½ kg)
		water
1	(1)	medium size onion
1	(1)	medium size carrot, peeled
1	(1)	bay leaf
10	(10)	whole peppercorns
		salt to taste

Cut chicken into serving pieces, put in a large pot, add remaining ingredients, then water to cover, and bring to a boil. Skim off foam, then turn down heat and simmer until chicken is tender, but still very firm. Cool in the pot.

Sauce:

5	(5)	*chilies anchos* or other red chilies (less quantity if a hotter variety, see write-up on chilies pages 335 to 337)
1	(1)	medium onion, chopped (¾ cup or 180 mL)
2	(2)	cloves garlic
2	(2)	medium size tomatoes, peeled, seeded and chopped
2 tbs	(2 *tbs*)	sesame seeds
½ cup	(125 mL)	blanched almonds
½ cup	(125 mL)	unsalted, shelled and hulled peanuts
¼ cup	(60 mL)	raisins
¼ ts	(¼ *ts*)	ground cloves
¼ ts	(¼ *ts*)	cinnamon
¼ ts	(¼ *ts*)	coriander seeds
½ ts	(½ *ts*)	anise seeds
1	(1)	tortilla, coarsely chopped *or* one slice of toasted bread, chopped
3 tbs	(3 *tbs*)	lard
2 cups	(500 mL)	chicken stock
1 oz	(28 g)	unsweetened chocolate (one square)
		salt to taste

In a bowl first stir together all ingredients for the sauce except chicken stock, chocolate, salt and sugar, then blend it all to a purée in a blender (or if not available, chop the nuts finely, then pound the whole mix into a purée with a mortar and pestle— quite a job. I'll admit.) Either way,

(*Continued on next page*)

(Chicken with Chilies, cont.)

you will have to do it in more than one batch.

Heat the lard in a large frying pan and fry the purée for 5 minutes, stirring constantly. Add chicken stock, chocolate, salt and sugar and cook until chocolate has melted. The consistency of the sauce should be like heavy cream. If it is too thick, add a bit more chicken stock.

Either add chicken pieces to the sauce in the pan, or put them in a large saucepan or flameproof casserole and pour the sauce over. Heat until chicken is thoroughly hot, about 20 minutes. Serve with rice and beans to 5-6. (Sometimes unfilled tamales are also served with this dish).

It improves in flavor if it is made a day ahead of serving and kept in refrigerator overnight, then just heat until hot before serving.

PORK CHOPS

Mexico (*Chuletas de Cerdo*)

Getting away from the spices we normally connect with Mexican cooking, here is a wonderful way of making pork chops, flavored with lemon and orange juice.

6–9	(*6–9*)	pork chops (about 3 lbs or 1½ kg) (depending on size and thickness)
2 tbs	(*2 tbs*)	butter or margarine
1 ts	(*1 ts*)	dry mustard
		salt and pepper to taste
1	(*1*)	clove garlic, finely minced
1	(*1*)	medium size onion, thinly sliced
1	(*1*)	green pepper, cut into thin strips
½ ts	(*½ ts*)	oregano
½ cup	(*125 mL*)	orange juice
2 tbs	(*2 tbs*)	lemon juice
1 tbs	(*1 tbs*)	flour, mixed with ¼ cup (60 mL) cold water

Sprinkle pork chops with dry mustard, salt and pepper then brown in one tbs butter or margarine. Set aside. Sauté onion and garlic in remaining butter until onion is transparent, then add pork chops, pepper, orange and lemon juice and simmer over low heat until pork chops are tender, about 30–45 minutes, depending on thickness. Turn them over once during cooking.

When chops are tender, add flour mixed with water to skillet, blend with remaining contents and cook about 5 minutes. Serve with rice or potatoes in any form.   For 6.

PORK STEW WITH RED CHILI SAUCE

Mexico   (*Puerco en Adobo Rojo*)

A very flavorful pork stew.

4	(4)	chiles anchos
2 lbs	(1 kg)	boneless pork, cut into 1½″ (38 mm) cubes
1	(1)	medium size onion, whole, stuck with 2 whole cloves
1	(1)	small onion, chopped (½ cup or 125 mL)
1	(1)	clove garlic, chopped
½ ts	(½ ts)	cumin
5	(5)	whole peppercorns
1	(1)	1″ (25 mm) piece of cinnamon stick
½ ts	(½ ts)	oregano
1 tbs	(1 tbs)	sugar
1	(1)	large tomato, peeled, seeded and chopped
2 tbs	(2 tbs)	lard

If dried chilies are used, soak them in water for one hour.

Put pork with whole onion and water to cover (about 2 cups or 500 mL) in a large saucepan and bring to a boil. Skim off foam, then turn down heat and simmer meat until tender, 1–1½ hours, but do not let it get so overcooked that it falls apart.

Remove seeds and veins from fresh chilies, or from dried ones after soaking. In a blender, combine chilies, onion, garlic, spices and herbs, sugar and tomato and blend until well combined, if too thick add a ¼ cup (60 mL) pork stock. Blending may have to be done with half the mixture at a time.

Heat lard in a small frying pan, then add chili mixture and cook for about 5 minutes, and stir to avoid scorching. Drain stock from meat. Add 1 cup (250 mL) of stock to chili mixture and mix, then add it to the meat. Stir to get meat covered and simmer an additional 15 minutes. If too thick, add about ½ cup (125 mL) more stock.

Serve with tortillas or rice to 5–6.

STUFFED PEPPERS

Mexico   *(Chiles Rellenos)*

This way of stuffing peppers is a bit more time consuming than we are used to, but that's the way they do it, and results are very good.

6	*(6)*	poblano chiles, or green peppers
½-¾ cup	*(125-180 mL)*	flour for dredging
2	*(2)*	eggs, separated

Filling:

1½ lbs	*(¾ kg)*	ground pork or beef
2 tbs	*(2 tbs)*	salad oil, or olive oil
1	*(1)*	large onion, finely chopped (1 cup or 250 mL)
1	*(1)*	clove garlic, finely minced
1	*(1)*	apple, peeled, cored and chopped
¼ cup	*(60 mL)*	raisins
2	*(2)*	medium size tomatoes, peeled, seeded and chopped
2	*(2)*	canned Jalapeño chiles, seeded and chopped (or ¼ ts dried hot peppers)
		salt and pepper to taste
		pinch of cinnamon
		pinch of cloves

Toast the peppers by holding them with a fork over fire until pepper skin blisters, (if skin gets black, it will not matter), then wrap them in a damp cloth. After 15 minutes, carefully peel off outer skin. Cut into halves length-wise and remove seeds and white membranes.

For filling, sauté the onion and garlic in oil for 5 minutes, then add meat and brown slightly, breaking up large pieces with a fork. Add remaining ingredients and cook over low heat for about 30 minutes. Beat egg yolks until thick, then beat egg whites until stiff and carefully fold yolks into whites.

Fill slit peppers with this meat mixture, pressing it in with a spoon, dredge in flour then dip in egg mixture being careful to get peppers all covered. Fry in oil (350° F or 175° C) a few at a time until peppers are golden brown, then lift them out and drain off excess oil on paper toweling. Serve as they are on a bed of shredded lettuce, or with tomato sauce. (See page 358)   Serves 6.

CHILI CON CARNE

Mexico   (*Chiles con Carne*)

*There is quite a controversy about this traditional Mexican dish, whether or not
to use tomatoes in it. Some connoisseurs insist that the real Mexican way is to
make it without tomatoes, but I have often eaten it with tomatoes in Mexico and
I have a feeling most Americans would like it better that way.*

5	(5)	dried *chiles anchos or* 3–5 tbs powdered chili
1½ lb	(¾ *kg*)	stewing beef, cut into ½″ (12 mm) cubes
2 tbs	(*2 tbs*)	salad oil
1	(*1*)	medium size onion, chopped (¾ cup or 180 mL)
1	(*1*)	clove garlic, finely minced
½ ts	(½ *ts*)	cumin
½ ts	(½ *ts*)	oregano
2	(*2*)	medium size tomatoes, peeled and chopped (optional)
		salt and pepper to taste
2 cups	(*500 mL*)	cooked red kidney beans

If using dried whole *chiles anchos* rinse them in cold water, remove veins, stems and seeds, soak them in a bowl with 1 cup (250 mL) hot water for about 1 hour, then purée them in an electric blender or pass them through a foodmill.

Slightly brown meat in salad oil, and set aside. Add onion and garlic to oil and sauté for about 5 minutes, then add puréed chilies and cook for 5 more minutes, stirring constantly. If tomatoes are used, add them at this time, then add meat and seasonings and bring to a boil. Turn down heat to very low and simmer for about 45 minutes. Add beans and cook for an additional 20 minutes.   Serves 6.

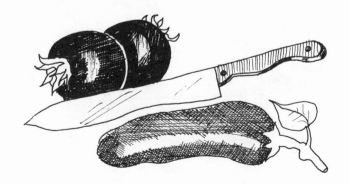

TORTILLAS

Mexico

Many Mexican households have their own tortilla presses, but I have seen women in Mexico making them with their hands. And it looks so easy. But it really is not. However, if you make them every day through many years, I guess you'd get the knack of it. There are, however, ready-made tortillas to buy in most super-markets today, if you need them for a recipe or to make a Mexican meal, and prefer not to make them. They are eaten in so many ways with all meals and as snacks that I think they are one of the most important parts of the Mexican cuisine.

2 cups	*(500 mL)*	*masa harina* (Mexican corn flour, not corn meal)
1 ts	*(1 ts)*	salt
1¼ cups	*(310 mL)*	warm water

Mix together all ingredients into a soft dough. Shape into walnut size balls and roll flat between two sheets of wax paper or, which I feel is even better, between two plastic bags, into very thin cakes of about 4–5″ (100–130 mm) diameter. If you do have a tortilla press, of course, you will use this. You may also use hands directly, dampening them slightly with water for each cake. If the tortillas stick to the wax paper or your hands, this may mean that the dough needs a little more flour, so add it by the tablespoonful until sticking stops.

Cook on medium heat on an ungreased griddle, for about one minute on each side, or until they are slightly browned. Makes about 1 dozen tortillas.

But if you intend to use them for appetizers, make smaller balls and flatten them out to about 2″ (50 mm) in diameter.

Tortillas of any size may be kept warm in a 150° F (65° C) oven by wrapping them first in paper toweling, then in a slightly damp towel or cloth napkin.

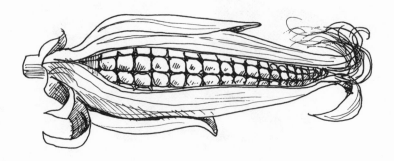

WHEAT FLOUR TORTILLAS

Mexico (*Tortillas de Harina de Trigo*)

Tortillas made with ordinary flour are used in the north of Mexico and are sometimes referred to as Tortillas del Norte.

2 cups	(*500 mL*)	flour
¼ cup	(*60 mL*)	lard or shortening
⅔-¾ cup	(*160-180 mL*)	cold water
1 ts	(*1 ts*)	salt

Cut lard or shortening into flour until very crumbly, add salt to water and add to flour mixture. Work into a stiff dough, knead it for a couple of minutes, then let it rest at least 1 hour at room temperature. Make balls the size of a walnut, then roll out into 4"-6" (100-150 mm) rounds, between two plastic bags or wax paper.

Bake on an ungreased griddle over medium heat about one minute on each side, or somewhat less on the second side. Makes about 1 dozen 5" (125 mm) tortillas.

Mexico **TACOS**

Although they do have sandwiches and bread rolls of the American style in Mexico, tacos must be considered as *the* Mexican sandwich, as their popularity and general use is so much greater.

They are just tortillas that are warmed up slightly, filled, then rolled up, or simply folded over if there is a lot of filling. They are often eaten just that way, but they may also be fried, baked or broiled.

Preferably the tortillas for tacos should be freshly made, as they otherwise have a tendency to crack when they are rolled up. However, if only pre-made ones are available, just heat them slightly to prevent cracking.

They make a nice meal when eaten together with a salad, or simply shredded lettuce and fried beans.

Some suggestions for taco fillings follow, but use your own imagination as just about anything goes, just like in a sandwich:

Shredded chicken with shredded lettuce, grated cheese and chili sauce.
Shredded pork, tomato sauce (page 358) and shredded lettuce.
Sliced or shredded turkey with Mole Poblano (see page 342).
Picadillo (page 351) with shredded lettuce and tomato slices.

(*Continued on next page*)

Fried beans, strips of canned chili and strips of Monterey Jack or Muenster cheese.

Chorizo (Spanish or Mexican sausage)—Remove the skin then chop and fry the meat. Add equal amounts of Monterey Jack cheese or Muenster cheese, and chopped chilies or strips of chilies.

Mexico   TOSTADAS

Tostadas are tortillas that are cooked first, then fried in hot oil until golden in color and crisp. If made ahead of time, keep in oven so that they remain crisp and do not get tough.

For appetizers, use 2″ (50 mm) tortillas, but do not assemble them until just before serving, as they otherwise would lose their crispness. You just pile on top, whatever you wish, for example:

Fried beans (or just plain mashed kidney beans); some cooked chicken slivers; fried chorizo sausages; shrimp; sárdines; slices of roasted meat; almost always with a few very small pieces of canned hot chilies, some shredded lettuce, sliced tomato, grated cheese or sour cream. There are no set rules of what to use, as long as you can balance it on them and are able to open your mouth wide enough to bite into them without making a mess.

TOSTADITAS (or TOTOPOS)

These are tortillas that are cut into wedge-like pieces and fried crisp as above. Instead of piling anything on them, they are used as "scoops" for dips, such as guacamole, and also to decorate and eat fried beans. They may come out either crisp or chewy.

QUESADILLAS

Quesadillas make a nice luncheon dish when served with a salad. They also make good appetizers but then 2″ (50 mm) tortillas should be used instead.

Use the recipe for dough for tortillas and make them about 4″ (100 mm) in diameter. Put filling on one half of the raw tortilla, then fold over to make a half circle, seal the edges well and cook in about ½″ (12 mm) hot lard or oil until they are golden brown in color. Drain on paper towels and serve hot.

(*Continued on next page*)

Filling suggestions:

Strips of Monterey Jack or Muenster cheese and a few small pieces of
  canned, peeled chilies.
Picadillo (see below).
Pork *adobo* cut into shreds (see Pork Stew, page 345).
Chorizo sausage, skinned, cut up and sautéed in a little oil together
  with some chopped onion, chopped tomatoes and chopped chilies.
Beans, with cheese and chopped chilies.
Sardines with chopped chilies.

VARIATION:

Quesadillas may also be made from tortillas that are already made. If
they are cold or from the freezer, they should be heated slightly to
make them more pliable as they otherwise might break when you fold
them over. Put the filling in the middle as above, fasten together with a
tooth-pick, then fry in hot lard as above.

PICADILLO

Mexico

1 lb	(½ kg)	ground chuck
1	(1)	large onion, finely chopped (1 cup or 250 mL)
1	(1)	clove garlic, finely minced
2 tbs	(2 tbs)	salad oil
1	(1)	large tomato, peeled, seeded and chopped
1	(1)	apple, peeled, cored and chopped
⅓ cup	(80 mL)	raisins
1-2	(1-2)	canned Jalapeno peppers, seeded and finely chopped
		salt and pepper to taste
¼ ts	(¼ ts)	each of cinnamon and ground cloves

Brown meat, onion and garlic in oil, breaking up chunks of meat with a fork. Add remaining ingredients, mix well, bring to a boil, then turn down heat to low and simmer for 25 minutes. Use for filling of tacos, tostadas, quesadillas etc. or serve with rice as a main meal.

ENCHILADAS

Mexico

Enchiladas are another tortilla dish that is very popular. It is almost always part of a meal in a Mexican restaurant in our country.

12	(12)	tortillas (about 4" or 100 mm size)

Filling:

2 cups	(500 mL)	cooked cubed chicken or turkey
½ cup	(125 mL)	chopped black olives
¼ cup	(60 mL)	chopped blanched almonds
2 tbs	(2 tbs)	finely chopped scallions

In a bowl mix together all ingredients until well blended.

Assembly:

2 cups	(500 mL)	tomato sauce (see page 358)
½ cup	(125 mL)	grated Parmesan or Cheddar cheese

For serving:	Sour cream (if desired)

Heat sauce and put tortillas into it for about 30 seconds, a few at a time. Remove and place about ¼ cup (60 mL) filling on each one and roll up. Place with seam side down in a well greased shallow baking dish, pour sauce over them, sprinkle with cheese and bake in a 350° F (175° C) oven for 15 minutes. Serve immediately to 4–5.

VARIATIONS:

Instead of chicken mixture, use 3 cups (750 mL) of Picadillo (see page 351) or 1 lb (½ kg) chorizo (sausage) fried and broken up.

Instead of adding the tomato sauce to the baking dish use 2 cups (500 mL) of cooked and mashed beans.

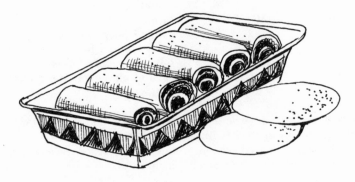

TORTILLA AND CHEESE CASSEROLE

Mexico   *(Chilaquiles)*

A nice cheese casserole for a meatless meal.
The "green tomato sauce" variation is not made from green tomatoes. The Mexican tomatitos verdes is a different fruit entirely, and unripened tomatoes cannot be substituted.

12	*(12)*	baked tortillas, 4 or 5″ (100–125 mm) lard for frying
2 cups	*(500 mL)*	tomato sauce (see page 358) chopped chilies to taste, or chili powder
½ lb	*(¼ kg)*	Monterey Jack, Muenster or American cheese, cubed
1 cup	*(250 mL)*	sour cream
½ cup	*(125 mL)*	Parmesan cheese, grated

Cut each tortilla in about 8 pieces, then fry lightly in hot lard, drain on paper toweling. Place a layer of tortillas in the bottom of a 1½ qt (1½ L) buttered baking dish, then make layers of tomato sauce, cheese and sour cream. Repeat layers until all ingredients are used up, ending with the sour cream.

Bake in a 350° F (175° C) oven for 30 minutes, sprinkle with Parmesan cheese, and bake until this has melted, about 10 minutes.

Serves 4–5.

VARIATION:

Instead of the above tomato sauce, use Mexican green tomato sauce, otherwise proceed as above.

Green Tomato Sauce:

1	*(1)*	small onion, finely chopped
1	*(1)*	clove garlic, finely minced
1 tbs	*(1 tbs)*	salad oil
2 cups	*(500 mL)*	*tomatitos verdes* (2 cans of about 8 oz or 250 mL)
2	*(2)*	small green chilies pinch of sugar salt to taste

Sauté onion and garlic in oil until onion is wilted, but do not let it brown. Put in a blender together with the tomatoes and chilies and liquid from cans and blend into a purée.

TAMALES

Mexico (*Tamales*)

Tamales are usually filled and eaten as a meal in themselves. If unfilled, they are served with Chicken Mole Poblano or similar dishes. They are very popular in Mexico, but eaten chiefly on special occasions, as they are a little more elaborate to prepare than other corn products. Packaged corn husks may be hard to obtain in many places in the U.S. but if you should acquire a taste for tamales, I do not see why you could not save the husks when you prepare corn on the cob, dry them and keep them for making tamales.

Some cookbooks recommend using either parchment paper or aluminum foil, but somehow I feel that this way the Mexican *flavor of the meal is lost.*

2 cups	(500 mL)	masa harina (Mexican corn flour)
1½ ts	(1½ ts)	salt
1 ts	(1 ts)	baking powder
⅓ cup	(80 mL)	lard
1½ cups	(375 mL)	lukewarm chicken broth (approximately)
2 dozen	(2 dozen)	dried cornhusks

Sift together *masa harina,* salt and baking powder. Cream lard until very light and fluffy, then add flour mixture a little at a time while beating constantly. Add broth gradually and mix until a rather soft and mushy dough has been obtained.

Spread about 1 tbs of dough in the center of each corn husk, then add 1 tbs of filling in the center and fold dough over filling, then the exposed sides of corn husks over the dough, then ends of the husks on top and bottom are folded over. Tear a couple of corn husks into strips and use these to tie the tamales at the top. Place in a steamer with the bottom ends of the corn husks down, and steam for about 1½ hours over medium heat. Check off and on, and add a little boiling water if the pot is going dry.

Fillings:

Picadillo (see page 351)
Monterey Jack or Muenster cheese with chopped chilies to taste.
Refried Beans with cheese.
Chicken Mole Poblano (see page 342).
Pork Adobo, shredded (see page 345).

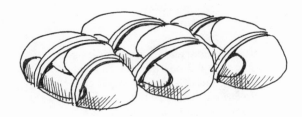

TAMALE CASSEROLE

Mexico   (*Tamal de Casuela*)

Filling:

1 lb	(½ kg)	ground chuck
1 tbs	(1 tbs)	butter or margarine
1	(1)	small onion, finely chopped
		(½ cup or 125 mL)
½ cup	(125 mL)	finely diced green pepper
½ ts	(½ ts)	oregano
½ ts	(½ ts)	cumin, crushed
1 tbs	(1 tbs)	chili powder
		salt and pepper to taste
2 cups	(500 mL)	canned tomatoes (1 lb or 500 g can)

Sauté onion in butter or margarine in a skillet until onion is transparent then add green pepper and meat and brown meat well, breaking up lumps with a fork. Add spices and tomatoes, simmer uncovered for 15 minutes.

1½ cup	(375 mL)	yellow cornmeal
1½ cup	(375 mL)	cold water
3 cups	(750 mL)	boiling water
2 ts	(2 ts)	salt
1	(1)	egg, well beaten

Mix cornmeal with cold water, then gradually stir into salted boiling water. Stir continuously until mixture has thickened. Remove from heat, let cool for a minute, still stirring, and add egg.

Spread half of it in a thin layer in a square baking dish 8 x 8 or 9 x 9″ (200 x 200 or 220 x 220 mm). Add meat filling and smooth it out to cover evenly. Spread remaining corn mixture thinly over the top and bake in a 350° F (175° C) oven about 25 minutes.

Serve immediately, to 5–6.

BEANS

Mexico (*Frijoles*)

Beans are eaten with practically every meal in Mexico, even for breakfast. They are often cooked in large quantities and then fried as they are needed. (When you hear the expression re-fried beans, this is actually a mis-translation of refrito (fried with emphasis) as the beans have not actually been fried before.)

2 cups	(*500 mL*)	red kidney, black or pinto beans
1	(*1*)	large onion, finely chopped
		(1 cup or 250 mL)
1	(*1*)	clove garlic, finely chopped
1-2	(*1-2*)	chilies, seeded and finely chopped
2 tbs	(*2 tbs*)	lard or salad oil
		salt and pepper to taste

Soak beans in cold water overnight. Add onion, garlic, chilies and water to cover beans a little more than 1″ (25 mm). Bring to a boil, turn down heat and simmer for one hour. Add lard or oil, salt and pepper, and add a little more hot water if beans appear very dry, however, they should be on the dry side. Cook until beans are tender, then remove about ½ cup (125 mL), mash this thoroughly, then return to pot and stir to get mixture evenly thickened.

Serves 6–8.

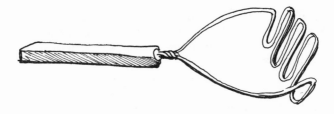

FRIED BEANS

Mexico (*Frijoles Refritos*)

		all the beans from the above recipe
		(about 6-8 cups)
½ cup	(*125 mL*)	lard

Heat about ⅓ of the lard in a frying pan, add a small quantity of beans, mashing with a spoon over low heat, then add more lard and beans and continue cooking and stirring until mixture is creamy and is paste-like in appearance.

YELLOW RICE

Mexico

(Arroz Amarillo)

Saffron is what is usually used to make a yellow rice both in Spain and elsewhere. However, in Mexico they make a yellow rice using tomato instead which makes it flavorful—and it is more economical than saffron.

1	*(1)*	medium size onion, chopped (³⁄₄ cup or 180 mL)
1	*(1)*	clove garlic, chopped
3 tbs	*(3 tbs)*	olive oil or salad oil
1	*(1)*	large tomato, peeled, seeded and chopped (about 1 cup or 250 mL)
1½ cups	*(375 mL)*	rice
3 cups	*(750 mL)*	chicken stock
		salt and pepper to taste

In a heavy skillet sauté onion and garlic in 1 tbs oil over low heat about 5 minutes, then put it into a blender together with chopped tomato and blend until puréed. (Or pass it all through a sieve.) Heat remaining oil, add rice and sauté rice until it is golden in color, stirring it to get all the grains coated with oil and evenly colored.

Add contents from blender, salt, pepper and stock and bring to a boil, cover, turn down heat and cook about 15 minutes or until rice is tender and all liquid has been absorbed. Stir only once during this period.

Serves 5–6.

SCRAMBLED EGGS

Mexico

(Huevos Revueltos)

One of the standard breakfast dishes in Mexico, usually served with beans and tortillas.

½ cup	*(125 mL)*	tomato sauce (see page 358)
10	*(10)*	eggs
		salt and pepper to taste

Heat the sauce in a large skillet. Beat eggs slightly and add to sauce stirring constantly with a wooden spoon until eggs are set. Serve immediately with hot tortillas, beans (plain or fried) and some canned chilies. Serve 5–6.

| *Mexico* | | TOMATO SAUCE | *(Salsa di Jitomate)* |

1	*(1)*	medium onion, finely chopped (³⁄₄ cup or 180 mL)
1	*(1)*	clove garlic, finely minced
2	*(2 tbs)*	salad oil
2 cups	*(500 mL)*	tomatoes, peeled, seeded and chopped (about 2 large ones)
1-3	*(1-3)*	chilies, seeded and veins removed, then chopped salt and pepper to taste

Sauté onion and garlic in oil, until onion is translucent, add remaining ingredients and cook for 30 minutes. Check seasonings and serve either hot or cold.   Makes about 2 cups.

CHRISTMAS EVE SALAD

Mexico   *(Ensalada de Noche Buena)*

A simple but remarkably good mixture of fruit and vegetable salad, tradition- ally eaten on Christmas Eve.

2	*(2)*	apples, peeled cored and cubed
2	*(2)*	oranges, peeled and cut into sections (or one 7 oz (200 g) can of mandarin oranges)
2	*(2)*	peeled and sliced bananas
3	*(3)*	medium size cooked beets, cubed
2	*(2)*	slices fresh or canned pineapple, cubed
2 tbs	*(2 tbs)*	lemon juice
¹⁄₃ cup	*(80 mL)*	chopped peanuts pomegranate seeds (optional) mayonnaise lettuce (whole leaves or shredded, as desired)

Mix together fruits and lemon juice and chill thoroughly. Line a salad bowl with either whole lettuce leaves or shredded lettuce, then add the fruits. Sprinkle with peanuts and pomegranate seeds, if used. Put may- onnaise in bowl and serve separately.

VARIATION:

Sometimes this salad is served with brown sugar and light cream instead of mayonnaise.

ROYAL EGGS

Mexico   *(Huevos Royales)*

A classic among Mexican desserts.

6	*(6)*	egg yolks
2 ts	*(2 ts)*	water
		pinch of salt
1 tbs	*(1 tbs)*	raisins
¼ cup	*(60 mL)*	sherry
⅔ cup	*(160 mL)*	sugar
⅔ cup	*(160 mL)*	water
1	*(1)*	stick of cinnamon (about 2″ or 50 mm)
1 tbs	*(1 tbs)*	pine nuts or blanched and chopped almonds

Beat egg yolks with water and salt until very thick and creamy, at least five minutes on high speed of an electric mixer. Pour into a shallow greased pan, about 7″ x 7″ (180 x 180 mm) or a round 8″ (200 mm) pan. Place in a larger pan, filled with hot water, and bake in a 350° F (175° C) oven for about 20 minutes, or until eggs are set.

In the meantime soak raisins in half the sherry, and put sugar, water and cinnamon in a saucepan, bring to a boil, and boil briskly for 5 minutes. Remove cinnamon.

When eggs are set, cut into 1½–2″ (40–50 mm) squares, using a heated knife, and carefully add these squares to hot syrup and poach until they are saturated with syrup. Remove egg pieces to a serving dish, add raisins with sherry to syrup, and poach for about 3 minutes. Remove from heat, add remaining sherry and pour over egg pieces. Sprinkle with pine nuts or almonds and let cool. Serves 4–6.

"PILLOW" FRITTERS

Mexico (*Sopaipillas*)

These fritters are popular in the north of Mexico and some say they actually originated in the state of New Mexico. The ones I have tasted in Mexican restaurants in the U.S. have been very large in size, about 4–5" (10–12 cm), but in Mexico they have been the small squares in this recipe.

2 cups	(*500 mL*)	flour
2 ts	(*2 ts*)	baking powder
½ ts	(*½ ts*)	salt
1 tbs	(*1 tbs*)	shortening
⅔ cup	(*160 mL*)	water
		oil for deep-frying

For sprinkling: confectioners' sugar

Sift together flour, baking powder and salt. Cut in shortening with a pastry cutter until coarsely crumbly. Add water and work into a ball. Scrape up flour mixture around the sides of the bowl, then work dough until smooth on a lightly floured baking board. Divide dough in two then roll out each half to about ⅛" (3 mm) thickness. Cut into 2" (50 mm) squares.

Fry in deep fat at 375° F (190° C) until they puff up and turn golden brown, then turn over and cook for a few seconds on the other side. Drain on paper toweling. When cool, sprinkle with confectioners' sugar.

Makes about 3 dozen.

VARIATION:

Add some cinnamon to sugar, before sprinkling.

ANISE-SESAME COOKIES

Mexico (*Pastelitos con Anis y Sesamo*)

2 tbs	(*2 tbs*)	sesame seed
1 tbs	(*1 tbs*)	anise seed (or ⅓ ts anise extract)
2 ts	(*2 ts*)	boiling water
⅔ cup	(*160 mL*)	sugar
¾ cup	(*180 mL*)	butter or margarine
1	(*1*)	egg
2 cups	(*500 mL*)	flour
¼ ts	(*¼ ts*)	baking soda
For brushing:		1 egg beaten with 1 tbs milk

(*Continued on next page*)

(Anise-Sesame Cookies, cont.)

Toast sesame seeds by spreading them in a baking pan in a 350° F (175° C) oven for about 5 minutes, stirring once or twice to obtain an even golden color. Mix anise seed with boiling water and let it steep about 20 minutes.

In an electric mixer beat butter or margarine with sugar until light and fluffy, add egg and mix well. Strain liquid from anise seed mixture, discarding the seeds, then add to batter. Stir in flour mixed with baking soda, a little at a time, and mix well. Chill dough for at least 2 hours in refrigerator, or overnight, if desired.

Shape dough into 1/2" (12 mm) balls and place widely apart on an ungreased cookie sheet, then flatten with the bottom of a glass, dipped in flour each time to make a cookie about 1 1/2" (37 mm) in diameter. Brush with egg and milk mixture and sprinkle with the toasted sesame seeds.

Bake in a 375° F (190° C) oven 8–10 minutes, or until golden in color.   Makes 60–70 cookies.

RICE PUDDING WITH ALMONDS

Mexico   (*Budin de Arroz con Almendra*)

1/3 cup	(*80 mL*)	rice
		pinch of salt
1 cup	(*250 mL*)	water
		grated rind of one orange
2 cups	(500 mL)	milk
1/2 cup	(*125 mL*)	sugar
1/4 cup	(*60 mL*)	almonds, blanched and ground
2	(*2*)	egg yolks
For sprinkling:		cinnamon (optional)

Bring rice to a boil with salt, water and orange rind, then turn down heat and cook for 15 minutes over low heat. Add milk, sugar and almonds, bring to a boil again, then turn heat to very low and cook without cover until all milk has been absorbed, stirring often to prevent scorching.

Beat egg yolks slightly in a bowl, add some of the pudding, then return all of it to the pot, stir, and cook for a few minutes longer, but do not let it boil vigorously as it might then curdle. Put into a serving dish and sprinkle with cinnamon if desired.

Serves 4–6.

WEDDING COOKIES (or BRIDE'S COOKIES)

Mexico   (*Polverones de Boda*)

*There are two accepted names for these cookies. Maybe they are made by
Mother for the wedding festivities—or maybe they are one of the first things a
bride will bake for her new husband? Anyway, any husband, old as well as
new, would be happy to eat them.*

1 cup	(*250 mL*)	butter or margarine, at room temperature
½ cup	(*125 mL*)	confectioners' sugar
1 ts	(*1 ts*)	vanilla extract
2 cups	(*500 mL*)	flour
1 cup	(*250 mL*)	pecans, ground or chopped very fine
For dusting:		confectioners' sugar

Cream butter and sugar until very
light and fluffy, add vanilla, flour and
nuts and work together into a ball.
Make 1″ (25 mm) balls and put on a
greased baking sheet, well apart from
each other. Use the bottom of a glass,
flatten each cookie to about 2″
(50 mm), dipping the glass in flour
each time. Bake in a 350° F (175° C)
oven for 12–15 minutes, or until
golden brown. Cool on wire racks,
then dust rather heavily with confectioners sugar.

SWEET ROLLS

Mexico   (*Pan Dulce*)

*Every visitor to Mexico will have a lingering memory of the light, sweet rolls
that are served for breakfast. Here is one variety.*

1 pkg	(*1 pkg*)	dry yeast
⅓ cup	(*80 mL*)	lukewarm water
½ ts	(*½ ts*)	salt
½ cup	(*125 mL*)	sugar
3 tbs	(*3 tbs*)	butter or margarine, melted
1 cup	(*250 mL*)	milk, lukewarm
1	(*1*)	egg, slightly beaten
3½-4 cups	(*900-1000 mL*)	flour, sifted
For brushing:		2 tbs melted butter
For sprinkling:		3 tbs brown sugar

(*Continued on next page*)

(Sweet Rolls, cont.)

Soften yeast in lukewarm water with half the sugar in a large bowl of an electric mixer, about 5 minutes. Add remaining sugar, melted butter, milk and egg, beat on mixer medium speed until well blended. Add sifted flour, a little at a time while beating and continue until the mixture gets too heavy for the mixer, then add remaining flour and beat with a wooden spoon until mixture is smooth and elastic.

Cover and let stand in a warm place until double in bulk, about one hour. Turn out onto floured baking board and divide dough into four parts, then make each of these parts into 6 balls of equal size and place on a greased baking sheet. Cover and let them rise in a warm place for 1 more hour.

Brush with melted butter, sprinkle with brown sugar and bake in a 400° F (200° C) oven 12–15 minutes or until done. Remove from baking sheet and let cool on a wire rack.

SANGRIA

Mexico

Sangria, a wonderfully refreshing drink, especially in the Summer, can be bought already mixed in the liquor stores. However, it is so easy to make yourself and this way I think it has an extra zing to it.

1 bottle	(*1 bottle*)	dry red wine (⅘ qt–24 oz or 750 mL)
1	(*1*)	large lemon, thinly sliced
1	(*1*)	large orange, thinly sliced
2 tbs	(*2 tbs*)	sugar (or more to taste, if desired)
¼ cup	(*60 mL*)	brandy
2–3 cups	(*500–750 mL*)	club soda

Mix together all the ingredients except the club soda in a large pitcher and let stand for at least four hours. Stir carefully if sugar has not dissolved by this time. Just before serving, add club soda, then serve over a lot of ice cubes in tall glasses.

VARIATION

This drink is often used without the club soda and served just over ice cubes.

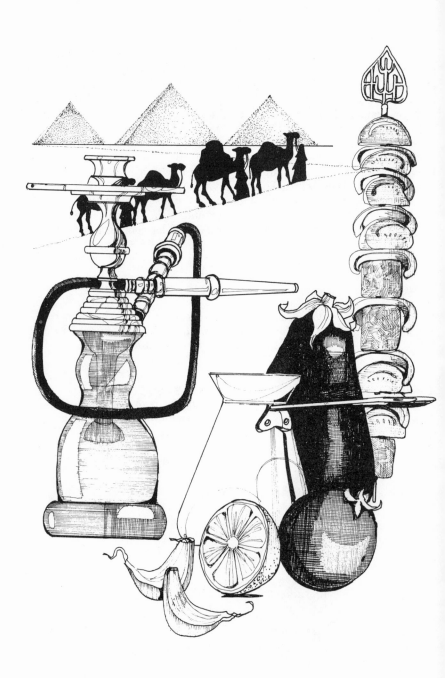

Middle East
and
Northern Africa

GEOGRAPHICALLY, this section certainly covers a lot of ground, especially if you look from east to west. The reason why I have lumped all this area together is that the Moslem countries along the Mediterranean are closely related to the Middle East in their culinary habits. But, having also included a recipe from Afghanistan, I am not even sure it is correct to call all that end *Middle East*. But what else?

There are several similarities that strike you when you study the cuisine of these areas. One is, of course, that most countries are strictly Moslem and thus pork is not eaten, but there are others, such as their prominent use of cracked wheat (*burghul*) and chickpeas for carbohydrates, the predominance of lamb among the meats, their use of fruits or nuts in cooking poultry and meat, and popularity of cinnamon as a seasoning for meats. And in practically all these countries there is an almost universal use of the flat type bread, called *pitta* (*pide*, Arabian bread, Armenian bread, Sahara bread etc. etc. depending upon where it was baked.) This is a traditional bread, which in many places is baked in out-in-the-open clay ovens that are very different from ours. However, in the larger cities, most of these flat breads are now baked commercially in modern ovens.

All through these countries as well as in Greece and Turkey a favorite dessert is the delectable pastry *baklava*, and there are other pastries of similar types drenched with sugar syrups and honey. Another important dessert is *halva*. Quite often rosewater or orangewater is sprinkled over desserts such as puddings. This does not give a flavor but a fragrance, and may be somewhat objectionable to some of us in the U.S. who are not used to such added odors. I judge by my family, who liked one of the desserts containing rosewater all right, but "next time," they asked me "please don't put perfume in it". So go easy on the rosewater until you are sure it will be accepted.

BURGHUL (CRACKED WHEAT) APPETIZER	*Tabbouleh*	Lebanon
CHICK PEA APPETIZER	*Hummus*	Lebanon
IRANIAN APPETIZERS (FETA CHEESE & LENTIL PURÉE)		Iran
LAMB SOUP	*Balsagan Kufte*	Armenia
ROASTED CHICKEN WITH FRUIT STUFFING		Tunisia
VEAL PATTIES		Egypt
COUSCOUS		Morocco
LAMB AND KIDNEY BEAN STEW	*Abgushte Lubia Germez*	Iran
BEEF STEW WITH PRUNES	*Khoresh Alu*	Iran
WITH PEACHES	*Khoresh Holy*	Iran
WITH APPLES	*Khoresh Sib*	Iran
WITH RHUBARB	*Khoresh Rivas*	Iran
CHOPPED MEAT CAKE	*Menazzeleh*	Syria
EGG-FILLED MEAT BALLS	*Kufteh Tabrizi*	Iran
GROUND LAMB KEBAB	*Luleh Kabab*	Iran
CAULIFLOWER CASSEROLE	*Maqlub el Qarnabit*	Jordan
BULGHUR CASSEROLE	*Kibbeh Bissanieh*	Lebanon
SPLIT PEA PATTIES	*Shami-e Pook*	Iran
STEAMED RICE	*Chelo*	Iran
PERSIAN STRING BEAN SOUFFLE	*Kuku-ye*	Iran
LENTIL AND VEGETABLE STEW		Tunisia
LEEK TURNOVERS	*Boolaunee*	Afghanistan
CHEESE SALAD	*Michoteta*	Egypt
ORANGE SALAD	*Munkaczina*	Saudi Arabia
SAHARA (ARABIAN) BREAD	*Pitta*	Tunisia
PERSIAN BREAD	*Nan-e Barbari*	Iran
BAKLAVA (HONEY PASTRY)		
MIDDLE EASTERN PRUNES		

BURGHUL (CRACKED WHEAT) APPETIZER

Lebanon (*Tabbouleh*)

A very refreshing and unusual appetizer that is easy to prepare.

³⁄₄ cup	(*180 mL*)	**burghul** (cracked wheat)
1	(*1*)	medium size onion, finely chopped (³⁄₄ cup or 180 mL)
2	(*2*)	scallions, finely chopped (include green part)
1 cup	(*250 mL*)	finely minced parsley
¹⁄₂ cup	(*125 mL*)	finely chopped fresh mint leaves (or 2 ts dried ones)
2	(*2*)	medium size tomatoes, peeled, seeded and chopped
		salt and pepper to taste
¹⁄₃ cup	(*80 mL*)	lemon juice
²⁄₃ cup	(*160 mL*)	olive oil

Put burghul in a bowl and cover with cold water and let stand for 1–2 hours. Drain off water, and press with a spoon to remove as much excess water as possible. Add all remaining ingredients and mix well. Keep in refrigerator for at least 2 hours before serving, as an appetizer on small plates.

Serves 5–6.

Lebanon ## CHICKPEA APPETIZER (*Hummus*)

Tahini (sesame paste) gives this appetizer its very special flavor. It can be bought in cans in specialty stores for Middle East products. Beware however, that you do not get the sesame oil which is used in Chinese cooking.

1¹⁄₄ cup	(*310 mL*)	cooked chickpeas (one 10 oz or 300 g) can
¹⁄₃ cup	(*80 mL*)	sesame paste (tahini)
¹⁄₄ cup	(*60 mL*)	lemon juice
1	(*1*)	clove garlic, chopped
		salt to taste

For garnish: chopped parsley

Put all the ingredients into a blender and work until smooth. If blender is not available, pass chickpeas through a sieve, then mix well with the remaining ingredients. Chill for a couple of hours. Put into a bowl and garnish with chopped parsley. Serve as an appetizer, a spread on crackers, or as a buffet dish. Serves 4–6.

IRANIAN APPETIZERS

Iran

Feta Cheese

This cheese, which is available in most of our cheese stores, and in supermarkets that have a good cheese selection, is used all over the Middle East both as a cooking ingredient and an accompaniment for bread. It is somewhat salty in flavor and crumbly in texture. It is sometimes soaked in water, if a blander taste is desired. It is also often mixed with any one of the following: chopped fresh dill, mint, tarragon or parsley, or sour cream or soy-sauce. Serve with flat bread or crackers.

Lentil Purée

1 cup	*(250 mL)*	lentils
2 cups	*(500 mL)*	water
1	*(1)*	medium size onion, finely chopped (³⁄₄ cup or 180 mL) salt and pepper to taste

Cook lentils until tender, 20–30 minutes. Drain off excess water then purée in a blender or pass through a sieve. If too thick, add a little of the cooking liquid. Season with salt and pepper and serve as a spread for crackers.   Serves 6.

LAMB SOUP

Armenia   *(Balsagan Kufte)*

This is soup in its native land, but elsewhere it is likely to be called a stew.

1½ lbs	(³⁄₄ kg)	lean ground lamb
1	*(1)*	medium onion, chopped (³⁄₄ cup or 180 mL)
3 tbs	*(3 tbs)*	finely minced fresh parsley
½ cup	*(125 mL)*	raw rice, well rinsed
1 ts	*(1 ts)*	dried basil
		salt and pepper to taste
3	*(3)*	eggs
½ cup	*(125 mL)*	flour
		juice of 1 small lemon
5 cups	*(1250 mL)*	meat stock

(*Continued on next page*)

(Lamb Soup, cont.)

Mix together lamb, onion, parsley, rice, seasonings and one egg and blend well. Shape into small meatballs, about 1″ (25 mm) in diameter. Dredge in flour. Bring stock to a boil and carefully drop meatballs into the broth, a few at a time so that mixture does not stop boiling. When all the meatballs have been added, turn down heat and simmer about 20 minutes.

Beat remaining 2 eggs together with the lemon juice and put into a soup tureen. Stir in some of the hot broth to make a creamy sauce, then add remaining broth and meatballs and stir well. Serve in deep soup bowls with pitta bread (see page 382) if desired. For 4–6 people.

ROASTED CHICKEN WITH FRUIT STUFFING
Tunisia

The fruits give a nice flavor to the chicken and also make the meat juicy.

1	(*1*)	roasting chicken, 4-4½ lbs (2-2¼ kg)
½ lb	(¼ *kg*)	prunes
½ lb	(¼ *kg*)	dried apricots
½ cup	(*125 mL*)	seedless raisins
1	(*1*)	medium size onion, finely chopped (¾ cup or 180 mL)
2 tbs	(*2 tbs*)	butter or margarine
1	(*1*)	medium size apple, peeled, cored and chopped
1 ts	(*1 ts*)	ground cinnamon
		salt and pepper to taste

Soak prunes, apricots and raisins in water overnight or at least 6 hours, then remove pits from prunes and chop all the fruit. Sauté onion in butter or margarine until translucent, but do not let it get brown. Add chopped fruits to onion, add seasonings and heat.

Clean and wipe chicken, then fill stomach cavity with fruit, fasten with skewers or sew it together. Rub it with salt and pepper and roast in a covered pan in a 350° F (175° C) oven for 1½ hours, turning several times during roasting so that fruit juices can penetrate the meat all over. Remove cover and roast an additional 15–20 minutes, until it is golden brown and crisp. Carve chicken and serve with the fruit stuffing and rice.

Serves 5–6.

VEAL PATTIES

Egypt

A patty which is chewy in a nice way, thanks to all the nuts mixed with the meat. And they add a very special flavor, too.

1 lb	(½ kg)	ground veal
1	(1)	large onion, finely chopped (1 cup or 250 mL)
½ cup	(125 mL)	coarsely chopped almonds
½ cup	(125 mL)	coarsely chopped filberts
½ cup	(125 mL)	raisins
1	(1)	egg, slightly beaten
		salt and pepper to taste

Mix together all the ingredients and shape into 8–10 oval patties. Put into a shallow baking dish and bake in a 350° F (175° C) oven about 45 minutes. Serve with rice.   Serves 4–5.

COUSCOUS

Morocco

Couscous is a semolina type wheat cereal, available in specialty stores, that is used to make the dish with the same name, and is almost the national dish of Morocco and other North African countries. If you like a hearty down-to-earth stew, this is it, and the couscous that is steamed on top makes it a really exotic dish.

½ lb	(¼ kg)	couscous (about 1½ cups or 375 mL)
1½ cups	(375 mL)	cold water
1 ts	(1 ts)	salt
2 lbs	(1 kg)	lamb (part of leg, neck or shoulder, cut into 1″ or 25 mm cubes)
2 tbs	(2 tbs)	salad oil
4-6 cups	(1-1½ L)	water
2	(2)	large onions, peeled and quartered
2	(2)	ribs celery, sliced into 2″ (50 mm) lengths
½	(½)	small yellow turnip, peeled and cut into 1″ (25 mm) cubes
2	(2)	medium size potatoes, cut into 1″ (25 mm) cubes
		salt and pepper to taste
½ ts	(½ ts)	ground ginger
1 cup	(250 mL)	canned chickpeas
⅓ cup	(80 mL)	raisins
3 tbs	(3 tbs)	butter

Add salt to cold water and add to couscous in a bowl. Let it stand for at least 30 minutes. If mixture should appear lumpy, break up lumps with your hand and add a bit more water, if necessary. In a so-called couscous cooker, or a large 6 qt (6 L) Dutch oven, brown lamb slightly in oil, then add water and bring to a boil. Place the couscous in a colander, lined with a single layer of cheese cloth in case the holes of the colander are so large that couscous pieces may fall through, and put this colander on top of meat in Dutch oven. Cover pot and colander, and let meat cook so that it steams, checking off and on to make sure it is steaming properly.

After 1 hour, remove colander and add carrots, turnips, celery, potatoes to meat, then return colander on top and continue cooking and steaming until vegetables are almost tender, about 30 minutes. Remove colander again and add chickpeas and raisins and continue steaming an additional 20 minutes. Place couscous in a large serving dish, add butter on top and stir until well blended. Make a hollow in the center of the piled up couscous and put the vegetables and meat in it. Serve immediately, to 5–6.

LAMB AND KIDNEY BEAN STEW

Iran   (*Abgushte Lubia Germez*)

Dried beans of every size and kind are used liberally. They go very well in this lamb stew type of dish.

3–4 lbs	(*1½–2 kg*)	stew lamb, cut into pieces
½ cup	(*125 mL*)	kidney beans
2 tbs	(*2 tbs*)	butter or margarine
1	(*1*)	large onion, finely chopped (1 cup or 250 mL)
1 cup	(*250 mL*)	water
⅓ cup	(*80 mL*)	tomato sauce
1 ts	(*1 ts*)	oregano (may be omitted if tomato sauce contains this herb)
¼ ts	(*¼ ts*)	cinnamon
		salt and pepper to taste

Soak beans overnight or for at least 6 hours in cold water to cover. Slightly brown lamb pieces in butter or margarine, then remove and put into a stewing pot or large saucepan. Sauté onion until transparent, about 10 minutes, and add to pot together with remaining ingredients.

Bring to a boil, then turn down heat and simmer for 1½–2 hours, or until meat and beans are tender and meat comes away from the bones. If stew should turn out to be too thick, add a bit more water. Accompany with rice.

Serves 5–6.

Iran   **BEEF STEW WITH PRUNES**   (*Khoresh Alu*)

In Iran these wonderful stews, containing different fruits, are known as "sauces." They are almost always served with rice.

1½ lbs	(*¾ kg*)	stewing beef, cut into 1″ (25 mm) cubes
2 tbs	(*2 tbs*)	butter or margarine
1	(*1*)	large onion, finely chopped (1 cup or 250 mL)
		salt and pepper to taste
¼ ts	(*¼ ts*)	cinnamon
¼ ts	(*¼ ts*)	nutmeg
10	(*10*)	medium size prunes
1 cup	(*250 mL*)	water
2 tbs	(*2 tbs*)	lemon juice

(*Continued on next page*)

(Beef Stew with Prunes, cont.)

Soak prunes in water for about 1 hour. In a large skillet brown meat in butter or margarine, add seasonings and onion and brown slightly. Cook prunes in a small saucepan with the water for 10 minutes, then remove pits and purée them in a blender or just chop them finely. Add to meat together with lemon juice, then bring all to a boil, turn down heat to very low and simmer until meat is very tender, 1–1½ hours. Serve with rice.

VARIATIONS:

Beef Stew with Peaches—(Khoresh Holy)

Follow the directions for the above recipe but instead of prunes use 4 large slightly unripe peaches. Peel them, remove pits, slice them, and sauté in 2 tbs butter for 10 minutes before adding to the meat.

Beef Stew with Apples—(Khoresh Sib)

Proceed as for the preceding recipe but instead of peaches, use 3 tart apples, peeled, cored and sliced.

Beef Stew with Rhubarb—(Khoresh Rivas)

Proceed as the preceding recipe but instead of apples, use 1 cup (250 mL) sliced fresh rhubarb. If less tart dish is desired, add 1–2 ts sugar.

Syria   **CHOPPED MEAT CAKE**   *(Menazzeleh)*

A quick and simple dish when you are in a hurry.

1 lb	(½ kg)	ground chuck
1	(1)	large onion, finely chopped (1 cup or 250 mL)
1	(1)	clove garlic, finely minced
1 tbs	(1 tbs)	salad oil
		salt and pepper to taste
2	(2)	medium size tomatoes, peeled and chopped (or 1 cup (250 mL) canned tomatoes, cut up finely)
3 tbs	(3 tbs)	finely minced parsley
½ ts	(½ ts)	cumin
2 tbs	(2 tbs)	finely chopped fresh mint (or 1 ts dried mint)
4	(4)	eggs, well beaten

In a skillet brown meat in oil until it loses its red color, add onion and garlic and sauté until onion is transparent. Add salt, pepper, tomatoes, parsley, cumin and mint and simmer until mixture is well blended, about 15 minutes. Stir beaten eggs into meat mixture, all at once, blending it well together, then cook over low heat until eggs are completely set. Cut into pie-shape wedges to serve.

For 4–6.

EGG-FILLED MEAT BALLS

Iran   *(Kufteh Tabrizi)*

Tabriz is a town in northwestern Iran which seems to specialize in meatballs of different sizes—sometimes up to 1 lb of meat. I guess at that size we would call them meat-loaves instead.

1½ lbs	(¾ kg)	chopped lamb
⅔ cup	(160 mL)	yellow split peas
2 cups	(500 mL)	water
1	(1)	medium size onion, finely chopped (¾ cup or 180 mL)
1	(1)	egg
½ ts	(½ ts)	cinnamon
¼ ts	(¼ ts)	nutmeg
		salt and pepper to taste
3	(3)	hard boiled eggs, shelled
9	(9)	prunes, pitted
¼ cup	(60 mL)	water

Cook the peas in water until soft, then remove from heat and mash them. Cool slightly, then add chopped meat, onion, egg, and seasonings and mix well. Divide meat mixture into three parts, then each part into two. Shape each piece into an oval. On three of them, place an egg in the center, surrounded by three prunes. Cover with the remaining meat ovals and press together into egg shapes. Put them all into a buttered baking dish, add ¼ cup (60 mL) water and bake in a 350° F (150° C) oven for 45 minutes. Serve with plain rice.   For 6.

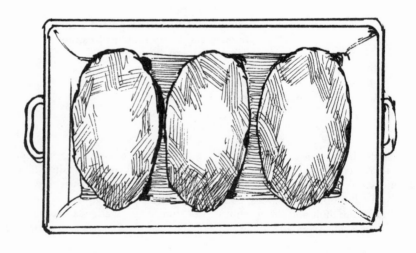

GROUND LAMB KEBAB
Iran (*Luleh Kabab*)

I had a big surprise when I first had this dish in Iran. I had ordered kababs and thought it would be chunks of meat, but here arrived something shaped like a sausage. I found that this is a very common way of making kababs, which apparently can mean anything that is small and is cooked on skewers. They can also be made from ground beef.

1½ lbs	(¾ kg)	ground lamb
1	(1)	large onion, finely grated
1	(1)	egg, slightly beaten
		salt and pepper to taste
¼ ts	(¼ ts)	cinnamon
1 tbs	(1 tbs)	cooking oil

In a large bowl work together all the ingredients, except the oil, with a wooden spoon until well mixed. Take handfuls of this mix and shape into oblong, sausage shapes about 1″ (25 mm) in diameter and about 4″ (100 mm) long. Brush skewers with oil, push through the meat lengthwise, then brush surface with oil. Cook over charcoal or under the broiler, 5–10 minutes, according to desired doneness, turning the skewers over to get the meat evenly broiled.
Serves 4–5.

CAULIFLOWER CASSEROLE
Jordan (*Maqlub el Qarnabit*)

1½ lb	(¾ kg)	ground chuck
2 tbs	(2 tbs)	salad oil
		salt and pepper to taste
½ ts	(½ ts)	cinnamon
1	(1)	medium size cauliflower
1 cup	(250 mL)	rice
½ cup	(125 mL)	tomato juice

Brown meat slightly in a skillet in 1 tbs oil, breaking up any lumps with a fork. Add salt, pepper and cinnamon. Cut cauliflower right through the head in flat ½″ (12 mm) slices (the end pieces will of course not be flat), and sauté them in remaining oil for 10 minutes but let them get only lightly brown. Cook rice in slightly salted water for 10 minutes, then drain off excess water. Smooth out top of meat in first skillet, arrange cauliflower slices over this and the rice on top. Smooth and press down slightly. Sprinkle tomato juice over and cook over very low heat 45 minutes. When ready, turn over skillet and carefully unmold on a serving platter.
Serves 5–6.

BULGHUR CASSEROLE

Lebanon   (*Kibbeh Bissanieh*)

In some Middle East countries rice is expensive and the grain most commonly used is cracked wheat, known as bulghur, which is found in specialty stores and some markets in the U.S. It makes a nice change from our more common accompaniments to meat dishes or casseroles.

½ lb	(¼ *kg*)	bulghur (cracked wheat) (1½ cups or 375 mL)
1 lb	(½ *kg*)	ground lean lamb
1	(*1*)	medium size onion, finely chopped (¾ cup or 180 mL)
3 ts	(*3 ts*)	salt
		pepper to taste
¼ ts	(¼ *ts*)	cinnamon
2 tbs	(*2 tbs*)	butter or margarine

Soak *bulghur* in water to cover for 30 minutes. Add lamb, onion and seasonings and mix well.

Filling:

1	(*1*)	medium size onion, finely chopped (¾ cup or 180 mL)
1 tbs	(*1 tbs*)	salad oil
½ lb	(¼ *kg*)	ground lean lamb
3 tbs	(*3 tbs*)	pine nuts (or coarsely chopped walnuts)
		salt and pepper to taste

Sauté onion in oil until transparent. Add lamb and cook until meat loses its pink color, breaking up large pieces with a fork. Add nuts, salt and pepper and cook until meat is lightly brown.

Assembly:

Put half of *bulghur* mixture in the bottom of a greased 9 x 9″ (220 x 220 mm) baking pan. Cover with all the filling then add remaining *bulghur* mixture on top, pressing Dot with butter and bake in a 375° F (190° C) oven for 30 minutes, then reduce heat to 300° F (150° C) and bake an additional 30 minutes. Serve immediately to 5–6.

SPLIT PEA PATTIES

Iran   *(Shami-e Pook)*

The original recipe I got for these meat patties did not contain an egg. However, I found that they had a tendency to fall apart and therefore added the egg as a remedy.

1 cup	(*250 mL*)	yellow split peas (½ lb or ¼ kg)
1 cup	(*250 mL*)	water
1 lb	(½ kg)	ground chuck
2	(*2*)	large onions, finely chopped (2 cups or 500 mL)
		salt and pepper to taste
¼ ts	(¼ *ts*)	cinnamon
¼ ts	(¼ *ts*)	nutmeg
½ ts	(½ *ts*)	baking soda
1	(*1*)	egg (optional)
3 tbs	(*3 tbs*)	butter or margarine

Pulverize the peas in a blender (or, if not available, cook the peas in slightly salted water until well done and mash them or press them through a sieve). Mix with water and let stand for 30 minutes. Then mix with meat, onions, seasonings, baking soda and egg, and work the mixture until very smooth. Shape into round patties and make a hole through the middle.

(This is the traditional way of making these patties in Iran). Sauté patties in butter or margarine until brown on both sides and done. Serve either hot or cold.

VARIATION:

Use chick-pea flour, if available, or make your own in the blender, proceeding as above.

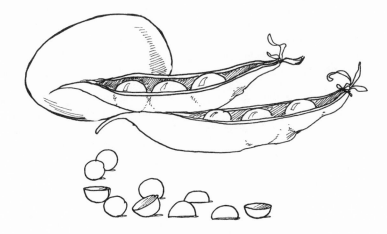

STEAMED RICE

Iran   *(Chelo)*

Iran has one very special way of preparing rice. We, who are used to just boiling it, may think it is a lot of fuss fixing rice in the way described here, but Iranians feel this is the best way. The crust that will form on the bottom of the pan is considered the best of all. Rice prepared by this method is called chelo, but they also make rice dishes named polo, in which it is mixed with other ingredients. But sometimes, they just plain boil it and call it kateh.

1½ cups	(375 mL)	rice
2 tbs	(2 tbs)	salt
6 cups	(1½ L)	water
⅓ cup	(80 mL)	melted butter

For serving: 1 raw egg (optional)

Wash rice well in several luke-warm waters until it runs clear, then soak it in cold water, with 1 tbs salt added, overnight. Bring 6 cups (1½ L) water with remaining salt to a boil. Drain off water in which rice was soaked then add rice to the boiling water, remove from heat and leave rice for 15 minutes, stirring a couple of times to avoid rice sticking to the bottom of the pot. Pour rice and water into a colander, then rinse with luke-warm water.

Put 2 tbs of melted butter into cooking pot, add 1 tbs of water then add rice, spoonful by spoonful. First spread it around the bottom of the pot, then mount it into a cone shape. Pour remaining melted butter over the rice, attempting to distribute it evenly. Put a layer of paper toweling on top of pot, then put the lid on top of this, and then two dish towels on top of the lid. Cook for 10–15 minutes over low heat, then turn down heat even lower and cook for 30–35 minutes.

By this procedure, a crisp crust of a golden color should develop on the bottom of the pot, while the rest of the rice remains white. (This crust is the highly esteemed reason for cooking rice this way.) To make it easier to remove, when ready, put the pot in a sink filled with cold water for a few minutes, which should loosen the crust.

For the table, make rice into a pyramid shape on a large platter and either top it with more melted butter, or make an indentation on top of the pyramid and add a whole raw egg, which is mixed in with rice just before it is served individually. This type of rice usually goes with the meat sauces (or stews) described on page 372.

Serves 6.

PERSIAN STRING BEAN SOUFFLÉ

Iran   *(Kuku-ye)*

Here follows a dish that is a little difficult to describe—it is not an omelet and not a soufflé but something in between. With different things added to it— vegetables as well as meat or fish—it makes a nice buffet or luncheon dish and the beautiful thing is that although it is like a soufflé, it does not sink but stays high and fluffy.

1 lb	(½ kg)	string beans
1	(1)	medium onion, finely chopped (¾ cup or 180 mL)
3 tbs	(3 tbs)	butter or margarine
6	(6)	eggs
¼ ts	(¼ ts)	baking soda
		salt and pepper to taste

Cut string beans in ¼" (6 mm) long pieces, cook in salted water until tender, then drain. Sauté onion in 1 tbs butter until transparent. Beat eggs until light and fluffy, add salt and pepper, baking soda, onion and drained beans. Heat remaining butter in a large skillet or omelet pan, pour in egg mixture and cook over medium heat until light brown on the bottom, about 8 minutes. Then turn over carefully, using a cover to catch the omelet (or soufflé), then slide it upside down back into pan to brown the other side. Cut into wedges and serve to 4–5.

VARIATIONS:

String Bean and Ground Beef Soufflé:

Use the same ingredients as in the preceding recipe but add ½ lb (¼ kg) ground chuck. After the onions have been sautéed, remove them from pan and add meat and cook until well browned, using a fork to break up meat that sticks together. Instead of pouring all the egg mixture in the skillet, add only half of it and cook until set, then spread meat on top of it and then remaining egg mixture. Continue cooking over low heat for 15 minutes then turn over soufflé and brown the top side.

Cauliflower Soufflé:

Instead of using string beans, use one small head of cauliflower, cut into small flowerets and cooked until tender, then mash coarsely with a potato masher or a fork before mixing in with egg and onion.

LENTIL AND VEGETABLE STEW

Tunisia

Lentils are one of the first foods mentioned in the bible and have nourished mankind over the ages. And there are many good ways to serve them, as in this recipe with a fresh lemon flavor.

1 cup	*(250 mL)*	lentils
2	*(2)*	medium size potatoes, diced
1	*(1)*	medium size carrot, thinly sliced
1	*(1)*	stalk celery, thinly sliced
1	*(1)*	leek, sliced (optional)
1	*(1)*	medium size onion, finely chopped
2	*(2)*	cloves garlic, finely minced
1 tbs	*(1 tbs)*	salad oil
		juice of 1 lemon
2 tbs	*(2 tbs)*	parsley, finely chopped
		salt and pepper to taste

Soak lentils for at least 4 hours, then cook in 2½ cups (625 mL) water for 30 minutes. Add potatoes, carrot, celery and leek and cook for 10 minutes. Sauté onion and garlic in oil, until onion is translucent, then add to lentils together with lemon juice, parsley and seasonings. Cook for an additional 10 minutes, or until all vegetables are tender. Serve either hot with meat, or cold as an appetizer.

Serves 4–5.

Afghanistan **LEEK TURNOVERS** *(Boolaunee)*

A giant size turnover, eaten as a side dish with meat.

2 cups	*(500 mL)*	flour
½ ts	*(½ ts)*	salt
½–⅔ cup	*(125–160 mL)*	water

Mix all ingredients until a stiff dough has been obtained, then turn out on a floured baking board and knead until smooth and elastic. Set aside for 30 minutes.

(Continued on next page)

(Leek Turnovers, cont.)

Filling:

2 cups	(500 mL)	leeks, cut into ¼″ (6 mm) lengths
½ ts	(½ ts)	salt
		pinch of cayenne pepper
2 ts	(2 ts)	salad oil
		oil for deep-frying

Parboil leeks for 5 minutes, then mix with remaining ingredients.

Assembly:

Pinch off a piece of dough, the size of a walnut, then roll out into a 8–9″ (200–220 mm) circle not more than ¹⁄₁₆″ (1½ mm) thick. Spread 3–4 tbs filling in the middle, then fold over into a crescent shape. Moisten the edges with water and seal. If desired, use a fork to press down to facilitate sealing. Fry in 375° F (190° C) hot oil, two at a time on both sides until golden brown. Keep hot until all are done.

Serves 4–5.

CHEESE SALAD

Egypt   *(Michoteta)*

Equally good as a salad or an appetizer. Or especially as something good to eat while you are counting calories.

1 cup	(250 mL)	feta cheese or cottage cheese (about ½ lb or ¼ kg)
		juice of 1 lemon
1	(1)	medium size red onion, finely chopped (¾ cup or 180 mL)
1½ cups	(375 mL)	peeled and diced cucumber (about ½ large one)
1½ tbs	(1½ tbs)	olive oil
		salt and pepper to taste

Crumble the cheese, then add lemon juice and oil and mix well. Stir in onion, cucumber, salt and pepper and blend. Let stay in the refrigerator for at least 1 hour for flavor to develop.

Serve as a salad or as an appetizer, to 4–6 people.

ORANGE SALAD

Saudi Arabia (*Munkaczina*)

A simple enough salad, but nice and refreshing.

3	(3)	large oranges
2	(2)	medium size onions
2 tbs	(2 tbs)	salad oil
3 tbs	(3 tbs)	vinegar
		pinch of cayenne pepper
½ ts	(½ ts)	salt
10	(10)	pitted black olives, sliced

Peel oranges and onions, slice very thinly. Arrange alternate layers in a serving bowl, pour over a dressing made from remaining ingredients, except olives, and let marinate for at least 1 hour. Decorate with sliced black olives.

Serves 5–6.

SAHARA (ARABIAN) BREAD

Tunisia (*Pitta*)

There are many names for this type of bread (pide among others). I visited a Bedouin village in Tunisia where I saw how it was baked in a cone-shaped, or rather beehive-shaped clay oven out in the open. On the bottom dried camel dung was used as fuel. The freshly shaped cakes were somewhat wetted and then "glued" on to the walls of the oven until they were ready after about 10 minutes. They claimed that the camel dung gave the bread the real good flavor. I could not argue against the goodness of the bread, but I guess most of us have to forgo this addition to the flavor, and bake it in the oven. And it is not bad that way either!

5–5½ cups	(1250–1375 mL)	flour (preferably unbleached)
1 tbs	(1 tbs)	salt
2 tbs	(2 tbs)	sugar
1	(1)	pkg dry yeast
2½ cups	(625 mL)	lukewarm water

Dissolve yeast with 1 ts sugar and ½ cup (125 mL) luke-warm water. In a bowl of an electric mixer blend 2 cups (500 mL) flour with 2 cups (500 mL) water at medium speed until smooth. Keep adding more flour, a little bit at a time, until the dough gets too heavy for the mixer, then work with a wooden spoon and add more flour to make a light dough.

Turn on to a floured baking board and knead for 10 minutes, adding

(Continued on next page)

(Sahara Bread, cont.)

enough flour to make an elastic dough, that does not stick to hands or board. Place dough in a well greased bowl, turn over once to cover bottom with grease, cover with plastic wrap and let rise in a warm place about 1 hour.

Punch down dough and divide into 12 balls. Let rest for 10 minutes, then with the knuckles of your hand, flatten out balls into ½" (12 mm) thick circles, about 5-6" (120-150 mm) in diameter. Bake on a greased pre-

heated baking sheet, 4-5 cakes to a sheet, in a 425° F (220° C) oven for 8-10 minutes, or until golden in color. Remove and let cool on a rack.

The cakes will puff up during baking, making a sort of pocket in the center. To eat, split cakes in half horizontally so that this pocket is opened, and fill the inside with cheese, or other sandwich makings, or just eat them plain without splitting. These cakes may be easily frozen, and re-heated for use.

PERSIAN BREAD

Iran   *(Nan-e Barbari)*

This bread does not keep well and should preferably be eaten while still very fresh.

1 pkg	(1 pkg)	dry yeast
1 cup	(250 mL)	luke-warm water
1 tbs	(1 tbs)	salad oil
4 cups	(1 L)	flour
2 tbs	(2 tbs)	butter, melted
1 tbs	(1 tbs)	sesame seeds

In a large bowl dissolve yeast in water, add oil. Add 1 cup (250 mL) flour and beat in an electric mixer until smooth, then keep adding additional flour until it slows the mixer. If dough is too soft, add additional flour and mix with a wooden spoon, then turn out onto a floured baking board and knead until smooth and elastic, about 10 minutes.

Put in a greased bowl, turn over dough to get all sides greased, cover

with plastic wrap and let it rise in a warm place until double in bulk, about 1½ hours.

Divide dough into two parts, then with the palms of your hands flatten each piece into an oval on a greased baking sheet, about ¼" (6 mm) thick. Brush surface with melted butter and sprinkle with sesame seeds. Let rise for 30 minutes then bake in a 350° F (175° C) oven for 20-25 minutes, or until golden brown. Serve hot.

BAKLAVA (HONEY PASTRY)

Middle East

The classic dessert of both Greece and Middle East. It might be a bit tedious to make, but the result and the ahs and ohs you will receive when people taste it make it worth-while.

¾ lb	*(400 g)*	phyllo pastry (available in specialty shops and some super-markets)
1 cup	*(250 mL)*	butter, melted
2 cups	*(500 mL)*	finely chopped nuts (walnuts, pecans, almonds or mixed)
3 tbs	*(3 tbs)*	sugar
¼ ts	*(¼ ts)*	cinnamon

Brush a 9 x 15" (220 x 380 mm) baking dish with melted butter then add 5 phyllo sheets, carefully smoothing them out and brushing each one well with melted butter, letting part of them hang over the edge of the baking dish. Mix together nuts, sugar and cinnamon and spread half of this mixture on top of phyllo sheets, then add 5 more phyllo sheets, again brushing each one carefully with butter. Add remaining nuts and phyllo sheets, repeating brushing each sheet with butter, then tuck in excess phyllo underneath. Finally brush top with butter and bake in a 325° F (165° C) oven for 1 hour.

When pastry is golden brown and ready, pour the following hot syrup over it immediately, spreading it evenly over the surface. Let cool at room temperature and let it rest in pan at least 6 hours before cutting into either triangles or squares of about 1½" (38 mm) size. (The traditional shape is a triangular one.)

Syrup:

1 cup	*(250 mL)*	honey
1 cup	*(250 mL)*	sugar
1 cup	*(250 mL)*	water
2 tbs	*(2 tbs)*	lemon juice

Mix together honey, sugar and water and bring to a boil, turn down heat and add lemon juice, then cook for 10 minutes.

MIDDLE EASTERN PRUNES

This is a recipe I got from someone, which I filed under Middle East. I am embarrassed to confess that I did not note which country and have completely forgotten who gave it to me. But I thought it was too good to leave out even though it has to remain doubly anonymous.

½ lb	(¼ kg)	prunes
½ cup	(125 mL)	hot tea
¼ cup	(60 mL)	Cointreau or other orange liqueur
1 cup	(250 mL)	heavy cream
		sugar to taste
½ ts	(½ ts)	vanilla extract

Put prunes in a small bowl and pour hot tea over. Push prunes down into liquid to get them all covered and if necessary use a little more hot tea. Let stand for at least 8 hours or over-night. Add liqueur and mix well. Whip cream with sugar and vanilla and serve on top of prunes.

Serves 4–5.

Norway

As in so many other countries in Europe with a long coastline, fish plays a dominant role in the culinary habits of Norway. And because there are many kinds and qualities of fish to choose from, people are very particular about both its type and its freshness. They expect their fishermen to bring in the fish they want for dinner, that very morning. Cod is considered a delicacy, and the very large variety, called the "western sea cod" (*vesterhavstorsk*), that is caught in these waters, is very good indeed. They usually eat it just poached with melted butter, and it really needs no other accompaniments.

Norway has a large fish canning industry and the Norwegian sardines are well known to us in the U.S. They also can a lot of herring of different types, and shrimp.

The eating habits of the Norwegians are very similar to those of the rest of Scandinavia with a few specialties of their own. For example, Norway is the only Scandinavian country where lamb plays an important part. I would even consider lamb and cabbage as their most popular dish. Legs of lamb are also cured and smoked, in a manner similar to Virginia hams, then stored for some time before they are used, sliced very thin to be eaten with bread and butter. The *flatbröd* is also peculiar to Norway—it is a paper thin crisp bread, often eaten just plain or with cheese.

Norway has many excellent cheeses and Jarlsberg is one of them which is very popular in the U.S. The Norwegian goat cheese (*geit-ost*) is very different from the goat cheeses of southern Europe. It is light brown in color, somewhat sandy in texture and pungent in flavor. Once you have acquired a taste for it, you can really get quite hooked on it.

Desserts follow the pattern of the other Scandinavian countries, with soups and puddings made from berries and fruits. One berry that is abundant in some places in Norway is the cloud-berry—*multer*—which looks somewhat like a pale yellow blackberry, but it has an almost divine flavor all its own. Even the Norwegians themselves sound almost reverent when they talk about them. The most popular cake of Norway—blöte-kake—is quite an unforgettable eating experience when made with these berries as a filling.

PEA AND BARLEY SOUP	*Bettagryn*
FISH PUDDING	*Fiskepudding*
LAMB AND CABBAGE	*Faar i Kaal*
SOUR CABBAGE	*Surkaal*
FARINA APPLE PUDDING	
DUKE'S TART	*Fyrstekake*
APPLE MERINGUE CAKE	
CREAM CAKE	*Blötekake*

Norway   **PEA AND BARLEY SOUP**   *(Bettagryn)*

This is a soup from far back and may be considered old-fashioned by calorie-conscious modern Norwegians. To be really authentic the meat should consist of salt-cured lamb, but as this is practically unobtainable in the U.S. I have substituted corned beef. The soup is still delicious as well as being the stick-to-the-ribs kind.

⅔ cup	*(160 mL)*	whole yellow peas (or if not available, whole green peas)
⅓ cup	*(80 mL)*	barley
6 cups	*(1½ L)*	water
		salt to taste
½ lb	*(250 g)*	corned beef, cut in small chunks
1 cup	*(250 mL)*	turnip, cut into ¼″ (6 mm) cubes
1½ cups	*(375 mL)*	carrots, cut into ¼″ (6 mm) cubes
1½ cups	*(375 mL)*	potatoes, cut into ¼″ (6 mm) cubes
¼ cup	*(60 mL)*	chopped leeks
2 tbs	*(2 tbs)*	chopped parsley

(Continued on next page)

(Pea and Barley Soup, cont.)

Soak barley and peas in water for at least 6 hours, or overnight. Add salt and bring to a boil, turn down heat, skim off surface and cook for 1½ hours. Add meat and cook for 1 hour. Add turnip and carrots and cook for 20 minutes, then add potatoes and cook until tender, about 15 minutes. Add leeks and cook for 5 minutes. Check to make sure all ingredients are tender, otherwise cook a little while longer. Serve immediately sprinkled with parsley.

Serves 4–6.

FISH PUDDING

Norway
(*Fiskepudding*)

This is one of the classical dishes of Norway where they always have such wonderful, fresh fish.

1 lb	(½ kg)	fish fillets (sole, flounder, cod or haddock)
2	(2)	eggs
		salt and pepper to taste
		pinch of nutmeg
⅓ cup	(80 mL)	milk
1 tbs	(1 tbs)	flour
½ cup	(125 mL)	heavy cream

Either put the fish through a meat grinder (medium blade) or cut it against the grain into very thin strips. Beat eggs, salt, pepper, nutmeg, milk and flour. If a blender is available, take a small amount of fish and a small amount of egg mixture at a time and purée same, putting each batch in a bowl. Continue until all has been puréed, then beat vigorously with a wooden spoon, adding cream, a little at a time.

If you do not have a blender, grind mixture three times in a meat grinder using the fine blade, then beat together with the egg mixture until it is smooth. Put mixture in a 1 qt (1 L) buttered and floured ring-mold, cover with aluminum foil, and set it in a larger pan with about 1″ (25 mm) of boiling water. Bake in a 325° F (165° C) oven for 1 hour, or until knife inserted into the pudding comes out dry.

Serve with melted butter or with this sauce:

(*Continued on next page*)

(Fish Pudding, cont.)

Shrimp (or lobster) sauce:

2 tbs	(2 tbs)	butter or margarine
2 tbs	(2 tbs)	flour
1½ cups	(375 mL)	light cream, half and half, or milk
1	(1)	can of shrimp (or lobster) about 7 oz (200 g)
1 ts	(1 ts)	lemon juice
		salt and pepper to taste

Melt butter in a small saucepan, add flour stirring vigorously. Add cream or milk, and liquid from can, a little at a time, stirring continuously until a smooth sauce has been obtained. Cook for 5 minutes. Add salt, pepper, lemon juice and shrimp. Heat only until shrimp is hot through and use immediately.

Serves 4–5.

LAMB AND CABBAGE

Norway (*Faar i Kaal*)

This is one of the more popular dishes in Norway. It may seem like a simple meal, but it is delicious and is considered good enough for any guest. I remember reading some place that the wife of Harry Brandt, former Premier of West Germany, used to serve this to her guests at the chancellery. Of course, she is Norwegian and knows how good this meal is.

4–5 lbs	(2-2½ kg)	stewing lamb (shoulder or breast)
1 tbs	(1 tbs)	butter or margarine
		salt and pepper to taste
10	(10)	whole allspice
½ cup	(125 mL)	water
1	(1)	medium head of cabbage (6 cups (1½ L)

Cut lamb into serving pieces and brown in butter in a heavy skillet, a few pieces at a time. Sprinkle with salt and pepper, put meat in a heavy saucepan and add whole allspice and water. Bring to a boil, turn down heat to low and simmer about 1 hour or until meat is quite tender. Trim the outside leaves off the head of cab- bage, divide into four quarters, re- move core and slice into rather coarse pieces. Remove the meat and skim off fat that has accumulated on top. (If desired, at this point the liquid can be put into the refrigerator and chilled

(Continued on next page)

(Lamb and Cabbage, cont.)

until the fat congeals and can easily be lifted out).

Make layers of meat and cabbage in the pan, add the skimmed pot liquid, and bring to a boil again, then cook gently for 10–15 minutes, or until cabbage is tender (the exact time depends upon how fresh the cabbage is, a very fresh head of cabbage may cook even faster). Serve with boiled potatoes.

For 5–6.

SOUR CABBAGE

Norway (*Surkaal*)

On Christmas day in Norway the traditional meal consists of a fresh ham roast and it is almost always served with this kind of cabbage.

1	(*1*)	medium size head of cabbage, finely shredded (about 6 cups or 1½ L)
2 tbs	(*2 tbs*)	butter or margarine
¼ cup	(*60 mL*)	vinegar
2 tbs	(*2 tbs*)	caraway seeds
1 tbs	(*1 tbs*)	sugar
1 tbs	(*1 tbs*)	flour

Melt butter in a large saucepan, add cabbage and stir to get fat distributed throughout. Add vinegar and caraway seeds and bring to a boil, turn down heat to very low and simmer for about 1 hour, or until cabbage is very tender. Sprinkle flour over cabbage and stir to mix, then cook for an additional 5 minutes.

Serves 5–6.

FARINA APPLE PUDDING

Norway

A nice substantial dessert—perfect to be served when soup is the main meal.

½ cup	(*125 mL*)	farina
2½ cups	(*375 mL*)	milk
½ ts	(*½ ts*)	salt
2 tbs	(*2 tbs*)	sugar
1	(*1*)	egg, slightly beaten
4	(*4*)	tart apples, peeled, cored and sliced
¼ cup	(*60 mL*)	sugar (more if desired)
2 ts	(*2 ts*)	cinnamon
¼ cup	(*60 mL*)	chopped almonds
2 tbs	(*2 tbs*)	butter or margarine

Cook farina with milk, salt and sugar until thick, stirring constantly. Remove from heat, then add egg and mix well. Put half of farina in a buttered baking dish, spread apple slices on it, add sugar, cinnamon and almonds and dot with the butter. Put remaining farina on top. Bake in a 400° F (200° C) oven for 20 minutes. Serve warm with thin cream or whipped cream.

Serves 4–5.

DUKE'S TART

Norway *(Fyrstekake)*

An almond cake that is very popular—and for a good reason, as you will find out.

½ cup	*(125 mL)*	butter or margarine
¾ cup	*(180 mL)*	sugar
1	*(1)*	egg, slightly beaten
1½ cups	*(375 mL)*	flour
1½ ts	*(1½ ts)*	baking powder
½ ts	*(½ ts)*	salt

Cream butter and sugar until light and fluffy, add egg and mix well. Sift together flour, baking powder and salt and add to butter mixture, a little at a time. If you use an electric mixer, use only while mixture is light enough for it, then add remaining flour and stir with a wooden spoon. Turn onto a floured baking board and knead into a smooth dough. Let rest in refrigerator for about 30 minutes.

Filling:

1 cup	*(250 mL)*	almonds or filberts
1 cup	*(250 mL)*	confectioners' sugar
1	*(1)*	egg
2 tbs	*(2 tbs)*	water

Prepare filling by grinding nuts, either in a nut-grinder or electric blender. Add confectioners sugar and mix well, then add egg and water and blend into a smooth paste.

Assembly:

Remove dough from refrigerator, set aside about ⅕ of it, then roll out remaining dough to fit a 9″ (220 mm) pie plate. Line pie plate with sheet of dough, place filling on top and smooth out. Bake in a 350° F (175° C) oven 35–40 minutes.

Make thin rolls of remaining dough. Remove cake from oven, add rolls in a criss cross pattern on top, then return to oven and bake an additional 30 minutes.

APPLE MERINGUE CAKE

Norway

A nice addition to the recipes of apple fanciers.

1	*(1)*	single layer sponge cake (see page 36)
5-6	*(5-6)*	apples
1 cup	*(250 mL)*	water
½ cup	*(125 mL)*	white wine (optional—if omitted increase water to 1½ cups (*375 mL*)
⅓ cup	*(80 mL)*	sugar

Peel and core apples, then cut them into halves. Make a syrup by boiling water with the sugar and half the wine. Poach apples gently in this until soft but not mushy, turning them over once during poaching. Put them directly on the sponge cake, cut side down. Add remaining wine to syrup then sprinkle over cake and apples.

Meringue:

3	*(3)*	egg whites
⅓ cup	*(80 mL)*	sugar
¼ cup	*(60 mL)*	chopped almonds

Beat egg whites until stiff, then add sugar a little at a time until well incorporated. Spread meringue on top of cake, sprinkle with almonds and bake in a 350° F (175° C) oven for 15 minutes. Cool away from drafts.

CREAM CAKE

Norway   *(Blöte-kake)*

This is the cake that greets visitors to Norway—and the one they often carry away with them in their memories.

4	*(4)*	eggs
1½ cups	*(375 mL)*	sugar
2 cups	*(500 mL)*	flour
2 ts	*(2 ts)*	baking powder
½ ts	*(½ ts)*	salt
¾ cup	*(180 mL)*	milk
4 tbs	*(4 tbs)*	butter or margarine
1 ts	*(1 ts)*	vanilla extract

(Continued on next page)

(Cream Cake, cont.)

Beat eggs until thick and foamy, gradually add sugar and keep beating until well incorporated, at least 10 minutes. Heat milk and butter until hot, but do not let boil. Sift together flour, baking powder and salt and add to egg mixture. Add the hot milk and stir batter only until mixture is smooth.

Pour batter into two greased and floured 9″ (220 mm) baking pans and bake in a 350° F (175° C) oven about 20–25 minutes, or until cakes test as done. Let rest in pans for 5 minutes, then turn out onto wire racks to cool.

Filling and assembly:

1-1½ cups (250–375 mL)	fresh berries, such as strawberries (whole or cut up) or raspberries mixed with sugar to taste *or* the same amount of frozen berries *or* canned or fresh peaches, cut up *or* crushed pineapple *or* fruit cocktail
1½ cups (375 mL)	heavy cream
For decoration:	A few of the fresh berries being used, or some sliced pineapple cut up, or maraschino cherries.

The Norwegian name for this cake, *blöte-kake*, means *moist* cake. You moisten it by sprinkling both layers of the cake with the excess fruit or berry juice. Spread the fruit evenly on the bottom layer, then place the second layer on top.

Whip the cream and cover entire cake. Put aside some cream and, using a cake-decorator set, squeeze it in an attractive pattern on top and on the sides.

Add any of the suggested decorations, if desired.

Poland

THE cooking of Poland has so many similarities to that of Russia that it is hard to say today which dish originated where—in Russia or Poland. And I am sure each of these countries likes to take the credit.

Thus *borscht* which we connect with Russia seems to be an almost national dish of Poland as well, and *pierogi* are just as popular in Russia as in Poland.

Polish hams are of the highest quality and are important exports to the U.S. and elsewhere. Their excellence is attributed to the Polish way of feeding and caring for the pigs.

I have here the recipes for a few dishes, more closely connected to Poland than anywhere else, which seem to be of special interest because of their distinctiveness.

<table>
<tr><td>PIEROGI</td><td>Pierozki</td></tr>
<tr><td>BERRY SOUP</td><td>Zupa Jagodowa</td></tr>
<tr><td>ROAST STUFFED CHICKEN</td><td></td></tr>
<tr><td>HUNTER'S STEW</td><td>Bigos Mysliwski</td></tr>
<tr><td>KIELBASA (POLISH SAUSAGE)
  WITH RED CABBAGE</td><td>Kielbasa z Czerwonej Kapuscie</td></tr>
<tr><td>NOODLES AND CABBAGE</td><td>Kluski z Kapusta</td></tr>
<tr><td>MUSHROOMS IN SOUR CREAM</td><td>Grzyby ze Smietana</td></tr>
<tr><td>BOW KNOTS</td><td>Chruszczik</td></tr>
<tr><td>BABA AU RHUM</td><td>Babka</td></tr>
</table>

PIEROGI

Poland   *(Pierozki)*

This type of little meat pastries exists in many countries, but I like them especially the Polish way, with mushroom sauce.

2	(2)	eggs
¼–½ cup	(60–125 mL)	water
3 cups	(750 mL)	flour
½ ts	(½ ts)	salt

For brushing: 1 beaten egg mixed
                                                 with 1 tbs milk

Beat eggs with ¼ cup (60 mL) water, add flour, sifted together with salt, mixing well and working into a firm dough. Add additional water, if dough is too stiff to handle. Turn onto a floured baking board and knead until smooth. Set aside in refrigerator for 15–20 minutes.

Filling:

½ lb	(¼ kg)	lean, chopped beef
1	(1)	small onion, finely chopped (½ cup or 125 mL)
2 tbs	(2 tbs)	butter or margarine
½ cup	(125 mL)	chopped fresh mushrooms
3 tbs	(3 tbs)	sour cream
		salt and pepper to taste

Sauté onion in butter until transparent, add meat, breaking up any lumps with a fork and cook until meat loses its red color. Add mushrooms and cook about 5 minutes more. Add sour cream and seasonings and mix into an almost paste-like texture.

Divide dough into three parts and roll out each one on a floured baking board to about ⅛″ (3 mm) thickness. Cut into rounds of about 3″ (75 mm), using a glass dipped in flour, if a cooky cutter of that size is not available. Place about ¾ tbs filling on each round, moisten edges with water and fold over, seal well by pressing together with a fork. Drop these *pierogis* into boiling salted water and cook about 5 minutes, then remove with a slotted spoon, drain and place in a buttered baking dish. Brush with beaten egg and bake in a 350° F (175° C) oven about 15–20 minutes or until golden brown. Serve hot with the mushroom sauce on the next page.

Serves 5–6.

(Continued on next page)

(Pierogi, cont.)

Mushroom Sauce:

2 tbs	(*2 tbs*)	**butter or margarine**
2 cups	(*500 mL*)	**chopped fresh mushrooms**
2 tbs	(*2 tbs*)	**flour**
1-1½ cups	(*250–375 mL*)	**light cream, or half-and-half**
1 tbs	(*1 tbs*)	**sherry (optional)**
		salt and pepper to taste

Melt butter in a sauce pan, add mushrooms and sauté about 10 minutes. Sprinkle with flour and stir well to mix, then immediately add cream, a little at a time, stirring continuously until mixture is smooth. Cook over low heat about 5 minutes. Add sherry and seasonings and serve.

BERRY SOUP

Poland (*Zupa Jagodowa*)

2 cups	(*500 mL*)	**blueberries, raspberries or blackberries**
		(or 1 pkg frozen berries, 10 oz or 300 g)
2 cups	(*500 mL*)	**water**
		grated rind of ½ lemon
		juice of ½ lemon
½ cup	(*125 mL*)	**sugar**
¼ ts	(*¼ ts*)	**cinnamon**
		pinch of ground cloves
1 tbs	(*1 tbs*)	**corn starch mixed with 2 tbs water**
1 cup	(*250 mL*)	**sour cream or fresh heavy cream, whipped**

Bring berries, water, grated lemon rind and juice to a boil and simmer until berries give up their juice. Press through a sieve, then return juice to pot, add sugar, cinnamon, cloves, bring to boil, turn down heat and cook for 5 minutes. Mix corn starch and water, add to juice and cook for one minute. Remove from heat. Either mix cream directly into soup while it is still hot, stirring to mix well, or chill the soup first and then serve it into soup bowls with dollops of either sour cream or whipped heavy cream.

Serves 4–6.

Poland   **ROAST STUFFED CHICKEN**

An unusual stuffing for a chicken—it turns out almost like a soufflé.

1	*(1)*	roasting chicken, 4–5 lbs (2–2½ kg)
1 cup	*(250 mL)*	day old bread, crusts removed, cubed
¼ cup	*(60 mL)*	milk
1	*(1)*	chicken liver
4 tbs	*(4 tbs)*	butter
1 cup	*(250 mL)*	parsley, finely minced
2	*(2)*	eggs, separated
		salt and pepper to taste

Rub chicken with pepper and salt, both inside and out. Soak bread cubes in milk and let rest for 15 minutes, then stir to remove any lumps. Chop chicken liver finely, mix with parsley and combine with bread. Cream butter until light and fluffy, add egg yolks and mix together with bread mixture. Beat egg whites until stiff, then carefully fold in. Fill the bird cavity with this stuffing and fasten opening with skewers. Roast in a 350° F (175° C) oven about 3 hours, basting off and on.   Serves 5–6.

Poland   **HUNTER'S STEW**   *(Bigos Mysliwski)*

Different types of the dish Bigos are extremely popular throughout Poland. They can be made in many ways with whatever left-over meat you have on hand, even frankfurters will do. Because of its good keeping quality Bigos has been a favorite with hunters who take it along to heat on wood fires in the forest. But this is a somewhat more sophisticated version.

2 cups	*(500 mL)*	**kielbasa,** (Polish sausage) diced into ½″ (12 mm) cubes
2 cups	*(500 mL)*	pork roast, diced into ½″ (12 mm) cubes (beef or lamb roast may be substituted)
1	*(1)*	large onion, finely chopped (1 cup or 250 mL)
1	*(1)*	clove garlic, finely minced
2 tbs	*(2 tbs)*	butter or margarine
1	*(1)*	small head white cabbage, shredded (4 cups or 1 L)
1	*(1)*	1 lb (½ kg) can sauerkraut
1 cup	*(250 mL)*	sliced fresh mushrooms (or one can, 8 oz or 250 g)

(Continued on next page)

(Hunter's Stew, cont.)

1 cup	*(250 mL)*	beef stock (bouillon cubes may be used, or left-over gravy from roast)
2	*(2)*	tart apples, peeled and diced
5	*(5)*	pitted prunes
1	*(1)*	can tomato paste (6 oz or 175 g)
1	*(1)*	bay leaf
		salt and pepper to taste
½ cup	*(125 mL)*	red wine

Sauté onion and garlic in butter until onion is transparent. Put all remaining ingredients, except wine, in a large, buttered casserole or a heavy Dutch oven, cover and either bake in a 325° F (165° C) for 1½ hours, or bring to a boil on top of the stove, then turn down heat and simmer over very low heat for the same amount of time.

Remove, add wine then continue baking or simmering for an additional ½ hour. Serve with rice, noodles or potatoes. Serves 5–6.

KIELBASA WITH RED CABBAGE

Poland

(Kielbasa z Czerwonej Kapuscie)

1	*(1)*	kielbasa (Polish sausage) about 1½ lbs (¾ kg)
1	*(1)*	small head red cabbage (about 2 lbs or 1 kg)
2 tbs	*(2 tbs)*	butter or margarine
¼ cup	*(60 mL)*	lemon juice
1 tbs	*(1 tbs)*	brown sugar
⅓ cup	*(80 mL)*	red wine or water
		salt and pepper to taste
1 tbs	*(1 tbs)*	corn starch, mixed with 1¼ cup (60 mL water)

Shred cabbage coarsely then sauté for a few minutes in butter or margarine in a large saucepan or Dutch oven, stirring constantly. Add lemon juice, brown sugar, wine or water, salt and pepper and bring to a boil, turn down heat to very low, cover pot and simmer for 30 minutes, stirring off and on. Add sausage and bring to a boil again and simmer under cover until sausage is heated through, about 30 minutes. Remove sausage. Mix corn starch and water and add, stirring to get it well mixed, bring to a boil and cook for 1 minute, then remove from heat and serve with sausages either cut into slices or into chunks. Serves 5–6.

NOODLES AND CABBAGE

Poland   (*Kluski z Kapusta*)

1	(*1*)	medium size onion, chopped (³⁄₄ cup or 180 mL)
2 tbs	(*2 tbs*)	butter or margarine
4 cups	(*1 L*)	coarsely shredded cabbage (about ¹⁄₂ medium head)
1 ts	(*1 ts*)	caraway seed
		salt and pepper to taste
¹⁄₂ lb	(¹⁄₄ *kg*)	egg noodles

Sauté onion in butter or margarine until onion is transparent. Add cabbage and stir-cook for 10 minutes, then add caraway seed and salt and pepper. In the meantime cook the noodles in another pot in salted water according to directions on package, then drain thoroughly. Combine noodles and cabbage and mix well, then cook for 5 minutes, stirring off and on.

VARIATION:

Just before serving, add ¹⁄₂ cup (125 mL) sour cream and mix well.

MUSHROOMS IN SOUR CREAM

Poland   (*Grzyby ze Smietana*)

Mushrooms are important in the Polish cuisine. Very often wild mushrooms, different varieties of which are abundant in their forests, are used. Our mushrooms are good for this dish too. It is popular either as an appetizer or as a side dish with meat.

1 lb	(¹⁄₂ *kg*)	mushrooms
1	(*1*)	small onion, finely chopped (¹⁄₂ cup or 125 mL)
4 tbs	(*4 tbs*)	butter or margarine
2 tbs	(*2 tbs*)	flour
2 tbs	(*2 tbs*)	milk
1¹⁄₂ cups	(*375 mL*)	sour cream
		salt and pepper to taste
		pinch of paprika

Clean and slice mushrooms. Sauté onion in butter or margarine until transparent, sprinkle with flour and stir to mix well. Add milk and mushrooms and bring to a boil, turn down heat and simmer for a few minutes. Season with salt and pepper, then add half amount of sour cream and cook for another few minutes. Just before serving, add remaining sour cream. Serves 5–6 as a side dish with meat, more as an appetizer.

WALNUT CAKE

Poland

A *Walnut Cake in one version or another is what is served in Poland for festive occasions. I think this is as good as any I have tasted, but, alas, it is so rich that for weight-conscious Americans it will be for very special occasions, indeed.*

2 cups	(*500 mL*)	walnuts, finely ground measured before grinding
6	(*6*)	eggs, separated
1 cup	(*250 mL*)	confectioners' sugar
2 tbs	(*2 tbs*)	fine dry breadcrumbs
1 ts	(*1 ts*)	vanilla extract

Beat egg yolks with confectioners' sugar until light and lemon-colored, then add walnuts, bread crumbs and vanilla extract. Beat egg whites until very stiff and fold into yolk mixture. Spread batter in two well greased and floured 9″ (220 mm) baking pans and bake in a 350° F (175° C) oven 20–25 minutes or until tested as done. Cool for five minutes in pans, then turn out onto wire racks to cool completely before filling.

Filling:

3 cups	(*750 mL*)	walnuts, finely chopped
1-½ cups	(*375 mL*)	confectioners' sugar
½ cup	(*125 mL*)	light cream or half and half

Mix together all the ingredients into a paste.

Assembly:

1 cup	(*250 mL*)	heavy cream (preferably unsweetened) whole or half walnuts for decoration

Spread about ⅔ of the filling between the layers and remaining ⅓ on top. Whip cream until stiff and swirl on top and sides and decorate with the whole or half walnuts. Serves 8–10.

BOW KNOTS

Poland   (*Chruszczik*)

Good cookies of a deep-fried variety.

1	(*1*)	egg
1	(*1*)	egg yolk
2 tbs	(*2 tbs*)	sugar
2 tbs	(*2 tbs*)	melted butter
1 tbs	(*1 tbs*)	cream
1½ cups	(*375 mL*)	flour
¼ ts	(*¼ ts*)	baking powder
		oil for deep-frying

For sprinkling: 2 tbs confectioners' sugar

Beat egg, egg yolk and sugar until light and fluffy, add melted butter and cream and mix well. Add flour, mixed with baking powder, a little at a time and work mixture into a firm dough. Knead on a floured board then roll out very thin and cut into strips, ¾″ x 2″ (18 x 50 mm). Cut a gash length-wise in the center, insert one end and pull through to make a bow-like knot. Deep fry in 350° F (175° C) oil, a few at a time, for 15–20 seconds, then turn over once and fry for a few seconds on the other side.

The cookies should be golden in color when ready. They cook very fast, so make sure they do not get too brown. Remove with a slotted spoon and drain on paper towels. When cool sprinkle both sides with confectioners' sugar. Makes about 3 dozen.

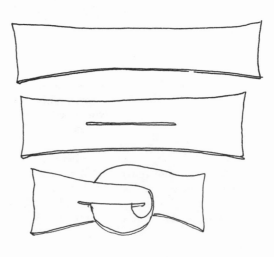

BABA AU RHUM

Poland (*Babka*)

The national cake of Poland—especially when baked in its own Turk's Head pan. It may, of course, be eaten without the rum syrup, if preferred.

1	(*1*)	pkg dry yeast
½ cup	(*125 mL*)	lukewarm milk
⅓ cup	(*80 mL*)	sugar
¼ cup	(*60 mL*)	butter or margarine
2 cups	(*500 mL*)	flour
3	(*3*)	eggs (at room temperature)
⅓ cup	(*80 mL*)	raisins
¼ cup	(*60 mL*)	mixed candied fruit

Dissolve yeast in ¼ cup (60 mL) of lukewarm milk mixed with 1 ts sugar. Melt butter or margarine in a small saucepan, add remaining milk and heat until warm, then put into bowl of an electric mixer. Add remaining sugar and 1 cup (250 mL) flour and beat for 2 minutes at medium speed. Add eggs, one at a time while beating, then add ½ cup (125 mL) flour and beat at high speed for a couple of minutes, scraping bowl off and on. Add remaining flour and beat again for a few minutes at high speed.

Cover bowl and let dough rise in a warm place for about 1 hour.

Stir in raisins and candied fruits and put dough either into a special Babka pan (sometimes called Turk's Head pan) or into an ordinary 2 qt (2 L) tube pan. Let rise again for 30 minutes, then bake in a 350° F (175° C) oven for about 35 minutes, or until done.

Before removing cake from pan, prick surface with a fork in many places and pour this rum syrup over it.

Rum Syrup:

½ cup	(*125 mL*)	sugar
⅓ cup	(*80 mL*)	water
¼ cup	(*60 mL*)	rum (or a little more, if desired)

Combine all ingredients in a small saucepan and bring to a boil. Pour over cake while hot.

After syrup has been absorbed, re-move cake from pan and cool on a wire rack. If desired, it may be iced with confectioners' sugar icing when cool.

Portugal

PORTUGAL has such an exposure to the Atlantic Ocean, that it is to be expected that fish plays a dominant role in its cuisine. What seems as a surprise, though, is the fact that with such a large fishing fleet, and such wonderful fresh fish, they use the salt, dried cod to such a great extent. This comes both from Iceland and the Scandinavian countries and is widely used in many varied recipes. I have even heard that there are 365 such recipes—one for each day of the year—but whether this is an exaggeration or not, I have not verified.

One product of Portugal, used all over the world, is Port Wine, which is used in the Portuguese cuisine for wine cookery with a distinctive flavor.

Portugal and Spain share a long border with the result that there are many similarities in both cooking methods and ingredients in these countries.

Being an adventurous seafaring people who have settled in many parts of the world, Portuguese influence can be found in the cuisines of South America, Africa and on many Pacific islands.

Among their desserts, the steamed pudding, of which many varieties exist, is the most distinctive.

SHRIMP SOUP	*Sopa de Camarao*
COD CASSEROLE	*Bacalhau a Portuguesa*
CHICKEN STEW	*Frango Guisado*
LIVER IN WINE	*Iscas a Portuguesa*
PORK WITH CLAMS	*Carne de Porco con Ameijoas*
WALNUT PUDDING	*Pudim de Noses*
BANANA PUDDING	*Pudim de Bananas*
SWEET BREAD	*Pao Doce*

SHRIMP SOUP

Portugal   (*Sopa de Camarao*)

In Portugal this soup is considered a very economical meal and is therefore favored by university students, who flock to restaurants featuring it.

1 lb	(½ kg)	fillets of flounder or sole
2 tbs	(2 tbs)	olive oil
5 cups	(1250 mL)	water
½ lb	(¼ kg)	raw shrimp, shelled and de-veined
1 tbs	(1 tbs)	fresh basil, finely chopped or ½ ts dried
2 tbs	(2 tbs)	finely chopped fresh parsley
¼ ts	(¼ ts)	oregano
1	(1)	medium onion, finely chopped (¾ cup or 180 mL)
		salt and pepper to taste
2	(2)	slices white bread, crusts removed and finely cubed (1 cup or 250 mL)
5	(5)	hardboiled egg yolks
For serving:		6 thick slices, toasted French style bread, rubbed with 1 clove garlic, cut in half

Cut fish fillets into bite size pieces and sauté in olive oil for a few minutes on each side, then remove. Sauté onion for a few minutes, then transfer into a large saucepan and add water, parsley, basil, oregano, salt and pepper and bring to a boil, turn down heat and boil for 8 minutes. Add shrimp and bring to a boil again, then turn down heat and boil for 3 minutes, add fish fillets, bread cubes and egg yolks and keep stirring gently until it becomes thoroughly hot, but do not let it boil again. Rub each slice of toast with garlic and place in the bottom of individual soup bowls, pour the soup and serve.

For 5–6 portions.

COD CASSEROLE

Portugal   (*Bacalhau a Portuguesa*)

In my childhood on the west coast of Sweden I remember 20–30 foot (7–10 meter) high racks with salted fish hanging to dry during the Summer months. I knew it was to be exported to many southern European countries. There they made good use of it, as this recipe will attest.

(Continued on next page)

(Cod Casserole, cont.)

1 lb	(½ *kg*)	salted dried cod
4	(*4*)	medium size potatoes, peeled and cut into ¼″ (6 mm) slices
4	(*4*)	medium size onions, sliced
4	(*4*)	medium size tomatoes, peeled and sliced
3	(*3*)	green peppers, cored and sliced
		pepper to taste
¼ cup	(*60 mL*)	olive oil

Soak codfish at least 10 hours in cold water, changing it at least once, and finally draining it off and discarding it. Cut fish into bite-size pieces, then put in a large casserole in alternate layers with the vegetables, making two layers of each. Sprinkle pepper on top and pour the olive oil over, then bake in a 350° F (175° C) for 1-1½ hours, or until both fish and vegetables are tender.

Serves 4–5.

CHICKEN STEW

Portugal

(*Frango Guisado*)

This is chicken with wine, but a different wine from what you generally use. The port makes it very nice, indeed.

1	(*1*)	frying chicken, about 3-3½ lbs (1½-1¾ kg), cut into serving pieces
3 tbs	(*3 tbs*)	olive oil
1	(*1*)	medium size onion, chopped (¾ cup or 180 mL)
1 cup	(*250 mL*)	fresh, peeled and chopped tomatoes (or same amount canned Italian plum tomatoes)
2 tbs	(*2 tbs*)	chopped fresh parsley
1	(*1*)	clove garlic, finely minced
¼ cup	(*60 mL*)	port wine
		salt and pepper to taste

Sauté onion and garlic in olive oil in an electric fryer or chicken fryer until onion is transparent. Add parsley and mix well. Push all of it to the sides of pan, add chicken pieces and brown well on all sides, add salt and pepper to taste, then blend in with onion mixture. Pour in port wine and simmer for 35–45 minutes, or until chicken is tender, turning pieces several times during cooking. Serve with rice.

For 6 people.

LIVER IN WINE

Portugal   *(Iscas a Portuguesa)*

As a child I loved fried liver and I still enjoy it very much. As it is such a nutritious and economical meal, I like to give many versions of serving it.

1½ lb	(¾ kg)	beef liver (or calves liver), sliced
¼ cup	(60 mL)	white wine
2 tbs	(2 tbs)	wine vinegar
		salt and pepper to taste
2 tbs	(2 tbs)	olive oil
1	(1)	bay leaf

Mix wine, vinegar, salt, pepper and bay leaf, and marinate liver in this about 2 hours. Remove liver and pat dry with paper towels. Fry it in olive oil in a hot pan for about 3 minutes on each side, then transfer slices to a serving plate and keep warm. Add marinade to the pan juices and bring to a boil, scraping fry pan to loosen particles that may be sticking to bottom. Serve the liver with mashed or boiled potatoes, and the pan juices in a separate bowl.

Serves 4–5.

PORK WITH CLAMS

Portugal   (*Carne de Porco con Ameijoas*)

1-½ lbs		boneless pork, cut from loin into ¾″ (18 mm) cubes
		salt and pepper to taste
½ cup	(*125 mL*)	dry white wine
2 tbs	(*2 tbs*)	salad oil
¼ ts		cayenne, or slightly more if desired
1 dozen	(*1 dozen*)	clams

Sprinkle pork with salt and pepper, then put in a bowl with the wine and marinate for about 4 hours, turning the pieces several times.

Drain off marinade and reserve, pat the meat dry with paper towelling, then brown well on all sides in a skillet.

Transfer meat to a heavy pot with a tight lid, then add cayenne and reserved marinade, bring to a boil, then turn down heat to low and simmer until meat is tender, about 30 minutes. Scrub clams and add to pot, turn up heat somewhat and steam them until they have opened (about 6–8 minutes), then remove shells and serve immediately.   Serves 4–5.

WALNUT PUDDING

Portugal   (*Pudim de Noses*)

5	(5)	eggs
⅔ cup	(160 mL)	sugar
1½ cups	(375 mL)	ground walnuts
½–1 ts	(½–1 ts)	cinnamon, according to taste

Beat eggs and sugar until light and fluffy, add ground nuts mixed with cinnamon and mix well. Pour into a buttered mold, cover with aluminum foil, and set this in a large saucepan with water up to 2″ (50 mm) on the mold and cover. The water should be kept simmering until the pudding is set, about 1½ hours. Chill and serve.

Serves 5–6.

BANANA PUDDING

Portugal   (*Pudim de Bananas*)

⅓ cup	(80 mL)	water
½ cup	(125 mL)	sugar
		grated peel of half a lemon
3	(3)	bananas, thinly sliced
3	(3)	eggs, separated
3 tbs	(3 tbs)	port wine
2 tbs	(2 tbs)	pine nuts

In a saucepan combine water, sugar and lemon peel, bring to a boil and cook until sugar is completely dissolved. Remove from heat and stir in bananas. Beat egg yolks until creamy and lemon-colored, then while still beating, add about half of the syrup to eggs, then pour this mixture, a little at a time, while stirring into banana mixture. Cook over very low heat until mixture thickens somewhat but do not let it boil, as it would then curdle.

Let mixture cool, then stir in wine. Beat egg whites until stiff and fold in. Toast pine nuts by putting them in a 350° F (175° C) for a few minutes. Put pudding either in individual dessert glasses or a serving dish and sprinkle with the pine nuts.

Serves 5–6.

SWEET BREAD

Portugal   *(Pao Doce)*

The first time I tasted this bread was on "my" island, Vinalhaven in Maine,
where an enterprising boy of about 14 years baked fresh loaves every day and
then walked along Main Street, selling them. I have also tasted the same bread
in Hawaii, where it is quite common. After all, the Portuguese people are sailors
and have roamed and settled all over, making good friends by bringing this
bread along with them wherever they have gone.

1	*(1)*	pkg dry yeast
¾ cup	*(180 mL)*	sugar
⅔ cup	*(160 mL)*	luke-warm milk
¼ cup	*(60 mL)*	butter
1 ts	*(1 ts)*	salt
3	*(3)*	eggs
4 cups	*(1 L)*	flour (or slightly more)
For brushing:		1 egg mixed with 1 tbs milk

Dissolve yeast in ¼ cup (60 mL) lukewarm milk with 1 tbs sugar. Melt butter and add milk and heat to lukewarm. In a bowl of an electric mixer beat eggs, then add sugar and beat until light and fluffy. Add butter and milk, mix well then add about 1½ cups (375 mL) flour, a little at a time and beat until smooth, about 5 minutes. Add remaining flour, a little at a time until the dough gets too heavy for the electric mixer, then beat with a wooden spoon until you get a light dough.

Turn out on a floured board. Knead about 10 minutes or until smooth and elastic, adding a little bit more flour if the dough should stick to the board or your hands. Put dough in a greased bowl, turn over once to get both sides greased and cover with a plastic wrap. Let it rise in warm place about 1½ hour or until double in bulk.

Punch down dough and divide into two round balls and place each one in an 8″ (200 mm) greased cake pan. Let rise until double in size, about 1 hour, then brush loaves with egg mixed with milk and bake in a 350° F (175° C) oven 35–40 minutes, or until golden brown.

Makes 2 loaves.

Russia

THE Soviet Union is a country that covers an area of $\frac{1}{7}$ of the land surface of the earth and it stretches approximately 6,800 miles (10,900 km) from east to west and 2,800 miles (4,500 km) from north to south. In a country of this size it goes without saying that there cannot be a cuisine that is the same all over. Therefore we will find quite a variety of both cooking methods and flavors, each one distinctive to the part of the country where it is used.

In the west there is some influence of Scandinavian cooking, maybe even going back to times when the Vikings from the eastern part of Sweden trekked through Russia on their way to the Black Sea. Many of them stayed on, and they settled whole villages. In the southeastern part of Russia they eat practically the same things as they do in the Balkan states, Turkey and Iran, and when we get far to the east, there is some Chinese and Mongolian influence.

So there is a great variety of food, and the Russians like food, not only in quality but in quantity. This may have to do with their climate, which is quite severe with cold, cold winters requiring extra calories to keep warm.

In Russia of today there are usually four meals a day—breakfast, lunch, dinner and a late snack. The dinner hour is on the early side—preferably between 3 and 5 P.M., that is, when it can be arranged that way. With so many women having outside jobs and coming home late, this favorite dinner hour may have to be saved for week-ends and holidays. Both breakfast and lunch are light meals, but the main meal is

415

more substantial and almost always consists of *zakuski* (hors d'oeuvres), soup, main dish and some sweet cake or similar for dessert.

Zakuski may consist of only one or two things, such as salted or pickled herring, salads and vegetables (cucumber is a favorite, both fresh in the summer and pickled or salted the remainder of the year, often served with sour cream), and for more festive occasions smoked salmon or sturgeon. There are also some hot *zakuskis* and on banquet occasions there are great varieties of both hot and cold ones.

With the soup course *piroshki* (sometimes called *pirogi* or in Poland *pierogi*) are often served and for everyday use *kasha,* which is a porridge made from buckwheat or other grains, is eaten with the soup. Sour cream (*smetana*) may also be served.

The main meal consists of fish, meat or poultry, prepared in many different ways.

Desserts, cakes and cookies are popular. Many of these are connected with traditional holidays, of which Easter is an important one, even without its religious connection. Then *pascha* is served, that wickedly rich but delicious cheese cake made in a pyramid shape and often decorated with colorful pieces of glacéed cherries or other fruits to look like bunches of jewels.

EGGPLANT SPREAD (EGGPLANT CAVIARE)	*Ikra Eze Baklajanov*
BEAN PURÉE	*Lobio*
BORSCHT	*Borstch*
CABBAGE AND SAUERKRAUT SOUP	*Shchi*
YEAST PANCAKES	*Blini*
CHICKEN PATTIES POJARSKI	*Kutleti Pojarski*
CHICKEN IN SOUR CREAM	
BEEF STROGANOFF	
LAMB PATTIES IN TOMATO SAUCE	*Izmir Keufta*
MEAT OR FISH PIE	*Koulebiaka*
MOSCOW CASSEROLE	*Selianka Moskva*
STUFFED CABBAGE	*Holubtsi*

(*Continued on next page*)

EGGPLANT SPREAD (EGGPLANT CAVIARE)

Russia   (*Ikra Eze Baklajanov*)

This appetizer spread is sometimes called Eggplant Caviare. However, I hesitated to use this name by itself, as many people might think I had inadvertently left out the fish roe.

1	(*1*)	medium size eggplant (about 1-1½ lb)
2 ts	(*2 ts*)	salt
1	(*1*)	medium onion, finely chopped (¾ cup or 180 mL)
1	(*1*)	clove garlic, finely minced
2 tbs	(*2 tbs*)	olive oil
1 tbs	(*1 tbs*)	lemon juice
		salt and pepper to taste

Peel eggplant and cut into ½″ (12 mm) cubes. Sprinkle with 2 ts salt and let stand for about 30 minutes, then squeeze liquid out of eggplant cubes. Sauté onion, garlic and eggplant in olive oil until very soft. Remove from heat. Chop very fine with a knife or spatula, then add salt, pepper and lemon juice. If mixture should be too dry, add 1-2 ts additional olive oil. Chill well before serving as an appetizer.   Serves 6.

BEAN PURÉE

Russia   (*Lobio*)

This dish is usually served on the side with meat, but I feel it lends itself perfectly to use as a dip with either chips or vegetables.

2 cups	(*500 mL*)	cooked kidney beans (1 1-lb or ½ kg can)
2	(*2*)	scallions, finely chopped
1-2	(*1-2*)	cloves of garlic, finely minced
¼ cup	(*60 mL*)	finely minced fresh dill
1 tbs	(*1 tbs*)	salad oil
½ cup	(*125 mL*)	chopped walnuts
		salt and pepper to taste

Put all ingredients except walnuts in a blender and beat into a smooth purée, or pass beans through a sieve, then mix well with remaining ingredients. Add walnuts and salt and pepper. Chill until ready to use. Serve with corn chips or fresh vegetables as a dip, or as a side dish with meat.
Makes about 2 cups.

Russia **BORSCHT** (*Borstch*)

This is the soup that immediately comes to your mind when you think of Russian soups. It is well liked and it is eaten either hot and cold, depending on the season.

3-4 lbs	(*1½-2 kg*)	soup beef with bones (such as shortribs or shin of beef)
8 cups	(*2 L*)	water
5	(*5*)	whole black peppercorns
2	(*2*)	bay leaves
5	(*5*)	medium size raw beets
4 cups	(*1 L*)	shredded green cabbage (about ½ medium head)
		salt to taste
2 tbs	(*2 tbs*)	lemon juice
1-2 ts	(*1-2 ts*)	sugar
1 cup	(*250 mL*)	sour cream
2-3 tbs	(*2-3 tbs*)	fresh dill, chopped

Trim excess fat from meat, add water and spices and bring to a boil. Skim off foam, cover and turn down heat, then simmer for 2–3 hours, or until meat is tender. Remove meat, strain liquid (stock) and skim excess fat off surface. (This can easily be done by cooling the broth for a couple of hours in the refrigerator, then lifting off the cake of congealed fat that has formed on top). Remove meat from bones and cut into bite-size pieces and reserve.

Clean beets, remove tops and cook in salted water until tender, 20–30 minutes for young beets, longer for older ones. Add shredded cabbage to stock and cook about 5 minutes. Peel cooked beets, cut into julienne strips, add to soup and cook about 5 more minutes. Add lemon juice and sugar. (The soup should be slightly tart, but not sour). Add meat to soup and heat thoroughly.

Serve soup and pass around a bowl of sour cream and a bowl of chopped dill and let everyone add a spoonful on top of the soup to be mixed in before eating.

Serves 5–6.

Russia   CABBAGE AND SAUERKRAUT SOUP   (*Shchi*)

Another soup popular in Russia but not well known outside that country.

1	(*1*)	small head of cabbage (about 1 lb or ½ kg)
1 cup	(*250 mL*)	sauerkraut (½ lb or ¼ kg)
1	(*1*)	medium size onion, chopped (¾ cup or 180 mL)
1	(*1*)	clove garlic, finely minced
2 tbs	(*2 tbs*)	butter or margarine
1 lb	(*½ kg*)	beef, short ribs or other cut with bone
5 cups	(*1250 mL*)	beef stock
		salt and pepper to taste
1 tbs	(*1 tbs*)	finely minced fresh dill or parsley, or both
½ cup	(*125 mL*)	sour cream

Shred cabbage coarsely and put in a large saucepan. Rinse sauerkraut in cold water, squeeze out water and add to cabbage. Sauté onion and garlic in butter or margarine until onion is transparent, then add to cabbage together with meat, beef stock and salt and pepper. Bring to a boil, then turn down heat and simmer over very low heat for 1½–2 hours, or until beef is tender and is loosened from the bones.

Remove bones from soup, then remove meat from bones, cut into bite size pieces and return to pot. Serve hot, sprinkled with dill or parsley. The sour cream may be stirred into the soup, just before serving, or may be served separately.

For 4–5 portions.

VARIATIONS:
Sometimes this soup is made with tomatoes also. If this is desired, add 1 cup (250 mL) canned tomatoes, with the onion and garlic. It also may be thickened with flour, by adding 1½ tbs flour stirred out with ¼ cup (60 mL) water after the cut-up meat has been added, then cooking for 5 minutes.

Russia   YEAST PANCAKES   (*Blini*)

Blini may also be made either with buck-wheat or plain flour. And if you have Russian caviar or smoked salmon to serve with it, you have a feast.

1	(*1*)	pkg dry yeast
¼ cup	(*60 mL*)	lukewarm water
½ cup	(*125 mL*)	butter or margarine

(*Continued on next page*)

(Yeast Pancakes, cont.)

1½ cups	(*375 mL*)	milk
3 cups	(*750 mL*)	flour (or buckwheat flour)
3 tbs	(*3 tbs*)	sugar
1 ts	(*1 ts*)	salt
3	(*3*)	eggs
For frying:		melted butter or margarine

Dissolve yeast in lukewarm water. In a small saucepan melt butter, add milk and heat to luke-warm. Sift together flour, sugar and salt. Beat eggs by hand or in an electric mixer until light and fluffy, stir in milk and butter mixture, yeast mixture and add the sifted dry ingredients a little at a time. Do not overmix, as it does not matter if batter is a bit lumpy. Cover with a towel and let rise in a warm place about 1 hour. Beat batter vigorously with a wooden spoon, cover and let it rise for another ½ hour. Heat griddle or teflon pan and brush with melted butter. Drop spoonfuls of batter to make pancakes of about 5" (125 mm) diameter. Cook for a little less than one minute, then turn over to brown the other side. When ready, stack pancakes on warm plate and keep them warm in the oven, while the rest of them are being made. Serve with melted butter, a bowl of sour cream and a bowl of caviar or thin slices of smoked salmon (lox).

Serves 8.

Russia   CHICKEN PATTIES POJARSKI   (*Kutleti Pojarski*)

Ground chicken meat is something quite unusual for us, but in Russia it is used to make these patties, which are always shaped to resemble chops.

1 lb	(½ *kg*)	skinned and boned chicken breasts
		salt and pepper to taste
½ cup	(*125 mL*)	butter
¼ cup	(*60 mL*)	flour, seasoned with salt and pepper to taste
1	(*1*)	egg, slightly beaten
1 cup	(*250 mL*)	dry bread-crumbs

Chop chicken breasts finely, using either a sharp knife or a food chopper. In a bowl mix together chopped chicken and seasonings, then melt 6 tbs of the butter and add, working it into the mixture, a little at a time. Chill thoroughly in refrigerator, then form into chop-like patties. Dredge in seasoned flour, dip in beaten egg and then in bread-crumbs. Fry in remaining butter in a large skillet or electric frying pan until golden brown on both sides. Serve immediately.

For 4 people.

CHICKEN IN SOUR CREAM

Russia

1	*(1)*	frying chicken, about 3–3½ lbs (1½–1¾ kg)
2 cups	*(500 mL)*	water
2 ts	*(2 ts)*	salt
1	1	small onion
1	1	carrot, peeled
3	3	celery tops
5	5	peppercorns
1 lb	*(½ kg)*	mushrooms
2 tbs	*(2 tbs)*	butter
1 cup	*(250 mL)*	sour cream

Cut chicken into serving pieces then bring to a boil with the salt, onion, pepper, carrot and celery tops, skim off surface, turn down heat and cook until tender, 30–40 minutes, depending on chicken. Remove chicken and cool until it can be handled. Remove skin and bones and cut into slivers. Slice mushrooms and sauté in butter for five minutes, add sour cream and blend, then mix well with chicken and heat but do not let it come to a boil as the sauce might then curdle. Serve with rice.   Serves 4–6.

BEEF STROGANOFF

Russia

This dish hardly needs an introduction, as it has become quite popular in our country.

1½ lbs	*(¾ kg)*	beef tenderloin, cut into ⅓″ (8 mm) strips (if less tender cut is used, use meat tenderizer)
3 tbs	*(3 tbs)*	flour
		salt and pepper to taste
3 tbs	*(3 tbs)*	butter or margarine
1	*(1)*	small onion, chopped (½ cup or 125 mL)
1	*(1)*	clove garlic, finely minced
1 cup	*(250 mL)*	thinly sliced mushrooms
1 tbs	*(1 tbs)*	tomato paste
½ cup	*(125 mL)*	beef broth
¾ cup	*(180 mL)*	sour cream

(Continued on next page)

(Beef Stroganoff, cont.)

In a skillet sauté onion and garlic in 1 tbs butter until onion is transparent. Add mushrooms and cook about 5 minutes. Remove from skillet, mix with sour cream and let stand for at least 1 hour. Dredge meat in 2 tbs flour mixed with salt and pepper then brown well in remaining butter or margarine, add beef broth and tomato paste and bring to a boil. Mix remaining flour with 2 tbs water and add to meat, mix well and bring to a boil again, turn down heat and cook for 5 minutes. Add sour cream mixture and heat thoroughly but do not let it come to a boil, as the cream would then curdle. Serve immediately with rice or noodles.

Serves 4–5.

LAMB PATTIES IN TOMATO SAUCE

Russia   (*Izmir Keufta*)

These lamb patties come from the very southern part of Russia. Even the name resembles that of similar patties eaten in Turkey, Iran etc.

1½ lbs	(¾ kg)	ground lamb
1	(1)	egg, beaten
1	(1)	clove garlic, finely minced
¼ cup	(60 mL)	dry bread crumbs
⅛ ts	(⅛ ts)	ground cinnamon
⅛ ts	(⅛ ts)	ground coriander
		salt and pepper to taste
1 tbs	(1 tbs)	butter or margarine
3	(3)	medium size tomatoes, peeled and finely chopped (or 1½ cups or 375 mL canned tomatoes, chopped)
1 tbs	(1 tbs)	water (or slightly more)

Mix lamb, egg, bread crumbs, garlic and seasonings and shape into oblong patties. Brown well on both sides in butter, then remove from pan. Add tomatoes and water to pan and cook, stirring vigorously to make a smooth sauce. If sauce tends to get too thick, add a bit more water. Return patties to pan and cook under cover for about 10 minutes. Serve with rice.

6 portions.

MEAT OR FISH PIE

Russia   (*Koulebiaka*)

This is more like a brioche than a pie because it uses a yeast dough for the shell.
The filling may be either fish or meat, both good and popular in their own way.

1	(1)	pkg dry yeast
1 tbs	(1 tbs)	sugar
1/4 cup	(60 mL)	lukewarm water
1/4 cup	(60 mL)	butter or margarine
1/2 cup	(125 mL)	milk
1	(1)	egg, lightly beaten
3 1/2 cups	(875 mL)	flour
1 ts	(1 ts)	salt

Dissolve yeast in lukewarm water mixed with sugar. In a saucepan melt butter, add milk and heat until lukewarm, then pour into a bowl of an electric mixer. Add egg. Sift together flour and salt and add 1 cup (250 mL) to bowl, then add yeast mixture. Blend at medium speed until well mixed, about 2 minutes, then add remaining flour a little at a time, until the mix gets too heavy for the electric mixer to handle, then continue beating with a wooden spoon. Turn out onto a floured baking board and knead until dough is smooth and elastic, about 10 minutes. Put in a greased bowl, turn over once, to get both sides greased, and let rise in a warm place for about 1 1/2 hours or until double in bulk.

Return to baking board, punch down dough and roll out into a rectangle, about 1/2" (12 mm) thick to fit into a loaf-pan about 5 x 12" (125 x 300 mm). Line the loaf pan with the dough, letting about 1 1/2" (38 mm) dough hang over the edge of the pan. Add filling and fold dough over, sealing the edges with water as neatly as possible. Brush with egg mixture and bake in a 375° F (190° C) oven for about 1/2 hour.

Serves 5–6.

Meat filling:

2	(2)	medium onions, chopped, 1 1/2 cups or 375 mL
2 tbs	(2 tbs)	butter or margarine
2 cups	(500 mL)	mushrooms, chopped
1 1/2 lbs	(3/4 kg)	chopped chuck or round steak
3	(3)	hard-boiled eggs, chopped
		salt and pepper to taste
2 tbs	(2 tbs)	sour cream
1/4 cup	(60 mL)	chopped fresh parsley

(Continued on next page)

(Meat or Fish Pie, cont.)

Sauté onion in butter until transparent, add chopped meat, breaking up lumps with a fork, and cook until the red color of meat has disappeared. Add mushrooms and cook an additional 15 minutes, then add eggs, parsley, seasonings and sour cream, and mix well.

Fish filling:

¾ lb	(350 g)	fresh salmon, or 1 lb (500 g) canned
1	(1)	small onion, finely chopped (½ cup or 125 mL)
3 tbs	(3 tbs)	butter or margarine
1 cup	(250 mL)	sliced mushrooms
2 cups	(500 mL)	cooked rice
2	(2)	hardboiled eggs, chopped salt and pepper to taste
2 tbs	(2 tbs)	finely chopped fresh dill (or 1 ts dried dillweed)

For poaching fish:

¾ cup	(180 mL)	water
¼ cup	(60 mL)	white wine
1	(1)	slice onion
3–4	(3–4)	peppercorns
½ ts	(½ ts)	salt

Bring fish to a boil, then cook over very low heat for about 5 minutes. Let fish cool in stock, then take out and remove skin and bones and flake fish (there should be about 2 cups or 500 mL). Sauté onion in butter or margarine until transparent, then add mushrooms and cook about 5 minutes more. Mix together fish, onion mixture, rice and hardboiled eggs, then add salt and pepper and dill.

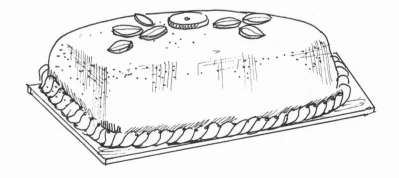

MOSCOW CASSEROLE

Russia   *(Selianka Moskva)*

Both cabbage and sauerkraut are popular in Eastern Europe. Here is a nice casserole using left-over meat.

1 lb	(½ kg)	sauerkraut (fresh or canned)
1	(1)	large onion, chopped (1 cup or 250 mL)
4 tbs	(4 tbs)	butter or margarine
		salt and pepper to taste
2 cups	(500 mL)	cooked sliced meat (left-overs of roast etc)
1	(1)	medium size dill pickle, thinly sliced
1 cup	(250 mL)	sliced fresh mushrooms
½ cup	(125 mL)	sliced, pitted black olives

Rinse and drain liquid out of sauerkraut and squeeze as dry as possible. Cook in salted water until tender. Drain off water. Sauté onion in 2 tbs butter or margarine until transparent, add sauerkraut, salt and pepper to taste and cook about 5 minutes.

Place half of sauerkraut mixture in a buttered baking dish, cover with a layer of meat, then with half of the dill pickle slices, mushrooms and olives. Repeat layers once more. Dot with 2 tbs butter or margarine and bake in a 350° F (175° C) oven 20–25 minutes. Serve piping hot.

Serves 5–6.

STUFFED CABBAGE

Russia   *(Holubtsi)*

This version of stuffed cabbage rolls is from the Ukraine and is very popular among Ukrainians in this country too, where it is always one of the side dishes in a holiday spread.

1	(1)	medium size head of cabbage
1	(1)	medium size onion, finely chopped (¾ cup or 180 mL)
1 tbs	(1 tbs)	butter
1 lb	(½ kg)	ground chuck
1 cup	(250 mL)	cooked rice
		salt and pepper to taste
1 cup	(250 mL)	tomato sauce (homemade or canned)
2 tbs	(2 tbs)	sour cream

(Continued on next page)

(Stuffed Cabbage, cont.)

In a large pot bring salted water to a boil. Trim off outside tough cabbage leaves, then with a paring knife carefully dig out the core as far in as is possible. Drop head of cabbage into the water and boil about 3–5 minutes. Remove, rinse quickly with cold water to cool slightly, then cut off as many leaves of cabbage as have been softened.

Return head of cabbage to pot and repeat procedure, cooking only 2–3 minutes each time, until the leaves that remain are too small to be used for stuffing. Pare off the main stems of the cabbage leaves to almost the same thickness as the leaves themselves.

Sauté onion in butter until transparent, then mix in meat and cook for about 10 minutes. Add rice and seasonings, and blend well. Put a heaping tablespoon of stuffing on each leaf, roll up and make a secure "package." Fasten with a tooth-pick or roll with clean cotton twine. Mix tomato sauce with sour cream, pour a thin layer on bottom of casserole, add stuffed cabbage, pour rest of sauce on top and bake in a 350° F (175° C) oven about 30 minutes.

Serves 5–6.

CAUCASIAN STUFFED PEPPERS

Russia

A nice version of stuffed peppers—this with ground lamb.

6	*(6)*	**medium size green peppers**
½ cup	*(125 mL)*	**rice**
1	*(1)*	**medium onion, finely chopped**
		(¾ cup or 180 mL)
1½ lbs	*(¾ kg)*	**ground lamb**
		salt and pepper to taste
2 tbs	*(2 tbs)*	**salad oil**
½ cup	*(125 mL)*	**meat broth or water**

Clean peppers, cut off tops and remove seeds and membranes. Blanch peppers by dropping them into boiling salted water for about 1 minute, then remove and rinse in cold water and drain. Cook rice in boiling water for 3 minutes, then rinse in cold water and drain. Mix rice with lamb, half the onion and spices and stuff into peppers, then brown them in oil in a frypan, open top first, then all over.

Place in greased baking dish preferably in one layer, add broth or water and bake in a 350° F (175° C) oven for about 30 minutes, or until peppers are tender. In the meantime add remaining half of the onion to frying pan, stir up pan juices and sauté onion for about 5 minutes. Pour over peppers just before serving.

Serves 5–6.

STUFFED PANCAKES

Russia

Stuffed pancakes—now more often called crêpes—are important in the Russian cuisine. The first recipe may not be as common as the second one, which is almost a classic.

Pancakes:

1 cup	(*250 mL*)	flour
1 ts	(*1 ts*)	salt
⅔ cups	(*160 mL*)	milk
½ cup	(*125 mL*)	water
2	(*2*)	eggs
2 tbs	(*2 tbs*)	butter or margarine

Sift together flour and salt, add milk and water and beat until smooth. Add eggs and mix until well blended. Let batter rest for 1 hour, then fry pancakes in a lightly buttered frying pan, about 6–8″ (150–200 mm) in diameter. (A teflon pan makes it easier as they are less likely to stick). Cook first until bubbles appear on the surface then turn over and fry slightly on the other side. Stack pancakes until they are all done.

Meat filling:

1	(*1*)	large onion, finely minced (1 cup or 250 mL)
2 tbs	(*2 tbs*)	butter or margarine
1 lb	(*½ kg*)	chopped chuck
½ lb	(*¼ kg*)	sliced mushrooms
1 tbs	(*1 tbs*)	flour
¼ cup	(*60 mL*)	sour cream

Sauté onion in butter or margarine for five minutes, add chopped meat and cook while stirring and breaking up lumps until the red color of the meat has disappeared. Add flour and mix well, then add mushrooms and sour cream and blend.

Put 1–2 tbs of meat mixture slightly towards you, off center of the pancake, then fold into a neat little package and put into a greased frying pan or baking dish. When they are all done, either heat carefully on top of the stove for about 5 minutes on each side, or put in a 350° F (175° C) oven for 15–20 minutes or until thoroughly warm.

Serves 4–6.

PANCAKES WITH COTTAGE CHEESE

Russia   *(Blintzes)*

Use the previous recipe for the pancakes.

Filling:

1½ cups	*(375 mL)*	cottage cheese
⅓ cup	*(80 mL)*	sugar
1	*(1)*	egg
1 ts	*(1 ts)*	vanilla extract
1 ts	*(1 ts)*	cinnamon (optional)

Optional for serving:

1 cup	*(250 mL)*	sour cream
1 tbs	*(1 tbs)*	sugar

Mix together all ingredients for filling in a large bowl, then assemble pancakes in the same manner as the previous recipe. These stuffed pancakes are often served with sour cream mixed with sugar.   Serves 4–6.

MACARONI CASSEROLE

Russia

1 cup	*(250 mL)*	macaroni
2 ts	*(2 ts)*	salt
4 cups	*(1 L)*	water
1	*(1)*	small onion, finely chopped (½ cup or 125 mL)
1 tbs	*(1 tbs)*	butter or margarine
1 lb	*(½ kg)*	chopped chuck
		salt and pepper to taste
2	*(2)*	eggs
½ cup	*(125 mL)*	milk
½ cup	*(125 mL)*	grated cheese

Cook macaroni in salted water until tender, then drain. Sauté onion in butter or margarine for five minutes, then add chopped meat and cook while stirring off and on with a fork to break up lumps. Add salt and pepper and mix well, then combine with macaroni. Pour into a greased baking dish. Beat eggs slightly, then mix with milk and pour over macaroni mixture. Sprinkle with grated cheese and bake in a 350° F (175° C) oven for 20–25 minutes. Serve hot, either with tomato sauce or with ketchup.

Serves 5.

QUICK CUCUMBER PICKLES
Russia

3–4	*(3–4)*	medium size cucumbers
1	*(1)*	small onion, thinly sliced
1	*(1)*	clove garlic, finely minced
1 tbs	*(1 tbs)*	fresh dill, finely chopped
		(or 1 ts dried dillweed)
2 cups	*(500 mL)*	water
⅓ cup	*(80 mL)*	wine vinegar
4 tbs	*(4 tbs)*	sugar
1 tbs	*(1 tbs)*	salt

Peel cucumbers and cut them lengthwise in eight pieces. Spread them in a shallow bowl in 2–3 layers. Cover with onion, garlic and dill, spread evenly over surface. Mix water, vinegar, sugar and salt, stir until dissolved, then pour over cucumbers. Chill for 6–8 hours or overnight before serving. Serves 6–8.

VEGETABLE SALAD
Russia   *(Rousski Salat)*

This usually goes by the name Russian Salad when it is served outside Russia.

3	*(3)*	medium sized potatoes, cooked, peeled and diced (about 2 cups or 500 mL)
1 tbs	*(1 tbs)*	salad oil
1 tbs	*(1 tbs)*	vinegar
1 cup	*(250 mL)*	cooked diced beets
1 cup	*(250 mL)*	cooked diced carrots
½ cup	*(125 mL)*	finely chopped dill pickles
1	*(1)*	large firm apple, peeled and diced (about 1 cup or 250 mL)
2 tbs	*(2 tbs)*	finely chopped onion
		salt and pepper to taste
2 tbs	*(2 tbs)*	mayonnaise
2 tbs	*(2 tbs)*	sour cream

Put potatoes in a large bowl then sprinkle with the salad oil and vinegar. Add beets, carrots, pickles, apple, onion, salt and pepper, and mix carefully. Mix together mayonnaise and sour cream and blend with the vegetables. Keep refrigerated for a couple of hours and serve cold.

Serves 4–6.

Russia   **BLACK BREAD**

One of my problems in visiting Russian restaurants is the black bread they
serve. I just love it. And I keep eating it so that there is hardly room for more
when the main meal arrives. Here is a version of that bread. It is somewhat
heavy in texture but very rich in flavor.

2	(2)	pkgs dry yeast
1 ts	(1 ts)	sugar
4 cups	(1 L)	rye flour
3–3½ cups	(750–825 mL)	flour
2 tbs	(2 tbs)	salt
1 cup	(250 mL)	wheat germ
2 tbs	(2 tbs)	caraway seeds, crushed
1 tbs	(1 tbs)	instant coffee
1 tbs	(1 tbs)	grated onion
2½ cups	(625 mL)	water
¼ cup	(60 mL)	vinegar
¼ cup	(60 mL)	molasses
3 tbs	(3 tbs)	cocoa
½ cup	(125 mL)	butter or margarine

For brushing: 1 ts corn starch, boiled with
                       ⅓ cup (80 mL) water

Dissolve yeast with sugar and ½ cup (125 mL) water. Mix together, but do not sift, rye flour and white flour. In a large mixing bowl, mix together 2 cups (500 mL) mixed flour, salt, wheat germ, caraway seed, instant coffee and onion. In a saucepan, mix together remaining water, vinegar, molasses, cocoa and margarine and bring to boil; cool to lukewarm.

Add to dry ingredients and mix well, either by hand with a wooden spoon or by an electric mixer. Add yeast mixture and continue to beat, then add enough flour to make a thick batter, mixing well. Stir in more flour to make a soft dough (it should take about the whole mentioned flour quantity) and turn out onto a floured baking board. Knead dough until smooth and elastic, about 10 minutes, using enough flour on hands and board so that dough will not stick.

Place in a greased bowl, turn over once to grease bottom of dough, cover with plastic wrap and let rise in a warm place until double in size, about 1 hour. Punch down dough and make two round balls about 6″ (150 mm) in diameter, place in 8″ (200 mm) round cake pans, cover and let rise again in a warm place for 1 more hour. Bake in a 350° F (175° C) oven 45–50 minutes, or until done.

In the meantime, prepare corn starch by combining with cold water in small saucepan and bring to a boil while stirring, turn down heat and cook for 1 minute. When bread is baked, brush tops of the loaves with mixture, return to oven for 2–3 minutes or until glaze has set. Then remove from oven and pans; cool on wire racks.   Makes 2 loaves.

FARINA OR SEMOLINA PUDDING

Russia

One of the Scandinavian influences on the Russian cuisine may be their fruit soups and fruit sauces. This type of pudding with fruit juice sauce is just as popular in Scandinavia.

2 cups	(500 mL)	milk
1/2 cup	(125 mL)	farina (or semolina)
1/2 ts	(1/2 ts)	salt
1/4 cup	(1/2 dl)	sugar
2	(2)	eggs, slightly beaten

Mix together milk, farina, salt and sugar and bring to a boil, turn down heat and simmer for 3–8 minutes, or until pudding thickens. Remove from heat. Put beaten eggs in a bowl, add some of the hot pudding to eggs then mix in with the pudding, stirring vigorously. Heat for a minute or so, but do not let it boil, as the eggs then would curdle. Put into a bowl or mold rinsed with cold water, and chill. Unmold it on a platter, or bowl. Serve with sauce made from fruit juice, or frozen strawberries or raspberries.   Serves 4–5

Fruit Juice Sauce (*Kisel*)

2 cups	(500 mL)	fruit juice (orange juice makes a good sauce. If too tart, add some sugar.)
1 1/2 tbs	(1 1/2 tbs)	corn starch
1/4 cup	(60 mL)	cold water

Bring juice to a boil, mix corn starch with cold water then add to juice and bring to a boil. Cook for about one minute, or until sauce becomes clear again, then remove from heat and chill. Serve cold.

EASTER CHEESE CAKE

Russia   *(Paschka)*

I would almost call this the "crown jewel" of desserts, be it in Russia or any part of the world.

1 lb	(½ kg)	cottage cheese
1 cup	(250 mL)	butter, at room temperature
1 cup	(250 mL)	sugar (preferably "veri-fine" granulated)
4	(4)	egg yolks
1 ts	(1 ts)	vanilla extract
1 cup	(250 mL)	golden raisins
½ cup	(125 mL)	finely chopped glacéed cherries
¼ cup	(60 mL)	finely chopped glacéed pineapple
1 cup	(250 mL)	chopped blanched almonds
		fresh or candied fruit for decoration

If the cottage cheese is on the moist side, let it drain for 15 minutes through a colander, while pressing down lightly with a spoon. Do not press too hard, as the cheese might then go through the holes too.

In a bowl, cream together sugar and butter until sugar is thoroughly dissolved, then add egg yolks, one at a time, and vanilla and continue mixing until smooth. Press cottage cheese through a sieve and add, little by little, and mix until well blended. Finally mix in all fruits and almonds.

Line a small colander or a 6″ (150 mm) wide well cleaned flower pot with a hole in the bottom with cheese cloth, put cheese mixture in it, fold cheese cloth over the top also and then put on a weight of 2–3 lbs (1–1½ kg). (A large filled vegetable or fruit can will do, if it presses the mixture down evenly.) This will make excess liquid drain out through the bottom so that the *pascha* will be firm.

Let it stand in refrigerator with a pan to catch the drippings underneath for at least 24 hours before you unmold it and remove the cheese cloth. Decorate with more candied fruit or with fresh fruit. Cut *pascha* into thin wedges when serving.

For 8–10 people.

Southeast Asia

This section covers many countries, but as their eating habits are similar in many respects, I have only a few of what I believe are representative recipes to cover this area. Furthermore, many of the recipes from this part of the world contain herbs, spices or vegetables that are practically unknown in our country and which may be impossible to obtain here, so they had to be weeded out no matter how exciting and good they might be.

All over this region spices seem to dominate the food, but that is only natural when you think of the fact that the equator runs right through some of these countries and the rest of them are close enough to it to have a really hot climate. Therefore, until recently, it was not possible for them to keep fresh tasting meats on hand at all times.

Singapore, which is a beautiful and modern city, is quite a melting pot of different nationalities—Malaysians, Indonesians, Indians, Chinese and also others in smaller numbers, so in this place you have quite a variety of cooking, depending upon the ethnic background.

The reason why I have no recipes for desserts is that they do not eat any to speak of, other than fresh fruits, of which there is a great abundance of all tropical varieties. Arriving on a ship in Singapore harbor at one time, I saw a freighter unloading mountains of cartons containing Washington State apples, so they apparently also import "exotic" fruits to add to their own abundance.

435

JAVANESE BROILED FISH	*Panggan Ikan Bawal Djawa*	Indonesia
MALAYSIAN FISH PUDDING	*Kuwe Ikan*	Malaysia
SINGAPORE CHICKEN		Singapore
BALINESE CHICKEN		Indonesia
CURRIED CHICKEN		Sri Lanka
SWEET AND SOUR CHICKEN		Thailand
BEEF IN SOY SAUCE	*Semur Daging*	Indonesia
PORK SATÉ		Singapore
SATÉ SAUCE		Singapore
PORK WITH PINEAPPLE	*Ma Ho*	Thailand
COCONUT HAMBURGERS	*Rempah*	Indonesia
EGGPLANT PATTIES		Malaysia
EGGPLANT CURRY		Sri Lanka
VEGETABLE SALAD	*Gado-Gado*	Indonesia
CURRIED FRIED RICE	*Nasi Goreng*	Indonesia
FRESH CUCUMBER PICKLE	*Atjar Ketimun*	Indonesia

JAVANESE BROILED FISH

Indonesia   (*Panggan Ikan Bawal Djawa*)

In Indonesia they even like the broiled fish hot.

2 lbs	(*1 kg*)	flounder or other flat fish
4	(*4*)	fresh red chilies, seeds removed and thinly sliced (or 2 ts dried chilies)
2 tbs	(*2 tbs*)	soy sauce
1 tbs	(*1 tbs*)	water
1 tbs	(*1 tbs*)	brown sugar
1	(*1*)	clove garlic, finely minced
1 tbs	(*1 tbs*)	butter, melted
		juice of ½ lemon

Make a marinade of soy sauce, brown sugar, chilies, water and garlic and pour over the fish. Marinate for at least one hour, then broil fish over a very low charcoal fire or in the oven until the fish is flaky, then remove it and place it on a serving platter. Pour over melted butter and sprinkle with remaining marinade, including chilies.   Serves 5–6.

MALAYSIAN FISH PUDDING

Malaysia   (*Kuwe Ikan*)

Coconut milk is used extensively in cooking in Southeast Asia. It is, of course, not milk at all, but whatever, it gives a nice subtle flavor to many things, including this fish pudding.

1 lb	(½ *kg*)	fish fillets (flounder, sole or haddock)
4	(*4*)	eggs
1 cup	(*250 mL*)	coconut milk (see page 70)
1 ts	(*1 ts*)	salt
1 ts	(*1 ts*)	turmeric
2 ts	(*2 ts*)	grated onion
1	(*1*)	clove garlic, finely minced
1 tbs	(*1 tbs*)	paprika

Cut fish fillets into thin strips and place on the bottom of a buttered baking dish. Beat eggs until light and fluffy. Mix coconut milk with remaining ingredients, then blend with beaten eggs. Pour over fish. Place baking dish in a larger pan, filled with hot water about 1½″ (38 mm) up the dish. Bake in a 325° F (165° C) oven for 45–50 minutes, or until knife inserted in center comes out clean.   Serves 5–6.

SINGAPORE CHICKEN

Singapore

A very flavorful chicken dish!

1	*(1)*	frying chicken, 3-3½ lbs (1½-1¾ kg)
2 tbs	*(2 tbs)*	salad oil
		salt and pepper to taste
1	*(1)*	medium size onion, finely chopped (¾ cup or 180 mL)
½ cup	*(125 mL)*	finely chopped celery
½ cup	*(125 mL)*	finely chopped carrot (about 1 medium)
1	*(1)*	medium size apple, peeled, cored and chopped
1-2 tbs	*(1-2 tbs)*	curry powder
1 tbs	*(1 tbs)*	flour
		grated rind of one orange
		juice of one orange
1 cup	*(250 mL)*	water
⅓ cup	*(80 mL)*	mango chutney, finely chopped

Cut chicken into serving pieces, season with salt and pepper, then brown lightly in a large skillet, remove and keep warm. Add onion, celery, carrot and apple to skillet and cook for five minutes while stirring. Sprinkle with curry powder, orange rind and flour and mix, add orange juice, water and chutney and stir till well blended. Add chicken pieces, bring all to a boil, turn down heat to very low then simmer until chicken is tender, 30–45 minutes.   Serve with rice to 4–5.

BALINESE CHICKEN

Indonesia

A nice chicken dish which can be made up ahead of time, or right before broiling.

1	*(1)*	frying chicken, 3-3½ lb (1½-1¾ kg)
1	*(1)*	small onion, finely chopped (½ cup or 125 mL)
2	*(2)*	cloves garlic, finely minced
2 tbs	*(2 tbs)*	salad oil
¼ ts	*(¼ ts)*	turmeric
1½ ts	*(1½ ts)*	coriander

(Continued on next page)

(Balinese Chicken, cont.)

½ cup	*(125 mL)*	coconut milk (see page 70)
1 ts	*(1 ts)*	sugar
1 tbs	*(1 tbs)*	vinegar
½ cup	*(125 mL)*	water

Cut chicken into serving pieces. In a skillet sauté onions and garlic in oil until onion is translucent, then add spices and continue simmering while stirring occasionally for about 10 minutes. Add chicken and sauté until it is slightly cooked on both sides. Add coconut milk, sugar, vinegar and water, bring to a boil, turn down heat very low and simmer for 20 minutes. Remove chicken from skillet, pat dry with paper towels and broil over hot charcoal or in the oven until nicely brown and crisp, basting several times with sauce from the skillet.

Serves 4–5.

CURRIED CHICKEN

Sri Lanka

1	*(1)*	frying chicken (about 3–3½ lbs (1½–1¾ kg)
2 ts	*(2 ts)*	turmeric
1	*(1)*	large onion, finely chopped (1 cup or 250 mL)
2	*(2)*	cloves garlic, finely chopped
1 tbs	*(1 tbs)*	salad oil
1	*(1)*	thin slice of fresh ginger, finely chopped (or ¼ ts powdered ginger)
2 ts	*(2 ts)*	ground chili powder
1 tbs	*(1 tbs)*	curry powder
		salt and pepper to taste
2 cups	*(500 mL)*	coconut milk (see page 70)
1 tbs	*(1 tbs)*	lemon juice
1 tbs	*(1 tbs)*	brown sugar (optional)

Cut the chicken into so-called "curry pieces," that are smaller than normal serving pieces. (Cut legs into two pieces, wings into 2, backs into 4, breast into 4–6). Rub turmeric into them and set aside for 20–30 minutes. Sauté onion and garlic in oil for 5 minutes, then add ginger, chili, curry powder, salt and pepper and mix well. Add coconut milk and blend. Add chicken pieces and bring to a boil, then turn down heat and let chicken simmer uncovered until tender, about 35–45 minutes. Just before serving, add lemon juice and brown sugar, and mix well. Serve with rice.

Serves 5–6.

SWEET AND SOUR CHICKEN

Thailand

For people who fancy sour-sweet dishes, here is a nice recipe from Thailand.

1 lb	($\frac{1}{2}$ kg)	skinned and boned chicken breasts
$\frac{1}{2}$ lb	($\frac{1}{4}$ kg)	chicken livers
1	(1)	medium size onion, sliced
3	(3)	cloves of garlic, finely minced
2 tbs	(2 tbs)	salad oil
2	(2)	carrots, peeled and cut into $\frac{1}{8}$" (3 mm) thick slices (about 2 cups or 500 mL)
$\frac{1}{2}$ cup	(125 mL)	chicken broth (may be made with bouillon cube)
1	(1)	medium size cucumber, peeled and cut in half lengthwise, then cut into $\frac{1}{8}$" (3 mm) slices
3	(3)	small tomatoes, peeled and cut into wedges
$\frac{1}{4}$ cup	(60 mL)	soy sauce
$\frac{1}{4}$ cup	(60 mL)	vinegar
2 tbs	(2 tbs)	sugar
1 tbs	(1 tbs)	corn starch, mixed with 2 tbs water

Slice chicken breasts into thin slices, then cut each chicken liver into 4–6 pieces. In a large skillet sauté onion and garlic for 5 minutes, but do not let it brown. Add chicken slices, livers, and carrot and sauté for 5 minutes, turning and stirring several times, then chicken broth and cook 5 minutes. Remove livers and set aside. Add cucumber and tomatoes, cover and cook 5 minutes. Mix together soy sauce, vinegar and sugar, and pour over skillet and mix well. Add corn starch mix while stirring and cook until thickened, then add chicken livers and cook only until these are heated through. Serve with rice and, if desired, chow-mein noodles. Serves 6.

BEEF IN SOY SAUCE

Indonesia   *(Semur Daging)*

Beef stew a different, very flavorful and exotic way.

2 lbs	(1 kg)	stewing beef, cut into 1" (25 mm) cubes
2 tbs	(2 tbs)	salad oil

(Continued on next page)

(Beef in Soy Sauce, cont.)

1	(*1*)	medium size onion, finely chopped ($\frac{3}{4}$ cup or 180 mL)
2	(*2*)	cloves garlic, finely minced
1	(*1*)	slice fresh ginger, finely minced or $\frac{1}{2}$ ts ground ginger
$\frac{1}{2}$ ts	($\frac{1}{2}$ *ts*)	nutmeg
		salt and pepper to taste
2	(*2*)	whole cloves
1 tbs	(*1 tbs*)	brown sugar
2 tbs	(*2 tbs*)	soy sauce
1 tbs	(*1 tbs*)	lemon juice

In a large skillet sauté onion, garlic, ginger, nutmeg and cloves in 1 tbs salad oil over low heat until onion is transparent, then remove from pan. Add remaining oil and brown meat on all sides, add salt and pepper then onion mixture, soy sauce, brown sugar and enough water to cover. Bring to a boil, then turn down heat and simmer under cover until meat is tender, $1\frac{1}{2}$ hours.

Serve with rice to 5–6.

PORK SATÉ

Singapore

In Singapore saté (or satay) stalls and vendors are as common as hot-dog carts and hamburger stands over here. Meat is threaded on thin wooden skewers, and served with a peanut-base sauce.

$1\frac{1}{2}$ lbs	($\frac{3}{4}$ *kg*)	pork tenderloin, cut into $\frac{3}{4}''$ (18 mm) cubes
1 tbs	(*1 tbs*)	ground coriander
1 tbs	(*1 tbs*)	brown sugar
		salt and pepper to taste
1	(*1*)	clove garlic, finely minced
$\frac{1}{4}$ cup	(*60 mL*)	soy sauce
3 tbs	(*3 tbs*)	lemon juice
For basting:		**salad oil mixed with marinade**

Trim excess fat off pork cubes. Mix remaining ingredients and pour over pork. Cover bowl and keep in refrigerator at least 8–10 hours, or overnight. Thread the meat on skewers and broil over a slow charcoal fire, or under broiler in oven, 4″ away from heat. Baste with marinade mixed with salad oil while broiling. Serve with rice, or in split frankfurter rolls, with or without the following sauce.

For 5–6 people.

SATÉ SAUCE

Singápore

1	(1)	small onion, finely chopped
1	(1)	clove garlic, finely chopped
1 tbs	(1 tbs)	salad oil
⅓ cup	(80 mL)	crunchy peanut butter
⅔ cup	(160 mL)	coconut milk (see page 70)
1 tbs	(1 tbs)	soy sauce
1 ts	(1 ts)	brown sugar
		salt to taste
1–2 ts	(1–2 ts)	red pepper flakes, according to taste
1 tbs	(1 tbs)	lemon or lime juice

Sauté onion and garlic in oil for 5 minutes, then put in an electric blender together with remaining ingredients and blend until a smooth sauce has been obtained. Put into a saucepan and heat only until warm. If sauce is too thick, add some water to it.

PORK WITH PINEAPPLE

Thailand   (*Mah Ho*)

A very simple-to-prepare dish, but good just the same. It has a very romantic name in translation—Galloping Horses, and you cannot help but wonder why?

1 lb	(½ kg)	ground pork
1	(1)	small onion, finely chopped (½ cup or 125 mL)
2 tbs	(2 tbs)	salad oil
2 tbs	(2 tbs)	sugar
		salt and pepper to taste
½ cup	(125 mL)	finely chopped roasted peanuts
1	(1)	fresh sliced pineapple or 1 can (about 1 lb or 500 g)
For decoration:		coriander leaves, chopped mint or shredded red chili

Sauté onion in salad oil for two minutes, then add pork, sugar, salt and pepper. Cook, while stirring off and on, breaking up lumps of meat with a fork, for 15 minutes then add peanuts and mix well. Put the pineapple slices on a serving plate and heap meat mixture on top, then garnish with any of the suggested items.

Serves 4–5.

COCONUT HAMBURGERS

Indonesia   (*Rempah*)

Really different hamburgers with a nice chewy consistency.

1 lb	(½ kg)	ground chuck
2 cups	(*500 mL*)	grated fresh coconut (about half a coconut)
1	(*1*)	clove garlic, finely minced
½ ts	(½ *ts*)	ground coriander
		pinch of ground cumin
		salt to taste
1	(*1*)	egg
2 tbs	(*2 tbs*)	salad oil

Mix all ingredients except oil until
well blended. Shape into hamburgers
and brown in oil in a skillet and cook
until done. Serve with rice or with
hamburger buns.

Serves 4–5.

EGGPLANT PATTIES

Indonesia

*Indonesia does have bland dishes too. Here is a good one with eggplant. This
vegetable sometimes is ornery when you cook it inasmuch as some of it gets
mushy and some of it is tough and will not mash. I find that it really does not
matter if it is not altogether mashed, I cut up the tough parts into very small
pieces and in this way get a difference in texture that is quite interesting.*

1	(*1*)	medium size eggplant, about 1½ lbs (¾ kg)
2 tbs	(*2 tbs*)	flour
		salt and pepper to taste
1	(*1*)	egg, slightly beaten
2 tbs	(*2 tbs*)	salad oil or butter

Peel and cut eggplant into cubes then
cook in slightly salted water until
tender. Drain off water and mash
eggplant, then cool. Add flour, seasonings and egg and mix well. Shape
into small patties and fry in oil or
butter, turning them once, until
slightly brown on both sides.

Serves 4–5.

EGGPLANT CURRY

Sri Lanka

2	(2)	medium size eggplants, (about 2 lbs or 1 kg)
		salad oil for frying
1	(1)	medium size onion, finely chopped (¾ cup or 180 mL)
1	(1)	clove garlic finely minced
½ ts	(½ ts)	ground chili
½-1 tbs	(½-1 tbs)	curry powder
1 cup	(250 mL)	coconut milk (see page 70)
2 ts	(2 ts)	lemon juice
		salt to taste

Slice unpeeled eggplants into ½″ (12 mm) slices and fry in some oil until they begin to brown, then remove, draining off excess oil. Sauté onion and garlic in remaining oil in the frying pan until onion is translucent, then add chili and curry powder and mix well. Add coconut milk and mix, then boil until thickened. Add eggplant slices and cook for 5 minutes, then add lemon juice and salt and cook until liquid has become quite thick.

Serves 5–6.

Indonesia **VEGETABLE SALAD** *(Gado-Gado)*

2 cups	*(500 mL)*	cooked but crisp green beans, cut into 1" (25 mm) lengths
2	*(2)*	medium sized new potatoes, cooked, peeled and sliced
2 cups	*(500 mL)*	bean sprouts (1 lb or 500 g can) or fresh ones, if available, steamed for one minute
2 cups	*(500 mL)*	finely shredded cabbage, cooked only for a few minutes so that it remains crisp
2	*(2)*	medium sized cooked but-still-crisp carrots, cut into strips length-wise
2	*(2)*	bean curds, fried in oil until golden brown on both sides, then cut into cubes
1	*(1)*	cucumber, unpeeled but seeded, cut into strips

Arrange all vegetables on a large platter in layers in the order they appear above. Pour over the following sauce.

Gado-Gado Sauce:

1	*(1)*	small onion, sliced
1	*(1)*	clove garlic, finely minced
2 tbs	*(2 tbs)*	salad oil
1 tbs	*(1 tbs)*	*trasi* (shrimp-paste) or anchovy paste
1	*(1)*	small red chili, seeded and finely chopped *or* $\frac{1}{4}$-$\frac{1}{2}$ ts red pepper (cayenne)
4 oz	*(125 g)*	crunchy peanut butter
$\frac{1}{2}$ ts	*($\frac{1}{2}$ ts)*	*laos* powder
1 cup	*(250 mL)*	coconut milk (see page 70)
2 ts	*(2 ts)*	paprika
2 ts	*(2 ts)*	brown sugar
1 ts	*(1 ts)*	lemon juice

Sauté onion, garlic and *trasi* in salad oil for 5 minutes. Transfer into a blender, together with remaining ingredients except lemon juice and blend until smooth. Transfer into a saucepan and cook until sauce has thickened, but is still of pouring consistency. (Add a bit of water, if it is too thick). Remove from heat and add lemon juice, then pour over vegetables and serve.

Serves 5–6.

CURRIED FRIED RICE

Indonesia   *(Nasi Goreng)*

Fried rice is a very popular dish in Indonesia and is usually part of a riis tafel *which is a bouffet style meal of many native dishes. It is most often made with fresh beef and with curry, so that it is different from the Chinese type of fried rice.*

3 cups	*(750 mL)*	cooked cold rice
1 lb	*(½ kg)*	boneless steak, shredded
½ lb	*(¼ kg)*	shelled and deveined fresh shrimp
1	*(1)*	medium onion, finely chopped
		(³⁄₄ cup or 180 mL)
1	*(1)*	clove garlic, finely minced
¼ cup	*(60 mL)*	salad oil
2 tbs	*(2 tbs)*	curry powder
		salt and pepper to taste
2	*(2)*	eggs, slightly beaten
½ cup	*(125 mL)*	chopped scallions

Sauté onion and garlic in 2 tbs oil for five minutes in a large frying pan or a wok, then push aside. Add shredded meat and stir-fry until it is cooked, then add curry powder, salt and pepper and mix well. Add remaining oil and rice and stir-fry until rice is slightly covered with oil, and is thoroughly hot, then add shrimp and cook only until pink, about 5 minutes. Mix together all contents of pan. In a small frying pan cook eggs in a little oil as you would a pancake or a thin omelette, only until set, then cut them into ½ x 2″ (12 x 50 mm) strips and add on top of rice mixture in a serving bowl.

Serves 5–6.

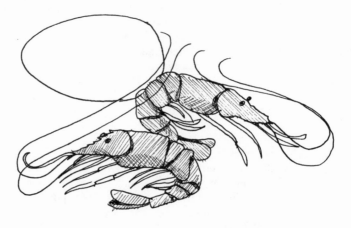

FRESH CUCUMBER PICKLE

Indonesia   (*Atjar Ketimun*)

Cucumber is always refreshing and in Southeast Asia it is often prepared this way.

1	(*1*)	medium size cucumber
1	(*1*)	small onion, thinly sliced
1	(*1*)	clove garlic, finely minced
		salt to taste
¼ cup	(*60 mL*)	white vinegar
1½ tbs	(*1½ tbs*)	sugar

Peel cucumber and cut in half length-wise. Scoop out seeds with a teaspoon and cut remaining cucumber into thin strips, then mix with onion slices in a bowl. Pour vinegar over, mixed with sugar and salt. Cover bowl and keep in refrigerator until well chilled.   Serves 5–6.

Spain

LIKE most visitors to Spain I came away with a great enthusiasm for the Spanish cuisine. As I only visited the southern and middle parts of the country, I did not get to enjoy their northern specialities. As the climate is more severe there, the food is a little bit on the heavier side, with stews, hot rich soups etc.

As over the centuries the Spaniards have traded with and been part of so many of the Mediterranean countries, a lot of the Spanish cooking is influenced by them. For example, olive oil is used almost exclusively in cooking and frying, and butter is used to only a very small extent. Their very high quality olives are used in many recipes and are also eaten pickled. Another feature is their use of almonds, not only in baking and desserts, but also as an ingredient in main dishes. Wines are also used liberally to give an extra flair to many foods.

All in all there is something festive and exuberant about Spanish cooking which you are apt to remember.

Practically surrounded by the sea as they are, sea food is important. Their way of mixing chicken with sea food produces what seems to be their most popular dish among foreigners. I am thinking of *Paella,* which is just out of this world.

Another thing one remembers about Spanish eating is their late hours for the meals, at least by our standards. After a breakfast of just coffee or chocolate with *churros,* the Spanish type of doughnuts, they are ready for a big lunch with many courses around 2–3 P.M. After that the siesta comes quite naturally. Then a late afternoon snack with *tapas*—hors d'oeuvres—and again a big meal for dinner which is served as late as 9 or 10 P.M.

MUSSELS IN SPICY SAUCE	*Mejillones con Salsa Picante*
HAM FRITTERS	*Buñuelitos de Jamon*
GARLIC SOUP	*Sopa de Ajo Caliente*
GAZPACHO	
POOR MAN'S LOBSTER	*Langosta del Pobre*
PAELLA VALENCIANA	
CHICKEN IN ALMOND SAUCE	*Pollo en Pepitoria*
STUFFED PORK ROAST	*Puerco Asado*
SPANISH OMELET	*Tortilla a la Espagñola*
BASQUE SCRAMBLED EGGS	*Piperade*
ANDALUSIAN RICE	*Arroz Andaluzo*
VEGETABLE MIXTURE	*Pisto Espagñol*
CARAMEL CUSTARD	*Flan*
ST. JOSEPH'S CUSTARD	*Crema de San José*
GYPSY CAKE	*Tarta Gitana*

MUSSELS IN SPICY SAUCE

Spain   **(*Mejillones con Salsa Picante*)**

Delicious, nourishing mussels exist in neglected abundance around our coasts. I believe that some day they will come into their own in this country. They have been harvested for centuries in Europe, where they are popular in most countries. Here is a nice way to serve them, Spanish style.

1 cup	(*250 mL*)	canned mussels (or steamed fresh ones, removed from the shell, about 4 dozen, depending upon size)
3 tbs	(*3 tbs*)	mayonnaise
1 ts	(*1 ts*)	mustard
1 tbs	(*1 tbs*)	sherry
1 ts	(*1 ts*)	lemon juice
⅓ cup	(*80 mL*)	canned pimientos, cut into thin strips

Mix together mayonnaise, mustard, sherry and lemon juice and blend well, then add pimiento. Place mussels in a serving dish, then spoon sauce over them and put in refrigerator for at least 2 hours. Serve as an appetizer.   For 4–6 people.
VARIATION:
If desired, clams may be substituted for the mussels.

HAM FRITTERS

Spain   (*Buñuelitos de Jamon*)

Light and tasty fritters, often served as tapas (*appetizers*).

1	(*1*)	small onion, finely chopped
		(½ cup or 125 mL)
2 tbs	(*2 tbs*)	olive oil or other salad oil
1 cup	(*250 mL*)	finely chopped ham
1	(*1*)	egg, slightly beaten
½ cup	(*125 mL*)	beer
⅔ cup	(*160 mL*)	flour
½ ts	(*½ ts*)	baking powder
		salt and pepper to taste
		oil for deep frying

Sauté onion in oil until transparent, add ham and cook for about 5 minutes. Let cool slightly. Sift flour with baking powder, salt and pepper, mix together with beaten egg and beer and blend until smooth. Add ham and onion mixture and mix well. Heat oil to 375° F (190° C), drop fritter mixture by teaspoonfuls into oil and cook about 2 minutes, or until golden brown. Drain on paper towels and serve as soon as possible as an appetizer.

For 5–6 people.

GARLIC SOUP

Spain   (*Sopa de Ajo Caliente*)

A traditional soup of Spain, so simple, so good and with ingredients you can easily have on hand.

3 tbs	(*3 tbs*)	olive oil
3	(*3*)	cloves garlic, coarsely chopped
4	(*4*)	slices white bread, crusts removed, cubed
4 cups	(*1 L*)	beef broth
		pinch of cayenne
		salt to taste

In a saucepan, sauté garlic in oil until lightly brown, then discard garlic. Add bread cubes and fry until lightly browned. Add broth, bring to a boil, season with salt and cayenne, then add to bread cubes. Simmer together 20–25 minutes. Serve immediately.

For 4–5 portions.

GAZPACHO

Spain

This national soup of Spain is very easy to make if you have a blender, otherwise it takes more effort as you have to pass the vegetables through a sieve. It is wonderfully refreshing in the summer when there are ample supplies of fresh ingredients.

3	(3)	medium tomatoes, peeled and chopped (about 2 cups or 500 mL)
1	(1)	small cucumber, peeled and coarsely chopped (about 1 cup or 250 mL)
1	(1)	green pepper, seeded and coarsely chopped
1	(1)	clove garlic, finely minced
2	(2)	slices white bread, crusts removed and cubed (about 1 cup or 250 mL)
2 tbs	(2 tbs)	olive oil
3 cups	(750 mL)	cold water
		salt and pepper to taste
For sprinkling:		1 cup (250 mL) each of chopped tomatoes and cucumber, ½ cup (125 mL) each of green peppers and onions

Combine tomatoes, cucumber, pepper, garlic, cubed bread, olive oil and the water in a bowl, then put a little at a time into an electric blender and blend at the highest speed. Strain mixture through a sieve and press with a wooden spoon to extract as much juice from the vegetables as is possible. Discard the solids left in the sieve.

Season with salt and pepper and chill for several hours before serving. Serve soup, putting the chopped vegetables separately into little bowls, so that each person can sprinkle them on top of his own portion of soup.

Serves 4–5.

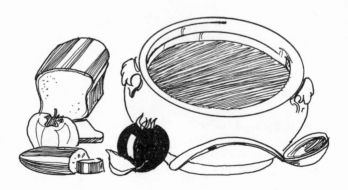

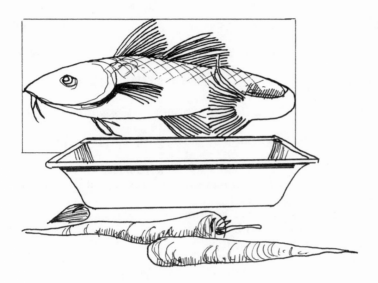

POOR MAN'S LOBSTER

Spain   *(Langosta del Pobre)*

Lobsters are rare in Europe and therefore expensive. Whether you really think this dish tastes like lobster or not, I leave up to you, but it is a nice way to prepare fish fillets.

1–1½ lbs	(½–¾ kg)	cod fillets
2	(2)	cloves garlic, finely minced
2 tbs	(2 tbs)	olive oil
1 tbs	(1 tbs)	paprika
2	(2)	medium size carrots, peeled and thinly sliced
1	(1)	bay leaf
1 ts	(1 ts)	salt (or more, if desired)
1 cup	(250 mL)	water

Cut fish into bite size pieces. Mix together garlic and olive oil and coat fish, then sprinkle with paprika and put into a shallow baking dish. Add remaining ingredients and bake in a 350° F (175° C) oven without cover for 20–25 minutes, or until fish is flaky. Remove fish and bay leaf from baking dish, then purée the remaining liquid and vegetables in an electric blender, or lacking this, press them through a sieve, and pour over fish.

Serves 4–5.

PAELLA VALENCIANA

Spain   *(Paella Valenciana)*

One of the most popular dishes of Spain—and it certainly deserves to be.

1	*(1)*	frying chicken, 2-3 lbs (1-1½ kg)
4 tbs	*(4 tbs)*	olive oil
½ lb	*(¼ kg)*	*chorizos* (Spanish sausages) or hot Italian sausages
1	*(1)*	medium onion, finely chopped (¾ cup or 180 mL)
2	*(2)*	cloves garlic, finely minced
2	*(2)*	medium size tomatoes, peeled and chopped
2 cups	*(500 mL)*	rice
3 cups	*(750 mL)*	chicken stock or water (approximately)
½ cup	*(125 mL)*	white wine
12	*(12)*	small clams
12	*(12)*	mussels (optional)
1 lb	*(½ kg)*	shrimp, medium size, shelled and de-veined
1	*(1)*	lobster, cooked (1-1½ lb, or ½-¾ kg) *or* 2-3 frozen rock lobster tails *or* one 8 oz (250 g) can of lobster meat
½ ts	*(½ ts)*	saffron
		salt and pepper to taste
1 ts	*(1 ts)*	paprika
1 cup	*(250 mL)*	fresh or frozen peas, cooked
¼ cup	*(60 mL)*	pimentos, cut into strips

Cut chicken into small serving pieces, then brown in a large skillet in 2 tbs olive oil. Add sausages and cook with chicken pieces 15 minutes, then remove them and cut sausages into ¼" (6 mm) slices and set them and the chicken aside. Sauté onion and garlic over low heat for 10 minutes, stirring off and on so that onions do not get brown, then add tomatoes and cook for 5 more minutes. In a paella pan or a large Dutch oven heat remaining oil and add rice, while stirring, to get it evenly coated with oil. Add chicken

stock or water, wine, chicken, onion mixture, saffron, paprika and salt and pepper, bring to a boil, then turn down heat and cook slowly for about 20 minutes.

In the meantime steam the mussels and clams in ½" (12 mm) of water in a small saucepan until they open up. If any of them should fail to do so, discard them. Remove the meat from the shells and set aside. Cook shrimp in the same saucepan for 2-3 minutes, but only until they turn pink, then strain liquid into the rice pot. Re-

(Continued on next page)

(Paella Valenciana, cont.)

move meat from lobster shell and cut into small pieces. Check to see if the rice mixture is now moist enough, otherwise add a little more stock or water.

Combine the rice mixture with the shellfish, peas and pimientos and stir to mix well. Cook uncovered over low heat until all is well heated through, about 15 minutes. Serve directly from pan and decorate with pimientos and some of the seafood shells.   Serves 8–10.

CHICKEN IN ALMOND SAUCE

Spain   (*Pollo en Pepitoria*)

A very good way to fix chicken, especially if you like almonds.

1	(*1*)	frying chicken, 3–3½ lbs (1½–1¾ kg), cut into serving pieces
2 tbs	(*2 tbs*)	olive oil
1	(*1*)	small onion, finely chopped (½ cup or 125 mL)
1	(*1*)	clove garlic, finely chopped
½ cup	(*125 mL*)	water
½ cup	(*125 mL*)	white wine
1	(*1*)	bay leaf
¼ ts	(*¼ ts*)	saffron
½ cup	(*125 mL*)	almonds, blanched and slivered
		salt and pepper to taste
1 tbs	(*1 tbs*)	flour, mixed with ¼ cup or 60 mL cold water

Brown chicken pieces in olive oil, in a chicken fryer or large skillet, remove and set aside. Sauté onion and garlic in the same pan, until onion is transparent, then add chicken, water, wine and seasonings. Simmer chicken until almost done, about 35–40 minutes, depending on how tough or tender it is, then add almonds and flour-and-water mixture. Stir contents in pan and cook about 5 minutes longer. Serve with rice or potatoes.

For 4–5 people.

STUFFED PORK ROAST

Spain   *(Puerco Asado)*

3-4 lbs	*(1½-2 kg)*	loin of pork
		salt and pepper to taste
1 tbs	*(1 tbs)*	olive oil
1	*(1)*	medium size onion, finely chopped
		(¾ cup or 180 mL)
1	*(1)*	clove garlic, finely minced
3	*(3)*	medium size tomatoes, peeled, seeded
		and chopped (or 1½ cup or 375 mL,
		chopped, canned tomatoes)
1 ts	*(1 ts)*	chili powder
6	*(6)*	black olives, pitted and chopped
⅓ cup	*(80 mL)*	raisins
1½ cup	*(375 mL)*	cooked rice
½ cup	*(125 mL)*	white wine
1 lb	*(½ kg)*	small potatoes, peeled
1 lb	*(½ kg)*	small white onions, peeled

Cut a deep slit in the pork loin to make a "pocket" for the stuffing. Rub outside with salt and pepper. Sauté onion and garlic in olive oil until onion is transparent, add tomatoes and chili powder and cook about 8–10 minutes, then add olives and raisins. Mix half of this mixture with the rice and put it into the "pocket". Either tie the meat together in a couple of places with cotton twine, or secure it with skewers.

Roast in a 350° F (175° C) oven uncovered about 1 hour, then stir the wine into the remaining tomato mixture, and pour around the roast. Add peeled potatoes and onions and continue baking an additional 1½ hour, or until pork is tender. Baste meat off and on with pan drippings and add a little more wine or water, if sauce should get too thick. Skim off fat before serving.

Serves 6–8.

SPANISH OMELET

Spain   *(Tortilla a la Española)*

A nice egg dish for a meat-less meal. It is sometimes called a Spanish peasant omelette.

1	(*1*)	small onion, finely chopped (about ½ cup or 125 mL)
¼ cup	(*60 mL*)	olive oil
4	(*4*)	medium potatoes, peeled and thinly sliced salt and pepper to taste
6	(*6*)	eggs

In an omelette pan or small skillet sauté onion in oil for a few minutes over low heat, add potato slices, salt and pepper and cook over low heat until tender and golden brown in color. Beat eggs in a bowl, add salt and pepper to taste, then pour mixture over the potatoes, moving potato slices here and there to let egg mixture penetrate to bottom of pan. When almost set, ease omelette out of pan and turn over to slightly brown the top. Serve with a salad.

For 4 people.

BASQUE SCRAMBLED EGGS

Spain   *(Piperade)*

3	(*3*)	large onions, sliced
2 tbs	(*2 tbs*)	olive oil
3	(*3*)	green peppers
3	(*3*)	red peppers, or if unavailable, 3 more green ones)
3	(*3*)	large tomatoes, peeled and coarsely chopped salt and pepper to taste
6	(*6*)	eggs, slightly beaten

Sauté onions in oil until transparent. Cut peppers in slices, remove seeds and white parts, then add to onions and cook until peppers are tender, 10–15 minutes. Add tomatoes and continue cooking, stirring off and on until a smooth mixture has been obtained. Add eggs, all at once and stir as for scrambled eggs and cook only until eggs have coagulated.

Serve hot to 4–6.

ANDALUSIAN RICE

Spain   *(Arroz Andaluzo)*

1	*(1)*	small onion, finely chopped (about ½ cup or 125 mL)
2 tbs	*(2 tbs)*	butter or margarine
1 cup	*(250 mL)*	rice
2 cups	*(500 mL)*	chicken stock (may be made with bouillon cubes)
1	*(1)*	bay leaf
		salt and pepper to taste
1 cup	*(250 mL)*	cooked green peas
¼ cup	*(60 mL)*	chopped pimiento

Sauté onion in butter or margarine until transparent. Add rice and stir to coat with the butter, add chicken stock, a little at a time, then bay leaf, salt and pepper. Bring to a boil, turn down heat to low and simmer until rice is tender, about 15–20 minutes, depending on what kind of rice is used, and all the liquid is absorbed. Discard bay leaf and stir in peas and pimiento and serve immediately.

Serves 4–6.

VEGETABLE MIXTURE

Spain   *(Pisto Espagñol)*

A simple but satisfying casserole.

¼ lb	*(125 g)*	boiled or baked ham
1 tbs	*(1 tbs)*	olive oil
2	*(2)*	medium size onions, chopped (1½ cups or 375 mL)
2	*(2)*	green peppers, chopped
3	*(3)*	small zucchinis, sliced
2	*(2)*	medium size tomatoes, peeled, seeded and chopped (about 1 cup or 250 ml)
		salt and pepper to taste

Cut ham into small pieces and fry for a few minutes in oil, then add onions and peppers and sauté about 10 minutes, or until onions are transparent. Add zucchini and tomatoes and bring to a boil (no water needed), turn down heat and simmer for about 25 minutes, or until all vegetables are tender.   Serves 4–5.

VARIATION:

Place the vegetable mixture on a serving dish and put one fried egg for each serving on top.

CARAMEL CUSTARD

Spain   *(Flan)*

The classical Spanish dessert—popular not only in Spain but practically everywhere that Spanish speaking people live.

2 cups	(500 mL)	milk
⅓ cup	(80 mL)	sugar
2	(2)	eggs, slightly beaten
1 ts	(1 ts)	vanilla extract

Rinse mold in which custard is to be baked in cold water, then sprinkle 2 tbs sugar over the bottom and melt over low heat, tipping mold so that the sides gets coated with the melted sugar. Set aside and let caramel harden. Heat milk and remaining sugar until sugar is melted, then pour, little by little over eggs in a bowl, beating until well mixed. Add vanilla, pour into mold and place in a larger dish with warm water in a 350° F (175° C) for about 45 minutes or until a knife comes out clean, when stuck slightly off center into the custard. Unmold and serve either slightly warm or chilled.   4–5 portions.

VARIATION:

Instead of making the custard in one mold, use 4–5 individual molds. Use a frying pan to melt the sugar and then pour the melted sugar into the molds. Then proceed as above.

ST. JOSEPH'S CUSTARD

Spain   *(Crema de San José)*

A flan-like custard with a bit of a difference.

3	(3)	egg yolks
½ cup	(125 mL)	sugar
2 tbs	(2 tbs)	corn starch
2¼ cups	(560 mL)	milk
1	(1)	cinnamon stick
		thinly sliced peel of one lemon

Beat egg yolks and half the sugar until light and fluffy. Stir corn starch in ¼ cup (60 mL) cold milk. Bring remaining milk together with thinly sliced lemon peel and cinnamon stick to the scalding point, then strain hot milk into egg and sugar mixture. Add corn starch mixture and stir well. Return mixture to saucepan and bring to almost a boil over low heat, but don't let it boil, as it would then curdle.

Remove from heat and pour into a 9" (220 mm) pie plate and chill for 3–4 hours. Sprinkle with remaining sugar and put under a pre-heated broiler for 5 minutes, which will cause the sugar to caramelize and harden. Allow custard to stand for 5 minutes before serving. Serve either plain or with whipped cream.

Serves 4–5.

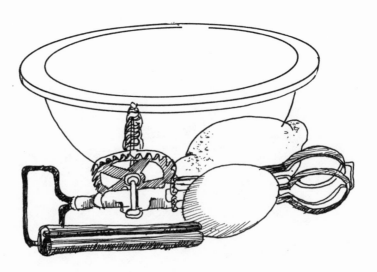

GYPSY CAKE

Spain   (*Tarta Gitana*)

2 cups	(*500 mL*)	flour
1/2 ts	(*1/2 ts*)	salt
1/2 cup	(*125 mL*)	sugar
2/3 cup	(*160 mL*)	brown sugar
1 ts	(*1 ts*)	cinnamon
1/3 cup	(*80 mL*)	vegetable shortening (or lard)
2/3 cup	(*160 mL*)	chopped dates
1/4 cup	(*60 mL*)	chopped almonds
2/3 cup	(*160 mL*)	sour milk or buttermilk (if not available, add one ts vinegar to fresh milk and let it sit for 10 minutes)
1 ts (scant)	(*1 ts scant*)	baking soda

Sift flour into a mixing bowl then mix with salt, sugar, brown sugar and cinnamon. Cut in shortening with a pastry cutter until mixture resembles coarse crumbs. Set aside 1/3 cup (80 mL) of this mixture together with one tbs of the chopped almonds to be used for topping.

Add dates and remaining almonds to cake mixture and mix well. Add baking soda to milk and stir to mix, then combine with the flour mixture and blend well. Spread batter in a greased and floured baking dish, 9 x 9" (220 x 220 mm) and bake in a 350° F (175° C) oven for 25–30 minutes or until cake tests as done.

Serves 6–9.

Sweden

It hardly matters where you are in the world, if you mention that you are Swedish, the other person's face will light up and out will come the word "Smörgåsbord," pronounced in many different ways. And the funny thing is that the *smörgåsbord* has just about disappeared as an eating custom in Sweden itself. It is, of course, true that there are restaurants still serving it in Sweden, but they are mainly geared towards the tourist trade.

However, there is usually a tendency to serve something like it at Christmas time. As this holiday is a much drawn out affair, with several little holidays connected with it, people will get their fill of *smörgåsbord* at that time. Within the family, it is not just to get together once during the holidays, but everyone has to take their turn to entertain, so it will be repeated many times.

A real Swedish *smörgåsbord* (literal translation: Sandwich Table) consists of pickled herring and other fish in many varieties, then more fish and shellfish prepared in other ways, such as aspics and salads. There is always a variety of cold cuts, liver paté and jellied meats. Then there are some warm dishes, such as omelets with different fillings, Jansson's Temptation, small meatballs and kidney sautée with wine. Finally there are several varieties of cheese, and throughout the whole meal many types of bread, from *limpa* (a Swedish rye bread) and pumpernickel to crisp-bread and crackers. The *smörgåsbord* used to be considered only an appetizer, but in these days of eating in smaller amounts, most people will have had enough after having partaken of the above mentioned foods and will be satisfied with just some dessert and coffee.

463

In setting up a *smörgåsbord*, the hostess takes special pride in decorating the food to the best of her artistic ability to make it pleasing to the eye as well as to the palate.

Instead of *smörgåsbord* as an appetizer these days, so-called *snittar* are provided. These are tiny open-faced sandwiches, often of a triangular shape, and almost always in threes, one with pickled or canned herring and egg, one liver paté or meat and one cheese. But often some other dish is served, such as a herring gratin (Jansson's Temptation), a sea-food salad or similar.

And there are so many good things to eat in Sweden that I have had a difficult time in weeding out what I did not have room for (after all this is a book of cooking from many countries). And maybe I would have had the same difficulty in every other country if I were just as familiar with the cooking of each.

Of many excellent baking recipes that I have, only a handful are in this book. And today people in Sweden are weight-conscious, and this reflects in their eating habits. Gone are the days when you had to have seven kinds of cakes or cookies in order to have a coffee-klatsch. This custom still prevails, though, in the countryside when birthday celebrations and other festivities are held. And even today few people really feel comfortable in serving just one kind of treat when they have company.

PICKLED HERRING (WITH VARIATIONS)	*Inlagd Sill*
ANCHOVY CASSEROLE (JANSSON'S TEMPTATION)	*Jansson's Frestelse*
ANCHOVY ROLL	*Ansjovisrulle*
CHEESE ROLL	*Ostrulle*
PICKLED SALMON	*Gravad Lax*
PICKLED SALMON SAUCE	*Gravlaxsås*
WEST COAST SALAD	*Västkustsallad*
LIVER PATÉ	*Leverpastej*
MEAT BALLS	*Köttbullar*
BEEF PATTIES A LA LINDSTROM	*Biff a la Lindström*
LOIN OF PORK WITH PRUNES	*Plommonspäckad Fläskkarré*
CASTLE POT ROAST	*Slottstek*

LEG OF LAMB	*Lammstek*
BOILED LAMB WITH DILL SAUCE	*Lammkött med Dillsås*
STUFFED CABBAGE ROLLS	*Kåldolmar*
CHEESE AND CAULIFLOWER CASSEROLE	*Ost-och Blomkålslåda*
SWEDISH PANCAKES	*Plättar (Pannkakor)*
APPLE SOUP	*Äpplesoppa*
BIBI'S DELIGHT	*Bibis Förtjusning*
RICE A LA MALTA	*Ris à la Malta*
MERINGUE SUISSE	*Marängsuisse*
MOCHA TORTE	*Mockatårta*
DREAM CAKE	*Drömtårta*
MAZARIN CAKE	*Mazarinkaka*
RYE BREAD (LIMPA)	*Rågbrödslimpor*
RYE BREAD WITHOUT YEAST	*Rågbröd utan jäst*
FILBERT CRESCENTS	*Nötgifflar*
QUICK-BAKE CRESCENTS	*Snabbgifflar*
LUCIA BUNS	*Lussekatter*
TYRA'S PASTRIES	*Tyras Bullar*
THE KING'S SPICE COOKIES	*Kungens Pepparkakor*
SPRITZ COOKIES	*Spritsar*
OATMEAL LACE COOKIES	*Havreflarn*
ALMOND TARTLETS	*Mandelmusslor*
HOT CHRISTMAS DRINK	*Glögg*

PICKLED HERRING

Sweden *(Inlagd Sill)*

Pickled herring is popular all over Scandinavia. The fact that these recipes are presented as Swedish may not be quite fair, as practically the same recipes exist in Norway, Denmark and Finland as well. There is no real smörgåsbord without it, and it must be considered the number one appetizer in these countries.

2	(2)	salt herrings

Marinade:

½ cup	(125 mL)	vinegar
⅔ cup	(160 mL)	water
½ cup	(125 mL)	sugar
1	(1)	small onion, sliced
10	(10)	peppercorns, crushed

Soak herrings in cold water for 24 hours, then remove skin and bones and make each into two fillets. Bring all the marinade ingredients to a boil, let cool for a few minutes then pour over fish fillets, cover dish, and place in refrigerator for at least 8 hours or overnight. Cut fillets diagonally into slices. Herring may now be served as it is or made more fancy with one of the following:

CURRIED HERRING

(Curry-Sill)

2 tbs	(2 tbs)	mayonnaise
2 tbs	(2 tbs)	heavy cream
1 ts	(1 ts)	curry
1 ts	(1 ts)	akvavit (a Scandinavian liquor), optional

Mix together ingredients and pour over the sliced herring fillets and refrigerate several hours, or overnight. Serve with rye bread.

HERRING IN TOMATO SAUCE

Sill i Tomatsås

¼ cup	(*60 mL*)	marinade
1 tbs	(*1 tbs*)	ketchup
2 tbs	(*2 tbs*)	tomato paste

For garnish: about 2 tbs each of capers and finely chopped onion

Mix together marinade, ketchup and tomato paste and stir till well blended and pour over sliced herring. Refrigerate, preferably overnight, and serve with rye bread.

HERRING IN MUSTARD SAUCE

Sill i Senapsås

⅓ cup	(*80 mL*)	mustard
3 tbs	(*3 tbs*)	sugar
⅓ cup	(*80 mL*)	sour cream
⅓ cup	(*80 mL*)	mayonnaise
3 tbs	(*3 tbs*)	finely chopped fresh dill

Garnish: a few fresh dill sprigs

Mix together all ingredients and spoon over sliced herring pieces. Chill in refrigerator for at least 6 hours or overnight.

ANCHOVIES CASSEROLE
(JANSSON'S TEMPTATION)

Sweden   *(Jansson's Frestelse)*

This appetizer is one of the best. The name is supposed to have come about in this manner: If a girl has a boyfriend who cannot make up his mind to marry her, she makes this dish for him and then he cannot resist her any more.

8	(8)	anchovy fillets (1-3¼ oz or 110 g can) of Scandinavian type
2	(2)	medium size onion, thinly sliced
3 tbs	(3 tbs)	butter or margarine
3-4	(3-4)	large potatoes, cut into julienne strips
1 cup	(250 mL)	light cream
		pepper to taste

Sauté onion in 2 tbs butter until transparent, and set aside. Arrange half the potatoes in one layer in a buttered baking dish, add one layer of sautéed onion, one layer of anchovy fillets and finish with a layer of remaining potatoes. Sprinkle with pepper and anchovy brine, then pour half the cream over and dot with remaining butter. Bake in a 375° F (190° C) oven for 15 minutes, then add remaining cream and bake another 45 minutes.

Serve directly from the baking dish either as an appetizer or as part of a buffet or *smörgåsbord*.

4–6 servings.

ANCHOVY ROLL

Sweden *(Ansjovisrulle)*

These soufflé type rolls make very delicious appetizers, but also do quite well as luncheon dishes, with a crisp salad as accompaniment. They would then serve fewer people, however.

4 tbs	(4 tbs)	butter or margarine
½ cup	(125 mL)	flour
1 cup	(250 mL)	milk
1 cup	(250 mL)	light cream
½ ts	(½ ts)	salt
3	(3)	eggs, separated
½ ts	(½ ts)	baking powder

Melt butter or margarine in a saucepan, add flour and stir, add milk, a little at a time while stirring, then cream. Cook until mixture has thickened. Remove from heat and add egg yolks, one at a time and mix until well blended, and let mixture cool, stirring occasionally. Beat egg whites until stiff, stir in baking powder, then carefully fold into batter. Spread on a greased and floured wax paper in a baking pan, about 11 x 13" (270 x 320 mm) and bake in a 400° F (200° C) oven 15–20 minutes, or until done. Carefully turn out on a clean towel, peel off wax paper and cool for a few minutes, then roll up with the towel and let cool slowly.

Filling:

3	(3)	medium size onions, chopped (2¼ cup or 625 mL)
2 tbs	(2 tbs)	butter or margarine
1	(1)	can Scandinavian type anchovies (about 4 oz or 125 g) or 2 cans (2 oz ea or about 60 g) of Portuguese anchovy fillets
½ cup	(125 mL)	grated Parmesan cheese
½ cup	(125 mL)	finely chopped parsley

Sauté onion in butter or margarine until onion is translucent, chop anchovies finely, add and mix well. Unroll cake in towel and spread onion mixture evenly on the surface, then sprinkle with parsley and half the cheese. Roll up as a jelly roll and sprinkle remaining cheese on top. Bake in a 450° F (230° C) oven 6–8 minutes or until cheese on top is melted. In case the roll has been made ahead of time and therefore is thoroughly cold, bake in a 425° F (220° C) oven for 15 minutes instead to make sure it gets heated throughout. Serve hot, cut into slices, as an appetizer to 5–6.

CHEESE ROLL

Sweden *(Ostrulle)*

The "cake" is the same as in previous recipe.

Filling:

2	(2)	medium size onions, finely chopped (1½ cups or 375 mL)
½ cup	(125 mL)	chopped pimiento (or one fresh red sweet pepper finely chopped)
2 tbs	(2 tbs)	butter or margarine
½ cup	(125 mL)	finely chopped dill weed
10	(10)	medium size black olives, pitted and chopped
1 ts	(1 ts)	curry powder
4 oz	(125 g)	mild cheese (Monterey Jack, Munster or American)
		salt and pepper to taste
¼ cup	(60 mL)	grated Parmesan

Sauté onion and pimiento in butter or margarine until onion is soft. Add dill, olives and curry powder and mix. Either grate cheese coarsely or cut into strips, depending upon the kind of cheese, then add to onion mixture and cook until cheese is melted.

Spread evenly on surface of cake and roll up jelly-roll fashion. Sprinkle with grated Parmesan and bake in a 400° F (200° C) oven for 6–8 minutes or until cheese on top is melted. If the roll has been made ahead of time, and is therefore cold, bake in a 375° F (190° C) oven for 15–20 minutes to make sure the cheese inside also gets melted. Serve hot, cut into slices, as an appetizer for 5–6.

Sweden ## PICKLED SALMON *(Gravad Lax)*

I wish I could think of a more exciting American name for this—it sounds too mundane for the delicacy it is. It is considered one of the top culinary achievements in Sweden, and I have had nothing but ahs and ohs from the Americans to whom I serve it.

2 lbs	(1 kg)	piece of salmon, if possible, the middle cut
4 tbs	(4 tbs)	salt
4 tbs	(4 tbs)	sugar
½ ts	(½ ts)	peppercorns (preferably white pepper), crushed

(Continued on next page)

(Pickled Salmon, cont.)

1	(1)	large bunch of fresh dill (or two smaller bunches) a few twigs of spruce or pine, if available
For serving:		one lemon, cut into wedges

Split the fish open and separate it into two pieces. Carefully remove the backbone and also pull out smaller bones. Mix together salt, sugar and pepper and rub into the fleshy side of the fish.

Place some of the twigs and some dill on the bottom of a shallow dish, large enough to hold the whole piece of fish in a flat position, then place the fish, skin side down in it, add more dill and the other piece of fish, flesh side down on top of the dill to make a sandwich-like arrangement. (If you use the end piece of salmon, one end would be thinner than the other in such a case, put the thinner part over the thicker to make it as even as possible). Add remaining dill and more twigs on top, put a small carving board or a plate over the fish pieces, then put a weight on top of the board and refrigerate for 48 hours.

Remove from the marinade that has formed during the curing and scrape off the pepper. Slice very thin on a bias, just as smoked salmon is done. Serve as an appetizer, or a main meal, garnished with fresh dill and lemon wedges. It is delicious just plain but in Sweden it is traditionally served with the following sauce, to 6–8 as an appetizer, 4 as a main meal.

PICKLED SALMON SAUCE

Sweden   (*Gravlaxsås*)

3 tbs	(*3 tbs*)	prepared mustard
1 tbs	(*1 tbs*)	sugar
⅓ cup	(*80 mL*)	salad oil
2 tbs	(*2 tbs*)	vinegar
		salt and pepper to taste
1 tbs	(*1 tbs*)	fresh chopped dill

Mix together all ingredients and stir until well blended. (It may be done in a blender, but in such a case do not add dill until after the blending). Serve with pickled salmon, or with boiled shrimp, lobster or crab.

WEST COAST SALAD

Sweden   *(Västkustsallad)*

A wonderful prelude to a dinner, and a dish where you may substitute one or more of the ingredients according to what you have on hand. But it is mainly a shell-fish salad and this should not be forgotten, or you may not have a West Coast Salad at all.

¼ lb	*(125 g)*	fresh mushrooms or one small can mushrooms, thinly sliced
½ lb	*(¼ kg)*	boiled shrimp
1	*(1)*	boiled lobster, or 2–3 rock lobster tails or 1 8 oz (250 g) can of lobster meat or same size can of crab meat
15	*(15)*	fresh steamed mussels, or clams, or one can of same, about 4 oz (120 g)
½ cup	*(125 mL)*	chopped celery
1 cup	*(250 mL)*	cooked green peas
1	*(1)*	head of lettuce, shredded
2	*(2)*	hard-boiled eggs
2	*(2)*	tomatoes, cut into wedges
For sprinkling:		chopped fresh dill

Dressing:

2 tbs	*(2 tbs)*	wine vinegar
⅓ cup	*(80 mL)*	salad oil
		salt and pepper to taste
1 ts	*(1 ts)*	paprika

If whole lobster is used, split same and remove meat from body and claws and cut into pieces. If fresh mussels or clams are used, steam them (procedure, see recipe on page 307) then remove meat from shells. If canned ones are used, drain off liquid. Put shellfish and mushrooms into a bowl and sprinkle with dressing, then chill in refrigerator at least one hour.

Half an hour before serving, arrange shredded lettuce in a bowl, add shellfish, mushrooms, celery and peas and decorate with hard-boiled egg wedges and tomato wedges. Sprinkle freshly chopped dill on top. Salad may also be assembled into individual salad bowls in a similar manner.

Serves 6.

LIVER PATÉ

Sweden   (*Leverpastej*)

Liver paté is one of the favorites for open-face sandwiches in Scandinavia. It is also very good with crackers as an appetizer. It used to be a tedious dish to make, but if you have a blender, it is very easy. Although pork liver is preferred, calves' liver may be used instead. (For some time I had trouble finding pork liver in the stores, and was finally told that it was practically all exported to France for their use in making liver paté. Sweden is evidently not alone in its preference for this kind of liver in paté).

1 lb	(½ kg)	pork liver (or calves')
½ lb	(¼ kg)	fresh pork fat (or bacon fat)
4	(4)	Scandinavian type anchovy fillets (Anchovy Sprats) or 2 ts anchovy paste
2 tbs	(2 tbs)	chopped onion
1 tbs	(1 tbs)	butter or margarine
1 ts	(1 ts)	salt
½ ts	(½ ts)	pepper
1½ cups	(375 mL)	light cream or half-and-half
2 tbs	(2 tbs)	flour
3	(3)	eggs, well beaten
2 tbs	(2 tbs)	brandy (optional)

Sauté onion in butter until transparent. Grind liver, bacon, anchovy fillets and onion with the finest blade of the meat grinder, then place mixture in a bowl. Mix together flour and cream until smooth, add eggs and blend well, then add to liver mixture. Add salt and pepper. Blend in an electric blender, about one cup at a time, or press through a sieve. Add brandy, if used.

When all has been blended put mixture in a 3½ x 7" (90 x 180 mm) loaf pan. Cover pan with aluminum foil and bake in a 325° F (165° C) oven with the loaf pan placed in a larger pan with hot water up to about 2" (50 mm) from the top of the loaf pan. Bake about 1½ hours, or until a thin knife inserted in the center of the paté comes out clean. If water in the larger pan should evaporate during baking, add additional boiling water. Chill thoroughly before serving as an appetizer, or as open-face Scandinavian sandwiches.   Serves 8–12.

VARIATION:

This paté is also good when made with chicken livers. They are not a traditional ingredient in Sweden, probably because chickens (and their livers) were available only in limited numbers until recently.

MEAT BALLS

Sweden (*Köttbullar*)

There are hundreds of versions of meatballs and it is always a matter of concern for the new bride to have to match her husband's "Mother's meatballs." In Sweden they are always made either au jus or with pan gravy, never with sour cream etc. for which you will find recipes in this country. And the meatballs you serve with smörgåsbord are almost always just plain, without any gravy at all.

1 lb	(½ kg)	chopped meat, preferably a mixture of ½ beef and ¼ each of pork and veal
1	(1)	small onion, finely minced
2 tbs	(2 tbs)	butter or margarine
⅓ cup	(80 mL)	dry bread crumbs
¾ cup	(180 mL)	milk
1	(1)	egg
		salt and pepper to taste
¼ ts	(¼ ts)	ground allspice

Sauté onions in 1 tbs butter until transparent. Soak bread crumbs in milk for 5 minutes, then add ground meat, onion, egg and seasonings. Mix well. Shape meatballs with hands into balls 1½″ (30 mm) in diameter, rinsing hands with cold water to avoid meat mixture sticking to them. Brown meatballs on all sides in remaining butter. Shake pan off and on to keep their round shape.

When evenly brown, turn heat down to low and simmer for about 10 minutes, then remove from pan, and add a little hot water, stirring briskly to mix in loose particles and pan juices. Serve this pan gravy with meatballs as it is "au jus," or add 1½ tbs of flour mixed with 2 tbs water and 1 cup beef broth and make a regular gravy. When smooth, return meatballs to gravy and cook together about 5 minutes.

Small Meatballs for *smörgåsbord:*

Use the same ingredients as above, except that ¼ cup (60 mL) cream and ½ cup (125 mL) water should be substituted for the milk. Shape meatballs into very small rounds, about 1 ts for each meatball for a ½″ (12 mm) diameter. Brown well on all sides, they are then cooked and do not need any simmering. Serve on tooth-picks without any gravy, as an appetizer, or in a serving dish as part of a buffet or *smörgåsbord.*

BEEF PATTIES A LA LINDSTROM

Sweden   (*Biff à la Lindström*)

A type of hamburger patty that is quite different. Who would ever think of putting pickled beets with hamburger meat? Well, I guess some Mr. or Mrs. Lindstrom did, probably without dreaming that it would be so popular.

1½ lbs	(¾ kg)	ground round steak or sirloin
1 cup	(250 mL)	mashed potatoes (2 medium size potatoes) mashed with ½ cup (125 mL) milk
1	(1)	egg
		salt and pepper to taste
¾ cup	(180 mL)	finely chopped pickled beets
1	(1)	small onion, finely chopped (½ cup or 125 mL)
2 tbs	(2 tbs)	capers, chopped
2 tbs	(2 tbs)	butter or margarine

In a large mixing bowl mix together meat, potatoes, egg, salt and pepper and work mixture with a wooden spoon until smooth. Add beets, onion and capers and blend to get them evenly distributed in the meat mix. Shape into round or oval patties, about ¾" (20 mm) thick.

Fry in butter or margarine in a hot skillet until nicely brown, about 5 minutes on each side. Remove patties onto a warm serving platter. Add a little water to skillet, stir to remove brown particles on bottom and pour these pan juices over the meat patties. Serve immediately with potatoes prepared in one way or another, (just boiled, or mashed, scalloped, creamed, cheese'd etc.).

For 4–6 portions.

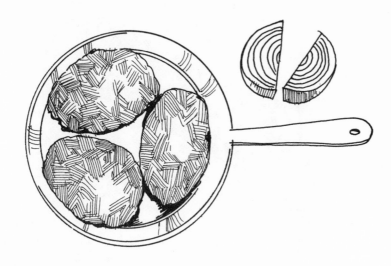

LOIN OF PORK WITH PRUNES

Sweden   *(Plommonspäckad Fläskkarré)*

A way to make a pork roast (which is sometimes on the dry side) both juicy and flavorful by adding prunes. It makes quite an attractive piece of meat.

4–5 lbs	(2–2½ kg)	loin of pork
10	(10)	prunes
½ cup	(125 mL)	hot water
		salt and pepper to taste

Soak prunes in hot water about 20 minutes, then cut them in halves and remove the pits. Save the soaking water. With a sharp paring knife make deep ½″ (12 mm) wide cuts into the loin of pork and insert prunes into these openings. Or you may make a deep slice length-wise in two places in the pork-loin, insert the prunes at equal intervals, then tie the meat together with cotton twine. When you cut the roast, it looks very nice this way as the prunes appear in a sort of pattern.

Rub salt and pepper into meat surface, and roast in a roasting pan in a 325° F (165° C) oven about three hours or until meat thermometer registers 185° F (85° C). Put meat on a serving platter and remove string, if it is used. Add water left over from soaking prunes to the roasting pan and stir with a spoon or a whisk to loosen all pan drippings. Strain drippings and remove excess fat. Put 2 tbs fat into a sauce-pan and blend in 2 tbs flour and stir until well mixed. Add strained pan drippings, a little at a time and stir until a smooth gravy has been obtained. If desired, add ¼ cup (60 mL) cream to gravy. Slice meat into chops, or, if desired, remove the backbone and carve into thinner slices. Serve with gravy, to 5–6.

CASTLE POT ROAST

Sweden   *(Slottstek)*

Pot roast is generally a very satisfying meal. Here it is upgraded in flavor to the extent that it is called Castle Pot Roast.

4–5 lbs	*(2–2½ kg)*	top or bottom round roast
		salt and pepper to taste
2 tbs	*(2 tbs)*	butter or margarine
3–4	*(3–4)*	anchovy fillets (preferably the Scandinavian type)
2 tbs	*(2 tbs)*	wine vinegar
2 tbs	*(2 tbs)*	brown sugar
2	*(2)*	medium onions, chopped (1½ cups or 375 mL)
2	*(2)*	bay leaves
10	*(10)*	whole allspice
6	*(6)*	peppercorns
¼ cup	*(60 mL)*	red wine
1½–2 cups	*(400–500 mL)*	beef bouillon or water

Rub meat with salt and pepper and brown well in butter or margarine in a Dutch oven. Put anchovies on top of meat, add onions, bay leaves, vinegar, sugar, spices, wine and a small amount of bouillon. Simmer over low heat until meat is thoroughly tender, about 3 hours, turning it over about three times during cooking, and adding remaining bouillon gradually each time. When meat is done, remove it and keep it warm. Strain pot liquid, skim off fat on top, and use to make a gravy as follows:

Gravy:

3 tbs	*(3 tbs)*	fat
4 tbs	*(4 tbs)*	flour
		pot liquid
½ cup	*(125 mL)*	heavy cream

In a saucepan add flour to fat, stirring vigorously to make it smooth, add pot liquid gradually while stirring until a smooth gravy has been obtained. Just before serving add heavy cream and mix well. To serve, cut meat in thin slices, and pour a little gravy on top, then serve remainder from a gravy bowl. This meat is often served with red cabbage.   Serves 8–10.

LEG OF LAMB

Sweden (*Lammstek*)

The difference in the Swedish way of preparing leg of lamb is the gravy which contains a cup of coffee with cream and sugar. Surprising, yes, but it makes a very flavorful gravy and takes away the "woolly" flavor that you sometimes get if the lamb is aging into mutton. . .

1	(*1*)	leg of lamb, about 6 lbs (3 kg)
2	(*2*)	medium size onions, quartered
		salt and pepper to taste

Rub meat with salt and pepper then place in a baking pan together with the onions. Bake in a 325° F (160° C) oven until done, about 30–35 minutes to the pound (175° on meat ther-mometer, if one is used). Remove meat and keep warm. Add 2 cups (500 mL) of water to pan drippings and scrape to loosen all particles, then skim off fat on top and strain into a saucepan.

Gravy:

2 cups	(*500 mL*)	pan drippings
4 tbs	(*4 tbs*)	flour
1 cup	(*250 mL*)	coffee with cream and 1 ts sugar
		salt and pepper to taste

Heat 3 tbs of removed fat, add flour and stir until browned, then add pan drippings a little at a time, while stirring constantly. When mixture is smooth, add coffee with cream and sugar. Taste gravy for seasoning and serve from a sauce bowl.

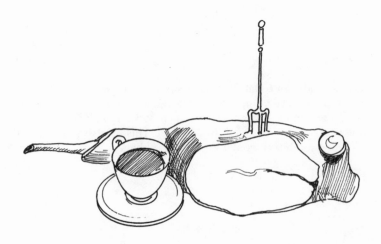

BOILED LAMB WITH DILL SAUCE

Sweden   (Lammkött med Dillsås)

A very good way of preparing lamb stew—especially if you like dill.

3-4 lbs	(1½-2 kg)	stewing lamb (shoulder or breast)
2 cups	(500 mL)	water
		salt to taste
6	(6)	whole peppercorns
6	(6)	whole allspice
1	(1)	bay leaf
4-5	(4-5)	fresh dill sprigs

Cut meat into serving pieces and put it into a heavy saucepan or Dutch oven and bring to a boil. Skim foam off surface, then turn down heat to low, add seasonings and dill sprigs and simmer until meat is tender, 1–1½ hours. If meat is very fat, it is a good idea to cook it early in the day, then cool meat and stock until the fat rises to the surface where it hardens, and can easily be removed. However, it is good for the flavor to leave a little bit of the fat. Just before serving, re-heat until bubbling hot, and make sauce out of the stock.

Dill Sauce:

2 tbs	(2 tbs)	butter or margarine
2 tbs	(2 tbs)	flour
1½ -2 cups	(375-500 mL)	stock
2 ts	(2 ts)	vinegar
2 ts	(2 ts)	sugar
1	(1)	egg yolk, beaten
2 tbs	(2 tbs)	chopped fresh dill

Melt butter in a saucepan, blend in flour while stirring, then gradually add stock and blend until smooth. Remove from heat and add vinegar, sugar and dill. Add about ½ cup (125 mL) of the sauce to the beaten egg yolk and stir, then return it all to the sauce. Serve immediately.

Serves 4-5.

STUFFED CABBAGE ROLLS

Sweden *(Kåldolmar)*

Stuffed cabbage rolls are popular in the Balkan countries, as well as Russia and Poland, but the Swedes have a way with them that I think is special—or maybe it is because I grew up loving them.

Filling:

1½ lb	(¾ kg)	ground chuck
½ cup	(125 mL)	rice
1 cup	(250 mL)	water
1	(1)	egg, slightly beaten
¼ cup	(60 mL)	milk
		salt and pepper to taste

Cook rice in salted water until tender, about 15 minutes, then let it cool slightly. Add milk, egg, raw meat and seasonings and mix well.

Assembly:

1	(1)	medium size head of cabbage (about 2 lbs or 1 kg)
2 tbs	(2 tbs)	brown sugar

Gravy:
pan juice
2 tbs flour mixed with ½ cup (125 mL) cold pot liquid, in which cabbage was cooked.

Bring water to a boil in a large pot. Trim off outside tough cabbage leaves, then with a small paring knife carefully dig out the core as far in as is possible. Drop head of cabbage into the water and boil for about 3–5 minutes, then remove, rinse quickly with cold water until it is cool enough to handle. Cut off as many leaves as have softened. Return head of cabbage to pot and repeat procedure until the leaves are too small to stuff.

Pare off the main stems of the leaves to make the thickness as close as possible to the rest of the leaf. To stuff, spread out each leaf and put a heaping tablespoon of stuffing on it, roll up into a neat, small "package" then secure with a tooth-pick or use clean cotton twine to tie around it. Place the stuffed cabbage rolls in a roasting pan, sprinkle with brown sugar.

Bake them covered in a 350° F (175° C) oven about one hour, remove from oven and pour pan juice into a saucepan, while keeping the cabbage rolls hot. Add flour and water mixture and bring to a boil, then simmer about 5 minutes. If

(Continued on next page)

(Stuffed Cabbage Rolls, cont.)

gravy should be too thick, add a little more of the cabbage water. Taste gravy for seasoning and add more salt and pepper, if necessary. Serve as a main dish, with gravy either poured on top of the cabbage rolls in a serving dish, or brought separately in a gravy bowl. Serves 5–6.

CHEESE AND CAULIFLOWER CASSEROLE

Sweden (*Ost och Blomkålslåda*)

This makes a nice luncheon or dinner meal, especially when you have house guests and are doing something with them in the hours before you eat. It can be put together ahead of time, even the day before it is baked.

8	(8)	slices white bread
2–3 tbs	(2–3 *tbs*)	butter or margarine
2–3 tbs	(2–3 *tbs*)	of a good mustard, preferably Dijon or similar type
2 cups	(500 mL)	cooked cauliflower, broken into flowerets, (or 1 pkg frozen cauliflower)
½ lb	(¼ kg)	cheddar cheese
3	(3)	eggs, slightly beaten
3 cups	(750 mL)	milk
		salt and pepper to taste
		pinch of nutmeg

Spread bread slices with butter or margarine, then with mustard. Put four slices of the bread, buttered side up, in a 9 x 9″ (220 x 220 mm) square, buttered baking dish. Cover bread slices with half the cheese, cut into thin slices, then add the cauliflower, well drained, on top. Add remaining cheese slices and on top of these, the remaining four slices of bread, this time with the buttered side down.

Scald milk, remove from heat, then add slightly beaten eggs and season-ings. Beat vigorously with a wire whisk or electric beater till mixture foams, then pour over bread. Let rest for at least 5–6 hours, or overnight in the refrigerator. Bake for 1 hour in a 375° F (190° C) oven and serve immediately to 5–6.

VARIATION:

If you have left-over ham, cut 1–2 cups (250–500 mL) cubed ham and add on top of the first layer of cheese.

SWEDISH PANCAKES

Sweden   (*Pannkakor* or *Plättar*)

*In Sweden there is a saying: "With meatballs and pancakes you can feed a man
from the cradle to the grave." This shows their popularity. Swedish pancakes are
always of the type that is referred to as "crepes" here and they are usually one
of the first things you learn to cook as a child, as they are especially easy to
make if you have the Swedish type plätt-panna. This is a special frying pan that
cooks seven 3" (75 mm) pancakes at a time. At this size they are easy to turn
over and therefore suitable for a child's first culinary efforts. Pancakes are a
very versatile food. In Sweden they are eaten as either main meals or desserts
but very seldom for breakfast.*

1¼ cups	(*310 mL*)	flour
½ ts	(½ *ts*)	salt
2 cups	(*500 mL*)	milk
2	(*2*)	eggs
2 tbs	(*2 tbs*)	sugar (use sugar only when pancakes are used for dessert)

For frying: butter or margarine

Mix together flour, salt and milk until smooth. Add eggs and mix well. If pancakes are intended for dessert, add sugar. Let batter rest for at least ½ hour.

Melt a little butter or margarine in a small frying pan, preferably Teflon, and make sure bottom is all covered with a thin layer of the fat. Stir batter and add a thin layer, about 3 tbs for a 7" (180 mm) pan, and tip pan slightly to get batter to cover the whole bottom. Cook first on one side until a few small bubbles start to appear on top, then turn over and cook on the other side until golden brown in color on that side also. From time to time stir batter in the bowl to avoid flour sinking to the bottom, making the top part too thin. Stack the pancakes on a warm plate, either flat or folded over twice, and keep warm. Serve warm, as they are, with jam or thawed frozen berries, or use them in some manner described below. Makes 10–12 7" (180 mm) pancakes.   Serves 4–5 for dessert.

VARIATIONS:

Put flat pancakes on a pie plate that is kept hot over a pot of boiling water. Spread each pancake with some warmed up apple sauce, about 1½ cups (375 mL) in all. When they are all done, cover the top of the stack (and the edges if desired) with whipped cream immediately before serving. Makes a nice warm cake.

Mix whipped cream with fresh or frozen sweetened berries and put 1–2 tbs in each pancake and roll up and serve.

If pancakes are used as a main meal, add either ½ lb (¼ kg) fried crumbled bacon, or finely cubed ham, by sprin-

(*Continued on next page*)

(Swedish Pancakes, cont.)

kling some on each pancake as soon as it has been poured into the pan. Serve with cranberry or lingonberry sauce.

OR

Fill each pancake with creamed seafood, mushrooms or other vegetables, and put in a baking dish. Sprinkle with grated cheese and heat until cheese has melted.

APPLE SOUP

Sweden   *(Äpplesoppa)*

In Sweden fruit soups are quite popular desserts, especially in the Summer when they are wonderfully refreshing served ice cold. I have chosen an apple soup to represent them.

4 cups	*(1 L)*	tart apples (about 4 large apples), peeled, cored and cut into small pieces
2 cups	*(500 mL)*	water
¼ cup	*(60 mL)*	sugar, or more, if desired
1	*(1)*	piece of stick cinnamon (optional)
2 tbs	*(2 tbs)*	corn starch, mixed with ½ cup (125 mL) cold water

Put the apples with the water, sugar and cinnamon into a saucepan, bring to a boil and cook about 3–5 minutes, depending upon the hardness of the apples. They should not be completely dissolved, but remain partly in pieces. Remove from heat, stir in corn starch mixed with water, then return pot to heat and bring to a boil, stirring continuously. Remove from heat and serve, either luke-warm or well chilled.   For 4–5 people.

BIBI'S DELIGHT

Sweden (*Bibi's förtjusning*)

Quite often you will see people eating apple-pie carefully scraping the apple filling out of the crust and leaving the crust on the plate. This should be a good dessert for them—apple-pie á la mode minus the crust. My daughter enthusiastically brought me this recipe after a visit with my sister Bibi in Sweden.

4–5	(*4–5*)	medium size apples, peeled and sliced
2 tbs	(*2 tbs*)	butter or margarine
¼ cup	(*60 mL*)	light syrup
1 ts	(*1 ts*)	cinnamon (optional)

In a large skillet melt the butter or margarine, add apple slices and sauté for 5 minutes. Add syrup and cinnamon and continue cooking over low heat until apple slices are tender but not mushy. Serve directly out of skillet, if it is nice enough, or transfer to serving dish and serve immediately with scoops of ice-cream on top.

Serves 4–5.

RICE À LA MALTA

Sweden (*Ris à la Malta*)

In Sweden Santa Claus does not come through the sky on a sleigh drawn by reindeer but instead on the snowy ground in a sled pulled by goats. And on Christmas Eve you are supposed to put out a dish of left-over rice porridge from the family supper for him to eat. But in my home, instead of giving all the leftovers to Santa, some were saved to use for dessert on Christmas Day, and this is the way it was made.

½ cup (*125 mL*) rice
1 cup (*250 mL*) water
3 tbs (*3 tbs*) sugar
½ cup (*125 mL*) milk
1 cup (*250 mL*) heavy cream
1 cup (*250 mL*) cut up orange sections (membranes removed)
        or canned mandarin oranges or fresh
        or canned pineapple, cut into small chunks
1 ts (*1 ts*) vanilla extract

(Continued on next page)

(Rice à la Malta, cont.)

Rinse rice well in cold water then cook it together with the water and 2 tbs sugar for 15 minutes, add milk and stir well then cook over very low heat an additional 10 minutes. Let rice cool in refrigerator for several hours. Whip cream together with remaining 1 tbs sugar, add vanilla extract, then fold in cold rice, carefully blending to make an even mixture. Drain fruit pieces, set aside a few of them for decoration, then fold the balance into rice mixture. Put into a serving dish and decorate with remaining fruit.

Serves 5–6.

MERINGUE SUISSE

Sweden   (*Marängsuisse*)

A simple dessert to make and usually a great favorite of children.

20	(*20*)	meringue tops ("kisses")
1 cup	(*250 mL*)	heavy cream, whipped
½ cup	(*125 mL*)	chocolate syrup

Crumble meringues and put a layer in 4–5 sherbert glasses or small serving bowls, dribble some chocolate syrup on top, then a layer of whipped cream. Continue these layers until all of it is used up.

Makes 4–5 servings.

VARIATION: (Mandarine Suisse)

| 1 | (*1*) | 11 oz (310 g) can of mandarin oranges |

Drain off liquid and add oranges to the above layers.

MOCHA TORTE

Sweden *(Mockatårta)*

This confection is a must for me to taste each time I visit Sweden as it was always my favorite cake while I lived there. No wonder I am always afraid to step on the scale upon my return to the U.S.

Meringue layers:

4	(4)	egg whites
¾ cup	(180 mL)	sugar
¼ ts	(¼ ts)	cream of tartar

Put the egg whites in a bowl and place it over a bowl of hot water, then beat until mixture is stiff. Add sugar, a little at a time and continue beating until well mixed. On a greased parchment paper or waxed paper, outline three 9″ (220 mm) circles, or squares, then spread meringue evenly on these. Bake in a 225° F (110° C) oven for 1½ hours, then leave them in the oven until completely cold.

Filling and frosting:

1 cup	(250 mL)	butter (two sticks), at room temperature
2 cups	(500 mL)	confectioners' sugar
2	(2)	egg yolks
⅓ cup	(80 mL)	very strong coffee

Cream butter until light and fluffy. Sift confectioners' sugar and gradually add it alternately with egg yolks and coffee, beating until well mixed.

Assembly:

¼ cup	(60 mL)	blanched, flaked almonds Maraschino cherries, cut into strips, halved green grapes or flaked chocolate, if desired

Put almonds on a baking dish in a 350° F (175° C) oven for 10 minutes, then remove. Set aside about ⅓ of the filling and frosting. Put remaining filling between the three layers, on top and on the sides. Put the filling that was set aside in a cake decorating tube or bag, using the star-like opening, then squeeze the frosting in a nice pattern on top and on sides. Decorate with the almonds, and also with one of the other suggested decorations. Serves 8–10.

DREAM CAKE

Sweden   (*Drömtårta*)

A cake looking like a jelly-roll but made with a chocolate base and a creamy filling.

3	(3)	eggs
½ cup	(125 mL)	sugar
3 tbs	(3 tbs)	flour
2 tbs	(2 tbs)	corn starch
1 ts	(1 ts)	baking powder
2 tbs	(2 tbs)	cocoa
2 tbs	(2 tbs)	sugar, for towel

Beat eggs and sugar until light and fluffy. Sift together flour, corn starch, baking powder and cocoa and add to egg mixture. Spread batter in a jelly-roll pan, 12 x 16" (300 x 400 mm), lined with greased wax paper, and bake in a 425° F (220° C) oven for 5 minutes. Remove from oven, carefully peel off wax paper and put cake upside down on a clean kitchen towel, sprinkled with sugar. Roll up towel and cake together while cake is still warm, and let it cool.

Filling:

½ cup	(125 mL)	butter or margarine
1 cup	(250 mL)	confectioners' sugar
1	(1)	egg yolk
1 ts	(1 ts)	vanilla flavoring

Stir butter and sugar until light and fluffy, add egg yolk and vanilla and mix well.

Assembly:

For sprinkling: **confectioners' sugar**

Unroll cake and towel and spread filling over cake, then roll it together without the towel, either length-wise or cross-wise, depending upon if you wish to have a short fat cake or a long thin one. Cover it with foil or plastic wrap and put in refrigerator for 1 hour or longer. Before serving, sprinkle cake with confectioners' sugar and cut into either thin or thick slices, according to taste.

MAZARIN CAKE

Sweden   *(Mazarinkaka)*

When I bake something I like, I get sort of hooked on it, and this cake brings back the days of my early marriage when it was the one I made most of the time—partly because of the nice compliments it always brought, and also because I like the "almondy" flavor myself.

Flan pastry:

1 cup	*(250 mL)*	**flour**
2 tbs	*(2 tbs)*	**sugar**
½ cup	*(125 mL)*	**butter or margarine**
1	*(1)*	**egg yolk**

Sift together flour and sugar, then cut in butter until mixture is crumbly. Add egg yolk and work dough together into a ball. If it should be too dry, add 1 tbs cold water. Chill in refrigerator 20–30 minutes. Roll out onto a floured baking board and cut to fit into either an 8″ (200 mm) cake pan with removable bottom, or an 8″ (200 mm) pie plate.

Filling:

⅔ cup	*(160 mL)*	**almonds**
5 tbs	*(5 tbs)*	**butter or margarine**
⅔ cup	*(160 mL)*	**confectioners' sugar**
2	*(2)*	**eggs**

Blanch and grind the almonds. Cream sugar and butter until smooth and fluffy, add eggs, one at a time and continue mixing until smooth. Fold in almonds. Put filling over pastry and bake in a 375° F (190° C) oven about 30 minutes. Cool, then either cover with water icing below, or sprinkle with confectioners' sugar.

Icing:

2 tbs	*(2 tbs)*	**confectioners' sugar**
1 ts	*(1 ts)*	**water**
1 drop	*(1 drop)*	**green food coloring**

Mix together and spread on top of cake after it has cooled somewhat but is still slightly warm.

RYE BREAD (LIMPA)

Sweden

(Rågbröd)

This is the most popular of Swedish breads in this country. It can be made in many versions, is delicious just plain, and also responds well to flavoring of many kinds, of which several examples are given.

1	*(1)*	envelope dry yeast
¼ cup	*(60 mL)*	lukewarm water
1 ts	*(1 ts)*	sugar
1 cup	*(250 mL)*	cold water
2 tbs	*(2 tbs)*	butter or margarine
4 tbs	*(4 tbs)*	molasses
⅓ cup	*(80 mL)*	brown sugar
2 ts	*(2 ts)*	salt
1 tbs	*(1 tbs)*	vinegar
½ ts	*(½ ts)*	baking soda
1 cup	*(250 mL)*	buttermilk (if not available, add 1 ts vinegar to 1 cup (250 mL) fresh milk and let stand 5 minutes)
4 cups	*(1 L)*	rye flour
2 cups	*(500 mL)*	sifted flour, approximately
Flavoring:		2 ts crushed anise seeds or 2 ts crushed fennel seeds or 1 ts each of crushed anise and fennel seeds or 1 ts caraway seeds or 2 ts finely chopped candied citron peel Any flavoring is optional

Dissolve yeast in lukewarm water with sugar. Combine cold water, butter or margarine, molasses, brown sugar, salt and vinegar in a saucepan and bring to a boil, then turn into a mixing bowl. Add baking soda and buttermilk, then rye flour and beat until well mixed, either by hand with a wooden spoon or in an electric mixer. Add yeast mixture, flavoring, if used, and sufficient flour to make a dough that does not stick to your hands. If electric mixer is used, keep adding flour until the mixture gets too heavy for it, then continue beating with a wooden spoon. Turn onto a floured baking board and knead for 10 minutes, adding flour as needed, or until dough is smooth and elastic.

Place in a greased bowl, turning dough over once to get both sides greased, cover with plastic wrap and let rise in a warm place until double in bulk, about 2 hours. Punch down dough and shape into three loaves, place either in greased loaf pans or

(Continued on next page)

(Rye Bread (Limpa), cont.)

close to each other on a greased baking sheet. Cover with a clean towel and let rise again in a warm place for 1 hour.

Then bake in a 350° F (175° C) oven for 45 minutes, brush the top of the loaves with some lukewarm water, then return to the oven and bake an additional 15 minutes, or until done. Brush tops once more with lukewarm water when taken out. Cover with clean towel, and cool on wire rack.

Makes 3 loaves.

RYE BREAD WITHOUT YEAST

Sweden   (Rågbröd utan jäst)

All over Sweden you can buy an almost black bread, called skånsk kavring. *The name indicates that it comes from the southern part of Sweden. I have always loved this bread and wanted to be able to bake it here in the U.S. But for some reason or another no recipe seems to exist in any of all the Swedish cookbooks I have scanned for it. But never give up hope—to my surprise this recipe, given to me by a friend who did not know about my futile search but wanted me to have a good bread recipe, seems to taste exactly like* skånsk kavring. *It is so easy to make—no fussing with yeasts, raising etc. and I have had nothing but nice comments about it from my guests.*

6 cups	(1½ L)	rye flour
3 ts	(3 ts)	baking soda
1 ts	(1 ts)	baking powder
2 ts	(2 ts)	salt
3 cups	(750 mL)	buttermilk (if unavailable, add 3 tbs vinegar to fresh milk and let stand for 5 minutes)
⅓ cup	(80 mL)	molasses
2 tbs	(2 tbs)	caraway seeds (or, if preferred, use 1 tbs each of crushed fennel and anise instead)

Mix together all the dry ingredients, then add buttermilk and molasses and stir together into a smooth dough. Work it for a few minutes on a floured baking board and shape into two loaves. Put these in greased bread pans about 3½ x 8″ (87 x 200 mm), and bake in a 210° F (100° C) oven for 20 minutes.

Then increase heat every 20 minutes, first to 260° F (125° C), then 300° F (150° C) and finally to 350° F (175° C). Keep temperature at this until bread is done, about 1 hour and 10 minutes. Towards the last 15 minutes, brush crust with water a couple of times. Let cool, wrapped in clean kitchen towels.   Makes 2 loaves.

FILBERT CRESCENTS

Sweden   (*Nötgifflar*)

Crescent shaped pastries, absolutely delicious with coffee or tea.

1 tbs	(*1 tbs*)	dry yeast (one half package)
¼ cup	(*60 mL*)	lukewarm milk
½ cup	(*125 mL*)	butter or margarine
1½ cup	(*375 mL*)	flour
1	(*1*)	egg, slightly beaten
2 tbs	(*2 tbs*)	sugar

Mix yeast with milk. Cut butter into flour with a pastry blender, until mixture is coarsely crumbly, then add milk mixture, egg and sugar. Blend dough until smooth and elastic, first in bowl then on floured baking board.

Make into a ball, place in a greased bowl, cover with plastic wrap and let rise until double in size, about 1 hour. (Or instead of letting it rise at this point, you may keep it in refrigerator for up to 10 days.)

Filling:

¼ cup	(*60 mL*)	butter or margarine
½ cup	(*125 mL*)	filberts
½ cup	(*125 mL*)	sugar

Grind nuts, either in a nut-grinder or in an electric blender. Stir butter until light and fluffy, add sugar and nuts and mix well.

Assembly:

For brushing: 1 egg yolk mixed with 1 tbs milk

Cut dough into three pieces, and make three flat round cakes of about 9″ (220 mm) diameter. Divide each into 8 parts. Put a little filling on each small piece near the base and roll up toward the center. Put them on a greased baking sheet, seam side down, and bend into a crescent shape. Let rise for about 45 minutes. Brush with egg mixture and bake in a 450° F (230° C) oven 6–8 minutes. Cool on a wire rack.

Makes 24 crescents.

Sweden **QUICK-BAKE CRESCENTS** *(Snabbgifflar)*

A good standby when you get guests for tea or coffee on short notice. Their look has a certain elegance which belies their simple ingredients.

½ cup	(125 mL)	butter or margarine
¼ cup	(60 mL)	sugar
1	(1)	egg
1-½ cups	(375 mL)	flour
2 ts	(2 ts)	baking powder
½ ts		salt
¼ cup	(60 mL)	cream
For filling:		orange marmalade (or apricot preserve) approximately 5 tbs
For sprinkling:		confectioners' sugar

Cream butter and sugar until light and fluffy, add egg and mix well. Add flour, sifted together with baking powder and salt, alternately with cream and mix only until thoroughly incorporated.

Place the dough on a floured baking board and divide it into two balls. Flatten each one out to an 8–9″ (20–22 cm) circle and cut each one into eight wedge shaped pieces. Put about ½ ts orange marmalade on the wide part of the wedge, then roll up and place on a greased baking sheet, seams down, then bend into the shape of a crescent.

Bake in a 425° F (220° C) oven for 5–6 minutes, or until golden in color. Remove and cool on wire rack then sprinkle with confectioners' sugar.

Sweden **LUCIA BUNS** *(Lussekatter)*

On December 13th Sweden celebrates the Santa Lucia Day. Long ago, before people paid real notice to calendars, it was believed this was the darkest night of the year. To brighten up the dark Nordic night, one of the young maidens of the house would dress up in a long white nightgown, wear a wreath of lingon-berry leaves with lit candles on her head and wake up the rest of the family with coffee and Lucia buns.

The name of the day was chosen for St. Lucia, who was a Christian martyr—a young girl whose eyes were pierced by the Romans so that she became blind, but then became a symbol of light. This custom of celebrating her day still prevails, and very early in the morning on December 13th you will see little girls and big girls scurrying around the cities and countryside, dressed up as described above, to bring treats to their teachers and friends, after caring for their own families.

While they always serve these traditional buns, the shape varies somewhat in different sections of the country.

(Lucia Buns, cont.)

1 pkg	(*1 pkg*)	dry yeast
1 cup	(*250 mL*)	lukewarm milk
½ cup	(*125 mL*)	butter or margarine
¼ ts	(*¼ ts*)	salt
¾ cup	(*180 mL*)	sugar
2 ts	(*2 ts*)	ground cardamom
1	(*1*)	egg, slightly beaten
4 cups	(*1 L*)	flour (approximately)

Put the yeast with ¼ cup (60 mL) lukewarm milk and 2 tbs sugar in the bowl of an electric mixer and let stand until yeast is completely dissolved. Melt butter or margarine in a saucepan and add to yeast mixture together with the remaining lukewarm milk, salt, sugar, cardamom and egg. Mix well.

Add about one half of the flour, a little at a time while beating on medium speed until well blended, then keep adding additional flour until the mixture gets to be too heavy for the mixer, then work with a wooden spoon, adding the remaining flour, and working until the dough is smooth and shiny. Turn onto lightly floured board and knead by hand about 10 minutes.

Put the dough in a clean, greased, bowl, turn over once and cover with plastic wrap. Put in a warm place to rise until double in size, about 1½–2 hours. Punch down dough and roll out to about ½" (12 mm) thickness. Shape into Lucia-buns by cutting strips of dough and rolling them into about ½" (6 mm) thick rolls, about 6" (150 mm) long and shape them this way:

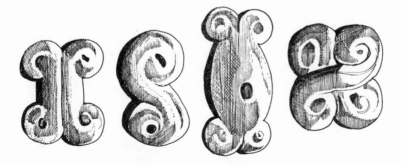

Put buns on a greased baking sheet, cover with a clean cloth, let rise for another ½ hour, then brush with egg mixture and bake in a 400° F (200° C) oven about 8–10 minutes or until golden brown in color.

TYRA'S PASTRIES

Sweden *(Tyras Bullar)*

Tyra is a relative of mine in Sweden who can make magic with flour and other baking ingredients, and who can dream up the most wonderful concoctions. Here is one of her easy-to-make pastries.

½ cup	*(125 mL)*	butter or margarine
2¼ cup	*(560 mL)*	flour, sifted
1 pkg	*(1 pkg)*	dry yeast
1 tbs	*(1 tbs)*	sugar
⅔ cup	*(160 mL)*	milk
		flour for dusting baking board
For brushing:		½ egg mixed with 1 tbs milk

Mix together sifted flour, yeast and sugar then cut in butter or margarine with a pastry cutter until mixture resembles coarse crumbs. Add milk and work together into a soft dough. Roll out dough to about ¼″ (5 mm) thickness on a floured board and cut into 2½″ (60 mm) squares. Put about ½–¾ ts filling in the middle of each square, then fold each corner towards the center and put the pastry into a paper baking cup. Put them in a warm place to rise for about 1 hour, then bake in a 390° F (200° C) oven for 10–12 minutes.

Makes 15–16 pastries.

Filling:

3 tbs	*(3 tbs)*	butter or margarine
1 cup	*(250 mL)*	confectioners' sugar
1 ts	*(1 ts)*	vanilla flavoring
		a few drops of water

Beat butter until soft, add sugar and vanilla and a few drops of water to make a smooth paste.

THE KING'S SPICE COOKIES

Sweden   (*Kungens Pepparkakor*)

This is the Christmas Cookie above all others in Sweden. The popularity can be judged by the vast number of varieties of recipes that exist. Each family felt bound by their "own" recipe, and each tasted somewhat different. These are the ones we used to bake in my home. If the quantity seems large, I wish to tell you that I cut it in half—as we always made the full 600 cookies the original recipe provides. However, this dough freezes very well, so you may cut up and roll out only as much as you feel like, and save the rest for some future date.

4½ cups	(*1¼ L*)	flour
1½ ts	(*1½ ts*)	baking soda
1 cup	(*250 mL*)	butter (two sticks)
½ cup	(*125 mL*)	heavy cream
¾ cup	(*180 mL*)	Karo syrup (dark)
1 cup	(*250 mL*)	sugar
1 tbs	(*1 tbs*)	cinnamon
1 tbs	(*1 tbs*)	ginger
1 ts	(*1 ts*)	ground cloves
1	(*1*)	egg, lightly beaten

Sift together 4 cups (1 L) flour and baking soda, then cut in butter with a pastry cutter until mixture resembles coarse crumbs. Beat cream until thick, add syrup, sugar, spices and the egg. Mix the flour into the batter and work together first in a bowl, then on a floured baking board until the dough is smooth. Leave it in the refrigerator for at least 8 hours, or overnight. Cut out pieces as large as an orange and roll out very thinly on a floured board, even less than ⅛" or 2 mm if possible. (This can be done by lifting the rolled out dough with a spatula, and then dusting the board again before turning it over.) The thinner the cookies are, the better they taste.

Use cookie cutters of different shapes. After cookies have been cut, squeeze remaining dough on baking board into a ball and put in refrigerator until it chills before rolling it out again.

Put the cut cookies on well greased cookie sheets and bake in a 375° F (190° C) oven for about 8 minutes or until lightly browned, but watch carefully that they do not get too dark, as this happens very suddenly. Let the cookies cool on the baking sheets for 3–5 minutes before removing. Makes 250–300 cookies.

SPRITZ COOKIES

Sweden   *(Spritsar)*

There are many recipes in this country for Spritsar but I think that this Swedish version, which is just about the simplest one, is one of the best. It is my husband's favorite cookie, and he considers himself an expert on spritz cookies.

1 cup	(250 mL)	butter or margarine
½ cup	(125 mL)	sugar
1 ts	(1 ts)	almond flavoring (or vanilla, if preferred)
2 cups	(500 mL)	flour (or slightly more)

Beat butter or margarine until light and fluffy, add sugar, a little at a time. Add flavoring, then sift flour and add, then blend well. Roll a little piece of dough in your hand and put in the oven (375° F) (175° C) and bake it for 5 minutes to test it. If it should float out, add a little bit more flour, but if it holds its shape put the dough into a cookie press. Use the attachment with a big star in the middle (see picture below) and press dough into rings, S's or bars, on greased baking sheets. Bake in the above temperature for about 6–8 minutes, or until cookies are golden in color. Let rest for about 2 minutes on the baking sheet before they are removed.

Makes about 6 dozen.

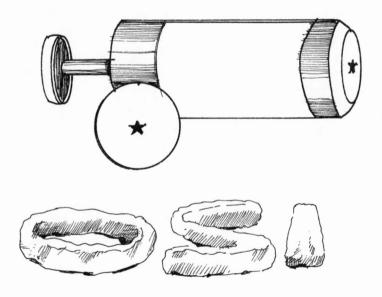

OATMEAL LACE COOKIES

Sweden   *(Havreflarn)*

*A simple cookie that looks so elegant, and as if it were much more complicated
to make than it is. However, a word of warning. Do not bake these on a damp
and muggy day—they will not keep their shape under those weather conditions.*

½ cup	*(125 mL)*	butter or margarine
1 cup	*(250 mL)*	oatmeal
1	*(1)*	egg
½ cup	*(125 mL)*	sugar
2 tbs	*(2 tbs)*	flour
½ ts	*(½ ts)*	baking powder

Melt butter in a small saucepan, remove from heat, add oatmeal and mix well. Beat egg and sugar until light and fluffy, then add oatmeal mixture and flour, sifted with baking powder, and stir until well blended. Drop by teaspoonfuls onto a well greased baking sheet, very widely apart as these cookies float out (spread) during baking. Put only about 10 cookies on the sheet at a time. Bake in a 375° F (190° C) oven 5–6 minutes, or until they are golden in color.

Prepare a broom handle or similar size and shape stick by covering with aluminum foil. Take cookies from oven and let them remain on baking sheet for 1 minute, but *no longer*, then remove them with a wide spatula and place them on the broom handle, carefully pressing down to get a bent shape. Work fast, because the cookies harden quickly, and if they should be too hard to bend, return them to the oven for 30 seconds to make them pliable again. Remove from broom handle when cool and keep in an air-tight container.

Makes about 40 cookies.

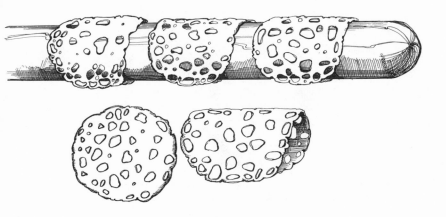

ALMOND TARTLETS

Sweden   *(Mandelmusslor)*

These tartlets can be used as they are as cookies, and are very often part of the Christmas assortment of cookies in Swedish homes. But they are also often filled with either a custard or whipped cream with berries and fruit. One word of warning though, be very careful in greasing the tartlet tins, as they are so tender that they are hard to get out whole. I often have trouble—and then I know I am guilty of rushing it, and not taking enough time in greasing the tins.

1 cup	*(250 mL)*	flour
¼ cup	*(60 mL)*	sugar
5 tbs	*(5 tbs)*	butter or margarine
½ cup	*(125 mL)*	blanched almonds, ground
1 ts	*(1 ts)*	almond extract
1	*(1)*	egg yolk

Sift together flour and sugar, then cut in butter or margarine with a pastry cutter until mixture resembles coarse crumbs. Add remaining ingredients and mix together into a ball and let dough rest for at least one hour.

Carefully grease small fluted tartlet tins, then add a piece of dough, the size of a large walnut. With your thumb dipped in flour press the dough up the side of the tin, thicker towards the top than the bottom. Bake in a 375° F (190° C) oven for 10–12 minutes or until golden in color.

Let cool for a few minutes before turning them out by tapping the bottoms of the tins until the tartlets come out. Makes about 20 (using the Swedish type tins) maybe less if another mold is used.

HOT CHRISTMAS DRINK

Sweden
(*Glögg*)

The smell of hot wine and spices from my husband's yearly batch of glögg *has become a part of the Christmas Eve aromas in our house. When the Christmas weather is cold and crisp, this drink will warm you in more than one way.*

1	(*1*)	bottle burgundy (24 oz or 750 mL)
1	(*1*)	fifth bottle vodka or whiskey
1 cup	(*250 mL*)	raisins
1 cup	(*250 mL*)	blanched almonds
3	(*3*)	sticks cinnamon
1 tbs	(*1 tbs*)	cardamom seeds, skinned
1 ts	(*1 ts*)	whole cloves
1	(*1*)	small piece of lemon peel, pith removed
1	(*1*)	pint bottle inexpensive brandy
½ lb	(*250 g*)	lump sugar

Pour wine, vodka or whiskey, raisins and almonds in a large sauce pan. Tie cinnamon, cardamom, cloves and lemon peel into a piece of cheese cloth and add to wine. Bring slowly to boiling point, then simmer over very low heat for 30 minutes. Remove from heat, then put a grill of some kind on top of pot and put sugar on it, then pour brandy over sugar and ignite letting the heat melt the sugar into the pot. Keep pouring brandy a little at a time until all sugar is melted. Serve very hot, and reheat it each time it is served, with a few raisins and almonds in each serving glass. This makes about 2½ quarts (2½ L).

Switzerland

PEOPLE in general associate Swiss food with cheese. There are, of course, many other tasty foods in Switzerland, but in quite a lot of food cheese is an ingredient—you can use it for or in appetizers, soups, vegetables, meats, meatless meals and desserts. The Swiss have outstanding cheeses, and a great variety of them, but when we speak of Swiss cheese in this country, we usually mean Emmenthaler with its firm texture and big holes. This type is copied by many countries, besides the U.S., but when you want to be sure of a well matured product, you are safe when you buy "Switzerland Swiss".

Switzerland is situated in just about the center of Europe, and the people speak mainly three languages (there is a fourth, called Romansch which is a variety of Latin but it is spoken by less than 1% and is thus of less consequence)—that is French, Italian and German (the German is called *Schwyzerdütsch* or Swiss-German, and is quite different from the language spoken in Germany). The population in the different parts also cook similarly to the ways of France, Italy and Germany. And you will notice that you can tell in what part of the country the dishes originate from their names.

Switzerland produces much milk, so it goes without saying that there have to be a lot of cows. By the law of nature all of them are not born to be cows but a substantial percentage turns out to be bull-calves. As the Swiss generally do not raise beef cattle, many bull calves are quickly used for their meat, so veal is much used and is prepared in many delicious ways.

Like their eastern neighbor—Austria, and also other middle European countries—they make cakes and pastries that are outstanding. All

501

kinds of nuts are used liberally in baking. And most of us also know of their wonderful chocolates, which are sometimes used as ingredients in desserts.

CEREAL MIX	*Birchermüsli*
BAKED SCRAMBLED EGGS WITH CHEESE	*Käse Rührei*
CHEESE TARTLETS	*Ramequins*
CHEESE CROQUETTES	*Croquettes au Fromage*
BROWN FLOUR SOUP	*Basler Mehlsuppe*
CABBAGE AND RICE SOUP	*Kabissuppe*
VEAL CUTLETS WITH SOUR CREAM	*Veau Emincé* or *Gschnetzlets*
LUGANO POT ROAST	*Stufato alla Luganese*
FONDUE BOURGUIGNONNE	
HOLLANDAISE SAUCE	
BEARNAISE SAUCE	
SOUR CREAM AND HORSERADISH SAUCE	
CHEESE FONDUE	*Fondue de Fromage*
POTATO CAKE	*Rösti*
POTATOES IN CHEESE CUSTARD	*Käsekartoffeln*
SAUTÉED CHEESE PATTIES	*Käseklösschen*
ONION OMELET	*Frittata di Cipolle*
GREEN BEAN SALAD	*Grüne Bohnensalat*
CARROT CAKE	*Aaergauer Rübli Torte*
ENGADINER NUT PIE	*Engadiner Torte*
COFFEE CREAM GATEAU	*Gâteau de Mocha*
KIRSCHTORTE	
EGG BRAID	*Zopf*
TRADITIONAL HONEY COOKIES FROM BASEL	*Leckerli*
JAM-FILLED COOKIES	*Spitzbuben*
CHOCOLATE FONDUE	*Fondue au Chocolat*

CEREAL MIX

Switzerland   *(Birchermüsli)*

The health-food cult may very well have been started in Switzerland by a Dr. Bircher-Benner, who did not like what the Swiss usually ate and created a well-balanced and nutritious meal that is eaten all over Switzerland today, in homes as well as restaurants. Here it is. Varieties of it are also manufactured, and some of it is exported to our country.

1 cup	*(250 mL)*	oatmeal (uncooked)
1 cup	*(250 mL)*	cold water
¼ cup	*(60 mL)*	fresh squeezed lemon juice
¼ cup	*(60 mL)*	sweetened condensed milk, or honey
3	*(3)*	large apples
½ cup	*(125 mL)*	chopped nuts (any kind)

Soak oatmeal in cold water. Soaking time depends upon whether "quick oats" or old fashioned oats are used. If quick oats are used, 10–15 minutes are enough, otherwise soak overnight. Just before serving add lemon juice, condensed milk or honey, grate the apple (peels and all) directly into the oatmeal and mix well. Sprinkle with nuts. Serves 4–5.

VARIATIONS:

Other fruits may be used, such as peaches, pears etc., chopped very fine.

BAKED SCRAMBLED EGGS WITH CHEESE
Switzerland   (*Käse Rührei*)

An interesting addition of cheese to the breakfast eggs. Makes a nice luncheon dish too.

5	(*5*)	eggs
½ cup	(*125 mL*)	milk
		salt and pepper to taste
6 tbs	(*6 tbs*)	butter or margarine
¼ lb	(*125 g*)	Swiss cheese, sliced
⅓ cup	(*80 mL*)	dry breadcrumbs

Melt half the butter. Beat eggs, milk, salt and pepper well and mix with melted butter. Butter a 9" (220 mm) square or round shallow baking pan with 1 tbs of butter and pour egg mixture into this. Bake in a 375° F (190° C) oven for 10–15 minutes, or until eggs start to coagulate. Then cover with cheese slices and bread crumbs, and dot with remaining butter. Continue baking for about 10 minutes or until golden brown on top. Cut in squares or wedges and serve immediately to 4–5.

CHEESE TARTLETS
Switzerland   (*Ramequins*)

The best of appetizers from Switzerland—what would they contain if not cheese? Here are two different types.

For crust, use your favorite pie crust recipe for single crust, or use recipe on page 54)

Filling:

1 cup	(*250 mL*)	grated cheese (cheddar, or ½ Swiss and ½ Parmesan or Romano)
½ cup	(*125 mL*)	sour cream
2 ts	(*2 ts*)	flour
1	(*1*)	egg
		salt and pepper to taste
		pinch of cayenne pepper

Roll out pie crust and cut out to line tartlet pans or cup-cake pans. Mix all ingredients for the filling until well blended, then fill tartlets ¾ full. Bake in a 375° F (190° C) oven about 15 minutes and serve immediately as appetizers.

Makes 10–12 tartlets.

CHEESE CROQUETTES

Switzerland   *(Croquettes au Fromage)*

3 tbs	*(3 tbs)*	butter or margarine
5 tbs	*(5 tbs)*	flour
1¼ cups	*(310 mL)*	milk
		salt and pepper to taste
⅓ lb	*(150 g)*	Swiss cheese, coarsely grated or cubed
2	*(2)*	egg yolks, lightly beaten
1	*(1)*	egg
		flour for dredging
		dry breadcrumbs for dredging
		oil for deep frying

Melt butter in a saucepan over low heat, add 4 tbs flour, stir until well blended, then add 1 cup (250 mL) milk, a little at a time, stirring continuously until a smooth sauce is obtained. Cook over low heat for 5 minutes. Season with salt and pepper and remove from heat, then add cheese and stir until it has melted. Add egg yolks and mix well. Spread mixture in a well greased shallow pan, and chill for at least 2 hours. When ready to use, cut mixture into about 15 pieces and shape into patties or regular croquette shapes.

Beat egg with remaining flour and milk. Dredge each patty first with flour, then dip it into the egg mixture and drain off excess liquid, then dip into bread crumbs and chill for about 20 minutes. Heat the oil to 350° F (175° C) then deep-fry until golden in color, turning them over once during cooking. Serve immediately with tomato sauce, either home made (see page 350) or canned.

Serves 5–6 as an appetizer.

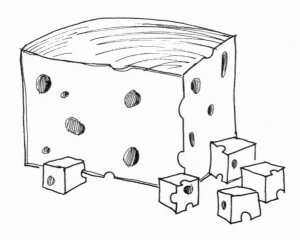

BROWN FLOUR SOUP

Switzerland   *(Basler Mehlsuppe)*

Flour soup certainly does not sound either exciting or appetizing. But just try it. Or you may have already done so if you have visited Basel during early spring, where it is served at the start of Lent. And it is eaten in many farm kitchens as the most common breakfast food.

5 tbs	(*5 tbs*)	butter or margarine
4 tbs	(*4 tbs*)	flour
4 cups	(*1 L*)	boiling water
1	(*1*)	small onion
4	(*4*)	cloves
1	(*1*)	small bay leaf
		salt to taste

Brown 4 tbs butter lightly in a heavy saucepan, add flour and stir to a smooth paste. Keep cooking over medium heat, stirring very often to prevent scorching, until mixture has the light brown color of milk chocolate. Add the hot water, first a small amount, while stirring vigorously to make a smooth mixture, then in bigger amounts. Stick the cloves into the onion and add together with the bay leaf, then salt to taste and simmer over very low heat about 45 minutes.

Before serving, remove onion and bay leaf and add the remaining butter. Serve plain, or add 1 ts tomato paste or 1–2 tbs grated Swiss cheese. For 4–5.

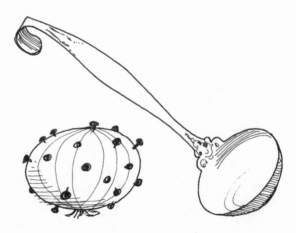

20

Switzerland　　　　CABBAGE AND RICE SOUP　　　(*Kabissuppe*)

A simple but good and satisfying soup.

4 cups	(*1 L*)	finely shredded cabbage (about 1 small head)
1	(*1*)	medium size onion, thinly sliced
2 tbs	(*2 tbs*)	butter or margarine
4 cups	(*1 L*)	chicken or beef stock (may be made with bouillon cubes)
¼ cup	(*60 mL*)	rice
		salt and pepper to taste
		pinch of nutmeg
For serving:		Grated Swiss or Parmesan cheese to taste

Sauté onion in butter or margarine in a large saucepan for 5 minutes, add cabbage and cook over slow heat, stirring off and on, until cabbage has wilted, about 15 minutes. Add soup stock, rice and seasonings, bring to a boil, then turn down heat to very low and cook under cover until rice is tender, 12–15 minutes (if you use converted rice, the cooking time is somewhat longer). Serve with grated cheese. Serves 4–5.

VEAL CUTLETS WITH SOUR CREAM
Switzerland　　　　　　　(*Veau Emincé or Gschnetzlets*)

Veal in Switzerland, as well as in most European countries, is of high quality and requires very little cooking to be tender and delicious. And here is a way to bring out the best in veal.

1½ lb	(*¾ kg*)	veal cutlet
1 tbs	(*1 tbs*)	butter
1 tbs	(*1 tbs*)	salad oil
1 cup	(*250 mL*)	dry white wine
1 cup	(*250 mL*)	sour cream
1	(*1*)	medium size onion, finely chopped (¾ cup or 180 mL)
2 ts	(*2 ts*)	flour
		salt and pepper to taste

Cut the meat against the grain into fine slivers, about ¼″ x 1″ (6 x 25 mm). Sauté onions in the butter and oil over low heat until transparent and golden. Turn up heat, add the veal and cook over high heat until the meat changes color, then add the wine and cook for a few minutes. Mix sour cream with flour and add, mix well and heat just to a boil, then serve immediately.

Serves 5–6.

LUGANO POT ROAST

Switzerland   (*Stufato alla Luganese*)

The Italian influence in this recipe makes itself known not only in its "Swiss" name but in the wine that goes into it. However, a dry sherry may be substituted.

4–5 lbs	(2–2½ kg)	boneless top or bottom round or chuck roast
3	(3)	slices bacon, chopped
1	(1)	large onion, chopped (1 cup or 250 mL)
		salt and pepper to taste
2	(2)	bay leaves
½ cup	(125 mL)	water
1 cup	(250 mL)	dry Marsala (or sherry)
2 tbs	(2 tbs)	flour, mixed with ¼ cup (60 mL) water

Cook bacon in a large skillet over low heat until crisp, then add onion and sauté for five minutes. Remove onion and bacon with a slotted spoon and set aside, but let bacon fat remain in skillet. Turn up heat and brown the meat on all sides, then sprinkle with salt and pepper. Put meat in a roasting pan. Add water to the skillet and scrape bottom to remove loose particles and add to roasting pan together with onion, bacon and bay leaves. Roast in a very slow oven, 275° F (135° C) for 3–4 hours, or until meat is tender. Add wine gradually, about ¼ cup (60 mL) at a time starting after one hour of roasting. Remove meat when done and keep it warm.

Skim fat off the top of pan juice and strain into a saucepan. Add flour and water mix and bring to a boil, turn down heat and cook gravy five minutes. Slice meat and put on a platter, then pour some gravy over the slices and serve additional gravy from a gravyboat.   Serves 6–10.

FONDUE BOURGUIGNONNE
Switzerland

Serving fondue is a nice intimate way of entertaining that came into the U.S. cooking scene in a big way a couple of years ago. And why not let the guests do some of the work?

3 lbs	(1½ kg)	fillet of beef, lean sirloin or other tender cut of beef

For cooking:

3 cups	(750 mL)	cooking oil *or* half oil and half clarified butter (see ghee, page 258)

Cut the meat into about ¾″ (18 mm) cubes and place it in a mound on a serving platter. Heat the oil until bubbling, then set it on a heating unit (use a fondue pot or chafing dish or if these are not available, an electric frying pan) and add a small piece of bread to prevent splattering. Let each guest spear some meat on a fondue fork then dip-cook it to his liking (rare, medium rare or well done) in the hot oil, then transfer immediately to his plate to eat with a dinner fork.

Let each guest choose the sauce or sauces he prefers to eat with the meat. The following sauces may be served. (There should be several, but it is not necessary to have all of them.

Bearnaise or Hollandaise sauce (below), Cumberland (page 142), sour cream with horseradish, mustard (hot or mild), or tomato ketchup—plain or mixed half and half with mayonnaise.
Serves 6.

HOLLANDAISE SAUCE
Switzerland

Hollandaise Sauce is a pretty common one in the U.S. and many have their own favorite recipies. But if not, here is one.

½ cup	(125 mL)	butter
2	(2)	egg yolks
2 tbs	(2 tbs)	hot water
2 tbs	(2 tbs)	lemon juice
¼ ts	(¼ ts)	salt
		pinch of cayenne

Melt butter over low heat until it bubbles, but do not let it brown. Beat egg yolks thoroughly in a small bowl, then slowly pour melted butter into bowl beating constantly. Add hot water, still stirring. Pour from bowl into a double boiler to keep hot, add lemon juice and seasonings to the sauce.
Serve warm to 4–6.

BEARNAISE SAUCE
Switzerland

1 cup	(250 mL)	butter (½ lb or ¼ kg)
2 tbs	(2 tbs)	wine vinegar or tarragon vinegar
3 tbs	(3 tbs)	water
2 tbs	(2 tbs)	finely chopped onions
5	(5)	whole peppercorns, crushed
1 tbs	(1 tbs)	finely chopped fresh tarragon or
		1 ts dried
3	(3)	egg yolks
		salt and cayenne pepper to taste

Melt butter in a saucepan, but do not let it get brown. In another small saucepan mix together vinegar, water, onion, peppercorns and tarragon and cook until liquid has been reduced to about ⅓. Then cool slightly. Strain mixture and put in a double boiler. Add egg yolks and beat vigorously over hot water until the mixture starts to thicken. Add the melted butter carefully, a little at a time, continuously beating until sauce is thick and foamy. Season to taste with salt and cayenne and serve immediately.

If sauce has to be reheated, do so in a double boiler or over hot water, as it would curdle if it were to boil.

Serves 4–6.

SOUR CREAM AND HORSERADISH SAUCE
Switzerland

1 cup	(250 mL)	sour cream
1-1½ tbs	(1-1½ tbs)	prepared horseradish
		(or grated fresh, if available)
		salt to taste

Mix all ingredients together and let stand for 30 minutes before using.

CHEESE FONDUE

Switzerland *(Fondue de Fromage)*

In this recipe it is necessary to follow directions as to kind of cheese, dry wine etc. as otherwise the result may be a curdled hunk of inedible stuff. I have a bad memory of this happening—guests sitting waiting in the dining-room anticipating the dunking and me frantically calling my Swiss neighbor asking what to do about the mess in the pot—like a big hunk of chewing gum. Nothing, she said, just throw it out. . . . Catastrophe!

1 lb	(½ kg)	Swiss cheese (preferably imported such as Switzerland Swiss, (Emmenthaler) or half each of Emmenthaler and Gruyere)
3 tbs	(3 tbs)	flour
1	(1)	clove garlic
1½ cups	(375 mL)	dry white wine (the Swiss Neuchatel is best, but a dry Rhine or Chablis type will do also)
1 tbs	(1 tbs)	fresh lemon juice
3 tbs	(3 tbs)	Kirsch or brandy salt, pepper and nutmeg to taste
For serving:		1-2 loaves French or Italian bread, cut into chunks with some crust on each one

Cut cheese into small cubes or shred it, then mix with flour. Cut the garlic clove in half, then rub the cooking pot with it. Pour wine into pot and put over medium heat until air bubbles rise to surface, then add lemon juice and mix. Add cheese by the handful, stirring constantly with a wooden spoon after each addition, and continue cooking until the cheese has melted and starts to bubble. Add seasonings (very sparingly) and Kirsch or brandy and mix well.

Transfer contents of cooking pot into a fondue pot or chafing dish. Keep contents bubbling hot over low heat and start the guests dunking by spearing bread chunks onto long fon-due forks and swirling around. Each one should take his turn, with the constant swirling keeping the fondue at the right consistency. Towards the end it has a tendency to get somewhat thick which can be fixed by adding a couple more tablespoons of wine and mixing well. The bottom crust that will form eventually is considered a delicacy by the Swiss. When it is evident, the heat should be turned off, and the crust scraped out with a spoon.

Most Swiss drink hot tea with fondue, as cold drinks, even wine, are considered inappropriate for digestion when eating it.

Serves 4–5.

Switzerland   POTATO CAKE   *(Rösti)*

The secret of getting this recipe right is to be sure you get a good crust on the bottom to hold it together, before you either turn over the potatoes or serve them. This is the most common way of serving potatoes in Switzerland.

5	(5)	medium size potatoes (about 1½ lbs or ¾ kg)
3 tbs	(3 *tbs*)	butter or margarine
		salt and pepper to taste

Boil potatoes in their jackets until done, then cool and peel them. Shred coarsely, or cut them into fine julienne strips. Heat butter in a skillet, then add potatoes gradually. Add salt and pepper to taste and mix in with potatoes, then pat down with a spatula and cook over medium heat until potatoes are tender and a golden crust has formed on the bottom.

You may now serve the potatoes as they are, turning each portion to put golden crust up, or ease them onto a large platter or plate which has been inverted on top of the skillet and then ease them back into the skillet and fry until golden brown on the other side also. Serve hot to 4–5.

VARIATIONS:

Add 2 slices of bacon, fried and crumbled, and 1 small onion, finely chopped (½ cup or 125 mL) sautéed a few minutes in the bacon fat, to the raw potatoes then proceed as above. Or add ½ cup (125 mL) grated Swiss cheese to the raw potatoes, then proceed as in the main recipe.

POTATOES IN CHEESE CUSTARD

Switzerland   *(Käsekartoffeln)*

5	(5)	medium size potatoes
¼ cup	(60 *mL*)	butter or margarine (4 tbs)
		salt to taste
1 cup	(250 *mL*)	milk
2	(2)	eggs, slightly beaten
⅓ cup	(80 *mL*)	grated Swiss cheese

Peel potatoes then cut into thin slices, about ⅛″ (3 mm) thick. Heat butter in a large skillet, add potatoes and stir to get them all covered with butter, then sprinkle with salt. Cover skillet and cook over lowest possible heat until potatoes are tender, stirring off and on by lifting potatoes off bottom to prevent them from sticking to it.

Mix together milk, eggs and cheese and pour mixture over potatoes. Cook another 10–15 minutes or until a golden crust has formed on the bottom. Turn upside down (golden crust up, that is) on a serving platter and serve to 4–5.

SAUTÉED CHEESE PATTIES

Switzerland   *(Käseklösschen)*

These delectable cheese patties should be served very quickly after they are made so that the insides still consists of melted cheese. They can be served with just a vegetable or a salad, but I feel they are the perfect accompaniment to baked ham.

4	*(4)*	egg yolks
¾ cup	*(180 mL)*	sour cream
2 cups	*(500 mL)*	grated Swiss cheese (about ½ lb or ¼ kg)
3 tbs	*(3 tbs)*	flour
½ ts	*(½ ts)*	dry mustard
		salt and pepper to taste
3 tbs	*(3 tbs)*	butter or margarine

Beat egg yolks slightly, then add sour cream and cheese and mix well. Sift together flour and seasonings and add to cheese mixture and beat until well mixed.

Melt butter in a skillet and drop cheese mixture by tablespoonfuls and sauté over medium heat until golden brown on bottom, then turn over and sauté on other side.

Serve immediately to 4–6.

ONION OMELET

Switzerland   *(Frittata di Cipolle)*

3	*(3)*	large onions, finely chopped (about 3 cups or 750 mL)
6 tbs	*(6 tbs)*	butter or margarine
1 tbs	*(1 tbs)*	olive oil
		salt and pepper to taste
6	*(6)*	eggs
¼ cup	*(60 mL)*	water

Sauté onions in butter and oil over low heat in a skillet or large omelet pan until onions are transparent. Season with salt and pepper. Mix together eggs and water and beat slightly, only until well mixed. Pour eggs over onions, cover and cook over low heat until omelet is set, and golden on top. If desired, turn it over and cook for a few minutes to make it golden brown on both sides.

Serves 4–5.

GREEN BEAN SALAD

Switzerland   (*Grüne Bohnensalat*)

Bean salad is popular in Switzerland and this mustardy type of dressing is typical.

| 1 lb | (½ kg) | green beans |
| | | salt to taste |

Dressing:

⅓ cup	(80 mL)	olive oil (or other salad oil, if prefered)
2 tbs	(2 tbs)	vinegar
1 ts	(1 ts)	prepared mustard
1	(1)	small onion, finely chopped
1 tbs	(1 tbs)	finely chopped parsley
1 tbs	(1 tbs)	chopped chives (optional)
		salt and pepper to taste

Cook beans in salted water until tender but still crisp, then drain. Make dressing by mixing all ingredients well, then pour over beans while still hot and toss to cover them all with dressing. Let stand at room temperature for at least 1 hour, but preferably two, then serve without chilling.   Makes 4–5 servings.

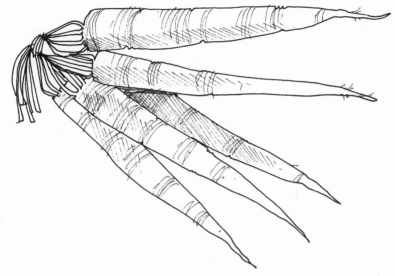

CARROT CAKE

Switzerland   *(Aaergauer Rübli Torte)*

A carrot cake out of this world, in which grated almonds just about take the place of flour. It is moist and has very good keeping quality.

1½ cups (8 oz)	375 mL (250 g)	unblanched almonds, grated
½ lb	(250 g)	raw carrots, finely grated
1 tbs	(1 tbs)	grated lemon rind
2 ts	(2 ts)	lemon juice
5	(5)	eggs, separated
1 cup	(250 mL)	sugar
2 tbs	(2 tbs)	flour
1 tbs	(1 tbs)	corn starch
¼ ts	(¼ ts)	salt
2 tbs	(2 tbs)	Kirsch, cognac or rum

Add lemon rind and juice to grated carrots and mix. Beat egg yolks with the sugar until very light and fluffy. Mix almonds with flour and corn starch, then fold into egg mixture together with grated carrots. Beat the egg whites with the salt until very stiff, carefully fold into the carrot-egg yolk mixture, then add the liquor.

Pour mixture gently into a 9″ (220 mm) greased and floured spring pan and bake in a 375° F (190° C) oven for 30–40 minutes. Test the cake for done-ness when the dough begins to shrink away from the walls of the cake pan.

This cake may be served with whipped cream, sprinkled with confectioners' sugar, or frosted when cool.

ENGADINER NUT PIE

Switzerland   *(Engadiner Torte)*

A wonderful torte or pie which is almost indecently rich, but crunchy and delicious.

Shell: (Basic short dough)

3 cups	(750 mL)	flour
1 cup	(250 mL)	sugar
1 cup	(250 mL)	butter
1	(1)	egg (or 2 egg yolks)
½ ts	(½ ts)	grated lemon rind
2 ts	(2 ts)	vanilla extract

For brushing: 1 egg yolk mixed
                               with 1 tbs milk

Sift flour twice then combine with sugar in a large bowl. Cut in butter with a pastry blender until mixture resembles coarse meal. Add egg (or egg yolks) and lemon rind and work together thoroughly, then transfer dough to a baking board. Cool your hands by running them under cold water, drying them quickly and immediately work the dough to a smooth ball. If the dough should be too crumbly add up to one tbs water.

Wrap dough in plastic wrap and chill at least 1 hour. (At this stage it may be kept even for several days). Take out of refrigerator and leave at room temperature for at least 20 minutes before rolling out. Line a 9″ (220 mm) pie pan with about half the dough and fill with the following:

Filling:

1 cup	(250 mL)	sugar
¾ cup	(180 mL)	heavy cream or evaporated milk
9 oz	(250 g)	coarsely chopped nuts (any kind, or mixture of different kinds)
2 tbs	(2 tbs)	honey

In a saucepan melt the sugar over low heat until it liquefies and becomes golden brown in color. Add the nuts, then stir in cream and honey.

Spread the filling over the dough in pie pan, then cover with a top crust made from remaining dough and pinch together top and bottom crust to seal the edges. Brush with egg yolk mixture and bake in a 350° F (175° C) oven about 45 minutes or until golden brown on top. Serve either warm or cold.

Switzerland COFFEE CREAM GATEAU (*Gâteau de Mocha*)

An elegant and most delectable cake.

½ cup	(*125 mL*)	hazelnuts (filberts)
½ cup	(*125 mL*)	almonds, blanched
1¼ cup	(*310 mL*)	confectioners' sugar
3	(3)	egg whites

Put hazelnuts on a baking sheet in a hot oven, 400° F (200° C), for a few minutes. Remove them and rub them in a towel until all the skins have been removed. If unblanched almonds are used, blanch them by putting them in boiling water for a minute or so, then slip off skins. Toast almonds lightly for a few minutes in the oven at 350° F (175° C). Grind almonds and hazelnuts and mix together. Beat egg whites until very stiff, add half the sugar and continue beating for a few minutes, then fold in remaining sugar and ground nuts.

Bake in two greased and floured 8″ (200 mm) layer cake pans, preferably with removable bottoms, otherwise cut wax paper to fit bottoms. Grease pans before adding wax paper, then grease and flour this. Bake in a 375° F (190° C) oven 20–25 minutes, or until cakes test as done. Remove cakes from pans while still hot and leave them to cool on a rack.

Filling and Frosting:

1 cup	(*250 mL*)	confectioners' sugar
3	(3)	egg yolks
4 tbs	(*4 tbs*)	strong black coffee (brewed or instant)
½ cup	(*125 mL*)	butter
		shaved dark chocolate (optional)

Put egg yolks, sugar and coffee in a bowl and place it over a pot with boiling water and beat while water is steaming, until mixture is thick. Remove from heat and let it cool, stirring from time to time. Cream butter until fluffy, then add egg mixture by the spoonful while beating vigorously. Put filling mixture between the layers and on top and sides of cake, using a tubular cake decorator, if desired. Or just swirl it on in a nice pattern, either leaving it plain, or sprinkling some shaved dark chocolate for decoration. 6–8 servings.

VARIATION:

Instead of the above cream mixture, whipped cream may be used as follows:

1 cup	(*250 mL*)	heavy cream
2 tbs	(*2 tbs*)	confectioners' sugar
1 tbs	(*1 tbs*)	very strong coffee

Whip cream until stiff, then add sugar and coffee and mix well.

Switzerland   KIRSCHTORTE

The most famous—and perhaps the most delectable—of all the delectable cakes of Switzerland. It entails some extra work but the ohs and ahs you get from your guests make it more than worth-while.

Meringue layers:

3	(3)	egg whites, at room temperature
⅛ ts	(⅛ ts)	cream of tartar
⅓ cup	(80 mL)	verifine sugar
1 cup	(250 mL)	blanched, finely ground almonds
		(weighing about 2 oz or 60 g)
2 tbs	(2 tbs)	flour

Beat egg whites with cream of tartar until very stiff, then add sugar, 1 tbs at a time, and keep beating until smooth. Mix almonds with flour and fold in. Line a cookie sheet with aluminum foil and butter the foil, then draw two 8″ (200 mm) circles on the foil and distribute egg white mixture on these. (They will be rather thin.). Bake in a 425° F (220° C) oven 8–10 minutes, or until the tops are golden brown. Remove from oven and let cool on sheet for a couple of minutes, then turn out upside down and carefully peel off the foil. Cool layers on a rack.

Sponge layer:

2	(2)	eggs
½ cup	(125 mL)	sugar
⅔ cup	(160 mL)	flour

Beat eggs until very light and fluffy. Beat in sugar, 1 tbs at a time and continue beating until smooth and thick. Carefully fold in flour. Bake in a greased and floured 8″ (200 mm) cake pan for 20 minutes in a 350° F (175° C) oven. Let cake cool in pan for 5 minutes, then remove from pan and cool on a rack.

Filling & Frosting:

1 cup	(250 mL)	butter
2½ cups	(625 mL)	confectioners' sugar
1	(1)	egg
1	(1)	egg yolk
3 tbs	(3 tbs)	Kirsch
1 ts	(1 ts)	vanilla flavoring
		red food coloring (optional)

(Continued on next page)

(Kirschtorte, cont.)

Cream butter until light and fluffy. Sift confectioners' sugar and gradually beat it in, alternately with egg, egg-yolk and Kirsch. If a pink frosting is desired, add a couple of drops of red food coloring.

Assembly:

| ⅓ cup | (80 mL) | **Kirsch** |
| ⅓ cup | (80 mL) | **chopped toasted unblanched almonds** |

Spread a thick layer of filling on one of the almond meringue layers. Sprinkle Kirsch on both bottom and top of sponge layer, then put it on top of filling over meringue layer. Add another thick layer of filling and put the second meringue layer on top. Use rest of filling to frost cake on sides and on top, using a cake decorator set to make rosettes etc. if desired.

Using the fingers, add the chopped almonds on the sides (and also in a small circle in the center of top, if desired). Leave cake in cool place for at least 8 hours, but preferably for 24, as it tastes better if you give the flavors a chance to really sink in.

Switzerland   **EGG BRAID**   (*Zopf*)

A rich and satisfying coffee cake or breakfast cake that is not too sweet. But make sure you knead the dough long enough, this gives the cake its best texture.

About 6 cups	(*1½ L*)	flour
½ cup	(*125 mL*)	sugar
2	(*2*)	packages dry yeast
2	(*2*)	eggs
1 cup	(*250 mL*)	milk
2 ts	(*2 ts*)	salt
½ cup	(*125 mL*)	butter or margarine

For brushing: 1 egg yolk mixed with 1 tbs water

In a large bowl thoroughly mix 2 cups (500 mL) flour, sugar, salt and yeast. Melt butter in a sauce pan, add milk and heat until luke-warm. Gradually add to dry ingredients and beat for 2 minutes at medium speed of electric mixer, or longer if by hand with a wooden spoon. Add eggs and enough flour to make a thick batter, then beat at high speed for 2 minutes. Stir in enough additional flour to make a soft dough.

Turn out onto lightly floured baking board, and knead until smooth and elastic, at least 10 minutes. Place in a greased bowl, turning once to get top greased. Cover bowl and let dough rise in a warm place until double in bulk, about 1–1½ hours.

Punch down dough, and divide in half. Make three long rolls out of each half, then shape these into braids. Place on a greased baking sheet and let rise again in a warm place for 1 hour. Brush with egg yolk mixed with water and bake in a 350° F (175° C) oven about 25–30 minutes. Makes 2 braids.

TRADITIONAL HONEY COOKIES FROM BASEL
Switzerland (*Leckerli*)

These cookies are chewy. Do not worry if they turn out to be rather hard to bite into. They should rest for several weeks in a container before they are eaten.

½ cup	(*125 mL*)	honey
½ cup	(*125 mL*)	sugar
¼ cup	(*60 mL*)	candied orange or lemon peel
1 ts	(*1 ts*)	grated lemon rind
2¼ cups	(*560 mL*)	flour
1 ts	(*1 ts*)	baking soda
½ ts	(*½ ts*)	ground cloves
1 ts	(*1 ts*)	cinnamon
1 cup	(*250 mL*)	blanched and slivered almonds

Cook honey and sugar in a saucepan over low heat while stirring, until mixture comes to a boil. Remove from heat and add candied peel and grated lemon rind. Mix flour with baking soda and spices and add to honey mixture, then add almonds, mix well and work together into a ball. (The dough will be quite stiff, but will soften after it has mellowed).

Cover dough and let it stand to mellow at room temperature for at least 2 days.

Roll out mellowed dough ⅓–½″ (8–12 mm) thick, then cut into bars 1 x 2″ (25 x 50 mm). Place them on a greased and floured baking sheet. Bake in a 325° F (165° C) oven about 20 minutes, or until lightly brown in color.

Glaze:

½ cup	(*125 mL*)	sugar
¼ cup	(*60 mL*)	water

Cook sugar and water in a small saucepan until it spins a thread (230° F or 110° C). Brush each cookie with this hot syrup. When completely cool, store cookies in an air-tight container. They will keep for many months and preferably should not be eaten until after they have "ripened" in flavor for a couple of weeks, at least. Makes about 3 dozen cookies.

JAM-FILLED COOKIES

Switzerland (*Spitzbuben*)

The Swiss name for these cookies means in translation "urchins". I am not sure why, but I can easily visualize little urchins sneaking into a jar of them, and filling up their mouths and their pockets.

1 cup	(*250 mL*)	butter or margarine
³⁄₄ cup	(*180 mL*)	sugar
2	(*2*)	eggs
1 cup	(*250 mL*)	blanched almonds, ground (about 4 oz or 120 g)
3-¹⁄₂ cups	(*875 mL*)	flour
For filling:		jam or jelly (about 1 cup or 250 mL)

Beat butter or margarine with sugar until light and fluffy, add eggs and continue beating until smooth. Add ground almonds and flour, and mix well until a soft dough has been obtained. Wrap in plastic and let rest in refrigerator for at least one hour.

Roll out dough on a floured baking board to about ¹⁄₈″ (3 mm) thickness and cut with a 1-¹⁄₂–2″ (37–50 mm) cookie cutter. Bake on a greased baking sheet in a 375° F (190° C) oven about 8 minutes or until golden in color. While still warm spread jelly or jam on the bottom of the cookie then another cookie on top of this, also bottom down. Let cool on wire rack.

Makes about 5 dozen.

CHOCOLATE FONDUE

Switzerland   *(Fondue au Chocolat)*

Chocolate fondue is one of those concoctions that originated in the U.S., then came to Switzerland and became popular there too. The Swiss chocolate bar Toblerone makes a very good fondue, so I think this belongs with other Swiss foods.

½ lb	(¼ kg)	sweet or semi-sweet chocolate (or chocolate bars with crushed nuts etc. The Swiss chocolate bar Toblerone which contains crushed almonds and also honey is excellent)
½ cup	(125 mL)	cream (light or heavy)
2 tbs	(2 tbs)	Kirsch, brandy or liqueur (mint, Cointreau etc.) (optional) if liquor is not wanted, use the same amount of strong coffee for flavoring instead.
For dipping:		Fresh fruits such as strawberries, bananas, pineapple, apples, pears, oranges—all cut into bite size pieces. Tiny cream-puffs (use recipe on page 182 but use teaspoonfuls of dough), sponge cake or lady-fingers cut into bite size pieces.

Break chocolate into pieces, then combine all ingredients in a sauce pan, fondue pot or chafing dish and melt over very low heat while stirring until chocolate has melted and mixture is smooth. Keep mixture melted by keeping in the chafing dish or such over low heat.

Serve by placing fondue pot in the middle of the table and letting each person help himself to fruits or cakes, dipping into the pot with long forks.

Turkey

GEOGRAPHICALLY, Turkey is almost all in Asia, but on the western shores of the Bosporous is the very small European part of the country that includes the very important city of Istanbul. Although the capital is now Ankara, right in the middle of Turkey, Istanbul was the capital for centuries, and is still the gateway between Asia and Europe. Only a few years ago a bridge was built there to connect the two continents. Istanbul has a very European flair—except when you watch the skyline, where instead of church steeples you see the domes and minarets of numerous beautiful mosques.

Because of geography the food is heavily influenced both by the exotic East and by the Balkan countries. And what you eat often seems to be a mixture of the best of everything from these two worlds.

Fish is a big item, and a favorite among the shellfish is mussels, which are often fried and sold on little wooden skewers by street vendors. And as in most of the Middle East, lamb is the number one among meats, most likely for the reason that the country is mountainous and can support lots of sheep, and among Moslems, pork is not eaten and can therefore not compete. A Middle East favorite is the marinated, broiled chunks of lamb which we know as shish-kebab. There is something in Turkey called *Döner Kebab*, however, that tops everything else. The meat from a leg of lamb is cut in slices and then wrapped around a tall vertical, rotating spit. As the meat is ready, it is cut off from the surface, and for some reason it is more tender and more tasty than in any other way. Unfortunately, this way of broiling cannot be duplicated in our homes.

525

Rice is also important, and there are *pilafs* of great variety, either plain, or using fish or meat.

Turkish desserts are very sweet, often made with nuts and drenched in honey or sweet syrups and with a little rose-water added for fragrance. Their favorite pastry is *baklava*, as it is in Greece and also other Middle East countries.

STUFFED MUSSELS	*Media Dolma*
GREEN PEPPERS WITH YOGURT	*Biber Yogurtly*
RED BEAN APPETIZER	*Barbunya Fasulye Zeytinyagli*
BEET SALAD	*Pancar Salatasi*
CHICKEN SOUP WITH YOGURT	*Tavuk Tshorbasi Yogurtly*
WEDDING SOUP	*Dügün Tshorbasi*
FISH BALLS	*Balik Köftesi*
SHISH KEBABS	
CIRCASSIAN CHICKEN	*Tsherkes Tavugu*
CHICKEN LIVER PILAF	*Isch Pilav*
YOGURT CAKE	*Yogurt Tatlisi*
YOGURT DRINK	*Ayran*

STUFFED MUSSELS

Turkey (***Media Dolma***)

Mussels are very popular in Turkey, as in other Mediterranean countries. As there is such an abundance of them around our sea shores, I think that eventually they will come into their own here also, as they are very good. If in doubt, try this appetizer which should prove their excellence.

4 doz	(*4 doz*)	mussels
1½ cup	(*375 mL*)	mussel liquid
2	(*2*)	medium onions, finely chopped (1½ cups or 375 mL)
4 tbs	(*4 tbs*)	olive oil
½ cup	(*125 mL*)	rice
2 tbs	(*2 tbs*)	currants
2 tbs	(*2 tbs*)	pine nuts (pignoli)
		salt and pepper to taste
¼ ts	(*¼ ts*)	ground allspice
¼ ts	(*¼ ts*)	ground cinnamon
For serving:		lemon wedges

(*Continued on next page*)

(Stuffed Mussels, cont.)

Clean mussels well by scrubbing and de-bearding them. Place them in the bottom of a large kettle, add about ½″ (12 mm) of water. Bring to a boil and steam until mussels open, then remove meat from shells. Strain liquid in kettle through several layers of cheese cloth and measure 1½ cups (375 mL). Chop mussels coarsely.

Cook rice in 1 cup (250 mL) mussel liquid for 15 minutes. Sauté onions in olive oil until transparent, then combine with rice. Add mussels, pine nuts and spices and simmer together, adding the remaining liquid a little at a time until it is all absorbed. Either stuff mixture back into mussel shells, or, if preferred, use larger scallop shells, and chill thoroughly before serving. Serve with lemon wedges.

For 5–6 people.

GREEN PEPPERS WITH YOGURT

Turkey   *(Biber Yogurtly)*

Yogurt is almost a staff of life in southeastern Europe and many Asian countries. It is used in many dishes besides being eaten as is, and it also makes a refreshing drink.

2	(2)	medium size green peppers, coarsely chopped (about 1½ cups or 375 mL)
2 tbs	(2 tbs)	olive oil
½ cup	(125 mL)	plain yogurt salt and pepper to taste

Sauté peppers in olive oil until tender, season with salt and pepper, then mix with yogurt. Chill for at least 2 hours and serve as an appetizer, to 4–5.

RED BEAN APPETIZER

Turkey   *(Barbunya Fasulye Zeytinyagli)*

1 cup	*(250 mL)*	dried red beans or kidney beans (about ½ lb or ¼ kg)
		or
1 can	*(1 can)*	cooked kidney beans (1 lb or 500 g size)
1	*(1)*	medium size onion, finely chopped (¾ cup or 180 mL)
2	*(2)*	cloves garlic, finely minced
2 tbs	*(2 tbs)*	olive oil
2	*(2)*	medium size tomatoes, peeled and finely chopped
1	*(1)*	medium size carrot, finely chopped salt and pepper to taste
For sprinkling:		chopped parsley

If dried beans are used, soak them overnight and cook in lightly salted water to cover until beans are soft but not mushy (1½–2 hours). Sauté onion and garlic in oil until onion is transparent, then add tomatoes, carrot and seasonings and cook over low heat about five minutes. Add beans and about 1 cup (250 mL) bean stock. (If canned beans are used, add ½ cup (125 mL) water to liquid from can.) Cook all of it together for about 10 minutes.

Chill for several hours in the refrigerator and serve cold, sprinkled with chopped parsley, as an appetizer or as a side dish to 4–5.

BEET SALAD

Turkey   *(Pancar Salatasi)*

4	*(4)*	cooked medium size beets (about ½ of a 1 lb or 500 g can)
1 cup	*(250 mL)*	yogurt (plain)
1 tbs	*(1 tbs)*	olive oil
1	*(1)*	clove garlic, finely minced salt and pepper to taste
For sprinkling:		1 tbs finely chopped fresh parsley (optional)

Cut beets into thin slices and put in a bowl. Mix together yogurt, olive oil, garlic, salt and pepper. Pour over beets, then stir around to get dressing to cover all slices. Let stand in refrigerator for at least 2 hours. Sprinkle with parsley, just before serving, if desired.   Serves 4–5.

CHICKEN SOUP WITH YOGURT

Turkey   (*Tavuk Tshorbasi Yogurtly*)

This is one of the most popular soups in the Middle East. It is a chicken soup with a difference.

4 cups	(*1 L*)	chicken stock
⅓ cup	(*80 mL*)	rice
⅔ cups	(*160 mL*)	plain yogurt
1	(*1*)	egg
		salt and pepper to taste

For sprinkling: 2 tbs fresh parsley, chopped
                       1 ts finely chopped fresh mint
                       (optional)

Rinse rice, then cook in chicken stock until tender. Beat egg and yogurt together, then add soup, little by little, while continuously beating. Heat soup carefully again, but make sure it does not boil, as it may then curdle. Serve hot sprinkled with parsley and mint.   Serves 4–5.

WEDDING SOUP

Turkey   (*Dügün Tshorbasi*)

I really do not know whether this soup is eaten at weddings or not—but it is a nice soup, nevertheless.

½ lb	(¼ kg)	coarsely ground lean lamb
2 tbs	(2 tbs)	butter or margarine
2 tbs	(2 tbs)	flour
		salt and pepper to taste
5 cups	(1¼ L)	beef, lamb or chicken broth
		juice of one lemon
2	(2)	egg yolk

For sprinkling: 1 ts paprika

Brown lamb in butter, breaking up large pieces with a fork and cook until pink color has disappeared. Sprinkle with flour and mix well. Bring broth to a boil, add meat and simmer for 1 hour. Mix lemon juice with egg yolk in a bowl and beat until well blended. Add a small amount of soup to bowl and mix well, then about ½ cup (125 mL). Take soup off heat and pour contents of bowl into soup and mix well. Then heat carefully but do not let it come to a boil, as the soup would then curdle. Serve in soup bowls and sprinkle with paprika.   Serves 4–6.

VARIATION:

Add one whole egg to meat mixture, then add pepper and salt and work together. Shape into tiny meatballs, the size of a filbert nut, add to broth, then proceed as above.

Turkey   FISH BALLS   (*Balik Köftesi*)

1 lb	(½ kg)	fish fillets (cod, haddock or flounder)
½ cup	(125 mL)	dry bread crumbs
1	(1)	small onion, finely chopped
1 tbs	(1 tbs)	finely chopped parsley
		salt and pepper to taste
¼ ts	(¼ ts)	cumin, crushed
1	(1)	egg, slightly beaten
		corn starch for dredging
		oil for deep-frying

Grind fish through the smallest blade in a food-grinder, then mix well with crumbs, onion, parsley, seasonings and egg and shape into ¾" (18 mm) size balls. Roll these in corn starch and fry in 375° F (190° C) until golden. Drain on paper towels and serve hot, either as a main course or as appetizers.

Serves four.

SHISH KEBABS
Turkey

Everyone who has visited Middle East countries must remember the delicious cooking aromas from various types of grills for kebabs of different kinds. The meat is marinated, and becomes so tender and delicious that it melts in your mouth.

2 lbs	(*1 kg*)	boneless lean lamb (preferrably from the leg, cut into 1″ or 25 mm cubes)
8	(*8*)	very small onions, or 3 medium size ones
1	(*1*)	large green pepper, cut into squares
2	(*2*)	medium size firm tomatoes, cut into 8 pieces each
8	(*8*)	mushroom caps

Marinade:

1	(*1*)	small onion, finely chopped (½ cup or 125 mL)
¾ cup	(*180 mL*)	lemon juice (or white wine, or a mixture of both)
¼ cup	(*60 mL*)	olive oil
2 ts	(*2 ts*)	dried mint
		salt and pepper to taste

Mix together all ingredients for the marinade in a bowl, then add meat, turning to cover all pieces. Cover bowl and chill for at least 6 hours, or overnight in refrigerator. Turn meat pieces a couple of times during marinating time.

Thread the meat on greased skewers alternately with the vegetables and grill the meat over hot charcoal, or under the oven broiler, for about 5 minutes on each side, turning and basting three times with the marinade while the kebabs are being cooked. Serve immediately by pushing the contents of the skewer directly on to the plates.

For 4–6 people.

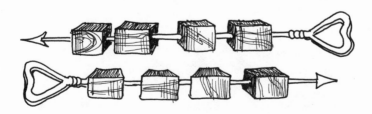

CIRCASSIAN CHICKEN
Turkey   *(Tsherkes Tavugu)*

You may have heard about Circassian chicken with a walnut sauce. It is a most unusual way of preparing the bird. If you want to fix chicken in a truly different manner, try it. It really is a wonderful dish.

1	(1)	frying or stewing chicken, 3½–4 lbs (1¾–2 kg)
1	(1)	medium size onion
1	(1)	carrot, scraped
		handful of celery leaves
		a few sprigs of parsley
1	(1)	bay leaf
10	(10)	whole peppercorns
		salt to taste
6 cups	(1½ L)	water

Cut chicken into serving pieces. Put into a large kettle together with remaining ingredients, bring to a boil, skim off surface, turn down heat and simmer chicken until tender, 45 minutes to 1½ hour, depending upon the size of chicken, and if it is a stewing chicken or a fryer. When ready, remove meat from bones and cut into fine slices, arrange on a platter and keep warm while the sauce is made.

Walnut Sauce:

2	(2)	slices white bread, crusts removed, and cubed
1½ cup	(375 mL)	shelled walnuts
1	(1)	clove garlic
1 cup	(250 mL)	chicken stock (or slightly more)
1 ts	(1 ts)	paprika

Put all ingredients in a blender and mix at high speed until a thick sauce is obtained. If the sauce should turn out too thick, add a little more chicken stock. Pour over sliced chicken and serve with rice or noodles.   Four to 6 portions.

CHICKEN LIVER PILAF

Turkey *(Isch Pilav)*

½ lb	(¼ kg)	chicken livers
4 tbs	(4 tbs)	butter or margarine
¾ cup	(180 mL)	chopped scallions
1 cup	(250 mL)	rice
2 tbs	(2 tbs)	raisins
2 tbs	(2 tbs)	pine nuts (*pignoli*)
2 cups	(500 mL)	chicken broth (may be made from bouillon cubes)
		salt and pepper to taste
2 tbs	(2 tbs)	chopped fresh dill (or, if unavailable, chopped parsley)

Cut chicken livers in half then brown slightly in a large skillet in 2 tbs butter or margarine, season with salt and pepper, then set aside. Sauté scallions for five minutes, but do not let them get brown, then remove. Add remaining butter and add rice while stirring to get butter evenly distributed, then add raisins and nuts. Heat chicken broth and add, about ½ cup (125 mL) at a time, adding more as rice absorbs it. When rice is tender, about 15 minutes cooking, depending on rice, carefully fold in chicken livers, scallions and fresh dill or parsley and cook over very low heat for an additional 10 minutes to get mixture hot. Serve by itself, or as an accompaniment to chicken or meat.

Serves 4–5.

YOGURT CAKE

Turkey   (*Yogurt Tatlisi*)

¾ cup	(*180 mL*)	butter (1½ stick)
⅔ cup	(*160 mL*)	sugar
⅔ cup	(*160 mL*)	yogurt
3	(*3*)	eggs, separated
2 cups	(*500 mL*)	flour
1 ts	(*1 ts*)	baking powder
For topping:		
2 tbs	(*2 tbs*)	melted butter
		confectioners' sugar

Cream butter and sugar until light and fluffy, then add yogurt and blend well. Beat egg yolks until light and lemon colored, then blend into batter. Sift together flour and baking powder and beat egg whites until stiff, then add flour and egg whites alternately to batter, folding in lightly with a wooden spoon. Bake in 8″ (200 mm) square or round baking pan in a 350° F (175° F) oven for 45 minutes to 1 hour, or until done. As soon as it is removed from oven, brush with melted butter and when cool, dust with confectioners' sugar.

VARIATION:

Make a syrup by boiling ½ cup (125 mL) sugar with 1 cup (250 mL) water until sugar has dissolved. Add juice of 1 lemon and mix well. As soon as the cake has been taken out of the oven, sprinkle with the syrup and serve warm.

YOGURT DRINK

Turkey   (*Ayran*)

I have been told that this yogurt drink is more popular than milk in Turkey. In the Summer vendors in the streets sell it and it is really a nice and thirst-quenching drink.

2 cups	(*500 mL*)	yogurt, plain or flavored
1 cup	(*250 mL*)	water
		pinch of salt, if desired

Beat together all the ingredients, either in a mixer or in a blender, then chill.

The drink may be made thinner by mixing equal amounts of yogurt and water, instead of the above mentioned ratio.

VARIATION:

Add 1 ts of finely chopped fresh mint to this drink and mix as above.

Appendix

AMERICAN AND METRIC MEASURES

VOLUME

	Teaspoon (ts)	Tablespoon (tbs)	Fluid ounce (fl. oz.)	Cup	Deciliter (dl)	Milliliter (mL)
Teaspoon	1	$\frac{1}{3}$	$\frac{1}{6}$	$\frac{1}{64}$	.05	5
Tablespoon	3	1	$\frac{1}{2}$	$\frac{1}{16}$	.15	15
Fluid ounce	6	2	1	$\frac{1}{8}$	.30	30
Cup	48	16	8	1	2.37	237
Deciliter	20.3	6.76	3.38	.42	1.00	100

1 pint = 2 cups   1 quart = 2 pints
1 liter = 10 deciliters = 1000 milliliters

WEIGHT

1 kilogram = 1000 grams   1 kilogram = 2.20 pounds
1 hectogram = 100 grams   1 hectogram = 3.52 ounces
1 pound = 16 ounces   1 gram = .035 ounce
1 pound = .45 kilogram   1 ounce = 28.35 grams

535

TEMPERATURE CONVERSION

Fahrenheit and Celsius (Centigrade) temperatures may be converted into each other by use of either of the following formulas:

$$\text{Temperature, Fahrenheit} = \frac{9 \times \text{Temperature, Celsius}}{5} + 32$$

$$\text{Temperature, Celsius} = \frac{5 \times (\text{Temperature, Fahrenheit} - 32)}{9}$$

This conversion works out to whole numbers every 5 degrees on the Celsius scale and every 9 degrees on the Fahrenheit scale, as in the table below, where equivalent temperatures on the two scales are placed beside each other.

Fahrenheit	Celsius	Fahrenheit	Celsius	Fahrenheit	Celsius
−40	−40	149	65	329	165
−31	−35	150	65.5	338	170
−22	−30	158	70	347	175
−13	−25	167	75	350	176.6
− 4	−20	176	80	356	180
0	−17.7	185	85	365	185
5	−15	194	90	374	190
14	−10	200	93.3	383	195
23	− 5	203	95	392	200
32	0	212	100	400	204.4
41	5	221	105	401	205
50	10	230	110	410	210
59	15	239	115	419	215
68	20	248	120	428	220
72	22.2	250	121.1	437	225
77	25	257	125	446	230
86	30	266	130	450	231.1
95	35	275	135	455	235
100	37.7	284	140	464	240
104	40	293	145	473	245
113	45	300	148.9	482	250
122	50	302	150	491	255
131	55	311	155	500	260
140	60	320	160	600	315.5

Where to get what you need

CALIFORNIA

Bazar of India, 1331 University Avenue, Berkeley, Ca. 94702—Indian and Indonesian foods. Mail orders accepted, catalog upon request.

Bezijian Grocery, 4725 Santa Monica Blvd., Los Angeles, Ca. 90029—Indian, Middle Eastern, Greek and Balkan foods. Mail orders accepted and catalog sent upon request.

Enbun Co., 248 East First St., Los Angeles, Ca. 90012—Japanese and Chinese foods. No mail orders.

Kwong On Lung Company, 680 North Spring Street, Los Angeles, Ca. 90012—Chinese, Japanese and South East Asian foods. Mail orders for a minimum of $20.00 plus $2.00 handling charge. Catalog no longer exists due to price fluctuations.

Olson's Delicatessen, 5660 West Pico Blvd., Los Angeles, Ca. 90029—Scandinavian foods. No catalog or mail orders.

Cannery Gourmet, 2801 Leavenworth Street, San Francisco, Ca. 94133—Foods from Scandinavia and 95 other countries. Mail orders on unbreakable items, limited requests for catalogs accepted.

Casa Lucas Market, 2934 24th St., San Francisco, Ca. 94110—Mexican, Caribbean, Central and South American, Spanish, Algerian and Indian foods. No mail orders or catalog at present but being considered for future.

Wing Sing Chong, 1076 Stockton St., San Francisco, Ca. 94108—Indian, South East Asian foods. Mail orders accepted, catalog sent upon request and 25¢ mailing and handling charge.

Little Mermaid, 174 E. 3rd St., San Mateo, Ca. 94401—Scandinavian, Swiss, German and French foods. No catalog or mail orders.

Olof Kristiansen, Norwegian Imports, 1231 S. Pacific Ave., San Pedro, Ca. 90731—Scandinavian and German foods. Mail orders accepted, no catalog at present.

DISTRICT OF COLUMBIA

Tuck Cheong, 617 H St. N.W., Washington, D.C. 20001—South East Asian, Chinese and Japanese foods. Mail orders accepted and catalog sent upon request.

Wang's Co., 800 7th St. N.W., Washington, D.C. 20001—South East Asian, Chinese and Japanese foods. Mail orders accepted and catalog sent upon request.

ILLINOIS

Ericksons Delicatessen, 5250 N.

Clark St., Chicago, Ill. 60640—Scandinavian foods. Not known whether mail orders accepted or catalog exists.

Franklin Food Store, 1309 E. 53rd St., Chicago, Ill. 60650—Japanese, Chinese and South East Asian foods. Mail orders accepted. No catalog available.

La Preferida, Inc., 177–81 West South Water Market, Chicago, Ill. 60608—Spanish, Mexican and Caribbean foods. No mail orders or catalog.

Star Market, 3349 North Clark St., Chicago, Ill. 60657—Japanese and Chinese foods. Mail orders accepted. Price list sent upon request with self-addressed, stamped envelope.

Wickstrom's Delicatessen, 5247 N. Clark St., Chicago, Ill. 60640—Scandinavian foods. Not known whether mail orders accepted or catalog exists.

KANSAS

Imported Foods, 1038 McCormick, Wichita, Ks. 67213—Japanese and South East Asian foods. Mail orders accepted. No catalog available.

LOUISIANA

Oriental Trading Co., 2636 Edenborn Ave., Metairie, La. 70002—Japanese, Chinese, and South East Asian foods. Mail orders accepted and price list sent upon request.

MINNESOTA

Byerly Foods, 7171 France Ave. South, Edina, Minn. 55435—Scandinavian, French, German, English, Spanish, Greek, Oriental, Indian and Mexican foods. No mail orders accepted and no catalog available.

Ingebretsens Scandinavian Center, 1603 E. Lake St., Minneapolis, Minn. 55407—Scandinavian foods. No mail orders for foods (cookware only) and no catalog available at present.

MISSOURI

Asia Food Products, 1509 Delmar Blvd., St. Louis, Mo. 63103—Chinese, Japanese, South East Asian foods. Mail orders accepted, catalog available upon request.

NEW YORK

Malko Brothers, 197 Atlantic Ave., Brooklyn, N.Y. 11201—Greek and Middle Eastern foods. Mail orders accepted, catalog upon request.

Sahadi Importing Co., Inc., 187 Atlantic Ave., Brooklyn, N.Y. 11201—Indian and Middle Eastern foods. No mail orders or catalog.

Schaller Manufacturing Corp., 22–35 46th St., Long Island City, N.Y. 11105—German foods. Mail orders accepted, catalog upon request.

Bremen House, 218 East 86th St., New York, N.Y. 10028—German, Austrian, Dutch, French and Scandinavian foods. Mail orders accepted, catalog upon request.

Casa Moneo, 210 West 14th St., New York, N.Y. 10011—Mexican, South American, some Chinese and many European foods. Mail orders accepted, catalog upon request.

Kalustyan Orient Export Trading Corp., 123 Lexington Ave., New York, N.Y. 10016—Indian, Near and Middle Eastern foods. Mail orders filled, catalog on request.

Kasso Brothers, 570 Ninth Ave., New York, N.Y. 10036—Greek and Middle Eastern foods. No mail orders or catalog.

Katagiri & Co., Inc., 224 E. 59th St., New York, N.Y. 10019—Japanese and Chinese foods. Mail orders accepted. Prices upon request.

Manganaro Foods, 488 Ninth Ave., New York, N.Y. 10018—Italian foods. Mail orders accepted and catalog sent upon request.

Nyborg & Nelson, 937 Second Ave., New York, N.Y. 10022—Scandinavian and many other European foods. Mail orders accepted and prices sent upon request.

Old Denmark, 133 E. 65th St., New York, N.Y. 10021—Scandinavian and many other European foods. Mail orders accepted and prices sent upon request.

Paprikas Weiss, 1546 Second Ave., New York, N.Y. 10021—Hungarian and many other European foods. Mail orders accepted and catalog sent upon request.

H. Roth & Son, 1577 First Ave., New York, N.Y. 10028—Hungarian, Dutch, German, French, Czechoslovakian and Chinese foods. Mail orders accepted and catalog sent upon request.

K. Tanaka Co., Inc., 326 Amsterdam Ave., New York, N.Y. 10023—Japanese and Chinese foods. Mail orders accepted and prices sent upon request.

OHIO

Soya Food Products, 2356 Wyoming Ave., Cincinnati, Ohio 45214—Japanese, Chinese and some South East Asian foods. Mail orders accepted in limited amounts, no catalog available.

Omura Japanese Foods, 3811 Payne Ave., Cleveland, Ohio 44114—Japanese, some Chinese and South East Asian foods. Mail orders accepted, no catalog available.

Spanish & American Food Market, 7001 Wade Park Avenue, Cleveland, Ohio 44103—Mexican and Caribbean foods. Mail orders accepted, no catalog available.

OREGON

Anzen Importers, 736 Northeast Union Ave., Portland, Or. 97232—Japanese, Chinese and some South East Asian foods. Mail orders accepted, catalog upon request.

PENNSYLVANIA

Heintzelman's, 1128 Northway Mall, Pittsburgh, Pa. 15237—Middle Eastern, Oriental, British, German, French foods. Mail orders not normally accepted, but exceptions are made. No catalog available.

TEXAS

Antones Import Co., 807 Taft St., Houston, Tx. 77001—Mexican, South East Asian, Middle Eastern foods plus foods from many other countries. Mail orders accepted and catalog sent upon request.

WASHINGTON

Johnsen's Scandinavian Foods, 2248 N W Market St., Seattle, Wash. 98107—Scandinavian foods. Mail orders accepted and catalog available upon request.

Norwegian Sausage Co., 8539 N W 15th Seattle, Wash. 98117—Scandinavian foods. Mail orders accepted and catalog available upon request.

Index

541

Library of Congress Cataloging in Publication Data

Wegener, Maj-Greth.
    International cooking made easy.

    Includes index.
    1. Cookery, International.   I. Title.
TX725.A1W37   641.5   78-71120
ISBN 0-8038-3422-5